National Identification Systems

ALSO BY CARL WATNER
WITH WENDY MCELROY

Dissenting Electorate:
Those Who Refuse to Vote
and the Legitimacy of Their Opposition
(McFarland, 2001)

National Identification Systems

Essays in Opposition

Edited by CARL WATNER
with WENDY MCELROY

McFarland & Company, Inc., Publishers
Jefferson, North Carolina, and London

#5Z738699

ISBN 0-7864-1595-9 (softcover : 50# alkaline paper) ∞

Library of Congress cataloguing data are available

British Library cataloguing data are available

Cover image photograph ©2003 Corbis Images

Manufactured in the United States of America

*McFarland & Company, Inc., Publishers
Box 611, Jefferson, North Carolina 28640
www.mcfarlandpub.com*

For two women
who gave important help
to this anthology:

Julie Watner
Claire Wolfe

Table of Contents

I would also remind my colleagues that national ID cards are a trademark of totalitarianism that contribute nothing to the security of the American people.

— Congressman Ron Paul,
Statement for the Government Reform Committee Hearing
on National ID Card Proposals, November 16, 2001

Preface

By Carl Watner

In the weeks and months that followed September 11, 2001, Americans heard more and more about the need for national identification systems. Amidst these calls for increased security, Wendy McElroy suggested I examine the morality and the practicality of these programs. Would giving each person in the United States a unique number for life actually make us safer or would it simply allow governments to track us from cradle to grave? Had these suggestions for monitoring individuals ever been made before? What were the precedents—both historical and philosophical? What were the assumptions, implications, and likely outcomes of such a system? Would they make us more secure from attack or would we simply become more visible to those who wanted to tax and control us?

This is more than a book about national ID. It is about all forms of government enumeration, from the census of antiquity, to government naming practices, fingerprinting, social security numbers, and drivers licenses, to cutting-edge biometric technologies such as DNA, iris scans, or subcutaneous microchips capable of allowing those in charge to know where we are twenty-four hours a day via global positioning satellites. This book looks at the big picture of national ID: what it is, how it has developed, and how it might potentially change our society. It is also about those who have chosen to resist or oppose national ID schemes—from Gandhi's satyagraha campaign in South Africa in 1906 to those Americans who refuse to be counted or carry a government number today. These "Essays in Opposition" are intended to honor those whose consciences and principles do not allow them to "roll over" and acquiesce.

As I began to research the topic of government enumeration it became readily apparent that this was a highly ideologically-charged subject—with most people believing that some sort of government intervention was a prerequisite to modern life. In fact, several potential contributors to this book

1

refused to give permission to reprint their work because they were opposed to the ideological drift of this anthology. Never before has there been a book devoted to the idea that the logical outcome of government involvement in these areas (from government birth certificates to governmental databases and surveillance) is *1984*-style population control. That is why national ID systems have been called a "trademark of totalitarianism." While Americans might be able to avoid the abuses that such systems have brought about in other countries (national ID cards always seem to facilitate genocide, as one of our chapters points out), there remains the telling point that national ID and enhanced governmental powers *always* go hand in hand.

As in all intellectual efforts, this book could not have been assembled without help from numerous people. Foremost to be mentioned is Claire Wolfe, whose depth of knowledge, personal contacts, and editorial assistance I found invaluable. The two books that I continually consulted during my year-long work on this anthology were Jane Caplan and John Torpey's *Documenting Individual Identity: The Development of State Practices in the Modern World*, and Simon Cole's *Suspect Identities: A History of Fingerprinting and Criminal Identification*. The Inter-Library Loan Departments at the Spartanburg County Public Library and Wofford College went far above and beyond the call of duty in helping me to locate hard-to-find materials, some of which are mentioned in "For Further Reading." I would like to thank the Center for Independent Thought and various subscribers to *The Voluntaryist* for their support of this project.

Readers, as you grapple with the questions presented by this book, please remember that I take responsibility for all its faults and errors. Whatever merit you find in its arguments, historical analysis, and conclusions belong to those contributors who were so generous in allowing me to use their work. I only hope that you, your children, or your grandchildren will one day offer thanks to those in the ranks of the opposition who saw fit to challenge government enumeration.

Men Ahead of Their Times

Jeremy Bentham *and*
Luis Reyna Almandos

GENEVA SWITZERLAND, DECEMBER 14, 2001:
     Refugees meeting hears proposal to register every human. Every person in the world would be fingerprinted and registered under a universal identification scheme to fight illegal immigration and people smuggling outlined at a United Nations meeting....[1]

Believe it or not, the calls for universal national identification are not new. Jeremy Bentham, in a posthumously published essay, advocated universal tattooing and a new naming system for the population of England. The excerpt by Jeremy Bentham found on page 6 is taken from Chapter XII, Problem IX, in "Principles of Penal Law" in Volume I of The Works of Jeremy Bentham, *reproduced from the Bowring Edition of 1838–1843 (New York: Russell & Russell, Inc., 1962, p. 557).*

During the early 20th century, numerous penologists agitated for nationwide fingerprinting. In the midst of World War II, Senator William Langer of North Dakota introduced unsuccessful legislation that provided for the fingerprinting of every American.[2] Even this was not a new idea, as evidenced by the excerpts from an earlier pamphlet by Dr. Luis Reyna Almandos, who was Director of the Vucetich Museum (Juan Vucetich was a famous Argentinean criminologist) of the Faculty of Juridical and Social Sciences at La Plata University (Buenos Aires). "The Personal Number and the National Book of Personality" was originally published in Spanish in a Brazilian journal in 1934, and then in an English language translation (by Dr. Ricardo Gumbleton Daunt) in Revista de Identificación y Ciencias Penales *(Numero 22, October 1936, pp. 3–21).*

From "The Personal Number and the National Book of Personality"
By Dr. Luis Reyna Almandos

I. Bases of the System of Personal Number

The aim of the present study is to unfold a special form — strictly scientific and simple in essence — of organizing, in any country, the individual and genealogical register of *personality* with the view of constituting or materially effecting what I call *The National Book of Personality*....

It would be, perhaps, wearisomely stretched out to analyze the observations which enabled me to conceive *The National Book of Personality*, such as I intend to explain in this study. But I may safely say that ever since the day in which, together with my immortal friend Vucetich, I made the first day-books of what afterwards became the *Law of the General Register of the Identification of Persons for the Province of Buenos Ayres* (1916), the fundamental idea of that book began to take shape in my mind with well-defined characteristics....

Vucetich had already the great idea of centralizing in one register the finger personal record prints of every individual in the country. He had done more: he proposed in the month of March 1901, to the Second Scientific Latin-American Congress, which met in Montevideo, the organization of international identification....

Having said so much, it is not necessary to demonstrate with further facts and arguments the near and universal generalization of the great identification, i.e., the civil one which comprehends all **men** from birth and without distinction of conditions. As soon as we get rid of the poor idea that identification is merely a social defense against delinquents, we begin to perceive the high conception that identification — much more than such a defense — is the only efficacious way of warranting every individual the free and full use of his rights, and, as an inevitable result, the only sure way of organizing public administration in all nations, and the relations of a certain order among them....

The last affirmation, ... makes us recognize the fact that without the dactyloscopical system it is impossible to have civil identification centralized in every country....

If this is the truth; if identify can be proved mathematically only by means of the digital impress; and if no individual records is possible without the dactyloscopical methods (and of these the most perfect) we have then to accept scientific methods as the essential and unique basis of any civil organization of identity,...

Thus the necessary bases of civil identification are: (1) *the system of papillary impressions* (digital or chiroscopical); [and] (2) *a law of civil identity, general and compulsory.*

II. THE PERSONAL NUMBER AND THE DACTYLOSCOPICAL SYSTEM

Without the adoption of digital impressions it is utterly impossible to have any organization of identity. Consequently, the method which I propose for filing finger-print records of *an illimited number* and thus making it possible to have a register or a National Book of Personality, has its foundation and life in that system....

What I am aiming at is precisely this: that every country possess this Book which is *a civil biography of everyone of its inhabitants,....*

... I conceived the method which I have called the Personal Number, which renders it feasible to hold an illimited file of dactyloscopical records, and thus to form the so-called National Book of Personality, a summary of the nation, and an exact report about all the persons living in a given country.

III. THE PERSONAL NUMBER

I give the name of *personal number* to the civil figure, personal and exclusive, of each individual in every nation, identified according to the dactyloscopical system.

This number is awarded by the State when any person applies for civil identification. It *runs in a series* from 1 onwards; it is perpetual, individual, untransferable and immutable; it is permanent *for life*, and may not be given to another person even after the death of the first holder; with him it is born and with him it dies; and by it shall be regulated all acts concerning him, judicial and otherwise, [even] after death....

IV. MECHANISM OF THE INSTITUTION

The central idea of this study is simply grand; yet, its realization is not impossible,....

The plan to which I refer has, as its substance; I. A national triple dactyloscopical file in the three parts of which being correlated, to wit: (a) A file of finger-print records kept in accordance with the dactyloscopical key, or **method of classification**. Each record should carry the successive civil number. (b) A file of equal records kept in successive numerical order beginning with 1. (c) A file of equal records kept in the alphabetical order of surnames, and numbered as indicated above.

A book whose leaves are numbered in order beginning with 1. The number of each leaf or page should be the same civil number given to each inhabitant by force of its law of civil identity. *This is the National Book of Personality,* for in it are consigned all persons with the respective personal number, the data belonging to each person, the reports of his actions taken from any of the dactyloscopical records kept on file, or from any other sources of information which comprehend the life of every individual....

V. FORMULARY FOR THE PERSONAL NUMBER

For an organization of this nature, a national law is *a sine qua non condition.* Thus the plan is of immediate possibility in the countries which have promulgated this law. In other countries it depends on an intervening stage. But I write for the future....

We know that a card of identity is granted by the State to the identified person, and that a corresponding dactyloscopical record is kept on file in the Central Identification Office.... The card carries the serial number, but the record does not. Therefore, there is no personal number which controls the filing of records, of the formation of the Book of Personality numbered according to the explanation above.

By the method or form that I am proposing, *the three equal dactyloscopical records of each person carry the same number that the identity card has....*

CHARACTERISTICS OF THE PERSONAL NUMBER

According to what has been expounded, The National Book of Personality (which in the course of time and by constant effort might become The International Book of Personality) will owe its future existence — which is possible at present in the countries where the law of *civil dactyloscopical identity* is in force — to two factors: the mathematico-anthropological and the mathematico-administrative. The first is the dactyloscopical formula (anthropologico-juridical). The second is the *personal number* (juridico-administrative)....

In fact, it would be impossible to assign to each individual within the dactyloscopical key — be it that of Vucetich or of any other author — a unique figure, *an exclusive number* in order to designate or isolate him,....

The *dactyloscopical number* which is as has been said, anthropological because it emanates from human morphology (papillary ridges of the hand) identifies mathematically, but besides being applied to one and many persons, it is a complex number made up inevitably of many digits.... This ... renders it impracticable to number arithmetically the records of the file or the pages of the Book of Personality. It is impossible therefore to number pages or records of identity in successive order by using the dactyloscopical number.

As a result, and beginning with miscellaneous indices, I conceived, *as a vital instrument* of the new system, a mathematical synthesis of the individual personality: *the unit number,* intimately bound to the dactyloscopical-anthropological. This *unit number* permits, among other things, the organization, in every country, of general identity in files and registers of easy composition and management.

With the *dactyloscopical number* or with *the personal number,* it is possible to organize colossal files of millions and millions of **individuals**....

The Personal Number is a numerical expression that corresponds to every human being. It is *civil because* it designates man as a person capable of acquiring rights and assuming obligation. It is also civil because its aim is to build, on a basis of perfect order, the civil institution of identification. It assumes *penal* character because, in case of delinquency or fault, the identity is civilly pre-established. It is an *administrative number* because by means of it the various State institutions will be kept in good trim. It is an *international number*....

... It is a number that is unique by its nature because it stands for an identity that is also unique.

It is an *exclusive number* because it belongs to one man only and it is impossible that it should belong to any other.

It is a *successive number,* as already explained.

It is *untransferable,* for the same reasons above;....

The personal number is *perpetual:* the State through the proper administrative agencies confers it on the citizen at his birth, and he will keep it during his life-time....

The personal number is peculiarly *social.* It is the only social number that may exist. It is so because its object is order in collective life....

The personal number has, in addition, marked *moral* character, because, if it be adopted, all judicial scandals that spread at the death of many a person will disappear; crimes abetted by the confusion of personalities will become impossible; the dramas of lost or confused personality will be acted no more....

[I]t will be possible to have a Permanent National Census without any violent effort, so characteristic of census-taking which is realized in one day throughout the country....

EXAMPLES...

A lost boy who does not recall his name or *have on his person his personal number* (it is presumable though that he might have it) may be able to go back to his home by means of the *civil dactyloscopical test* wherever he encounters a charitable soul.

This is the case of the purely dactyloscopical system. But, if he remembers or carries his number (*and this ought to become in the process of time a habit of healthy foresight — tattooing the personal number, for example)* the boy may be sure that the social protection of his fatherland follows him, and that to be straying in any part, does not mean more than the anxiety of one moment's lonesomeness....

When a country, with any number of inhabitants, owns its *National Book of Personality,* then *Man* in that country will be known and valued as such; relationships will be easy and perfect; public security will be more assured; income will be more solidly warranted; justice will be more certain; the family will be guarded against dissolution and despoilment; in a word, man will be guaranteed in the exercise of his civil and political rights by the State at all moments and to a surprising degree of exactitude.

From *"Principles of Penal Law"*
By Jeremy Bentham

CHAPTER XII.

Problem IX
To facilitate the Recognition and the finding of Individuals

The greater number of offences would not be committed, if the delinquents did not hope to remain unknown. Everything which increases the facility of recognizing and finding individuals, adds to the general security.

This is one reason why less is to be feared from those who have a fixed habitation, property, or a family. The danger arises from those who, from their indigence or their independence of all ties, can easily conceal their movements from the eye of justice.

Tables of population, in which are inscribed the dwelling-place, the age, the sex, the profession, the marriage or celibacy of individuals, are the first materials of a good police.

It is proper that the magistrate should be able to demand an account from every suspected person as to his means of living, and consign those to a place of security who have neither an independent revenue, nor other means of support.

There are two things to be observed with regard to this object: That the police ought not to be so minute or vexatious as to expose the subjects to find themselves in fault, or vexed by numerous and difficult regulations. Precautions, which are necessary at certain periods of danger and trouble, ought not to be continued in a period of quietness; as the regimen suited to disease ought not to be followed in a state of health. The second observation is, that care should be taken not to shock the national spirit. One nation would not bear what is borne by another. In the capital of Japan, every one is obliged to have his name upon his dress. This measure might appear useful, indifferent, or tyrannical, according to the current of public prejudices.

Characteristic dresses have a relation to this end. Those which distinguish the different sexes are a means of police as gentle as salutary. Those which serve to distinguish the army, the navy, the clergy, have more than one object; but the principal one is subordination. In the English universities, the pupils wear a particular dress, which restrains them only when they wish to go beyond the prescribed bounds. In charity schools, the scholars wear not only a uniform dress, but even a numbered plate.

It is to be regretted that the proper names of individuals are upon so irregular a footing. Those distinctions, invented in the infancy of society, to provide for the wants of a hamlet, only imperfectly accomplish their object in a great nation. There are many inconveniences attached to this nominal confusion. The greatest of all is, that the indication arising from a name is vague; suspicion is divided among a multitude of persons; and the danger to which innocence is exposed, becomes the security of crime.

In providing a new nomenclature, it ought to be so arranged, that, in a whole nation, every individual should have a proper name, which should belong to him alone. At the present time, the embarrassment which would be produced by the change would perhaps surpass its advantages; but it might be useful to prevent this disorder in a new state.

There is a common custom among English sailors, of printing their family and Christian names upon their wrists, in well-formed and indelible characters; they do it that their bodies may be known in case of shipwreck.

If it were possible that this practice should become universal, it would be a new spring for morality, a new source of power for the laws, an almost infallible precaution against a multitude of offenses, especially against every kind of fraud in which confidence is requisite for success. Who are you, with whom I have to deal? The answer to this important question would no longer be liable to evasion.

This means, by its own energy, would become favourable to personal liberty, by permitting relaxations in the rigour of proceedings. Imprisonment, having for its only object the detention of individuals, might become rare, when they were held as it were by an invisible chain.

There are, however, plausible objections to such a practice. In the course of the French revolution, many persons owed their safety to a disguise, which such a mark would have rendered unavailing. Public opinion, in its present state, opposes an insurmountable obstacle to such an institution; but opinion might be changed, by patiently guiding it with skill, and by beginning with great examples. If it were the custom to imprint the titles of the nobility upon their foreheads, these marks would become associated with the ideas of honour and power. In the islands of the South Sea, the women submit to a painful operation, in tracing upon their skin certain figures, to which they annex the idea of beauty. The impression is made by puncturing the skin, and rubbing in coloured powders.

Notes

1. http://www.smh.com.au/breaking/2001/12/14/FFX058CU6VC.html
2. See Harold Cummins and Charles Midlo. Fingerprints, Palms and Soles, New York: Dover Publications, Inc., 1961, p. 292.

Government Surnames
and Legal Identities

James C. Scott, John Tehranian,
and Jeremy Mathias
Yale University

What's in a name? Certainly more than meets the eye. For hundreds of years (at least since the Dooms Day book of William the Conqueror) governments have been determined to know the true identity of their subjects in order to tax, conscript, and subjugate them. This piece, which first appeared in Volume 44, Comparative Studies in Society and History *(January 2002), discusses the history of the last name and shows why "it is still the first fact on documents of identity." James C. Scott is the Eugene Meyer Professor of Political Science and Anthropology at Yale University. This chapter is reprinted with the permission of Cambridge University Press.*

> We name a thing and — bang! — it leaps into existence. Each name a perfect equation with its roots. A perfect congruence with its reality [Yolland and Owen].
> But remember that words are signals, counters. They are not immortal. And it can happen — to use an image you'll understand — it can happen that a civilization can be imprisoned in a linguistic contour which no longer matches the landscape of ... fact [Hugh].
> I'll decode you yet [Yolland[1]]

I. Introduction

State naming practices and local, customary naming practices are strikingly different. Each set of practices is designed to make the human and physical landscape *legible*, by sharply identifying a unique individual, a household, or a singular geographic feature. Yet they are each devised by very distinct agents for whom the purposes of identification are radically different. Purely local, customary practices, as we shall see, achieve a level of precision and clarity — often with impressive economy — perfectly suited to the needs of knowledgeable locals. State naming practices are, by contrast, constructed to guide an official stranger in identifying unambiguously persons and places, not just in a single locality, but in many localities using standardized administrative techniques.

THERE IS NO STATE-MAKING WITHOUT STATE-NAMING

To follow the progress of state-making is, among other things, to trace the elaboration and application of novel systems which name and classify places, roads, people, and, above all, property. These state projects of legibility overlay, and often supersede, local practices. Where local practices persist, they are typically relevant to a narrower and narrower range of interaction within the confines of a face-to-face community.

A contrast between local names for roads and state names for roads will help illustrate the two variants of legibility. There is, for example, a small road joining the towns of Durham and Guilford in the state of Connecticut. Those who live in Durham call this road (among themselves) the "Guilford Road," presumably because it informs the inhabitants of Durham exactly where they'll get to if they travel it. The same road, at its Guilford terminus, is called, the "Durham Road" because it tells the inhabitants of Guilford where the road will lead them. One imagines that at some liminal midpoint, the road hovers between these two identities. Such names work perfectly well; they each encode valuable local knowledge, i.e., perhaps the most important fact one might want to know about a road. That the same road has two names, depending on one's location, demonstrates the situational, contingent nature of local naming practices. Informal, folk naming practices not only produce the anomaly of a road with two or more names; they also produce many different roads with the same name. Thus, the nearby towns of Killingworth, Haddam, Madison, and Meriden each have roads leading to Durham which the inhabitants locally call the "Durham Road."

Now imagine the insuperable problems that this locally-effective folk system would pose to an outsider requiring unambiguous identifications for each road. A state road repair crew, sent to fix potholes on the "Durham Road" would have to ask, "Which Durham Road?" Thus it is no surprise that the road between Durham and Guilford is re-incarnated on all state maps and designations as "Route 77." Each micro-segment of that route, moreover, is identified by means of telephone pole serial numbers, milestones, and township boundaries. The naming practices of the state require a synoptic view, a standardized scheme of identification generating mutually exclusive and exhaustive designations.[2] And, this system can work to the benefit of state residents: if you have to be rescued on Route 77 by a state-dispatched ambulance team, you will be reassured to know that there is no ambiguity about which road it is that you are bleeding on.

All place names, personal names, and names of roads or rivers encode important knowledge. Some of that knowledge is a thumbnail history: e.g., Maiden Lane [the lane where five spinster sisters once lived], Cider Hill Road [the road up the hill where the Cider Mill and orchard once stood], Cream Pot Road [once the site of a dairy where neighbors went to buy milk, cream, and butter]. At one time, when the name became fixed, it was probably the most relevant and useful name for local inhabitants. Other names refer to geographical features: Mica Ridge Road, Bare Rock Road, Ball Brook Road. The sum of roads and place names in a small place, in fact, amounts to something of a local geography and history if one knows the stories, features, episodes, and family enterprises encoded within them.[3]

For officials who require a radically different form of order, such local knowledge, however quaint, is illegible. It privileges local knowledge over synoptic, standardized knowledge. In the case of colonial rule, when the conquerors speak an entirely different language, the unintelligibility of the vernacular landscape is a nearly insurmountable obstacle to effective rule. Renaming much of the landscape therefore is an essential step of imperial rule. This explains why the British Ordinance Survey of Ireland in the 1830s recorded and rendered many local Gaelic place names (e.g., Bun na hAbhann, Gaelic for "mouth of the river") in a form (Burnfoot) more easily understood by the rulers.

The conflict between vernacular, local meaning in place names and a higher order grid of synoptic legibility is, however, rather generic. It is heightened by cultural difference, but it rests ultimately on the divergent purposes for which a semantic order is created. In western Washington state, for example, county officials in the 1970s changed old street and road names (e.g., French Creek Grange Road, Rainwater Road, Picnic Road, Potato Road) to new names based on the comprehensive logic of serial numbers and compass directions (19th Avenue Northwest, 167th Avenue Southeast). The result was a standardized grid on which each house could be located with Cartesian simplicity.[4] As the title: "Towns in Washington Bringing Back the Poetry in Street Names," indicates, a small popular revolt had succeeded in recuperating the old street names to the consternation of planning officials whose planning geometry had enabled ambulances or firefighters to be dispatched with greater speed and reliability. For a planner, a transportation manager, a tax collector, or a police officer, the conveniences of such a grid over vernacular practices is obvious. "With all these strange names, for an engineer like me,

I go, 'Aw, this is awful.' With Killarney Blace or Baloney Whatever, cul de sacs [sic] and circular streets, finding our way around is really difficult."[5]

II. State-Naming as State-Making:
The Case of Individual Naming Practices

Like place-names, permanent surnames help to chart the human topography of any region. Names play a vital role in determining identities, cultural affiliations, and histories; they can help fracture or unify groups of people. They represent an integral part of knowledge-power systems. This paper will study surnames as a social construct — a system of knowledge spun in the webs of power. Although most Westerners take their existence for granted, fixed, hereditary surnames are modern inventions. Through a comparative analysis, we will argue that the use of inherited familial surnames represents a relatively recent phenomenon intricately linked to the aggrandizement of state control over individuals and the development of modern legal systems and property regimes. In particular, the creation and diffusion of inheritable surnames represented a critical tool in the power struggle between local and outside authorities in the development of the modern nation-state, the emergence of ethnonationalist identities, and the imposition of credible private property systems.

THE PROBLEM OF CONFUSION

> Where is our history?/What are the names washed down the sewer/In the ceptic flood?/I pray to the rain/Give me back my rituals/Give back truth/Return the remnants of my identity/Bathe me in self-discovered knowledge/Identify my ancestors who have existed suppressed/Invoke their spirits with … [Shakespeare, *Othello*, Act 3, Scene 2].

It is both striking and important to recognize how relatively little the premodern state actually knew about the society over which it presided. State officials had only the most tenuous idea of the population under their jurisdiction, its movements, its real property, wealth, crop yields, etc. Their degree of ignorance was directly proportional to the fragmentation of their sources of information. Local currencies and local measures of capacity (e.g., the bushel) and length (the ell, the rod, the toise) were likely to vary from place to place and with the nature of the transacting parties.[6] The opacity of local society was, of course, actively maintained by local elites as one effective means of resistance to intrusions from above.

Having little synoptic, aggregate intelligence about the manpower and resources available to it, officials were apt either to overreach in their exactions, touching off flight or revolt, or to fail to mobilize the resources that were, in fact, available. To follow the process of state-making, then, is to follow *the conquest of illegibility*. The account of this conquest — an achievement won against stiff resistance — could take many forms, for example: the creation of the cadastral survey and uniform property registers, the invention and imposition of the meter, national censuses and currencies, and the development of uniform legal codes.

Here we examine what we take to be one crucial and diagnostic victory in this campaign for legibility: the creation of fixed, legal patronyms. If vernacular landscape-naming practices are opaque and illegible to outside officials, vernacular personal naming practices are even more so. The fixing of personal names, and, in particular, permanent patronyms, as legal identities seems, everywhere, to have been, broadly-speaking, a state project. As an early and imperfect legal identification, the permanent patronym was linked to such vital administrative functions as tithe and tax collection, property registers, conscription lists, and census rolls. To understand why fixed, legal patronyms represent such a quantum leap in the legibility of a population to state officials, it is first necessary to understand the utter fluidity of vernacular naming practices uninflected by state routines.

Vernacular naming practices throughout much of the world are enormously rich and varied.[7] In many cultures, an individual's name will change from context to context and, within the same context, over time. It is not uncommon for a newborn to have had one or more name changes *in utero* in the event the mother's labor seemed to be going badly. Names often vary at each stage of life (infancy, childhood, adulthood, parenthood, old age) and, in some cases, after death. Added to these may be names used for joking, rituals, mourning, nicknames, school names, secret names, names for age-mates or same-sex friends, and names for in-laws. Each name is specific to a phase of life, a social setting, or a particular interlocutor. To the question, "What is your name?" the reply in such cases can only be: "It depends."

In the small vernacular community, of course, this cornucopia of names occasions no confusion whatsoever. Local residents know the names they need to know, the codes appropriate to their use, the room for maneuver within these codes, and the ways in which these codes might be transgressed. They are rarely in doubt about who is who.

How is local confusion avoided in the absence of permanent patronyms? Let us take the simplest case where there are a small number of fixed, given names (often called "first" or "Christian" names in western Europe). It is claimed, for example, that around the year 1700 in England, a mere eight given names accounted for nearly ninety percent of the total male population (John, Edward, William, Henry, Charles, James, Richard, Robert). Without permanent patronyms, local people had innumerable ways of unambiguously identifying any individual. A by-name, second-name, or (sur)name (not to be confused with a permanent patronym) was usually sufficient to make the defining distinction. One John, for example, might be distinguished from another by specifying his father's name ("William's John" or "John-William's-son"/Williamson)[8] — by linking him to an occupation ("John-the-miller," "John-the shepherd") — by locating him in the landscape ("John-on-the-hill," "John-by-the-brook" — or by noting a personal characteristic (John-do-little). The written records of the manor or the parish might actually bear notations of such by-names for the sake of clarity.

Local practice in a contemporary Malay-Muslim village, where there are no permanent patronyms and where the number of given names is similarly limited, follows much the same pattern. Kasim who owns a small store is distinguished from four other Kasims in the village by being called "Kasim-kedai" ("store" Kasim); Ahmad who can read the Koran is called "Lebai-[Ah]mat"; Mansor who was once tripped up when his sarong fell down while chasing children is called, only behind-his-back of course, "Mansur-terlon-deh" (Mansor of the accidentally falling sarong), and Zakariah who has a harelip is called, also behind his back, "[Zakar]iah-rabit" (Hare-lip Zakariah). In this Malay-Muslim village, each of these names is locally, but *only* locally, definitive; only a relative insider is likely to know who has the village reputation for laziness, who can recite the Koran, who tripped on his sarong, or which John is William's son. The vernacular system is perfectly discriminating for those with the requisite local knowledge to understand each reference. Without a 'local-tracker' to fill in the missing information for identification, the outsider is at a loss.

The vernacular communities of the past, in part because of their autonomous naming practices, were quasi-opaque to state officials. Access to individuals was typically achieved indirectly through intermediaries: the local nobleman, the village headman, the imam or the parish priest, the tavern keeper, the notary. Such intermediaries, naturally, had their own individual and corporate interests. They might profit handsomely from their gate-keeping role. In any case, their interests were never perfectly coincident with those of state officials and often at cross-purposes. It is for such reasons that locally kept census rolls have often under-reported the population (to evade taxes, corvée labor, or conscription) and understated both arable land acreage and crop yields. Wilfred Testier, in his classic account of the Marsh Arabs in southern Iraq, provides an instructive example of how official ignorance of local identities might be deployed for local purposes. The provincial police, acting as conscription officers come to a marsh village with a list of thirty-two presumably eligible young men, two of whom they plan to take with them as recruits. Unable to identify anyone properly, the officials are told that the boys they seek are all either too young, have moved away, or have died. Instead they are given two young men whom village leaders had, all along, selected for them.[9]

REMEDIES TO ILLEGIBILITY: THE TAMING OF CHANCE

The problem of naming and identification can be expressed generally. Let us imagine a police official (it could be a tax collector or a conscription officer) who is trying to locate a specific, unique individual. Assume further that he is faced with a situation not unlike that of a small English village in 1700, but with no surnames, let alone fixed, patronymic surnames. Take a comparatively simple case of a village with, say, 1,000 males bearing only one of eight names, which are, for the sake of this initial case, perfectly evenly distributed across the (male) population. How likely, in this case, is our police official to collar the man he is after? If he knows he is looking for a "Henry," there will be 125 "Henrys" in this village and 124 of them will be the wrong "Henry." Without local assistance and under the assumption, for the sake of argument, that he actually knows the true given names of all villagers, he will almost surely fail. What if we imagine that all males in this village have two names, which vary independently? In this case, the chances that the police official will grab the wrong "Henry" are much reduced, but still substantial, as there will be about 15 "Henry Thomases," 15 "William Jameses," etc. Once we move to three names (also varying independently), it is likely that the police official will get his man half the time on average. The opacity of the villagers to outside identification is reduced radically by the use of each additional identifying name.

Our hypothetical example is, in effect, a best case scenario with only eight given names. Assume, for a moment, that the names are not evenly distributed; assume that the name, say, "William" is so popular that half the men in the village bear it, and the other seven names are evenly distributed among the remainder. In that case, the police agent, looking for a particular William, will face 285 aliases if the villagers have only a single name, 81 aliases in a village with two names, and 39 aliases in a village with three names.[10] The point is that anything less than an even distribution of names appreciably raises the odds that the suspect with a more common name will elude identification.

If we impose, arbitrarily, on such a village a permanent legal patronym such that Thomas son of William is registered as Thomas Williamson and his son as, say, Henry Williamson, and his son as, say, Edward Williamson, and so on, we do not improve the odds for the police who want to identify an individual in his generation but we do vastly improve the odds of identifying his parents, grandparents, sons and daughters who must necessarily bear the same permanent patronym. Questions of inheritance, paternity, and household affiliation become far more transparent, but never entirely so.

Before the advent of internal passports, photographs, and social security numbers, personal names were the form of identification most germane to police work. The use of personal names to locate a person depended, of course, on the compliance of the individual and the community in revealing true names. Where the community was hostile and the individual evasive, state officials were stymied. Hence the official predilection for internal passports that must be carried at all times under penalty of fines, or, better yet, for fingerprints which are unique and hard to efface or, better yet, for DNA profiles, a unique marker present in any sample of tissue.

Let us assume, for the moment, both a high level of compliance and a world in which the personal name is the key identifier. The police — here used as a convenient shorthand for any authorities wanting to locate a specific individual — may have their task complicated in either of two ways. The smaller the number of names in use within a population, the more difficult becomes the process of identification. We might think of this as the needle part of the "looking for a needle in a haystack" problem. How many needles look just like the particular needle we are looking for? The size of the haystack is also crucial. Broadly speaking, the haystack problem is a problem of scale. Once police work becomes a matter of finding a unique individual in a large town, a province, let alone a nation, the confusion of identical names becomes an administrative nightmare. The nightmare is further compounded by geographical mobility, as we shall see. If people are moving with any frequency, it becomes well-nigh impossible to know in which of many haystacks to search them out.

The modern state — by which we mean a state whose ideology encompasses large-scale plans for the improvement of the population's welfare — requires at least two forms of legibility to be able to achieve its mission. First, it requires the capacity to locate citizens uniquely and unambiguously. Second, it needs standardized information that will allow it to create aggregate statistics about property, income, health, demography, productivity, etc. Although much of the synoptic, aggregate information officials of the modern state require is collected initially from individuals, it must be collected in a form that makes it amendable to an overall statistical profile — a shorthand map of some social or economic condition relevant for state purposes.

Officials of the modern state — and of large organizations generally — are, of necessity, at least one step removed from the society they are charged with governing. They "see" the human activity of interest to them largely through the simplified approximations of documents and statistics: tax proceeds, lists of tax-payers, land records, average income, income distributions, mortality rates and tables, price and productivity figures. Once in place the tools of legibility and synoptic vision are readily deployed as the basis for gauging the progress of an "improving" state.[11] Thus do trends in statistics on accidents, fertility, mortality, employment, literacy levels, and consumer-durable ownership serve as indices of the success of state policy. Programs of improvement, even more than mere identification, require a discriminating set of techniques to locate individuals and classify them according to the relevant criteria. The more intrusive and discriminating the level of intervention contemplated, the sharper the tools of legibility required. The demographic knowledge necessary, for example, to conduct a vaccination campaign during an epidemic, or to identify and locate all residents of a city who have engineering degrees or who have children with speech defects are cases in point.

The importance of statistics and measurement to legibility alert us to the fact that the permanent patronym is, as we have emphasized, only one of a larger series of state practices collectively designed to take a relatively illegible world of vernacular meaning and recast it in terms that are synoptically visible. The case of uniform, standardized measures, and the cadastral survey might as readily illustrate how the legibility of names [r]ests, logically, with other state-making initiatives.

PERMANENT PATRONYMS AND THE STATE: ORIGINS

Before the fourteenth century, if we confine our attention to Europe, permanent patronyms were very much the exception.[12] Surnames designating, say, occupation or some personal characteristic, were widespread, but they did not survive the bearer. The rise of the permanent patronym is inextricably associated with those aspects of state-making in which it was desirable to be able to distinguish individual (male) subjects: tax collection (including tithes), conscription, land revenue, court judgments, witness records, and police work.[13]

All of these activities require more or less elaborate lists. So it is hardly surprising that it is through such documents that the effort to render the population and its genealogy legible is best traced. The census [or catasto] of the Florentine state in 1427 was an audacious (and failed) attempt to rationalize the administration of revenue and manpower resources by recording the names, wealth, residences, land-holdings, and ages of the city-state's inhabitants. At the time, virtually the only Tuscan family names were those of a handful of great families [e.g., Strozzi] whose kin, including affines, adopted the name as a way of claiming the backing of a powerful corporate group. The vast majority were identified reasonably unambiguously by the registrars, but not by personal patronyms. They might list their father and grandfather (e.g., Luigi, son of Paulo, son of Geovanni)[14] or they might add a nickname, a profession, or a personal characteristic. It is reasonably clear that what we are witnessing, in the cataso exercise, are the first states of an administrative crystallization of personal surnames. And the geography of this crystallization traced, almost perfectly, the administrative presence of the Florentine state. While one-third of the households in the city declared a second name, the proportion dropped to one-fifth in secondary towns, and then to a low of one-tenth in the countryside. The small, tightly-knit vernacular world had no need for a "proper name": such names were, for all practical purposes, official names confined to administrative life. Many of the inhabitants of the poorest and most remote areas of Tuscany — those with the least contact with officialdom — only acquired family names in the seventeenth century. Nor were fifteenth century Tuscans in much doubt about the purpose of the exercise; its failure was largely due to their foot-dragging and resistance. As the case of Florence illustrates, the naming project, like the standardization of measurements and cadastral surveys, was very much a purposeful state mission.

ENGLAND, SCOTLAND, AND WALES: PRIVATE PROPERTY, PRIMOGENITURE, AND LAW ENFORCEMENT

Even in England and Scotland, where patronyms took several centuries to develop, there was a method to the madness. If patronyms emerged solely for local, individual recognition purposes, then a system of non-hereditary secondary appellations would have sufficed. However, the surname system that emerged involved the use of hereditary and fixed last names. This fact is crucial to understanding the importance of patronyms with respect to the state. Indeed, the development of patronyms helped enforce private property rights, advance primogeniture regimes, and secure the ability of the state to make its subjects legible to its gaze.

The use of last names did not become common until well after the Norman Conquest. Social norms developed by the twelfth century dictated that it was a disgrace for a proper gentleman not to have a last name.[15] The use of patronyms then spread, albeit unevenly, with the implementation of the poll tax under Richard II[16] and the legal requirement of baptismal registration by Henry VIII.

A closer analysis of the process of surname diffusion also reveals the link between the English naming system and the securing of private property rights. In a bargain that replicates itself in many other nations, the aristocracy gained security for their property rights in many other nations, by adopting heritable patronyms. Their new legal identity was a political resource in their claim to property in land and office. By the middle of the thirteenth century, a large proportion of large and medium landowners in England possessed hereditary last names. An examination of Exchequer and Chancery records listing feudal landholders reveals that most of these patronyms were derived from the lands possessed by their bearers.[17]

It is significant to note that in the century or two following the reign of William the Conqueror, there was a great deal of uncertainty regarding the status of large land grants made by the King. As Richard McKinley notes,

> How far his grants were grants of property in fee and inheritance was perhaps not clear. In these circumstances, anything which helped to stress the hereditary character of tenure was likely to be viewed with favour by landowners, and the acquisition of a hereditary patronym especially one derived from a landed family's estates, would obviously have this effect....
> [Thus, the adoption of patronyms was] part of a general trend from them to the consolidation of their position as hereditary property owners.[18]

The link between land and last names is further emphasized by the types of names introduced by the Normans when they invaded Britain: they were almost all territorial in derivation. Indeed,

> [t]he followers of William the Conqueror were a pretty mixed lot, and while some of them brought the names of their castles and villages in Normandy with them, many were adventurers of different nationalities attracted to William's standard by the hope of plunder, and possessing no family or territorial names of their own. Those of them who acquired lands in England were called after their manors, while others took the name of the offices they held or the military titles given to them, and sometimes a younger son of a Norman landowner on receiving a grant of land in his new home dropped his paternal name and adopted that of his newly acquired land.[19]

Patterns of surname adoption also reveal a close link between primogeniture and naming practices. For example, during the twelfth and thirteenth centuries it was not uncommon that a senior branch of a family would continue to use the hereditary surname while the junior branches would adopt new patronyms, since they no longer had any property right in the main family estate.[20] Furthermore, the reorganization of the system of land ownership, the establishment of a formal system of primogeniture, and the development of inherited copyhold tenure for manorial land under the reign of Edward I helped to accelerate the use of last names. The last name became, in this context, another way of displaying paternity and, hence, inheritance rights. More generally, the adoption of permanent patronyms retraced, geographically, the growing presence of the Crown and its agents. It occurred "sooner among the upper classes than the lower, and sooner in the south than the north,"[21] sooner in the large towns than in the countryside. The greater the contact with the Crown-crafted world of documents, rolls, taxes, conscription, wills, and deeds, the greater the need for unambiguous designations.

On rare occasions, one gets a glimpse, like a fly caught in amber, of the state-based process of crystallization. A Welshman who appeared before an English judge in the early sixteenth century during the reign of Henry VIII, was asked his name. He replied, in the Welsh fashion, "Thomas Ap[son of] William, Ap Thomas, Ap Richard, Ap Hoel, Ap Evan Vaughan." He was reprimanded by the judge to "leave the old manner ... whereupon he after called himself Moston, according to the name of his principal house, and left that name to his posteritie."[22] One imagines, however, that this newly minted administrative last name remained all but unknown to Thomas's neighbors.

This small episode from Wales alerts us to the fact that local, vernacular appellations persist and co-exist, often for long periods, alongside official naming practices. Each name is appropriate to a particular sphere of social relations, certain encounters, and situations. Local naming practices rarely if ever disappear completely; instead, they remain relevant to a diminishing social sphere. The slippage between official naming and vernacular practice is apparent in the institution of the telephone book in countries where permanent patronyms are recent creations.[23] As encounters grow with the extra-local world, the world of official documents and lists (e.g., tax receipts, military eligibility lists, school documents, property deeds and inventories, birth, marriage and death certificates, internal passports, court decision, legal contracts), so also does the social circumference of official patronyms. Large segments of social life that might previously have been successfully navigated without documents, and according to customary practice, are now impossible without the paper trail, stamps, signatures, and forms on which the authorities insist. The state creates irresistible incentives for calling oneself after its fashion.

CITIZENSHIP, IDENTITY, AND STATE ADMINISTRATION

The logic and geography of the adoption of surnames and, later, permanent patronyms in France was little different than in England or Florence. In medieval Languedoc, for example, only a few names (Guillaume, Bernard, Raimond, Pierre, Pons) might designate three quarters of the male population. Nobles increasingly adopted surnames (not yet a nom de famille) to distinguish the eldest, inheriting son. In this fashion, the use of surnames and, later, stable noms de famille proliferated, first among the nobility, in the large towns, and among the propertied. The professional agent of this transformation was the notaire who functioned as the local record-keeper and for whom precision of identity was essential.[24] The fifteenth century case of Martin Guerre, made famous in film, is precisely about the great difficulty of establishing identities, especially among mobile populations. When, much later, birth certificates became more common, it was forbidden for a subject to change his or her name without permission from the Crown.

More broadly, the link between state-making and state-naming is so strong that one might, in fact, use the synoptic legibility of permanent, registered patronyms as a reliable proxy for the degree of state presence. Here a long-run time-elapse record would show the fissures and breakpoint of state saturation. That record would show, for Britain, that projects of legibility tended to stumble in the hills, where they encountered ecologies and populations that were distinct culturally and linguistically. The hills were, as Braudel has emphasized, bastions of relatively autonomous local societies.

> For there man can live out of reach of the pressures and tyrannies of civilization, its social and political order its monetary economy. Here there was no landed nobility with ... powerful roots.... There was no tight urban network, so no administration, no towns in the proper sense of the word, and no gendarmes we might add.... The hills were the refuge of liberty, democracy, and peasant republics.[25]

Inaccessibility, demographic dispersal, poverty, and active resistance meant that permanent patronyms (not to mention standardized place names) came late to the hills of Wales and Scotland. The higher the hills, the further from lowland centers of administration, the later their arrival. At the risk of over-generalization, it might be said that the more precocious the state-making, the earlier the appearance of permanent patronyms.[26] Thus they appear comparatively early in Italy, France, and England and later in Sweden, Germany, Norway, and Turkey. In many colonized countries, it occurred even later; in some cases it has hardly begun.[27] Within each political context, it is reasonably clear that the permanent patronym radiates out from the administrative center at a tempo that is conditioned by "stateness": first in the capital, first at the top of the status ladder, first in modern institutions (e.g., schools) and last in marginal areas (mountains, swamps), among the lower classes, among the marginalized and stigmatized.

Once deeds, wills and testaments, property transfers, and certain contracts are subject to state validation, there are powerful incentives for becoming a legible subject. And yet, at the same time, the classic fear of the state as taxer and conscriptor continued to provide much of the population with continuing reasons for remaining illegible. As late as 1753, the British Parliament defeated a census bill over fears of more taxation and, five years later, a bill for the "mandatory registration of births, marriages, and deaths." Contrast this effective resistance in England with the Crown's colonial policy in Ireland nearly a century earlier when William Petty conducted a comprehensive survey of land, buildings, people, and cattle in order to facilitate seizure and control. Where autocracy or conquest permit state officials to pursue projects of legibility, unhampered by consultation, they are likely to proliferate earlier and more extensively, though they may provoke resistance and rebellion.

War, because of the exceptional demands it makes on the mobilization of resources, is the great handmaiden of all forms of legibility, including permanent patronyms. Mobilization for war, as Charles Tilly demonstrates, impelled the early modern state to abandon indirect, tributary rule through powerful, and often recalcitrant, intermediaries and, instead, directly seize the military resources it needed.[28] What the state requires, of course, is far more than just conscripts (who are hopefully, unambiguously identified).

Fielding a 60,000-man army in the late seventeenth century would have required, for its men and its 40,000 horses, nearly a million pounds of food a day: a quartermaster's nightmare. The task demanded impressive feats of organization and expenditure. The mere grain needed to keep this army in the field, let alone armed and clothed, cost the equivalent of the wages of 90,000 ordinary laborers. This last requirement meant taxation nets of finer and finer mesh to enumerate real property, wealth, commercial exchange, and above all, the individuals who would bear the responsibility for paying and fighting.

MODERN CITIZENSHIP AND STATECRAFT: THE UNEASY BARGAIN

If state-making for the purposes of taxation, police control, and war were the great incentives to projects of legibility in ancient regimes everywhere, the rise of democratic citizenship and modernist social engineering required entirely new forms of legibility. The reach of the modern state, together with its ambitions to social reform, gave rise to state lenses with far greater resolving power than any pre-modern regime.

The great emancipatory step of the French Revolution's Declaration of Human Rights created a new subject/citizen. Whereas, before, even the most intrusive absolutist regimes were obliged to work through social intermediaries—clergy, nobles, and wealthy burgers— the revolutionary regime sought a direct, unmediated relationship to the citizen. This new citizen was an abstract, unmarked individual who was the bearer of equal rights before the law. Universal citizenship implied, in turn, that a citizen be uniquely and reliably distinguishable as an individual and not as a member of a community, manor, guild or parish. Universal rights signified, in turn, universal duties vis-à-vis the state — duties which included direct, universal conscription and taxation.

This extension of citizenship, coupled with legibility, was part and parcel of the internationalization of the French Revolution carried by the forces of Napoleon. Prussia's law, passed in 1812, encouraged the adoption of patronyms by all members of the Jewish faith. Ostensibly in the progressive spirit of the Enlightenment, the Jewish population would receive citizenship in exchange. The connection between universal citizenship and the taking of a name proper to a legal state identity is nowhere clearer than for the Jews in Central Europe. Despite the widespread use of fixed and hereditary patronyms in Europe by the nineteenth century, one key group lacked last names— the Ashkenazim. The nomadic, Yiddish-speaking Jewish population of central and northern Europe, the Ashkenazim had managed to retain their ancient patronymic system since the Biblical era. However, during the nineteenth century, Austria, France, Prussia, Bavaria, and Russia all imposed modern surname systems on their Jewish populations. The motives for such policies varied, but generally focused on the adoption of a registered legal patronym as a condition of citizenship and emancipation. The new surname system enabled governments more easily to levy and collect taxes, regulate businesses, conscript for military service, and control movements,[29] in return for which the Jewish population would receive full citizenship for its cooperation. Drawing on Prussian councilor-of-war Christian Wilhelm von Dohm's memorandum "On the Civic Betterment of the Jews" from 1781, several plans were advanced to establish economic and legal equality for the Jewish population. Although these plans differed in a variety of ways, they all agreed on one point: "no proposed law fail[ed] to declare an official choice of name to be obligatory"[30] for citizenship rights. Indeed, the eventual edict that passed gave the Jewish population citizenship in Prussia but only if they bore firmly fixed patronyms.

Soon after 1812, more insidious motives came to light. As Dietz Bering points out, "immediately after the Jews had chosen fixed surnames, attempts were made to secure via the names the dwindling recognizability of the Jew as Jews."[31] The liberality of 1812 edict gave way to a new law passed on 22 December 1833, which required all Jews to adopt a surname, not just those who sought naturalization. Furthermore, the government took steps to assure that previously adopted last names by the Jewish population were in line with newly adopted ones. Government appointed committees forced the Jewish population to accept patronyms that the government chose for them, such as Himmelblau, Rubenstein, Bernstein, Hirsch, and Löew. Furthermore, numerous ministerial reports in the 1830s and 1840s demanded the enactment of a penal clause to prevent members of the Jewish faith from altering their last names. By 1845, laws were passed to render the Jewish patronym in Prussia a closed list. Jewish last names took upon an immutable quality. It was not long before "the Jews, for whom in 1812 the gates of the legal ghetto had been opened only half-heartedly and not even completely, were to be imprisoned again in another ghetto: one of names."[32]

By 1867, all loopholes were closed. A Royal Cabinet order signed on 12 July 1867 gave district presidents the right to confirm any patronym changes that resulted from members of the Jewish faith converting to Christianity. The order made it increasingly difficult to alter a surname through religious conversion. Thus, the democratizing revolutions of 1848 and other reforms played a role both in emancipating and in controlling the population that had previously been illegible. The Prussian state wanted permanent patronyms not only to identify unique citizens, but also to code for religious background. When Germany implemented the Final Solution, the closed list of Jewish patronyms made the task of genocide terrifyingly simple.

By the mid-nineteenth century the idea of universal manhood suffrage was joined, in the West, with a high-modernist ideology requiring entirely novel levels of intervention into society. Once the improvement of society

itself (its health, skills, well-being, intelligence, safety, community life, housing, morals, etc.) became an important state project, a wholly new level of
legibility was required. It is one thing to round up a handful of recruits and
seize part of the wheat harvest; it is quite another to vaccinate, block-by-
block, the poorer quarters of a teeming city, to send disability checks to those
(and only those) with a specific handicap, or to create an epidemiological
database to identify rare diseases. High modernist intrusions typically require
fine-grained, discriminating, unambiguous forms of identification. The pref-
erences of administrators, left to their own devices, are nearly always serial
numbers of one kind or another: an infinite, discriminating, continuous
series, simple to apply and designed for maximum synoptic legibility.

Two Colonial Cases

What happens when a modernizing state with large ambitions encounters a society that is largely opaque? The starkest version of this encounter is
met in colonial situations where an authoritarian, mobilizing state faces a
society at once resistant and uncharted. Here, confronting a population with
few, if any, formal rights to representation, state officials are free to invent
schemes of naming that suit their ends, though implementing them successfully is another matter altogether.

We examine two such colonial cases, separated from one another by
roughly a half century: the creation of permanent patronyms for Native Americans in the United States around the turn of the century and the attempt by
the Canadian government to craft legible identities for the Inuit population
in the 1950s. Each scheme, seemingly simple in conception, became in practice a baroque tangle of contradiction and confusion. The schemes were, of
course, intended to create unambiguous (male) personal identities legible to
officials. The immediate purposes animating each naming exercise varied:
the Bureau of Indian Affairs was hoping to create and stabilize a new, private
property regime and, not incidentally, seize more land from the reservations;
the Canadian officials hoped to intervene more discriminatingly to promote
their vision of welfare, health, and development. What the exercises share,
however, is an overarching cultural project: to fashion and normalize a standard patriarchal family-system deemed suitable to their vision of citizenship,
property rights, and civilized, moral conduct.

The Renaming of Native Americans

The story of conquest, particularly in European settler colonies where
the conquerors held overwhelming power, could be written as a vast project
of renaming the natural world. Presto! Native names for flora, fauna, insects,
mountains, valleys, birds were effaced and replaced by the nouns and tax-

onomies of the conquerors. This process, too, is a project of legibility, a transfer of knowledge in which the mystifying (to Europeans) hieroglyphics of native naming practices was replaced by imported practices transparent to Europeans and, now, mystifying to the conquered. Comprehensive re-labeling is a pre-condition for the transfer of power, management, and control.[33]

Nowhere is this hegemonic project more apparent than in the effort to rename the individual native subjects of this colonial enterprise in a fashion that would allow the colonizers to identify each (male!) unambiguously as a legal person. To grasp the importance and scope of this undertaking, its function in promoting legibility and its role as a civilizational discourse, it is helpful to appreciate just how illegible Native American naming practices were to Europeans.

ILLEGIBILITY

Officials encountered, among Indians, what they considered a radical instability and plurality of names. As in many small stateless societies, a person would have several names dependent on the situation of address (e.g. among age-mates, between generations, among close kin) and these names would often change over time. A child who ran screaming into the teepee on seeing a bear might be called "Runs-from-the-Bear." Later on, if she rides a horse from which others have been thrown, she might be called "Rides-the-Horse." A hunter who was called "Five Bears" may be called "Six Bears" when he has killed another.[34] Researchers tracing surname adoption among the Weagamow Ojibwa noted the plurality of names, in this case partly due to contact with Europeans. The same individual was variously known as Freed Smith, Banani, Nizopitawigizik, and Fredrick Sagachekipoo.[35]

The plurality of names, as the previous example illustrates, was not simply a consequence of indigenous naming practices; it was substantially increased by overlapping jurisdictions and by problems of transliteration. An individual might have one or another of his names recorded by several authorities: a trading post clerk, a missionary, a tribal scribe, or a military or civilian administrator. Each name might be different and, if the people in question were migratory, the places of registration would vary. Imagine trying to pin down the identity of persons who have five or six names and who are constantly on the move![36] Here, of course, it is important to recall that the recording of names was either an attempt at translation into English (e.g., Six Bears) or a stab at transliteration for which there were no fixed rules. The result, in both cases, were names that bore an indifferent relationship to the indigenous appellation they purported to transcribe.[37] In the case of translation, even an accurate one, the name became nothing more than a nonsense syllable for non–English speaking Indians. In the case of transliteration, the problems were compounded by large phonological differences between English and native tongues. Thus, in the case of the Severn Ojibwa, such differences produced exotic local renderings of English given names: e.g., Flora = Pinona; Hector = Ehkitah; Telma = Temina; Isabel = Saben; Amos = Thomas; Louise = Anoys.[38] In the case of direct transliteration of the indigenous names of different persons, as among the Crow at the Devil's Lake Agency in North Dakota, one imagines that the recorded names were only one of many possible phonetic renderings: "Eyaupahamini," "Iyayahamani," Ecanajinka," "Wiyakimaza," "Wakauhotanina," "Wasineausuwmani," "Tiowaste." Had there been standard rules for transliteration and had the recorders of names followed these rules rigorously, the results would have still been mystifying and unpronounceable to white officials.

There were two further problems from the point of view of government agents. First, even translated names that could be understood came in an incompatible format. Take, for example, the names "Barkley-on-the-other-side," "Alice shoots-as-she-goes," "Irvie comes out of fog" (Montana, Crow). The given name is clear, perhaps, but what should be taken as the surname: the whole phrase, the last word...?

Secondly, and more seriously, the indigenous naming system only rarely gave any indication of sex or family relationship. Among the Southern Cheyenne, the following "family names" were recorded:

Father Gunaoi	3rd Daughter Imaguna
Mother Deon	1st Son Inali
1st Daughter Halli	2nd Son Zepko
2nd Daughter Aisima	

The letter recording these names notes that they do not indicate the sex of the children; in fact, what the writer means is that, if sex is indicated, it is not a code that he understands. Even when translation into English names prevailed among the Cheyenne, they very rarely indicated roles in a nuclear family so prized by officials. Thus, "Crow Neck," his wife "Walking Road," their sons "Clarence Crow Neck," "Rested Wolf," and "Hunting Over." On the Arapaho roll: "Bear Lariat," his wife "Mouse," sons "Sitting Man" and "Charles Lariat," and daughter "Singing Above." As we shall see, such illegible naming practices were unsuited to the twin normative legal requirements of civilized life: property ownership and marriage by law.

PROPERTY: THE DAWES ACT

The experience of Native Americans in the United States also suggests an intimate link among the consolidation of the modern nation-state, ethnic assimilation, the development of a private property regime, and the imposition of a European-style surname system. In their study of the Native

Americans of the Oklahoma, Dakota, and Wyoming Territories, Daniel Littlefield and Lonnie Underhill examine the nature of this link in the late nineteenth and early twentieth centuries.[39] Prior to 1887, Native American tribes had held land in common. However, with the passage of the General Allotment Act of 1887, the United States government required Native Americans to receive individual title to land. Though represented as a pro-assimilation policy that would give Native Americans the ability to pursue the American Dream,[40] the imposition of a private property regime actually condemned Native Americans caught in the reservation system to generations of poverty.[41]

Just as significantly, the new regime also represented a major attack on the power of tribal authorities.[42] Property rights accompanied the right to national citizenship, making the Native Americans subject to the law of the United States and not the laws of their tribe. Furthermore, with the elimination of common property rights, the tribal governments lost a major source of their power. The intermediary of the tribe was removed, allowing the United States government to directly control individual Native Americans.

So long as the administrative regime governing Native Americans resembled indirect rule — so long as the aims of white officials were containment and military security — their seemingly promiscuous and illegible naming practices were inconvenient, but not fatal. Officials worked through their own Indian employees and a handful of chiefs. They were dependent on "native-trackers" for detailed information or for locating a particular individual.

All of this changed with the Dawes Act of 1887, which authorized the President to allot 160 acres to each family head (presumptively a male) on a reservation. The title to the land would be held in trust for twenty-five years (apparently to prevent victimization of the new landowners by speculators) after which it would revert to the allottee and his heirs. The goal, aside from seizing more tribal land for white settlers,[43] was the cultural assimilation of Native Americans. "[A]fter receiving his allotment, which signified his severance from the tribe and its communal ways, he would become subject to the laws of the state or territory in which he resided."[44] In this sense, the Dawes Act was "a mighty pulverizing engine for the breaking up of the tribal mass."[45]

Now that many Native Americans would become property-owning citizens, no longer exclusively under tribal jurisdiction, but citizens with rights and obligations under the laws of the larger society, their illegibility as (male!) individuals was no longer acceptable. Native American naming practices were suitable for a common-property regime with a loose family structure and nomadic ways. They were not suitable for a newly created, sedentary, property owning, citizen yeomanry. As legal persons, Native Americans now needed a legal identity proper to the state.

The immediate impetus behind a standardization of Indian names was the institution of private property in land. Allotments meant deeds, titles, cadastral surveys, and inheritance, and these, in turn, required an unambiguous legal identity — preferably one that reflected close kinship ties (i.e., the normative nuclear family). Reformers, who believed allotments were the route to a necessary and beneficial assimilation, were intent on avoiding the confusion and litigation that customary naming practices might encourage. They set about standardizing names to make sure that land was registered under an unambiguous identity: names with permanent patronyms that would reduce the legal confusion about exactly who a deceased landowner's heirs were.

What is noteworthy here is the unavoidable, not to say coercive, logic joining standardized legal identities on the one hand and property-ownership on the other. As one official wrote, the American system of naming was,

> a good system, for it fixes the name of each individual after an unvarying fashion, and establishes the same practically beyond alteration.... We cannot see how it could be otherwise than it is. Furthermore, and what makes it so important, it is practically the only system known to American law, and it is impossible not to see that in all things, prominent among which is the transfer of property or the bequeathing of the same to heirs, trouble must come to those who disregard his system.[46]

Once the allotments were decided on, a whole set of gears were inexorably set into motion. The process is a classic example of practical, systemic hegemony; after all, property deeds, land records, and property taxes require synoptic, standardized forms of identification.

The enormous diversity of Native American naming practices, varying degrees of contact and assimilation, and the huge variety of administrative arrangements under which they were governed, created nearly insurmountable problems of illegibility. The "Poet of the Prairie," Hamlin Garland, made "the naming of the Red Men as they became citizens" a personal mission, seeking the confidence of President Theodore Roosevelt in carrying it out successfully. Stressing the legal necessity of a legible surname system for private property purposes and promoting the assimilation of Native Americans into Anglo-American society, Garland brought the renaming project to the President's attention on 1 April 1902.[47] In a letter urging Roosevelt to place George Bird Grinnell (a naturalist and ethnographer of the Cheyenne) in charge of a committee to rename all Native Americans, he made his goals clear: he wanted to establish a secure legal identity for all Indians: "It is imperative that family names should be reasonable and according to some system. The whole list is an inextricable tangle.... They must be named according to their family relation in order to prevent endless legal complication.... The work should be done by a central committee and not by the various clerks of the agencies."[48]

With Roosevelt's blessing, Garland cooperated with various members of the executive branch to execute a thorough renaming project among the Native Americans residing in the Territories. The overriding concern with establishing a systematic, centralized formula for renaming was echoed by The Commissioner of Indian Affairs, Thomas J. Morgan, in 1890. Although "the command to give names to the Indians and to establish the same as far as possible by continuous use had been part of the Rules and Regulations for years past," it had not been widely applied or generalized.[49] Morgan proposed general guidelines for the renaming exercise. A further regulation deplored the lackadaisical efforts to systematize and enforce the new names, which left in their wake a host of confusing, unpronounceable, and insulting patronyms. He further scolded both his subordinates and his Native American charges:

> Such Indian agents and superintendents of Indian schools have not sought to impress the Indian people with the importance of having their names fashioned after the whites, consequently they have had in this direction the opposition instead of the cooperation of the Indians. In this thing, as in nearly all others, the Indians do not know what is best for them. They can't see that our system has any advantages over their own, and they have fought stubbornly against the innovation.[50]

Morgan, Grinnell, and Garland tried, by the standards of the time, to be as accommodating as they could to indigenous naming practices, so long as they conformed to minimal standards of legibility. Morgan and Grinnell were not opposed to retaining Indian names providing that they were not "too difficult to pronounce." The rub, of course, was that "difficult to pronounce" referred to the difficulty experienced by native English speakers. Otherwise English names and translations were to be substituted whenever the original name was long and/or difficult. Garland agreed. Easily spoken names such as "To-re-ach" or "Chonoh" might be retained while others would require translation and, frequently, shortening as well. "Black Bull" might be shortened to "Blackbill" or "Blackbell"; "Standing Bull" to "Stanbull"; "Albert Spotted-Horse" to "Albert Spotted"; "Black Owl" to "Blackall"; "Brave Bear" to "Bravber." A Christian "given name" was normally appended as a first name: e.g., "Charles Stanbull." The Garland proposal aimed to make all names "decent and reasonable," to show a legal connection to the family. Brevity, ease of pronunciation to whites, and "pleasantness" were emphasized values, all favoring legibility. Existing names would be adopted if they met this criteria. If not, family names might be abbreviated or even altered and spelling would be made uniform.[51] As Garland noted, the point was that "our Indians should be entirely renamed according to some general system," retaining the Indians' own name whenever possible, shortening or modifying it so that it can be spoken by the Red Man's neighbor," so that it name(s) all children after their father or a name chosen by their mother." In short, he desired "a system which will show family relations, which will meet the wishes of the red people and be comprehensible to the white people."[52] The aim, Garland wrote, was to start each allottee with a decent and reasonable name — names that, when translated, seemed demeaning (e.g., "Ghost-faced Woman," "Drunkard," "Let them Have Enough," "Nancy Kills a Hundred," "Rotten Pumpkin,") were to be avoided.[53]

THE CIVILIZATIONAL PROJECT

The renaming of Native Americans was a "civilizing project" in at least two respects. The first is most obvious. The "Red Man" was being inducted, through the Dawes Act, into a radically new life that would eventually lead, it was hoped, to complete assimilation. Just as the pre-condition of the emancipation and full citizenship of the Jews in Central Europe was the legal adoption of permanent patronyms along Christian lines, so was a fixed legal patronym a condition of post-reservation life. The creation of such a legal identity was the necessary universal gear which would then engage the other gears of the official machinery of the modern state.

In 1819, Congress had established a "Civilization Fund" to introduce the Indian to "the habits and arts of civilization." In general, the Fund's goal was to transform what were seen (often mistakenly) as exclusively "hunting-and-gathering" cultures dependent on nomadism and communal ownership of land into a sedentary, agrarian (and artisan) society based on private property. The former condition, requiring bravery, shrewdness, and honor were associated with savagery, whereas a settled life with cultivated property was seen as the handmaiden of civilization: "… you may look forward to the period when the savage shall be converted to the citizen, when the hunter shall be transformed into the mechanic, when the farm, the workshop, the school-house, and the church shall adorn every Indian village; when the fruits of industry, good order, and sound morals shall bless every Indian dwelling."[54] As the Director of the Bureau of Ethnology John Wesley Powell reasoned, accomplishing this work required new names which "tend strongly toward the breaking up of the Indian tribal system, which is perpetuated and ever kept in mind by the Indian's own system of names."[55] As a structure of physical confinement and surveillance, the reservation system was itself not conceived as a project of cultural autonomy but as a prelude to transformation. "Restricting the tribes to a limited and permanent area was a prerequisite to successfully civilizing them."[56]

The second civilizing project — one embedded in the formula for renaming the Indians— was the restructuring of the "family" to bring it into line with the normative patriarchy of their white Christian neighbors. Family and kinship practices varied widely among Native Americans, but it is safe to say that they rarely resembled the codified religious and legal forms of the dominant society.[57] Plural and serial unions, child rearing by the extended family, and changes in the composition of bands over time were common and only served to confirm the need for "civilizing" efforts.

The illegibility of Native American kinship nomenclature was frequently taken by the would-be civilizers as a direct indication of confusion and disorder among the Indians themselves about kinship relations, not as a sign of a different kinship order. Just as the Spanish Governor General of the Philippines in 1847 imposed permanent patronyms on the premise that they would help Filipinos figure out who their cousins were (and avoid marrying them), so did the namers of the "Red Men" imagine that they were helping their charges sort out the primeval mess of their savage ways. Hamlin Garland, for example, supposed that the mere absence of a common patronym joining siblings was evidence "that each child stands alone in the world."[58] Writing of the Southern Cheyenne tribal roll, he declared, "The whole list is an inextricable tangle. For example, practically only one man can straighten out the family ramifications among the Southern Cheyenne."[59] It is not entirely clear whether Garland imagined that the Cheyenne themselves were in doubt about their relationship to one another; but it is clear that he believed that they, as well as the white man, would be thankful for a kinship terminology that clarified matters. Reading the correspondence and official circulars of the time makes it appear that the reformers believed that if they just got the kinship terminology right, the actual practices of Native Americans would soon fall in line with white, "civilized" norms.[60]

BOARDING SCHOOLS

Nowhere was the civilizational project more evident than in the boarding schools set up for Native American school children. The logic behind the boarding school was precisely the logic of the total institution. One might flail away at effecting small changes among masses of Native Americans on the reservation or, alternatively, concentrate on removing a smaller number of children of an impressionable age away from the contaminating influence of the tribe and into highly controlled, disciplinary surroundings. By a reduction in scale, one achieved a commensurate increase in micro-control of the environment. Here the new elites could be shaped from the ground up, Pygmalion-fashion.[61] The results were also more legible: so many graduated, so many literate in English, so many taught certain crafts and mechanical skills, etc.

Like the military model they mimicked, school techniques were meant to be a shocking and comprehensive baptism. The clothes they arrived in were discarded and a "military kit" was issued in its place; their diet was changed to a Western one; their hair (often an important cultural badge) was forcibly cut; facial paint was forbidden; time discipline was imposed; conversation in native languages was severely punished; and, of course, new names were mandated. A Sioux memoir of naming in the boarding school captures the atmosphere:

The new recruit's acquisition of a uniform was followed by the acquisition of a new name. Most often this occurred on the first day of instruction. In the case of Luther Standing Bear, he remembers that one day there were a lot of strange marks on the blackboard, which an interpreter explained were whitemen's names. One by one the students were asked to approach the blackboard with a pointer and were instructed to choose a name. When a name was selected, the teacher wrote it on a piece of white tape, which was then sewn on the back of the boy's shirt. When Standing Bear's turn came, he took the pointer and acted as if he were about to touch an enemy. By the end of the class, all the students had the name of a white man sewn on their backs. In the case of Luther Standing Bear, he needed only to choose a first name and was able to keep part of his Indian name in English translation. Not all the board school students had this luxury.[62]

As in many utopian schemes of standardization, the project of renaming Native Americans was a messy affair. It was common for one authority to codify names without noting, in each case, the results of earlier naming exercises. Efforts to create new names in the boarding schools to indicate paternity were seldom coordinated with renaming on the reservation where the students' fathers lived, thus leading to nearly hopeless confusion. Two brothers named in separate exercises might not be given the same last name. But, as in the case of the Philippines, over several decades, the frequency of contact with officialdom ensured that most Native Americans had legal names that conformed to the Anglo-American normative patriarchal order. Practice, of course, was something else again.

SERIAL NUMBERS AND SYNOPTIC ORDER: THE CASE OF THE INUIT

Roughly half-a-century after the Dawes Act, Canadian Authorities set about identifying their most nomadic and illegible population: the Inuit. Thanks to the existence of one closely observed study,[63] some comparisons with surname creation among Native Americans in the United States are possible. The similarities are more striking than the differences, which arise, it would seem, from Canada's more developed and centralized federal administration.

The Inuit, like many Native American groups, had naming practices that, while perfectly adequate for Inuit purposes, baffled the officials in charge of ruling them. Most Inuit had a single name, one that might, furthermore, change more than once in the course of a lifetime. In common with many other peoples, the Inuit believed in appeasing the restless ghosts of the deceased and, to this end, they strove to ensure that a dead person's name was given to a newly born infant as soon as possible. Gender-specific names arose only under colonial rule and it was quite common to have a daughter given the name of an admired and recently deceased male, whether or not he was a close relative.

Inuit names sounded odd and unpronounceable to European ears (e.g., Itukusuk or Kilabuk) and, as in the United States, even when European and biblical names were adopted, phonological differences made transliteration a tenuous art. As early as 1935, well before a comprehensive renaming was proposed, the difficulties had been noted. One official charged with following migrating individuals from one part of Northern Canada to another complained to the Department of the Interior:

> There are five divisions to the settlement and I think that if I left it to get the names from the natives, each has a different spelling for each name.... It does not seem to ease our troubles any that [the Inuit] have in recent years taken their names from the Bible. A good example of this is the common name "Ruth." The native cannot get his sounding mechanism around the letter "R" at the first of a word. As a result, different persons would write down the following when the native gave the child's name, "Vrootee," "Olootie," "Alootah," and other alterations along the same line. To one who does not know them personally, this makes it rather difficult when it comes to putting them in alphabetical order.[64]

To the problem of variant transliterations must be added that of multiple jurisdictions. Names might be exotically and differently crafted by the Nursing Station personnel, the Royal Mounted Police, and the school administration.

Like Native American personal and place names, Inuit names offered a condensed reference-shelf of narratives which, taken in the aggregate and expanded on, amounted to local histories. Such names marked the landscape and its inhabitants and created a local habitat rich in order and meaning, but largely inaccessible to outsiders. Projects to re-label places and people in standardizing ways carry at least three implications: they facilitate identification and control by extra-local authorities; they help nest the locality in a larger pattern of regional and national meanings; and, finally, they overlay and often efface local systems of orientation. As systematic re-mapping ventures, they re-orient some actors, typically powerful state agents, and dis-orient others. The transfer of knowledge via synoptic legibility is, at the same time, always a cultural project of internal colonialism. Thus, the tidying up of Inuit nomenclature went hand-in-hand with the creation of boarding schools, the ban on Inuit drum dancing and, in the case of the Coppermine Inuit, a prohibition of lip ornaments — actions all intended to make the Inuit into national subjects and citizens.

Unlike the United States government, which, in the 1890s, was preoccupied with confinement, sedentarization, and legal order, the Canadian state, after the Second World War, was animated as much by the delivery of services as by the creation of legal persons. The Canadian welfare state, though in its infancy, was committed to providing social security, pensions, family allowances, vocational schooling, and medical services for everyone, including the nomadic, illegible Inuit. Such discriminating intervention required an equally discriminating system capable of pinpointing each individual.

Bureaucratically speaking, the simplest system of identification is the serial number. Anything else is second best. Given half a chance, administrators are drawn to the arithmetic beauty of a potentially endless series of consecutive numbers. It eliminates, at a stroke, all the ambiguity and discretion which plague any system of last names, for example how to transliterate names not previously written, what part of a name to consider as a patronym (e.g., "de la Fontaine, Oscar" or "Fontaine, Oscar de la"; "McArthur" or "MacArthur").

Inspired by the experience of military dog tags, the Ministry of the Interior at first devised for the illegible Inuit a disk system. Each small fiber disk had, printed in relief, a crown, the words, "Eskimo Identification–Canada" and then a letter and a number: e.g., "E-6-2155." The "E-6 would stand for "East Zone, District 6" indicating the administrative zone of the North where this particular Inuit had been sighted, registered, and tagged! The succeeding number "2155" was a personal identification reference (as a social security number might be in the United States) which directed an official to the appropriate dossier containing all the information of interest to the state (name, aliases, birth-date, civil status, vaccinations, criminal record, pension and welfare records, etc.).

The intention of the administrators was that each Inuit would wear his or her disk on a necklace; in fact, they were manufactured with a hole stamped in them for this purpose. Analogies with the military dog tag system were not implicit but quite conscious. The 1935 proposal noted that: "My humble suggestion would be, that at each registration, the child be given an identity disk along the same lines as the army identity disk and the same insistence that it be on at all times. The novelty of it would appeal to the natives."[65]

Nor is the analogy superficial. The military dog tag, like the hospital identification bracelet, is worn on the body precisely to identify someone who cannot, or will not, identify himself. It identified the dead or unconscious soldier, or the one whose remains are otherwise unidentifiable. The Inuit disk, like the military dog tags, was invented as a device for outsiders to keep track — in the face of muteness, death, or willful resistance — of the people or objects so ordered. Not expected to speak for themselves, the fugitive hunting and trapping Inuit were to be branded like migratory birds so as to track their movements. Had the technology of the age permitted, there is little doubt that officials would have preferred small electronic transmitters and global positioning systems to monitor all movement by satellite.

Imposition of the disk system was seen as the key to all development and welfare among the Inuit.[66] The disk numbers, distributed exclusively to the Inuit following the 1935 census, were the template for assembling all vital statistics about health, education, income, crime, and population. In order to make it stick, officials insisted that the disk number be used in all official correspondence and on all birth, marriage, and death certificates. Evidence that the Inuit did not like the disk system[67] and suggestions for alternatives were rebuffed by its supporters, who urged stricter enforcement: "In my opinion there is no necessity whatsoever to replace the present identification disk with a medal or token of any kind. As I have been pointing out for twenty years, once the Eskimo realizes that the white man wants him to memorize an identification number and use it in all trading and other transactions, the Eskimo will fall into line."[68]

It was a very rare Inuit, indeed, who wore the disk around his or her neck.[69] Many Canadian agencies did not insist on the use of disk numbers in their dealings with Inuit, and the utopian single identifying number fell gradually into disuse. The Inuit complained that their children at school were asked to call out their disk number rather than a name and that they occasionally got mail addressed to their disk number alone.

Finally, in 1969, the disk system was formally abandoned, and a three-member board was created to take charge of establishing family names and their consistent spelling. Thus was born "Project Surname," a crash program to create and/or register proper patronyms for all Inuit before the Centennial. Those officials for whom unambiguous identification was paramount argued for retaining the disk scheme — "the alternative would be an unacceptable level of confusion."[70] "What about variable spellings of the same name?" they asked. "What about people using the same name?" (One official pointed out that in Pongnirtung there were three women named Annia Kilabuk.) "How will we keep track of people who move around?" "How do we know we are paying the right person?"[71]

Unlike disk numbers, patronyms did not lend themselves to a smooth, unambiguous series. A brochure explained why European-style names were preferable: Inuit names were too hard to pronounce, too long, and too similar.[72] As with most crash programs, implementation was chaotic and coercion fairly high. One official told the startled Inuit that everyone had to have a last name by the time he left the settlement the same afternoon: "I was in Baker Lake... There were 800 people. It was just like a sausage factory... 'Do you have a surname? What's your father's name? OK. You're [new name]'... Project Surname ended up by creating a situation which is just horrendous."[73]

Serial numbers and permanent patronyms are each civilizational projects. But while the doling out of serial numbers bore an air of lofty abstraction, the choosing of surnames involved, as elsewhere, an implicitly cultural project. One primary reason why Inuit names did not reflect sex and paternity was because the Inuit simply did not live in standard normative European-style families. (Nor, of course, did many Canadians of European ancestry!) The scolding tone of the administrative summary of Project Surname admitted as much. It complained of

> a total lack of understanding among the Eskimo people about the legal,
> social, and moral aspects of names ... family- or sur-name, under which
> all members of a family are identified, is unknown. Legal usage, ownership
> of property under a family name is impossible ... Marriage customs have
> never developed in the sense of the "Western civilized ethic," as a family
> unit has no common name tying it together. Adoption of children has pre-
> sented extreme difficulty.[74]

Adoption among relatives was very common and many Inuit children were named to reflect their adoptive parents rather than their birth parents. Nor was the concept "head of family," even as a formal status, particularly germane in the Inuit context. The desire of officials to create a viable system of identification and get welfare checks to the right person (and avoid fraud) was germane; but the desire to create a modern Canadian identity for the Inuit and muster them, at least on paper, into a standard, normative family was at the very core of Project Surname's logic.

This exercise did not, of course, eliminate Inuit naming practices. What it did produce was rampant name pluralism. Many, perhaps most, Inuit had an administrative name that followed European usage but also one or more local Inuit names, not recorded in any document, by which he or she was known locally. Thus, most Inuit move back and forth between a local iden- tity with its own codes and an administrative identity with its own code. As the mother of a newborn son explained, "It [a child's Inuit name] won't go on any record at all. But he will be known as another name.... It's still fol- lowed today. Like right now my own baby is named by three different names, which aren't going to be on his birth certificate."[75]

These two spheres of naming can coexist for long periods. Unlike the Inuit register of names, however, the Canadian register of names is under- written by a state, an army, the police, and the law. The greater the necessity and frequency of the Canadian code in Inuit lives, the greater the practical, daily hegemony of European-style surnames.

III. Names and the Practical Hegemony of the State

Just as industrialized nations are extending long-standing projects of legibility to the far reaches of their periphery, new states, with modernizing agendas, have been inventing permanent patronyms for the first time. Other techniques of identification, as we shall see, are now available. Most of them are more discriminating, legible, and efficient than the proper name. Never- theless, to follow the progress of legal naming throughout the world is to fol- low, simultaneously, the rise of regimes, which have plans for the mobilization and/or improvement of their population.

MODERNIZATION PROJECTS

The modern Turkish republic of Kemal Ataturk decreed universal, legal patronyms in the context of one of the most comprehensive projects of modernization and Westernization the world has seen. Having reformed the clock and the calendar, adopted the metric system, abolished feudal tithes, created a national system of citizenship, and rewritten the legal code to bypass the shari'a, Ataturk ordered the adoption of permanent legal family names in 1934.[76] The creation of a powerful modern state required a system of meticulous taxation and conscription that improved on the techniques of the Ottomans. This objective, in turn, required legible, personal identities. As we have seen in other instances, however, the mandating of last names was part and parcel of a vast cultural project designed to transform Turkey into a modern European nation. To this end, Arabic script was replaced with Roman, words with Ural-Altaic roots were emphasized, the wearing of the fez and the veil was banned; Islam and, with it, the Islamic tithe (zakat) was dis-established. The adoption of distinctively Turkish names, as opposed to Islamic and, especially, Arabic names was encouraged.[77]

The brusque legal change was easier to bring about than the revolutionizing of naming habits. Turks (not to mention the many national minorities) had many different names, some of which might change in the course of a lifetime. Locally, this posed no confusion as local residents knew the names of their neighbors and could, if necessary, add qualifying nicknames to clear up any possible misunderstanding. The new names co-existed with older naming practices for a long time, especially where contact with the state was episodic. Even at the center, the adoption of novel patronyms threatened, if rigorously and suddenly imposed, to provoke commercial and administrative chaos. Very few citizens actually knew the new patronyms of their acquaintances[78] and, mercifully, the Istanbul telephone book listed subscribers alphabetically by first name until 1950, fourteen years after the patronym decree. Nor was Turkey unique in this regard. Authorities in Thailand, where permanent last names were instituted in the 1950s, also have a healthy respect for the importance of practical knowledge. Names in the Bangkok phone directory are still listed and alphabetized by first name.

FIXING NAMES, FIXING IDENTITIES

So far we have examined the creation of names as official legal identities only in the context of Western-style naming practices. It should be perfectly clear, however, that the legibility of names as legal identities is intrinsic to any project of governance requiring discriminating intervention in local affairs. Thus, the conflict between parochial and outside authority and the legibility questions prevalent in the naming process are not merely vestiges of our past. Witness, for example, the legal and policy issues surrounding the creation of fixed identities in the relatively anonymous world of the Internet. The development of Internet cookies to better track cyber-identities, the quest for a consistent domain-name registration system, and judicial reforms aimed at awarding jurisdictional authority over the Internet to the courts of modern nation-states all represent early efforts to make cyberspace legible.

Meanwhile, the older process of state-making through naming continues, often with non-Western wrinkles. In China for example, the contemporary regime confronts a host of nationalities (fifty-six by official codification). Some have no tradition of permanent patronyms at all, some have many names and surnames, and still others have family names that do not conform to Han-Chinese usage. The standardized Chinese administrative system is no more able to accommodate exotic minority names than was the Bureau of Indian Affairs able to absorb — even after translation — the Crow name "Irvie comes-out-of-fog." Confronted with Kachin minority naming practices at the southwest frontier in Yuna'an Province, Chinese authorities do what Hamlin Garland did. They shoehorn Kachin practices into the nearest available standard Chinese equivalent. An ethnographer from Taiwan, studying the Kachin, described how they were fitted into the grid.

> Names in official records have to be able to be written in Chinese characters; hence family names that are mono-syllables are changed into Chinese (usually single character) surnames. Among the Zaiwa [sub-division of the Kachin] "Muiho" is a common and important surname whose standard matching surname in Chinese is "he" [Wade-Giles "Ho"], my own surname.[79]

For many of the isolated Kachin who have thus been conjured by a Han administrator into "He(s)," the Chinese record-keeping is of little moment. Their Han administrative identity is invoked only on those infrequent occasions when they have official business (e.g., taxation, contracts, conscription, inheritance of property) with the state. For the rest, for daily transactions, local naming practices are perfectly satisfactory.

Initially, then, state schemes of naming may hardly touch the citizens whose identities they aim to fix. "Name pluralism" may persist for centuries, with state-devised identities being invoked for some purposes, and local vernacular identities for others. But we must not imagine that official and vernacular names are on an equal footing. Official names have, in the final analysis, the weight of the nation-state and its associated institutions arranged behind them. Here the concept of "traffic patterns" as applied by Benedict Anderson to state-sponsored identities is instructive. Traffic patterns are what make imaginary administrative identities into the solid realities of social life. Thus the Dutch colonizers in Indonesia "identified certain residents as Chinese [Chinezen] although they were part of a huge diaspora that did not think of themselves as Chinese," nor were they so thought of. Nevertheless, the

Dutch government, working on their ethnoscape, proceeded to organize, "the new educational, juridical, public-health, police and immigration bureaucracies it was building on the principle of ethnic-racial hierarchies. The flow of subject populations through the mesh of differential schools, courts, clinics, police-stations, and immigration offices created 'traffic-habits' which, in time, gave real social life to the state's earlier fantasies."[80]

Vernacular names, like vernacular identities, do not typically disappear; but state naming systems typically become hegemonic for several reasons, all having to do with the institution of the modern nation-state. The state can insist that one use one's legal name in all official acts: e.g. certification of birth, marriage, and death, inheritance, legal contracts, last wills and testaments, taxes, written communications to officials. Correspondingly, the greater the frequency of interaction with the state and state-like institutions, as we have seen, the greater the sphere of public life in which the official name is the only appropriate identity.

Take, for example, the birth certificate. Along with the death certificate, it is a remarkable and very recent innovation; even in the West, people managed, until quite recently, to be born and die without official notice! The birth certificate is the first official recording of a proper (paper) legal identity and it is governed by many regulations. Care is taken to devise a proper surname when the normal parental agreement is lacking: "In cases where the mother and father have joint custody of the child and disagree on the selection of a surname, the surname selected by the father and surname selected by the mother shall both be entered on the certificate, separated by a hyphen, with the selected names entered in alphabetic order."[81]

Notice, also, that the normal, modern, institutional setting for birth and, hence, for the birth certificate forms, is the maternity ward of a hospital, where state-like bureaucratic routines for collection of vital statistics prevail. When, by contrast, most children are born at home, with or without professional care, the official registration of births is that much more complex. Modern, formal institutions are handmaidens to the creation and hegemony of official patronyms. The hegemony of state-structured institutions such as schools, social security, military service, taxpaying, property registration and transfer provide the "traffic patterns" that ensure the dominance of state-identification practices. It is in most citizens' interest to be duly recorded whenever state institutions have the power to provide a benefit or to diminish or cancel a penalty. Official identities, then, constitute an iron cage enclosing a great deal of social life in the contemporary modern state.

IV. Vernacular Optics, State Optics

Central to the institutional hegemony of the nation-state has been the project of synoptic legibility. Its hard-won achievement against dogged resistance, an achievement requiring massive institutional investments in creating records and the personnel to manage them, represents the armature of state knowledge. Without this synoptic grasp, without the field of vision it affords officials, most of the activities of the modern state, from vaccinating schoolchildren to arresting criminals (or political opponents) would be inconceivable.

The early modern state faced a population whose land tenure practices, identity, production, wealth, and health were largely opaque. An exotic tangle of local measurement practices, nicknames, customary rights, and forms of local exchange thwarted any monarch's scheme to mobilize resources for war or for public works. At the very least, officials at the center were hostage to the cooperation of local authorities for what intelligence they chose to offer. We have examined the creation of the permanent patronym as an essential, though rudimentary, element in this project of synoptic legibility. In a larger study, the permanent patronym would take its place beside a host of other state optical technologies: the standardization of weights and measures, the centralization of the legal code, the creation of uniform cadastral maps and property registers, a uniform tax code, a common currency, and the promotion of a standard dialect.[82]

Each of these projects represents a transfer of power and a corresponding switch in codes. The transfer of power, in terms of state capacity, is obvious, as is the fact that it is achieved against opposition. As socio-linguists are fond of saying, the difference between a dialect and a national language is that a national language is a dialect with an army. Nation-states, even revolutionary ones, could not simply decree projects of synoptic legibility; they had to be enforced. In 1791, the Revolutionary State in France required all prefectures to furnish the "name, age, birthplace, residence, profession, and other means of subsistence of all citizens living in its territory."[83] Only *three* of 36,000 communes replied! While the Napoleonic State a decade later did achieve better results, it required heroic efforts against substantial odds.

The switch in codes is vital. Both vernacular systems and state systems of, say, naming and measurement, are codes. The question is who holds the key to the code, who can break it. In the case of vernacular naming, as with the Inuit or Native Americans in the United States, the keys to the code are held locally — and often, but not always, fairly democratically — while the code remains an opaque hieroglyph to outsiders. In the most synoptic forms of identification — for example the serial number — the keys to the code are held by specialists (clerks, lawyers, statisticians) while the code typically remains a hieroglyph to local, non-officials. Such specialists might be termed "trackers," but they track synoptic forms of knowledge that are proper to the modern state. Access to these trackers ordinarily depends on political influence, financial resources, or both.

The bird's-eye view achieved by official projects of legibility is best seen as a neutral instrument of state capacity. Synoptic views are by no means neutral in how they privilege and empower state officials over local citizens and subjects. But they are utterly neutral with respect to the purposes for which they are used. They are, as we shall see, the basis for beneficial interventions that save lives, promote human welfare, without which contemporary life is scarcely imaginable. On the other hand, they enhance the capacity of the state to carry out the most fine-tuned and gruesome projects of surveillance and repression. In between these extremes lie the vast majority of uses: uses with both beneficial and troubling consequences.

Let us take the unambiguous identification of individuals through systematic, standardized birth records. This capacity, along with hospital records of birth defects, has existed for some time in Norway and has allowed epidemiologists to learn rather precisely how likely it is that a mother with a birth defect herself will give birth to a child with a defect.[84] Having a complete record of nearly half-a-million births from 1967 to 1982 (8,192 of which involved birth defects), researchers were able to establish that while women with birth defects were more likely than women without to bear children with birth defects, the *added* risk was quite small (1.4 percent), and that the small risk applied only to the passing on of their own birth defect. The findings have obvious implications for more informed genetic counseling and social policy, not to mention women's decisions about child bearing. None of these statistical facts is even imaginable without the personal legibility — two generations long — that makes possible this correlation between the birth defects of mothers and their children.

The way in which massive projects of legibility are often driven by a laudable concern for public welfare is manifest in the recent debate in the United States about a "health identification number." Originally seen as a means to ensure that employees could retain medical insurance if they changed employers, the proponents of "portability" suggested an electronic code for *all* patients.[85] In the words of the Chairman of the National Committee on Vital and Health Statistics, this code would be "a way to identify people uniquely."[86] Existing procedures, they reasoned, were inadequate. Names were not unique; they changed and were subject to various spellings; drivers' license numbers were not universal nor unique except within a single state; the social security number, though unique, was not universal. Furthermore, the existing system of medical record keeping had all the charm and confusion of vernacular naming practices. The varying modes of identification and software programs of different health-management organizations, hospitals, clinics, and employers ensured a mutually unintelligible dialogue of the deaf.

Reaching for a utopian solution, planners suggested a comprehensive and unique number for each patient, consisting of date of birth, latitude and longitude of hometown, and additional digits unique to the individual. Others suggested bio-medical markers such as thumbprints, electronic scans of the retina, or DNA profiles. The advantages of this vast administrative simplification are obvious; all patient records will be tracked as patients change doctors or addresses (or names!); billing would be streamlined, patients could get their records expeditiously, and last, but not least, the system would create the kind of national data-base of which epidemiologists have long dreamed. For the Center for Disease Control, it promised comprehensive information on illnesses (as opposed to the Center for Disease Control's system of reporting hospitals), and, for the individual practitioner, it promised the possibility of matching a comparatively rare individual case with others like it nationwide and learning which treatments worked best.

The opposition to a unique and comprehensive health identification number came from those who were in no doubt about its efficacy as a project of legibility. It was, in their view, all too legible, especially for those who wanted to put it to other uses. Sensitive health information could be conveyed to employers (e.g., HIV status), it could be linked to financial data and used for blackmail; it might be used by the police to track down suspects or witnesses (thus driving them away from medical care). Patients, thinking that a medical history of depression, abortion, or sexually-transmitted disease might end up in a database available to their employers or creditors, would be reluctant to confide in their doctors in the first place.[87] Once a comprehensive project of legibility is in place, it represents a vastly expanded capacity for discriminating intervention by *whoever* commands and surveys the synoptic heights.

V. Conclusion: The Modernization of Identification

The accurate identification of individuals, let alone actually locating their whereabouts is, historically speaking, a very recent phenomenon. Lacking a comprehensive and standardized population registry, the best that most early-modern European states could hope for was a tolerably accurate census and cadastral survey to guide levies of grain, draft animals, and soldiers. The specification of individual identities was typically confined to the local level, where the state was hostage to the collaborators it could find. Even where permanent patronyms were already established, the vagaries of their recording, standardization, duplications, variant spellings, not to mention population movement, made accurate extra-local identification of a resident a tenuous affair.

One can sketch, roughly, something of a continuum of identification practices, ranged according to how legible, exhaustive, and unambiguous they were. At one end would be, say, the Inuit before the disks and before

"Project Surname": a population totally legible to local insiders and almost totally illegible, synoptically, to outsiders. The introduction of permanent patronyms, even with all the liabilities we have noted, is a substantial step forward. Standardization of record-keeping across jurisdictions and of spellings, as well as declining duplication of names, has made the name increasingly discriminating. The name remains, in most cases, the first element in most systems of identification (e.g., "name, rank, and serial number" in army parlance).

The next step is the unique identification number, of which the Social Security Number is the classic American example. Where it covers every citizen and is coordinated with other data (e.g., address, father's name, mother's maiden name, date of birth), it can be quite discriminating. Its major drawback is that officials are stymied when a citizen refuses or is unable to give his or her name and "serial number." Many nations have attempted to remedy this defect in legibility by imposing substantial penalties on citizens who fail to deliver their internal passport or piece of identification to an authority. It is for this reason that the first thing a gendarme says to someone he has accosted is, "*Vos papiers, Monsieur.*" One of the most notorious cases of requiring all subjects to carry an identity card was the "pass system" of South Africa under apartheid. Here the pass was used to authorize and control movement between the cities and white areas on the one hand and the 'native locations' on the other. Elsewhere, as in nineteenth-century France, the pass system was sometimes combined with a record of employment (including the notation of employers) as in the *livret de famille*.

The development of photography in the mid-nineteenth century made possible the photo-identification and, with it, the police mug shot.[88] The photograph aids formidably in the progressive elimination of possible misidentifications afforded by several forms of identification — a name, a social security number, and a signature. Here one thinks of the Wanted posters made famous by the Federal Bureau of Investigation (FBI) in U.S. Post Offices, with a photo (front view, side views), name, aliases, height and weight, fingerprints, and the location last seen. For most civilian purposes, however, name, photo-ID, social security number, and signature are sufficiently definitive.

The next step, of course, and one devised long before the advent of the modern state, is the indelible marking of the body. This practice too amounts to a document of identity: an identity mark one has no choice but to bear corporeally. Tattooing was, for example, used in pre-colonial Siam on commoners in much the same fashion as a cattle-brand — to indicate to whom the commoner was enserfed. Like the mutilations used elsewhere to identify criminals, runaway slaves or serfs — such as notching or severing the ear or distinctive scarring — they identified less the individual than a class of people, almost always in a stigmatizing way. More permanent than dress, such marks nevertheless served, like sumptuary laws, to make status legible to any observer. In principle, permanent marks, such as tattoos, could be made the basis for unambiguous personal identification. One need only imagine that Canadian authorities had thought of tattooing the disk number on each Inuit for handy reference.

One decisive advantage of an indelible identification marked on the body is that it does not require the cooperation of the subject. When physically present, he reveals his identity whether he wishes to or not. The most modern forms of identification — and therefore those most favored by administrators — are virtually definitive for personal identity as in the case of bio-medical markers — e.g., the fingerprint,[89] the iris scan, and the DNA profile. In the case of the DNA profile, it is definitive long after death; a bit of tissue from a 2,000 year-old corpse exhumed from the permafrost yields the same absolutely distinctive DNA signature.

The disadvantage of *all* these technologies is that they require the physical presence of the body to be identified. But, the trick to much police work is, of course, successfully locating a suspect or witness whose identity is already known. It is not a radical step from fingerprints and DNA profiles to imagine electronic bracelets transmitting distinctive signals to a global-positioning satellite, allowing the police to know, at any time, the precise location of every person of interest — just as naturalists and wildlife ecologists now track the movements of a particular individual of a migratory species. Such totalizing possibilities are close to being realized for certain felons on probation or on work release under the United States judicial system.

The capacity that a society made perfectly legible by meticulous policies of identification affords state officials is far beyond what the early modern state could achieve — though not beyond what its ministers could imagine. In fact, a chief distinction between the early modern state and the modern state is precisely the hard-won terrain of synoptic administrative legibility — of geography, people, property, goods, commerce, health, skills — that makes large projects of mobilization and transformation conceivable.[90] Nowhere is this more apparent than in modernist projects of extermination. The efficient deportation of most of the Jews (some 65,000) of Amsterdam to their deaths during the Nazi Occupation would have been unthinkable in the early nineteenth century. The roundup was made possible by a meticulous and comprehensive population and business registry — names, addresses, ethnicity/religion — and cartographic exactitude. A map produced by the city's Office of Statistics in May 1941 is titled "The Distribution of Jews in the Municipality." Each black dot represents ten Jews, making it clear which blocks, when surrounded, would yield most of the Jewish population.[91]

Under more controlled conditions — i.e. the concentration camps — schemes of synoptic legibility could be pursued ruthlessly. The very term "concentration camp" is, of course, a shorthand reference to the involuntary confinement and regimentation of prisoners in a miniaturized setting, allowing close surveillance and near perfect legibility. In Auschwitz, serial numbers were tattooed on the left arm of all Jews and Gypsies, in the order in which they had arrived: the handful of long-term survivors became known as "old numbers" (i.e., low numbers).[92] An elaborate "sumptuary" color code to mark the sub-sets of prisoners was introduced. In addition to the well-known Jewish star of David, sewn on the left breast and the right trouser leg, there were a series of triangles (apex down) affixed to clothing to make the taxonomy of prisoners legible at a glance: brown for gypsies, green for "criminals," red for "politicals," pink for homosexuals, mauve for Jehovah's Witnesses, blue for émigrés, and black for "asocial" elements. Prisoners were identified at roll call by number, not by name.

Many of the same technologies of concentration, identification, and control are also the basis for what we could consider humanitarian interventions. The operational procedures of the United Nations High Commission for Refugees (UNHCR) are a striking illustration of how a comparable state-like capacity to generate legible social landscapes can also be deployed to provide a safe-haven for victims of terror and/or feed famished civilians. A "Practical Guide for Field Staff" entitled "Registration" distills the experience of refugee administration over the past fifty years.[93] "Fixing the Population," a key term in the manual, refers to enumerating, concentrating, and identifying the people "of concern" to the UNHCR. It requires, though without the barbed wire and electrified fences, a secure perimeter with a single, easily controlled entrance and exit. As refugees arrive, they are given "fixing tokens"; then, if the situation permits, wristbands and temporary identification cards, all of which are serially numbered to facilitate a rough census. Both the wristbands and the temporary identification cards have numbers from one, to twenty-four or thirty, each of which can be punched like a railway ticket to indicate the receipt of certain supplies and rations, depending on the code established. One purpose of the wristbands and identity cards is to prevent double registration and fraud; another is to identify particularly vulnerable groups (e.g., women nursing infants, aged and infirm) for special attention. Together with orderly, barracks-style, shelter construction, enumerated also by "section/block/individual shelter," the identity cards permit a more-or-less complete census of individuals by location in the camp. This too facilitates locating a particular individual who, say, needs special medicine or rations, has received a letter, or who has special skills of value to the camp's operation.

Recent technological advances, however, have made camp organization easier and more efficient. The use of computer-generated bar codes on the wristbands and identity cards, read by laser guns, allow camp officials to monitor the refugees and the distribution of rations more efficiently.[94] In mid-1999, volunteers from Microsoft Corporation were being deployed to the refugee camps bordering Kosovo to establish a standardized, digitized, photo-ID to be issued to all refugees. The aim was to produce a single, instantly accessible, database, which, among other things, would allow individuals to locate relatives and friends lost in the scramble to leave.

Despite the radically different purposes of concentration camps and refugee camps, despite the fact that the former routinely employs violence to achieve its ends, the discriminating administration of large numbers of strangers requires practices of legibility that bear a family resemblance to one another. Thus, unless one wishes to make an ethical-philosophical case that no state ought to have such panoptic powers— and hereby commit oneself to foregoing both its advantages (e.g., the Center for Disease Control) as well as its menace (like fine-combed ethnic cleansing)— one is reduced to feeding Leviathan and hoping, perhaps through democratic institutions, to tame it.

Notes

1. Brian Friel, *Translations*, Act II, Scene 1. London: Faber and Faber, 1981.

2. Strictly speaking, governmental road designation systems vary by level of jurisdiction. Thus one has, moving step-wise from local to supra-local, town roads, county roads, state roads, and national roads. At this last level the Interstate system, built with military needs in mind, is logically calibrated with east-west highways designated by tens (Interstate Routes 40, 50, 60, 70, 80, 90) growing larger as one moves north, and north-south highways designated also by tens (45, 55, 65, 75, 85, 95) growing as one moves east. The older and smaller the jurisdiction, the greater the likelihood that its road and street system will have folk characteristics that will be difficult for a stranger to fathom.

3. Where a place has been named before the occurrence of events that will forever mark it, the unmarked association is nevertheless indelible: Katyn forest, Guenica, Selma, Pearl Harbor, Auschwitz, Place de la Bastille, Hastings, Hiroshima, Bandung. For a mobile or nomadic people, the place names that trace their trajectory through the landscape often represent, collectively, like a pilgrimage route, their history, their myths, and their moral orientations. See Keith Basso, *Wisdom Sits in Places: Landscape and Language among the Western Apache* (Albuquerque: University of New Mexico Press, 1996).

4. "Towns in Washington Bringing Back Poetry in Street Names." *The New York Times*, 8 June 1997, p. 40.

5. Ibid.

6. In much of pre-modern Europe, it was common for powerful lenders, aristocratic or secular, to insist on the use of a different, and larger bushel, for the repayment of loans of grain than the bushel used for advancing it. Where domainal power was stronger, the disparity was correspondingly greater. See Witold Kula, *Measures and Men*, transl. by R. Szreter (Princeton: Princeton University Press, 1986).

7. For a far more elaborate discussion of the range of naming practices, see Richard D. Alford, *Naming and Identity: A Cross-Cultural Study of Personal Naming Practices* (New Haven: HRAF Press, 1987).

8. Since this would not be a permanent patronym, if John's son was named Richard, then, that son would be called "Richard-John's-son" thus dropping the grandfather's name "William" altogether.

9. Wilfred Thesiger, *The Marsh Arabs* (Harmondsworth: Penguin Books, 1967), pp. 198–99.

10. We want to thank Lincoln Moses for helping us figure out the mathematics of identification in these hypothetical examples.

11. See the excellent account in Ian Hacking, *The Taming of Chance* (Cambridge: Cambridge University Press, 1990).

12. China, by contrast, had a centralized surname scheme as early as the Qin dynasty (fourth century B.C.E.), which tried to register the entire population of the kingdom, but it is not clear how universally it was applied. This initiative may well have been the origin of the term "laobaixing" meaning, literally, the "old one hundred surnames," and which, in modern China, has come to mean "the common people." Before this time, the fabled Chinese patrilineage was absent among commoners.

13. The role of surnames as an official state function is also revealed in female naming practices. This is especially the case when one examines the tradition of married women taking their husband's last name. Strangely enough, "no hunting, gathering, or fishing society, no society with nuclear family organization; and only one society without patrilocal residence requires" women to change their names at marriage. R. Alford, *Naming and Identity...*, op. cit., p. 88. Indeed, the only sociocultural variable that correlates with female name changes at marriage is the technological complexity of a society. In the Anglo-American tradition, women typically took the last names of their husbands, "as women did not pursue an occupation outside the home and inheritance typically passed through sons or other male heirs, women took upon marriage their husband's surname as their own. It was the name that *best described and identified women to local officials.*" See Ralph Slovenko, "Overview: Names and the Law," *Names*, 32, 2 (June 1984): 107–13, 109 (emphasis added).

14. Recalling the biblical: "And x begat y who begat z."

15. James Pennethorne Hughes, *How You Got Your Name: The Origin and Meaning of Surnames* (London: Phoenix House, 1959) p. 20. It is instructive to note that social norms of this kind continue to exist, especially with respect to namelessness. As Helen Lynd writes, "The wood in *Through the Looking Glass* where no creature bears a name is a place of terror" (qtd. In Harold R. Isaacs, "Basic Group Identity: The Idols of the Tribe," in *Ethnicity: Theory and Experience*, Nathan Glazer and Daniel P. Moynihan, eds., Cambridge: Harvard University Press, 1975, 29–52, p. 51). Moreover, as Isaacs points out, "The sanction of namelessness imposed on bastardy in our culture is one of the most fearful that a group can impose. Namelessness of any kind, indeed, is almost beyond bearing 'nameless fear' is worse than any other kind of fear. Names, like social norms, provide a certain minimum security, bearings that every individual must feel around him or else be lost" (ibid.).

16. See C. M. Matthews, *English Surnames* (London: Weidenfeld and Nicolson, 1966). Pp. 43–44; Beverly S. Seng, "Like Father, Like Child: The Rights of Parents in their Children's Surnames," *Virginia Law Review* 70 (1984): 1303, 1307–8, 1324–27, see supra note 24.

17. Richard McKinley, *A History of British Surnames* (London: Longman Group, 1990), pp. 29–30.

18. R. McKinley, *A History of British Surnames*, p. 30.

19. George Fraser Black, *The Surnames of Scotland* (New York: New York Public Library, 1946), p. xliv.

20. R. McKinley, *A History of British Surnames*, p. 30.

21. C. M. Matthews, *English Surnames*, pp. 43–44.

22. William Camden, *Remains Concerning Britain*, ed. R. D. Dunn, originally published in 1605 (Toronto: University of Toronto Press, 1984), p. 122.

23. Thus, while Ataturk obliged the population of Turkey to take permanent patronyms between 1934 and 1936, they were little used in daily society and hence, the telephone book entries began, until the 1950s, with the first, or given, name.

24. Monique Bourin, "France du Midi et France du nord: Deux systemes anthroponymiques," *L'Anthroponomie: Documents de l'histoire sociale des mondes mediterranienns medievaux* (*Actes du colloque international organize par l'Ecole francaise de Rome*, 6–8 October 1994 (Ecole francaise de Rome, Palais Farnese, 1996), pp. 179–202.

25. Fernand Braudel, *The Mediterranean and the Mediterranean World in the Age of Philip II*, Vol. I, transl. by Sian Reynolds (New York: Harper and Row, 1966), p. 38.

26. It appears (though the timing and comprehensiveness are in dispute), that by the fourth century B.C.E., the Qin dynasty had been imposing surnames on much of its population for the purposes of taxes, forced labor, and conscription. The imposition of surnames was, of course, also a cultural project to superimpose the patrilineage on commoners and give the new, male family heads legal jurisdiction over their wives, children, and juniors. Patricia Ebery, "The Chinese Family and the Spread of Confucian Values," in *The East Asian Region: Confucian Heritage and Its Modern Adaptation*, ed. Gilbert Rozman (Princeton: Princeton University Press, 1991), pp. 45–83.

27. For example, permanent surnames are mostly absent in Indonesia and Burma.

28. Charles Tilly, *Coercion, Capital, and European States, AD 990–1992* (Cambridge: Blackwell, 1990), pp. 25–30.

29. See Kaplan and Bernays, *The Language of Names*, p. 57.

30. Dietz Bering, *The Stigma of Names: Antisemitism in German Daily Life, 1812–1933*, transl. by Neville Plaice (Ann Arbor: University of Michigan Press, 1991), p. 29.

31. Ibid., p. 15.

32. Ibid., p. 51.

33. In the case of the United States, Native American names persist here and there, particularly in the names of rivers— the great arteries of early colonial trade. Interestingly enough, it seems that geographical features that were not fixed points but rather whole regions or great stretches of river had, perhaps because of the continuity of the native name, a better chance of retaining their indigenous name.

34. Frank Terry, Superintendent of the U.S. Boarding School for Crow Indians, Montana, "Naming the Indians," *American Monthly Review of Reviews* 3 (1897), pp. 301–2.

35. Edward S. Rogers and Mary Black Rogers, "Method for reconstructing Patterns of Change: Surname Adoption by the Weagamow Ojibwa, 1870–1950," *Ethnohistory*, 25, 4 (Fall 1978), p. 336.

36. Nor, of course, should we overlook the advantages of illegibility for subjects who might have had good reasons for remaining elusive. Colonial subjects have some of the same reasons as the underworld for multiple aliases.

37. Thomas Morgan, Commissioner of Indian Affairs at the Dept. of the Interior in 1890, related the story of a boy delivered to a government school by an Apache policeman. On being asked by the white schoolteacher what his name was, the policeman replied, "Des-to-dah," which, henceforth became his name and which, in fact, meant "I don't know" in that Apache dialect (qtd. In Frank Terry, Superintendent of U.S. Boarding Schools for Crow Indians, Montana, "Naming the Indians." Electronic Text Center, University of Virginia Library, p. 304, see http://etext.lib.virginia.edu/etcbin/toccernew2).

38. Edward S. Rogers and Mary Black Rogers, "Method for Reconstructing Patterns of Change...," op. cit., p. 343. The name recorded in one instance as "Chalie Kanate" was also rendered as "Johnnie Kenneth," "Cainet," "Kennet," and "Kunat."

39. Daniel F. Littlefield, Jr., and Lonnie E. Underhill. "Renaming the American Indian: 1890–1913," *American Studies*, (1971), 12, 2:33–45, p. 34.

40. Henry E. Fritz, *The Movement for Indian Assimilation, 1860–1890* (Philadelphia: University of Pennsylvania Press, 1963), p. 19.

41. Ibid., pp. 198–221.

42. Daniel F. Littlefield, Jr., and Lonnie E. Underhill. "Renaming the American Indian, 1890–1913," op. cit.

43. The impulse came because of the Organic Act for the Territory of Oklahoma in which Indian lands became part of the Territory. Land was allotted individually, for the most part, to Native Americans (among them Fox, Shawnees, Sac, Potawotomi, Cheyenne-Arapaho, Tonkawa, Pawnees, Kiowa-Commanche) with the left-over land going to white settlers. See Daniel F. Littlefield, Jr., and Lonnie E. Underhill, "Renaming the American Indian: 1890–1913," op. cit.

44. David Wallace Adams, "The Federal Indian Boarding School: A Study of Environment and Response, 1879–1918," Ph.D. thesis, Indiana University School of Education (Ann Arbor: University Microfilms, 1975), p. 44.

45. Ibid.

46. Frank Terry, "Naming the Indians," op. cit., p. 306.

47. See Hamlin Garland, *Companions on the Trail* (New York: Macmillan, 1931).

48. Letter from Hamlin Garland to President Theodore Roosevelt, 29 July 1902 or thereabout, in *Selected Letters of Hamlin Garland* (Lincoln: University of Nebraska Press, 1998), pp. 157–58.

49. Morgan was in favor of retaining Indian names and transliterating them into English script where they were reasonably short and pronounceable (to whites). The practice of renaming had, of course, begun with those Native Americans who were employed by Reservation authorities, because they figured first on payrolls and ration lists. Naming, as we have seen earlier, spread as a function of the intensiveness of contact with officials (Frank Terry, op. cit.).

50. Dr. W. N. Hailmann, General Superintendent of Indian Schools, "Naming the Indians," *American Monthly Review of Reviews* 15 (March 1897), p. 302.

51. Hamlin Garland to the Commissioner of Indian Affairs, 3 Nov. 1902, Letter-Book, 1901–1904, 112 *Hamlin Garland Collection*, University of Southern California Library, Los Angeles.

52. Letter from Hamlin Garland to Charles F. Lummis, 26 Nov. 1902, in *Selected Letters of Hamlin Garland*, op. cit.

53. Each of these colorful names, of course, were attached to narratives which, collectively, mapped much of the individual, family, and local history of a Native American society.

54. From a document of the United Foreign Missionary Society's Board of Managers, quoted in David Wallace Adams, "The Federal Indian Boarding School...," op. cit., p. 14.

55. Daniel F. Littlefield, Jr., and Lonnie E. Underhill, "Renaming the American Indian: 1890–1913," op. cit., p. 36.

56. David Wallace Adams, "The Federal Indian Boarding School...," op. cit., p. 17.

57. It should be clear that the pattern being imposed was the *normative* pattern of the nuclear, patriarchal family, not the great range of practices characteristic of late nineteenth-century white society.

58. Letter to Charles F. Lummis, 3 Dec. 1902, in *Selected Letters of Hamlin Garland*, op. cit. p. 164.

59. Letter to Charles F. Lummis, 29 July 1902, *Selected Letters of Hamlin Garland*, op. cit. p. 164.

60. This belief recalls the reformers of the Meiji Restoration in Japan who toured Europe examining constitutions, believing that, if they got the constitution "right" an enlightened modern government would follow.

61. There was, for example, great concern over "summer holidays" during which time the students returned to their families and reservations. The boarding school authorities thought that all their civilizational work was undone over the summer and that they had to begin again from scratch in the fall.

62. David Wallace Adams, "The Federal Indian Boarding School...," op. cit., p. 101.

63. Valerie Alia, *Names, Numbers and Northern Policy: Inuit, Project Surname, and the Politics of Identity* (Halifax, Nova Scotia: Fernwood Publishing, 1994). This section is based almost entirely on Alia's fine study.

64. Letter from D. A. J. MacKinnon to the Department of the Interior to protest the difficulty of following individuals from one part of Pangnirtung district [E–6] to another. Cited in V. Alia, *Names, Numbers and Northern Policy*, op. cit., p. 29. Emphasis added to highlight MacKinnon's recognition of how much of the identification problem is confined to outsiders with no local knowledge.

65. V. Alia, *Names, Numbers and Northern Policy...*, op cit., p. 32.

66. The same system was tried on the !Kung in South Africa. V. Alia, *Names, Numbers, and Northern Policy...*, op. cit., p. 75.

67. Here it is apposite to recall the social commentary embedded in the army slang "dog tags" in order to imagine what the Inuit might have thought about wearing disks around their necks.

68. V. Alia, *Names, Numbers, and Northern Policy...*, op. cit., p. 36. Many people suggested using the Canadian Social Insurance number as the standard identification formula as it was used for other Canadians.

69. The exception that proved the rule was one Qallunaaq (Canadian of European descent) who, desiring assimilation, wore his disk to prove he had been classed as Inuit.

70. V. Alia, *Names, Numbers, and Northern Policy...*, op. cit., p. 56.

71. Northwest Territories Document, 1971a: 12, cited ibid., p. 56. V. Alia (p. 80) reports the following conversation in the course of her research: "A territorial government employee told me disk numbers were needed because 'all Inuit had the same name or so close you couldn't tell the difference. You needed something logical. You had to have an order. There weren't any names.' I replied that there were names and they were not the same. He insisted that Inuit were 'impossible to identify.'"

72. V. Alia, *Names, Numbers, and Northern Policy...*, op. cit., p. 63.

73. V. Alia, *Names, Numbers, and Northern Policy...*, op. cit., p. 69. Elsewhere in the circum-polar region, the Yuit of Siberia had single names like Canadian Inuit but were given last names in the 1930s, under Stalin. In the 1960s the polar Inuit were given last names by the Danes—first by the Ministry of Ecclesiastical Affairs. There were mixed names (e.g. the hunter "Itukusuk Kristiansen"). "People got surnames for administrative convenience." V. Alia, *Names, Numbers, and Northern Policy...*, op. cit., p. 75.

74. V. Alia, *Names, Numbers, and Northern Policy...*, op. cit., p. 75. Note the remarkable assumption that the absence of an appropriate naming system, by itself, prevents anything like 'family feeling.'

75. Valerie Alia, *Names, Numbers, and Northern Policy...*, op. cit., p. 82.

76. The process was not, however, completed until 1936. The late Ottoman Empire itself had moved, during the period known as the "Tanzimat" toward codification, systematization, and more fine-tuned administrative control. See, in this context, Recep Boztemur, "State-Making and Nation Building: A Study of the Historical Relationship Between the Capitalist Development and the Establishment of the Modern Nation State," Ph.D., University of Utah, Languages and Literature, 1997, pp. 260–423.

77. For this discussion see: Robert F. Spencer, "The Social Context of Modern Turkish Names," *Southwestern Journal of Anthropology*, 17, 3 (Autumn 1961), pp. 205–218; Donald E. Webster, "State Control of Social Change in Republican Turkey," *American Sociological Review*, 4, 2 (April 1939), pp. 247–256; Bernard Lewis, *The Emergence of Modern Turkey* (New York: Longmans, 1994), pp. 136 et seq., Vanik D. Volkan and Norman Itzkowitz, *The Immortal Ataturk: A Psychobiography* (Chicago: University of Chicago Press, 1984).

78. Two brothers might, in the naming exercise, take different patronyms, thereby, in effect beginning two separate patrilineages so far as names were concerned.

79. Ts'ui-p'ing Ho, "Exchange, Person, and Hierarchy: Rethinking the Kachin," Ph.D. Thesis, Anthropology, University of Virginia, 1997, p. 23. Thanks to Magnus Fiskesjo for bringing this thesis to our attention.

80. Benedict Anderson, *Imagined Communities: Reflections of the Origin and Spread of Nationalism* (London: Verso, 1983), p. 169.

81. Lois Law Library, 10D–49.0192. "Naming of Child When Parents Disagree on the Selection of the Name." Jeremy Mathias, unpublished lecture, n.d.

82. One can imagine the overwhelming impact of this process in colonial possessions where the language of documents, law, and administration were suddenly switched from the local vernacular to the metropolitan language.

83. Tore Frangsmyr, J. L. Heilbron, and Robin E. Rider, *The Quantifying Spirit of the 18th Century* (Berkeley: University of California Press, 1990), p. 13.

84. "New Data on Babies of Women with Birth Defects," *The New York Times*, 18 Apr. 1999, p. A18.

85. There would also be electronic codes for employers, health providers, physicians, and hospitals. "Health Identifier for All Americans Runs into Hurdles," *The New York Times*, 19 July 1998, pp. 1, 11.

86. Ibid., p. 1.

87. The Social Security system is now linked to many records, and practical access to credit histories, medical records, wages, and employment records is within the grasp of most talented computer hackers. In addition there are a great number

of counterfeit cards. Opponents of the health identification number fear that the same abuses and unauthorized access to confidential information will quickly overtake a health identification number. For the United States, it is the closest thing to a national identification number (137 million numbers issued since 1936).

88. And, later, a series of techniques by which witnesses could attempt to build a likeness from various elements of a face with the help of trained specialists.

89. The fingerprint as a form of identification was developed around 1880 and first applied in Bengal to combat pension fraud. Like so many other advances in police-work, it was tried first in the colonies and then transplanted back to Britain. Most of the uses of fingerprints involve trying to match the fingerprints of a suspect in custody with fingerprints collected at the crime scene. The fingerprint was never universal (though attempts were made in the 1920s in the United States to make it universal), and, despite the patina of pure science about it, it requires specialists with long experience to match fingerprints definitively. Lecture by Simon Cole, Dept. of Anthropology, Stanford University, November 1998.

90. For an elaborate argument along these lines, see James C. Scott, *Seeing Like a State: How Certain Schemes to Improve the Human Condition Have Failed* (New Haven: Yale University Press, 1998), pp. 87–102.

91. Ibid., pp. 78–79. It is also true that this map could equally have been used to feed the Jews or to evacuate them secretly to the countryside. The map was only information; it was the Nazis and their collaborators who supplied the deadly purpose.

92. Anton Gill, *The Journey Back from Hell: Conversations with Concentration Camp Survivors* (London: Grafton Publishers, 1988), pp. 26–32. Each camp designated prisoners by number but it appears that only at Auschwitz was the number tattooed on the skin of gypsies and Jews. The designation "Z" (for "Ziegeuner") appeared before the number in the case of gypsies. Some thought was given to branding prisoners' names on their forehead.

93. United Nations High Commissioner for Refugees, *Registration: A Practical Guide for Field Staff* (Geneva, May 1994).

94. Letter from Bela Hovy, Statistician, Division of Operational Support, United Nations High Commissioner for Refugees, 10 July 1998.

Genocide and Group Classification on National ID Cards

Jim Fussell

Within their own cultures and countries, few people have distinguishing characteristics which would mark them apart from their own countrymen. How could the Nazis tell a Jew from a Christian; how could a militiaman tell a Tutsi from a Hutu? National ID cards, listing a person's religion, ethnicity, or race, have long been a facilitating factor in allowing the perpetrators of murder to identify their potential victims. Jim Fussell, the founder of the website Prevent Genocide International, looks at how national ID cards have contributed to mass exterminations in modern history. This paper was presented on November 15, 2001 to the Seminar Series of the Yale University Genocide Studies Program, and is presently found on the internet at: http://www.preventgenocide.org/prevent/removing-facilitating-factors/IDcards/[1]

The role played by group classification on national identity cards in crimes of genocide in Rwanda and in Nazi Germany should trouble all persons concerned with prevention of genocide. In Nazi Germany in July 1938, only a few months before Kristallnacht, the infamous "J-stamp" was introduced on ID cards and later on passports. The use of specially marked "J-stamp" ID cards by Nazi Germany preceded the yellow Star of David badges. In Norway, where yellow cloth badges were not introduced, the stamped ID card was used in the identification of more than 750 Jews deported to death camps in Poland.[2] Ethnic classification on ID cards in Rwanda instituted by the Belgian colonial government and retained after independence, was central in shaping, defining and perpetuating ethnic identity. Once the 1994 genocide in Rwanda began, an ID card with the designation "Tutsi" spelled a death sentence at any roadblock.[3] No other factor was more significant in facilitating the speed and magnitude of the 100 days of mass killing in Rwanda.

National ID cards of all kinds are controversial. In recent years in the United States, Britain, Canada and Australia proposals for introducing national ID cards and registry systems have raised debate about government control and privacy issues. Classification of ethnic, racial or religious groups on ID cards, however, is a distinctively different issue. Group classification on ID cards or other official personal documents (passports, residence permits, etc.) force a person to be affiliated with a governmentally-defined group and expose persons to profiling and human rights abuses based upon their group identity. In times of crisis such classifications facilitate the targeting of persons on the basis of group affiliation, making individuals readily identifiable for possible detention, deportation, or death.

The hazard posed by group classifications of ID cards has been recognized in specific instances. In July 1991, for example, consultants recommended to the Habyarimana regime that it eliminate the Hutu and Tutsi ethnic classifications from the Rwandan ID cards. Later the elimination of ID classifications was agreed upon as part of the 1993 Arusha Accords.[4] Action to eliminate these classifications was ultimately not taken until 1997 by the new post-genocide regime established in July 1994.

Survey of Classifications on ID Cards

In a majority of countries in the world, national identification cards are issued to all adult persons. The cards are typically issued to everyone over age 15 and in many places the law requires that the cards be carried in public at all times. From such ID cards a person's group affiliation can sometimes be extrapolated from characteristics such as family name, place of birth, place of residence or the person's face in a photograph. These elements are usually suggestive of a person's background, but do not provide a definitive answer to someone seeking to determine a group identity. In more than 20 nations, however, a line appears on the card stating an ethnic, racial or religious affiliation. Many of these nations are places where intergroup tension or violence is prevalent. Another set of nations, including some of those with group classifications on their national ID cards and some without, issue special cards to particular population groups.[5] These groups include native-born permanent alien residents who must show an additional card, a separate card, cards of a distinctive color, or a specially marked or stamped card distinct from the larger population. This kind of special card is also included in this survey. The survey does not include the many examples of special cards issued to individual immigrants, based upon their status as foreign-born non-citizens. An effort has been made to include all definite examples, including those where there appears to be no danger of violence.[6]

This summary chart, arranged by group category and ID card type shows which nations have ID cards with group classifications, based on a survey derived from human rights country reports and news accounts. Past examples appear in italics.

Table 1:
Summary of Nations with Classification on ID Cards, Arranged by Group Category and ID Card Type

Group Category	Group Classifications are listed on All National ID Cards	Special Card or Mark (Special ID Cards issued and/or a special mark on the standard ID card)
Nationality	Israel	Native-born residents issued special ID or documents: Cambodia (ethnic Vietnamese), Ethiopia (Ethiopians with Eritrean affiliation); Indonesia (Ethnic Chinese); Japan (alien residents, especially ethnic Koreans); Kenya (ethnic Somalians); United States (some Native Americans, ethnic Japanese during WWII)
Ethnicity	Bhutan, China, Ethiopia, Kenya, Vietnam, *Burundi, DRCongo, Russia (and other former republics of the USSR)*, Rwanda	Syria (Kurds). Text on National Id cards in Macedonia, in Serbia and Montenegro and in Slovenia appear in minority languages on some cards only.
Race/Color	Dominican Republic, Malaysia, Singapore; *South Africa, United States (some State Driver's Licenses only)*	*Nazi Germany and war-time occupied European countries (Jews, Roma Sinti); Free Blacks in the United States during the time of slavery.*
Religion	Afghanistan, Brunei, Egypt, Jordan, [Pakistan — see details], Turkey; Greece, *Lebanon*	Iran (Christians), Saudi Arabia (nonmuslim foreigners), Syria (Jews)
Multiple Categories Special Status (legal, residential or territorial status where such status impacts national, ethnic, racial, or religious groups)	Myanmar (Burma, Indonesia, Sri Lanka	**Territorial:** Israel (East Jerusalem), Spain (North Africa enclaves), *France (Alsace-Lorraine); Legal: Indonesia (ex–Tapol)*

More detailed descriptions and sources appear in the appendix and on a regularly updated website

In recent decades, partly as a result of international action against the former Apartheid policies in South Africa, ID cards or documents with racial categories have come to be viewed with international disapproval. At the same time ID cards displaying other group categories such as ethnicity and religion continue to be used in many parts of the world. Group classification on ID cards often reflects an aspect of national identity and tradition, but the cards are also a manifestation of governmental power. With or without ID cards, national traditions may favor or privilege one part of the population, while marginalizing others. Classification on cards, however, fixes or reifies group identities and takes the power to define group identity away from individuals, families and communities, putting that power in the hands of government authorities.[7]

Most countries in the world do some sort of official classification of their population by groups using one or more of categories such as national origin, race, ethnicity or religion. Most commonly this information is gathered during a census or on birth certificates. Such classification schemes treat group difference in overly simplified ways treating group identity as an unchanging constant not subject to ongoing changes in society. What classification on national ID cards does is take group classification schemes one step further—from the classification of populations as a whole (in aggregate)— to the classification of individual persons by group. The effect of policies which apply group classifications upon individuals is to make group identity more rigid and to make one form of societal affiliation excessively prominent (usually religion or ethnicity), highlighting that particular area of difference above others, such as regional or local identity, social class or others. In most pluralistic societies a particular person's highlighted identity and affiliations differ by context and the situation at the moment. In a rigid or polarized society that a single identity is being reinforced and articulated.

The presence of group classifications on national ID cards is usually viewed as a matter entirely of domestic concern. It is possible to consider it in the same manner as widespread forms of group classification, such as information gathered during a census or on birth certificates. But the fact that these classifications on National ID cards must actually be carried and used by individuals makes the practice unlike other classification practices. The ramifications of this form of classification for individual persons should cause the practice to become a matter of international concern. Such international concern played a role in the elimination of Tutsi, Hutu and Twa classification in post-genocide Rwanda in 1997 and also influenced Greece, which eliminated a religious classification from its national ID card in July 2000. This change in Greece was made amid great controversy and opposition from the leadership of the Greek Orthodox Church, but with the strong encouragement of the European Union, which had been in the process of standardizing identification cards of all member countries.[8]

In response to a controversial initiative in the former Soviet Republic of Georgia to restore the ethnic nationality category on national ID cards, Antti Korkaakivi, a senior official at the Council of Europe's Human Rights Division, stated on January 21, 1999 that the mandatory inclusion of an ethnicity category on public documents could violate the Council of Europe's 1995 European Framework Convention on National Minorities.[9] More recently a July 2001 conference of non-governmental organizations and people's organizations in Southeast Asia meeting in Bangkok, Thailand called on members of ASEAN to "be accountable for discriminatory policies and practices" such as using "racial/religious identification in national identity cards and official government documents, that promotes greater racial and religious segregation."[10] These examples show that governments may be influenced by international and regional concern over the practice.

Intergroup Polarization and Classification on National ID Cards

Group classification on national ID cards does not indicate a government will engage in massive human rights violations. Classifications on ID cards are instead a facilitating factor, making it more possible for governments, local authorities or non-state actors such as militias to more readily engage in violations based on ethnicity or religion. ID cards are not a precondition to genocide, but have been a facilitating factor in the commission of genocide. Additionally the presence of group categories on ID cards, used constantly in routine official and business transactions, can contribute to polarization that can lead to genocide or related crimes.

Classification on ID cards is only one method perpetrators might use to identify a population group during genocide or ethnic cleansing. Group classifications did not appear on ID cards in the former Yugoslavia, for example. Other means of identifying a group such as creation of lists, marking buildings or mandating the display of distinguishing cloth badges can be used instead of or together with ID cards. Unlike these other means of identifying groups, however, group classification on ID cards has been a more universally accepted or tolerated practice, perceived as a normal and legal governmental function. The world did not respond to the presence of religious categories on the Afghanistan ID booklet, but has responded vocally to the announcement in May 2001 that Hindus in that country would be required to wear distinguishing yellow badges. Where a particular identity is stigmatized or vilified, it is of minimal difference that a person must carry that identity on the outer clothes, or must display it upon demand on a card.

Table 2. Classification on Identification Cards and Three Types of Polarized Intergroup Relationships

Categories of Relationship:	Deindividualization	Dehumanization	Demonization
Form of polarization	Societal polarization	Institutional polarization	Eliminationist polarization
Us–Them Type of Relationship	They are different from us; We are different from them.	They are inferior, less than us; We are superior, better, than them.	They are a threat to us; We are endangered by them.
Types of language Used by Dominant Population Group	The "other" a negative reference group, "what we are" is defined in juxtaposition to the "other."	Members of the group are viewed as less human or subhuman, through hate speech, pejorative, ethnic and racial slurs. Fear and hate are combined.	Genocidal hate speech: emphasizing a threat from all members of the group (including children and elderly) and calling for the elimination or destruction of the group. Use of metaphoric nouns and verbs characterizing the targeted population groups as non-human, i.e. animals, insects, diseases, and/or demons.
Role Played by ID Cards	Card viewers profile the individual card bearers in terms of group affiliation. Classification on ID cards reifies group identity. The ability of the individual to determine when and how to identify self is constrained. Cards play a role in governmental, financial, employment seeking interactions.	Group classification on ID Cards is central in the enforcement of institutional and legal domination. Cards determine where a person is permitted to live, to work and restricts freedom of movement. Threat of confiscation of the ID card is an additional means of control.	Classification on ID Cards is central in selection of the targeted population group. Issuing and enforcing use of the ID cards is one segment of a destruction process. Persons who select or control a group prior to death contribute as much to their destruction as the immediate killers.
Actions and policies Implied for the Dominant Group	Social distancing ("keep to your own kind"). Defacto residential segregation, intermarriage disapproved – an individual in "them" group is perceived as representing the whole.	Domination, subordination, control, apartheid, enslavement, Defeat, conquest Legal segregation, reservations, Bantustans, ghettoization, partition	Isolation, absolute separation, concentration, walled ghettos, quarantine, internment, concentration camps Elimination, deportation, expulsion, forced relocation, Massacres, pogroms, "ethnic cleansing," partial genocide, extermination, total genocide
Groups Perceived and Portrayed Monolithically	Coexistence based on limited separation They are the same, we are all the same; Deindividualization forced upon both groups.	Coexistence is possible through domination. Rebellion or alleged criminal activities responded to with partial elimination.	Mutual coexistence is impossible. Groups portrayed as mortal enemies (Kill or be killed).

ID cards are public documents over which the bearer has very limited rights of privacy. From the information on the ID card a person with car viewing authority is usually required to make some judgment about whether the card bearer is eligible or permitted to engage in a given activity. When information about group identity (such as ethnicity or religion) becomes a factor in the interaction, that information alters the card-viewers judgment. At a minimum, the presence of group classification categories on national ID cards creates and reinforces heightened awareness of group differences.

Table 2 is an attempt to understand ways in which group classification on national ID cards can impact on society in the very diverse set of societies where this practice has been a factor. The category "Deindividualization," which could also be called depersonalization, represents societies where classification reinforces voluntary and traditional social separation of groups, as in Malaysia or Singapore. "Dehumanization" represents societies where the classification of groups is institutionalized, such as Apartheid-era South Africa. "Demonization" represents societies in an advanced stage of a genocidal or eliminationist process, such as Rwanda in 1993 and 1994, Nazi Germany after 1938, or countries engaging in mass expulsion such as Vietnam in 1978, Bhutan in 1991, Ethiopia in 1998. The special significance of classification on the ID cards may be heightened at moments of crisis or in regions of conflict, such as in May 1998 in Indonesia or in Tibet [or] in China.

Human rights reports sometimes mention the role group classifications on ID cards play in particular incidents, though often the significance of the ID cards are a secondary or tertiary aspect of the report. In such incidents ID cards play a role often early in the incident when authorities or a militia first encounter the victims. As an institutional structure ID cards are tremendously significant, curtailing and constricting individual actions that would not become part of an incident report. When smaller numbers of victims are targeted in order to intimidate or terrorize a group, ID cards are one of several ways to accomplish this end.

When all members of a group or a large portion of a group are targeted for special treatment, however, ID cards can have enormous significance in facilitating that crime. In the last decade, in addition to the role ID cards played in the Rwandan genocide, group classifications on ID cards also played important roles in facilitating the large-scale expulsions of tens of thousands of persons on account of their group identity from Bhutan in 1991 and Ethiopia in 1998. Acts of "ethnic cleansing" to eliminate or drastically reduce a group's population on a given territory require systematic methods to identify and select persons to be targeted.

Group Classification on ID Cards
in Genocide, Ethnic Cleansing and
Other Eliminationist Population Policies

Identification of individual members of a targeted population group is a necessary task for perpetrators of genocide and ethnic cleansing. To accomplish this task, perpetrators either adapt existing administrative structures to their new purposes or create new structures. Identity cards are often the key element in a larger identification system. Their central position in such a system is due to their role in attaching the identity of the targeted group onto individual persons, combining individual identity information with a group profile.

In his 1996 book *Ethnic Cleansing*, Andrew Bell-Fialkoff locates genocide and ethnic cleansing within a continuum of eliminationist population policies, offering the following as a definition of population cleansing:

> "Population cleansing is a planned, deliberate removal from a certain territory of an undesirable population distinguished by one or more characteristics such as ethnicity, religion, race, class, or sexual preference. These characteristics must serve as the basis for removal for it to quality as cleansing."[11]

An understanding of genocide and ethnic cleansing as the most extreme acts within a continuum is very significant from the perspective of prevention. Often genocide and genocidal massacres are preceded by deportations and mass expulsions. Until Nazi Germany closed off all borders in October 1941, the persecution of Jews in Germany and occupied Europe had features which we would now call "ethnic cleansing." Perpetrators may use ethnic cleansing and massacres to test the responses of internal and external bystanders before escalating to genocide. Additionally, perpetrators may claim to be engaging in relocation, resettlement or deportations and use the claim to disguise acts of genocide. Finally, the conditions under which a population is moved during the course of relocation may actually have the characteristics described in Article II, section 3 of the Genocide Convention: "Deliberately inflicting on the group conditions of life calculated to bring about its physical destruction in whole or in part."

The following chart takes many of the countries included in the survey and locates those countries according to policies facilitated by group classification on ID cards or by situations in which classification on ID cards was a factor.

Table 3
Governmental Population Policies Facilitated
by Group Classification on ID Cards

Eliminationist policies:

Genocide	**Nazi Germany** (1938–1945), **Rwanda** (1990–1994)
Mass Expulsion	**Ethiopia** (Persons with Eritrean affiliation 1998), **Bhutan** (Lhotshampas, 1991), **Vietnam** (Hoa ethnic Chinese 1978–1979), **France** (Alsace-Lorraine 1918–1920)
Forced Relocation	**USSR** (ethnic Koreans 1937, Volga Germans 1941, Kalmyks, Karachai, 1943, Crimean Tatars, Meshkhetian Turks, Chechens, Ingush, Balkars 1944, ethnic Greeks, 1949)
Group Denationalization	**Cambodia** (ethnic Vietnamese 1993), **Myanmar** (Rohingya Arakanese 1992), **Syria** (Kurds 1962)

Other situations where classifications on National ID Cards are present

Civil conflict	**Macedonia** (2001), **Israel** (2000 to present), **Georgia** (1992), **Myanmar (Burma)** 1988 to present, **Sri Lanka** (1983 to present), **Tajikistan** (1992–1997), **Lebanon** (1975 to 1989), **Indonesia**
Restrictions	**China** (Tibet, Uigahr), **Pakistan** (Amadiya), **Syria** (Jews), **Laos** (non-Buddhists), **Japan** (ethnic Koreans), **Iran** (Christians), **Indonesia** (ethnic Chinese), **Malasia**
Legacy of past ID Classification policy	**Burundi, former Czechosolvakia, Democratic Republic of Congo, Georgia, Germany, Greece, Russia, Rwanda, South Africa, former Soviet republics**
No reported problems with classification on IDs	**Brunei, Jordan, Kenya, Saudi Arabia, Singapore, Slovenia**

Under some of these policies and in many of these situations ID cards or internal passports were one element in a larger identification system, involving creation of lists and registration, marking of dwellings and sometimes mandatory display of badges. Systematic marking of buildings was reported in Rwanda in 1994 and the former Yugoslavia in 1992–1995 as well as during the May 1998 "riots" in Indonesia in which ethnic Chinese were targeted. In some instances a government introduces new national ID cards but withholds the cards from a targeted population group in an apparent effort at mass denationalization.

The most elaborate identification system created was that of Nazi Germany, though it was not applied uniformly in all territories occupied by Germany. Raul Hilberg describes that system and its impact upon Jews in especially great detail in his 1985 edition of *The Destruction of the European Jews*, summarizing as follows:

The whole identification system, with its personal documents, specially assigned names, and conspicuous tagging in public, was a powerful weapon in the hands of the police. First, the system was an auxiliary device that facilitated the enforcement of residence and movement restrictions. Second, it was an independent control measure in that it enabled the police to pick up any Jew, anywhere, anytime. Third, and perhaps most important, identification had a paralyzing effect on its victims. The system induced the Jews to be even more docile, more responsive to command than before. The wearer of the star was exposed; he thought that all eyes were fixed upon him. It was as though the whole population had become a police force, watching him and guarding his actions. No Jew, under those conditions, could resist, escape, or hide without first ridding himself of the conspicuous tag, the revealing middle name, the telltale ration card, passport, and identification papers. Yet the riddance of these burdens was dangerous, for the victim could be recognized and denounced. Few Jews took the chance. The vast majority wore the star and, wearing it, were lost.[12]

In the development of the identification system, the ID card and the yellow badge served different complimentary purposes. In most countries where the "J" stamps were introduced, they were typically added to already existing identity cards, passports and other personal documents soon after occupation. The yellow badges were mandated at a later time, usually in the months immediately preceding deportations. Among Nazi-occupied territories Salonkia Greece is notable because the stars worn on clothing display individual ID numbers corresponding to those numbers appearing on individual identity cards. Secondary personal documents were also used alongside the ID cards, including ration cards and work permits. During 1941 in the closed ghettoes of Nazi-occupied Poland "Schein" cards (work permits) were issued. Persons without the documents were rounded up and deported to death camps.[13]

Most writers on the 1994 Rwandan genocide note the introduction of group classification on ID cards by the Belgian colonial government in 1933, an action most significant because it introduced a rigid racial concept of group identity where it had not previously existed. Of great significance also, however, was the repeated decision by the post-colonial Rwandan authorities to retain the group classifications on ID cards. Prior to independence, nine Hutu leaders declared their intention to retain such classifications in the Hutu manifesto of March 24, 1957, writing: "we are opposed vigorously, at least for the moment, to the suppression in the official or private identity papers of the mentions 'muhutu', 'mututsi,' 'mutwa.' Their suppression would create a risk of preventing the statistical law from establishing the reality of facts." By "statistical" the authors meant dominance by the Hutu majority population group.

One of the nine authors of the 1957 Manifesto, Gregoire Kayibanda, became the first president of Rwanda in 1961 and under his leadership the Rwandan *carte d'identité* continued to display the *"ubwoko / ethnie"* group affiliation of the card bearer. His successor, after a 1973 coup, President Jevenal Habyarimana also retained the cards until November 13, 1990. On that day, at the same time he announced a new multi-party system, President Habyarimana announced his intention, which he never acted upon, to abolish ethnic identity cards. He was later encouraged in April 1991 to follow through with this statement by American Ambassador Robert A. Flaten, but according to Philip Gourevitch the French ambassador opposed the plan. Alison De Forges reports that in July 1991 independent consultants encouraged France and other governments giving aid to Rwanda to require the removal of group affiliation from ID cards be taken as a prerequisite for assistance, but those governments failed to take that advice.[14]

In massacres northwestern Rwanda in early 1993, ethnic categories on ID cards facilitated the identification of victims. When this event occurred negotiations were in progress for power-sharing under a Transitional Government. Among the provisions in the August 4, 1993, Arusha Accords was the following: "The Broad-Based Transitional Government shall, from the date of its assumption of office, delete from all official documents to be issued any reference to ethnic origin." This continued presence of group classification on ID cards, even after their role in facilitating genocidal massacres in 1993, should remind us of the very nature of the genocidal killing that later ensued in April 1994. The Rwandan genocide was not the indiscriminate or wanton slaughter as it was sometimes portrayed. Instead, like most actions taken by perpetrators of genocide, the killing process was segmented into multiple distinct steps, with persons involved as administrative accomplices as well as direct killers. The testimony of one witness concerning the actions of Captain Ildéphonse Nizeyimana, a man who is a fugitive at large, underscores the bureaucratic nature of the task.

> Soldiers had orders to take identity cards from those whom they killed. According to one witness, Nizeyimana regularly received these cards from his men as they reported on the progress of the killings. They often appeared at his house shortly after a volley of gunfire was heard and handed the cards to the captain with the report, "Mission accomplished." In the captain's absence, his wife received the cards.[15]

In addition to facilitating the identification of Tutsi victims, another role of ID cards in the genocide was that of psychologically distancing the killers from their victims and from the nature of their task as killers. This distancing of perpetrators from their targeted victims facilitated by group classification on ID cards occurs whether the task is genocide, deportation or applying discriminatory restrictions.[16]

Removing Group Classification from ID Cards

This paper is an attempt to creatively explore a possible area of action for early stage genocide prevention. The findings are tentative and they are suggestive of an approach for further research. This approach involves perceiving the crime of genocide as the worst possible scenario in a continuum of violations. Another approach, late stage response through humanitarian intervention, involves halting or mitigating genocide through interdicting it as an imminent crime or one already in progress.

Early stage genocide prevention will entail addressing the precursors and facilitating factors that precede genocide. In part this shifts the focus away from the crime of genocide to pursuing more general positive outcomes such as building social peace and a stable economy. Nevertheless, there are specific factors that contribute to genocide that can be addressed. It is more difficult to hold leaders of government accountable for complex factors over which they have limited or partial control, such as the economy or the actions of irregular militias. In comparison, governmental policies based in law may be more readily addressed and reversed. Group classification on national ID cards is one such policy.

Table 4
Recent Actions to Remove or to Add Group
Classification on National ID Cards

	Removal or action to remove	Adoption, partial adoption or action to restore
Change in Law	Full Removal: Greece 2000, Rwanda 1997, Georgia 1997	Malasia 1999, Thailand 1999, Kenya 1997
Incomplete removal or partial adoption	Reports of policy still in effect, despite removal: Indonesia 1998, Lebanon 1997, Russia 1997	Pakistan (Registration form for ID cards requires religion, Passports include religion)
Proposal for Changes	Israel (Legislative), Turkey (Legislative), Egypt (Court Action 1997), Malaysia (Court Challenge April 2001)	Georgia (Legislative proposal to restore), Greece (Orthodox Church advocates restoration)

In the last five years governments have eliminated group classifications from national ID cards in Greece in 2000, and during 1997 in Georgia, Lebanon, Russia and Rwanda. In the same period calls to end classification on ID cards have also been made in Egypt, Indonesia, Israel and Turkey. In the same time period, in Georgia, Greece, Israel and Russia forceful advocates for retaining religious or ethnic classification have also spoken out. In 1992 in Pakistan an attempt by the government to add religious classification to National ID cards was partially halted by domestic opposition, leaving the classification on the application form but not on the card itself. Also recently in Kenya, a country with continuing ethnic tension, the government added a line for "kabila / tribe" to new National ID Cards issued prior to the 1997 Presidential election.

The policy decisions related to adding, eliminating or retaining group classifications on national identity cards are several steps removed from the issue of genocide prevention. Nevertheless when more governments end the practice, those which continue to use ID card classifications will likely be those with greater polarization and intergroup conflicts. In such situations a call to abolish the classification on ID cards or special cards can be a rallying point for moderates who seek a less polarized society. Governments, regional and international organizations and nongovernmental organizations can support such efforts.

Over the past decade more people have come to recognize that genocide is not a rare, isolated or unique event, but instead is a crime that occurs with disturbing frequency. With that insight, the often-repeated phrase "never again" can become a motivation not only for commemorating victims or punishing the perpetrators of past genocide, but also a basis for rejecting and condemning policies that make genocide more likely.

Notes

1. An earlier version of this paper was presented on June 10, 2001 as "Group Classifications on National Identity Cards as a Facilitating Factor in Genocide, Ethnic Cleansing, and Massive Violations of Human Rights," at the National Association of Genocide Scholars Conference, University of Minnesota, Minneapolis, USA. [www.isg-ags.org/conferences/2001ags-schedule.html]

2. Transcript of the trial of Adolf Eichmann, Session 36 (11 May 1961), Testimony of Henrietta Samuel.

3. Prosecutor vs. Jean-Paul Akayesu (Case No. ICTR–96–4–T), Judgment, 2 September 1998, paragraph 123. The comparison between the Nazi and Rwandan ID cards and a call for further research on this topic was made by Henry R. Huttenbach in an article entitled "The Letter of the Law and the Mark of Cain: When 'J' was and 'T' is lethal," *Genocide Forum*, year 1 (1994), no. 5.

4. Alison Des Forges, *Leave None to Tell the Story* (Human Rights Watch, 1999), p. 92, note 60.

5. Questions about special cards for a single ethnic group or the inclusion of religious affiliation on a possible National ID card were asked by pollsters in the United States in the fall of 2001. Immediately after the September 11 attacks by hijackers on the World Trade Center and the Pentagon, a CNN/USA Today/Gallup poll of Americans conducted September 14–15, 2001 found 49 percent of the public in support and 49 percent opposed to special ID cards for Arabs living in this country — including those who are U.S. citizens. Persons were asked, "Please tell me if you would favor or oppose each of the following as a means of preventing terrorist attacks in the United States ... Requiring Arabs, including those who are U.S. citizens, to carry a special ID." The item was third of eight items asked. ("Poll

Analyses, The Impact of the Attacks on America, September 25, 2001," by Jeffrey M. Jones, Gallup News Service, Princeton, NJ. See www.gallop.com/poll/releases/pr 010914c.asp. In a second poll in mid-November at the height of the Anthrax letter scare, questions about religious affiliation appearing on a possible future U.S. National Identification card were asked in a NPR/Kaiser/Kennedy School Poll on Civil Liberties. In response to the question, "Would you favor or oppose the following measures to curb terrorism.... Requiring that all citizens carry a national identity card at all times to show to a police officer on request" a total of 70 percent favored and 26 percent were opposed to this measure. Those who favored a national identification card were asked what information they would favor having on it. Ninety-six percent favored a photograph; 88 percent were in favor of fingerprints; 59 percent favored religious affiliation; 73 percent favored criminal record information; and 64 percent were in favor of DNA information on the card. (NPR/Kaiser Family Foundation/Kennedy School of Government National Survey on Civil Liberties, 30 Nov 2001) See http://www.people-press.org/terrorist01que.htm and http://www.npr.org/programs/specials/poll/civil_liberties_/civil_liberties_static_results_7.html.

6. The survey does not include the many examples of special cards issued to individual immigrants, based upon their status as foreign-born non-citizens. Another practice, much harder to document, is the failure or refusal of authorities to issue national ID cards to a particular population group. This practice can make it impossible for such persons to receive services, conduct business, travel or vote depending on the extent to which ID cards are required for these activities.

7. "[S]tate-defined identity categories can have a substantial impact on people, altering pre-existing lines of identity divisions within the society.... The categories used by the state, writes James C. Scott, in his 1998 book *Seeing Like a State*, can become "categories that organize people's daily experiences precisely because they are embedded in state created institutions that structure that experience." James C. Scott, *Seeing Like a State* (New Haven: Yale University Press 1998), p. 81–83.

8. On January 21, 1993 and April 22, 1993 the European Parliament in Strasbourg urged Greece to remove all mention of religion from national ID cards. On June 27, 2000 the European Commission against Racism and Intolerance (ECRI) of the Council of Europe noted that "although the constitution provides for freedom of religion, non-Orthodox religious— notably other Christian — groups have faced administrative obstacles and legal restrictions on religious practice, and members often experience intolerant behavior and sometimes discrimination."

9. Antti Korkaakivi stated "The main rule of the Framework Convention on the Protection of National Minorities, which entered into force in early 1998 — its main rule and underlying idea is that a person belonging to a national minority has the freedom, or should have the freedom, to choose to be treated or not to be treated as such [see Article 3].... And if there is an ethnicity line included in an identification document, that should definitely reflect this rule — i.e., ethnicity should not in any way be imposed upon a person. If a person does not want to be treated as a member of a national minority, he or she should have the right to stay out of that" ("Georgia: Ethnicity Proposal Stirs Debate on Nationality and Citizenship," by Jeremy Bransten, Prague, 22 January 1999 [*Radio Free Europe/Radio Liberty* www.rferl.org]).

10. We, representatives of various non-governmental organizations (NGOs) and people's organizations in Southeast Asia ... call on members of ASEAN to ... [b]e accountable for discriminatory policies and practices: 1. Which force minori-

ties to change their surnames as in the tribal peoples in Thailand; 2. Which force minorities to carry national identity cards which eliminate or change people's distinct ethnic identities like in Burma; 3. Which uses racial/religious identification in national identity cards and official government documents, that promotes greater racial and religious segregation and or discrimination as in Malaysia." (Southeast Asian Peoples' Statement on Confronting Racism, Racial Discrimination, Xenophobia and Related Intolerance, Conference statement, 18 July 2001).

11. Andrew Bell-Fialkoff, *Ethnic Cleansing* (New York: St. Martin's Griffin, 1996); Barnett R. Rubin, "Russian Hegemony and State Breakdown in the Periphery: Causes and Consequences of the Civil War in Tajikistan." Paper prepared for the Carnegie Project on Political Order, Conflict and Nationalism in the Former Soviet Union, September 1995, p. 4.

12. Raul Hilberg, *The Destruction of the European Jews* (New York: Holmes & Meier Publishers, 1985), 173–180; Einführung der Juden ab 1.1.1939 (Introduction of the identification card for Jews starting from 1.1.1939), 23. Juli 1938, Reichgesetzblatt 1 I, 922; Verordnung Reisepässe von Juden vom (Regulation of passports of Jews), 5 Oktober 1938 Reichgesetzblatt 1 I, 1342.

13. Lucy S. Dawidowicz, *The War Against the Jews 1933–1945* (New York: Holt, Rinehart and Winston, 1975), 280–282, 297–298.

14. The full paragraph from the Hutu Manifesto reads: "Les gens ne sont d'ailleurs pas sans s'être rendu compte de l'appui de l'administration indirecte au monopole tutsi. Aussi pour mieux surveiller ce monopole de race, nous nous opposons énergiquement, du moins pour le moment, à la suppression dans les pièces d'identité officielles ou privées des mentions "muhutu," "mututsi," "mutwa." Leur suppression risqué encore davantage la sélection en le voilant et en empêchant la loi statistique de pouvoir établir la vérité des faits. Personne n'a dit d'ailleurs que c'est le nom qui ennuie le Muhutu; ce sont les privileges d'un monopole favorisé, lequel risqué de réduire la majorité de la population dans une infériorité systématique et une sous-existence imméritée" from "Manifeste des Bahutu: Note sur l'aspect social du problème racial indigene au Ruanda: 24 mars 1957" in C. M. Overdulve, *Rwanda: Un people avec une histoire* (Paris: l'Harmattan, 1997), pp. 98–111; Philip Gourevitch, *We Wish to Inform You That Tomorrow We Will Be Killed with Our Families: Stories from Rwanda* (New York: Farrar Straus and Giroux, 1998), p. 90.

15. Arusha Accord (Peace Agreement between the Government of the Republic of Rwanda and the Rwandese Patriotic Front), August 1993, Article 16: "Deletion of reference to Ethnic Group in Official Documents: The Broad-Based Transitional Government shall, from the date of its assumption of office, delete from all official documents to be issued any reference to ethnic origin. Documents in use or not yet used shall be replaced by those not bearing any reference to ethnic origin," Arusha Accord (Peace Agreement between the Government of the Republic of Rwanda and the Rwandese Patriotic Front), 4 August 1993. Alison Des Forges, *Leave None to Tell the Story*, p. 501, citing Human Rights Watch/FIDH interview, Brussels, December 12, 1995; Republique Rwandaise, Parquet de la Republique, P.V. no. 189 and no. 260. See also Timothy Longman, "Identity Cards, Ethnic Self-Perception, and Genocide in Rwanda" in the forthcoming book *Documenting Individual Identity: The Development of State Practices in the Modern World*, edited by Jane Caplan and John Torpey (Princeton University Press).

16. Christopher R. Browning, *Ordinary Men: Reserve Police Battalion 101 and the Final Solution in Poland* (Harper, 1993), chapter 18.

The Compulsory Birth and Death Certificate in the United States

Carl Watner

The state's contact with each and every person in its jurisdiction usually begins at birth, since the law requires that newborns be registered with the government, and that an official "certificate of live birth" be issued and recorded. How long has this practice existed and what is its history? This essay, newly written for this anthology, answers these questions. Carl Watner, editor of this anthology, is a father of four home-schooled children, manager of two small businesses, and has published The Voluntaryist *newsletter for the last twenty years. His most recently published books include* I Must Speak Out: The Best of the Voluntaryist 1982–1999 *and* Dissenting Electorate: Those Who Refuse to Vote and the Legitimacy of Their Opposition *(2000).*

Introduction

When the Constitution of the United States was finally adopted by the thirteen states of the Articles of Confederation, the new federal government had no power to collect direct personal income taxes from each citizen or to record their births and deaths except once every ten years (in conjunction with the decennial census which was required to determine the apportionment of congressmen in the House of Representatives). "There was not the remotest idea in the minds of the framers of the Constitution as to the necessity of a complete record of vital statistics...."[1] Even among the States at that time, there was little concern for the official, civil registration of births and deaths. As one commentator noted during the 1860s, it was probably impossible for a large portion of the American populace to prove that they were ever born, that "their parents were ever married, and that they have any legitimate right to the name they bear, ..."[2] Yet today, nearly every person has a state-issued birth certificate. The constitutional directive for the decennial census has been expanded to such an extent that serious consideration is now being given to assigning a federal identification number to each and every citizen and resident alien. How did we, in the United States, move from the point where very few of our ancestors were concerned about even having a record of their births (much less having a public official make that record) to the point where we are ready to accept a government number to identify us? The main purpose of this article is to answer that question by presenting an overview of the evolution of government-mandated birth and death certificates in the United States.

In the Beginning

When the colonists that settled at Jamestown, Virginia, and Plymouth Rock, Massachusetts, arrived in North America, there already existed a history of birth and death registration in the older European countries. For example, in 1538, Lord Thomas Cromwell had ordered that the English parishes be responsible for keeping registers to record baptisms and burials. Twenty-five years later, the Council of Trent made it a law of the Catholic Church that registers of births and marriages should be kept.[3] However, since the Puritans and Pilgrims took the view that marriage was a civil event, rather than a religious one, they held that the registration of births and deaths should be a government responsibility, rather than an ecclesiastical one. Therefore, in 1639 the General Court of the Massachusetts Bay Colony ordered that births and deaths should be reported to the town clerk by parents or household owners within one month of their occurrence. Thus Massachusetts holds the record for being

> the first state in the Christian world which recorded births, deaths, and marriages by government officers; ... the first state in the world which recorded the dates of the actual facts of births, deaths, and marriages rather than the subsequent ecclesiastical ceremonies of baptisms, burials, and weddings; and ... the first state in the world which imposed on the citizen the duty of giving notice to the government of all births, [d]eaths, and marriages occurring in his family.[4]

The Connecticut colony followed suit in 1644, and the New Plymouth colony did likewise in 1646. John Locke, in his "Fundamental Constitutions" for the government of the Carolinas, which was prepared in 1669, made provision for a "Registry in every Signiory, Barony, and Colony, wherein shall be recorded all the births, marriages, and deaths that shall happen."[5]

During the 18th century, there was little concern on the part of American governments, either federal or state, for the recording of vital statistics. In 1785, James Madison proposed a law in the Virginia Assembly which would have created a system of statewide birth and death registration. It was defeated in the Virginia Senate. Similarly, on the federal level, under the North West Ordinance of 1787 there was no provision for the registration of births and deaths. Only marriages were required to be recorded within three months. New York City first recorded deaths officially in 1803, but it was not until 1847 that the city began recording births and marriages. Very few people, except the most wealthy, who were concerned with their legal inheritance, had any real interest in official public records. Until the last half of the 19th century, the recording of births, deaths, and marriages was generally considered either a semi-religious or social function. Such events, if they were recorded at all, were more likely to either be entered in a family's Bible, or a church register, than registered by a clerk in a government office.

It was largely the development of the public health movement and the advancements of medical science which propelled the demand for official vital statistics in the United States. Until the early 1900s, the American States might as well have been foreign nations, so far as measured by the uniformity of their health codes and registration of vital events. As one historian put it, "Only as European nations created efficient mechanisms in the course of the nineteenth century did the uncoordinated condition of American state registration begin to reveal the extent of its shortcomings."[6] For example, the English Parliament had passed a registration law in 1836, which provided for the collection of vital statistics. The legislature of Massachusetts followed suit in 1842. However it was almost three decades later before any state in the Union had an official Board of Health (Massachusetts in 1869), and before the American Public Health Association was founded (1872).[7] The initial impetus for the improved collection of vital statistics usually came from public officials, doctors, public health officers, sanitary engineers, and statisticians who were concerned with enumerating the variety of sicknesses, infectious diseases, and epidemics prevalent within their state, and who began to scientifically study causes, containment, and control.

The States justified such activities under their police powers of providing for the public's health, safety, welfare, the prevention and detection of crime, and the need to collect data for sanitary purposes and analysis. Lewis Hockheimer, in his 1897 article on "Police Power" in the *Central Law Journal*, noted that "The police power is the inherent plenary power of a State ... to prescribe regulations to preserve and promote the public safety, health, and morals, and to prohibit all things hurtful to the comfort and welfare of society."[8] The constitutional basis of such state power was found in the Tenth Amendment, which reserved to the states all powers not explicitly delegated or prohibited in the Constitution. Firefighting regulations, quarantine laws,

laws governing weights and measures, inspection of flour, meal, beef and pork, control laws over strong liquors, and recordation of vital statistics: in short, "no aspect of human intercourse remained outside the purview of" the police power if it could be justified as beneficial to the happiness and welfare of the state's citizenry.[9]

Birth and Death Registration
in Massachusetts

Throughout the 19th century, the State of Massachusetts remained a pioneer in recording the vital events of its citizens. However at the beginning of the 1800s, probably not more than 50% of the births and deaths in the state were actually registered according to the laws in force. Until at least the early 1840s, the main justification of the registration laws in Massachusetts was that "lists of births and deaths would be useful in cases of probate."[10] In February 1842, when the state legislature appointed a committee to revise the law, increasing emphasis was placed upon the "importance of vital records in studying the public health, particularly in helping to chart the course of epidemic diseases through the State." Numerous factors affected the collection of vital statistics during the middle decades of the century. For one thing it was estimated that less than 50% of births in the state were attended by a midwife or physician. Many parents were not aware that it was their responsibility to report births to the town clerks, and there was a "widespread reluctance to require physicians and midwives to report births." State supervision of medical doctors had been "relaxed" from 1830 to 1850 (formal licensing was not resumed until 1894), and it was believed that involving "medical practitioners in the registration system again might require a state-sponsored program for distinguishing between competent and less expert physicians."[11] So not only were the medical doctors fearful of involvement with the State, they resented being forced by law to report births and deaths, a service for which either they would not be paid, or receive very little compensation.

In 1849, the legislature again appointed a committee to close loop-holes in the vital statistics law. Lemuel Shattuck authored the report, which has been referred to as "the first treatise on the subject of vital registration" published in the United States. The committee demanded that town and city clerks both be "authorized and required" to collect birth and death information; that "all towns appoint superintendents of burial grounds and undertakers, who would have the exclusive right to handle interments;" and that amount of fees paid to those who had the duty to collect birth and death information be augmented.[12] Although much of the committee's report was rejected by the legislature, the report served to bring publicity to the topic of public health and vital statistics. Nevertheless, there were still a number of ways that deaths went unrecorded. First of all, private farm burials had never been outlawed in Massachusetts, and they were especially prevalent in the rural counties. The legislature feared to prohibit such burials "for fear of offending the folk tradition that a farmer should be buried on the land he tilled." Secondly, there were no state regulations regarding removal of bodies from one town to another. Thirdly, there was no requirement that coroners report violent deaths to the town clerks; and finally it remained very easy for sextons and cemetery superintendents to avoid the law.[13] By the early 1870s, the state legislature addressed these issues, including an order to all towns and cities to license undertakers (who were threatened with loss of their license if they failed to report deaths). Thus by the end of the 1870s, there was near 100% accuracy in the recording of deaths within the state.

However at the same time, problems remained in approaching such accuracy in the reporting of births. There were still parents and householders who remained unaware of their obligations, and "because parenthood was obviously not a government office, there were great obstacles in making parents comply with the law.... Perhaps they could have been prosecuted" but the widespread apathy with regard to birth statistics resulted from the fact that fertility was not regarded as a social problem at that time.[14] Nevertheless, with the advent of the State Board of Health in 1869, and the establishment of city and town boards of health during the 1880s and 1890s, and changes to the law in 1883 (which increased the fees paid to physicians and midwives who reported births), gradually more and more births were recorded. Additionally, town and city clerks often resorted to conducting municipal-wide censuses once a year as a means of recording births that either were not attended by a midwife or physician or births which they attended, but failed to report.[15] Thus by 1890, it was safe to say that the "the main features of an adequate system had been adopted and put into operation. No more than one or two per cent of the births and deaths which occurred in the State were not registered."[16]

The Registration Area

With the State of Massachusetts as an example, the federal government tried to encourage other states and local governments to emulate its practices. In 1880, the Federal Bureau of the Census initiated a national registration area for the uniform collection of death statistics in order to provide a scientific basis for the study of public health problems in the states. The registration "area" was simply all or part of a State (such as a major city within the State) which complied with the federal guidelines for the collection of death statistics. In order to qualify for admission into the national registration area a State or municipality had to comply with two requirements. First it had to pass satisfactory a law and implement a suitable system for death registration, and secondly, it had to attain at least a 90% rate of completeness in recording deaths within its geographic boundaries. Wilson G. Smillie in his book *Public Health Administration in the United States* discusses the evolution of modern registration:

> Various checks [we]re used by the Federal Census Bureau to determine whether a given state ha[d] fulfilled all requirements. The national registration area began with Massachusetts and New Jersey, the District of Columbia, and nineteen cities. Gradually the various states were admitted by the Federal Census Bureau so that every state is now included in the National Registration Area for Deaths. The National Birth Registration Area was established in 1915. Criteria for admission were similar to those required for admission to the death registration area. All states have met the federal requirements, though a few states have difficulty in maintaining the national registration standards. This formation of national registration areas marks one of the progressive steps in public health administration in the United States. It was brought about through formulation of a model registration law which was first presented to the official Association of Public Health Officers and approved by it. This model law had gradually been adopted by the various states.
>
> Registration of all births and deaths within the state is a function of the state health department. The state health officer, or some other person on his staff, who is responsible to, and is designated by him, is the official state registrar of vital statistics.
>
> The basis for effective registration is the formation of an organization whereby each birth and death that occurs within the state shall be recorded immediately on an individual certificate. Standard uniform certificates may be used, as well as standard methods of collection of the certificates and standard methods of interpretation of the data. These certificates are filed as a permanent record, and become part of the state archives.[17]

The objects of the national registration areas was the uniform and standardized collection of birth and deaths throughout the entire United States, so that statistics from one part of the country could be accurately compared to that of another part. When the federal registration area for deaths began in 1880, it only embraced about 17% of the country's population. In 1900 it was estimated that about 40.5% of the population had their deaths recorded; in 1915, the figure was up to 66.9%, and by 1925 the figure was up to 88%. As the author of *Why Should Births and Deaths Be Registered?* (published by the American Medical Association in various editions during the early 1900s), observed: the work of registration could not be called "a complete success *until every birth and death in the United States shall be promptly recorded*."[18] The former Chief Statistician for Vital Statistics of the United States, in 1916, wrote of his hope of the "rapid expansion" of the registration areas, "not only for deaths ... but also for births, until the entire country shall have attained a condition of 100% efficiency in this respect."[19]

American commentators and health officials during the later half of the 19th century noted that "voluntary contribution of information by heads of families or physicians ... ha[d] always been a failure."[20] In a report prepared for the U.S. National Board of Health in 1882, Dr. John Billings, a surgeon in the United States Army, discussed the problems surrounding the accurate collection of birth and death statistics. Members of the general public were simply not informed enough to understand the importance of birth and death registration. They "suppose that it is merely a hobby of the doctors, who want the information for their own private purposes, and that this information can only be obtained by an unjustified amount of meddling with private affairs and by a system of espionage which will cause much trouble and difficulty."[21] In a report to the Kentucky legislature in 1853, it was noted that the vital statistic records in many European countries are universal and compulsory: "In this country they would, by many, be considered unreasonable, oppressive, and tyrannical."[22] When a birth registration law was passed in South Carolina "many of the citizens absolutely refused to" cooperate with the law.[23] It soon became obvious to public officials that "We cannot ... hope to obtain any entirely satisfactory system of registration of births until the people at large have become educated to the necessity for it, and are induced to seek such registration of their own accord in order to secure proof of legitimacy, title to property, &c."[24] How true this observation was is reflected in the following comment: "The national Social Security Act [1935] proved to be a great stimulus to accurate birth certification. Many people had never considered a birth certificate to be of any importance until old age assistance, unemployment insurance, and other ramifications of the Social Security Act demonstrated to them that it was necessary to have this official proof of their existence."[25] Another means of accommodating the people to the idea of registration was to use the public schools to instruct the up-and-coming generation about the importance of public health and the necessity of cooperating with governmental authorities for such purposes.

The 19th century movement for registration of vital statistics emphasized the recording of deaths, not births. Authorities perceived that it was easier to enforce regulations which required a government certificate of death than of birth, because birth registration was considered a more invasive practice. A newborn could go his or her entire life without a birth certificate, whereas a person's body had to be disposed of within a few days of death. The laws in most American jurisdictions eventually required that a government permit be issued for "every interment and removal of a dead body, and the community soon learns to consider any attempt at burial without a permit as a suspicious circumstance...." Another commentator noted that "The *corpus* of every deceased human being must somehow be disposed of. The central registration authority in each locality is the only person qualified to permit legal disposal. Therefore substantially all deaths must get registered."[26]

The City of New York first required a death certificate under its Act of April 2, 1803, "which established public health regulations for the metropolis." All physicians were required to leave a signed note, which provided the name, age, and cause of death, with some member of the deceased's household. Sextons (the church official responsible for the church graveyard) were required to have the physician's statement present before any burial could occur. Violations of the law subjected the physician to a $50 fine, and the sexton to a $25. fine.[27] Thus it was that the entire death and dying process was regulated, so that no dead person could be legally buried without the proper state-required or city-required paperwork.

The doctor was one of the most important functionaries in the system of collecting vital statistics. As a person licensed by the state to practice medicine, it became the responsibility and duty of the physician to assist the public health officers in each locale. "It is an onerous public duty of each physician to report promptly to the health department all births and deaths that occur in his private practice.... Th[e] simple procedure [of filling out birth and death certificates] is one of the primary obligations to his patients and to the community that a physician assumes when he is granted permission by the state to practice medicine."[28] However, this was not always the attitude of doctors during the 19th century. In an article in the *Chicago Medical Journal* of 1878, it was noted that

> In this country there is only the curiosity of a few scientific men that can be relied upon for the moral support of a registry law, and it is probable that in Chicago not more than 12 in every thousand would be found to care for the registration of their nativity even in a family Bible. The reason why physicians do not execute the law is because they not only have no personal interest in its execution, but [also] because of an invincible, though not always clearly recognized, feeling of revolt against the injustice of a law which inflicts a special tax on the physician in the shape of postage, time, and trouble, and affords no compensation for the extra labor and expense. People do not like to make a present to the Government in any shape or form. It is as unjust to the State to add fifty cents to the doctor's tax simply because he is a doctor as it would be to add fifty dollars. The State should pay for all such service and it need not incur any great expense. It might, as in the case of jury duty or military service by conscription, fix its own rate, but the obligation should be recognized. The payment would, of course, require increased general taxation, but the increase would be levied on all alike. The health officers are trying to get service from the doctors without paying for it.[29]

The Model Laws

Even after the Registration Areas for the recording of birth and death statistics were in place, it took government authorities many years to bring all of the United States into the system. In 1903, Congress officially endorsed the system by passing a resolution that called for nationwide support of "proper registration of all deaths and births."[30] Pennsylvania was one of the states that embraced the system, and it was reported that in that state there were "hundred of actual prosecutions [which] have been directed by state authorities" against those who failed to register births.[31] In 1907, uniform legislation patterned after the law in Pennsylvania was prepared. This law, which became known as the Model Law, was "endorsed by the Census Department of the U. S. Government, the American Medical Association, the American Public Health Association, the American Statistical Association, the Committee on Uniform Laws of the American Bar Association, American Child Hygiene Association, [and] the American Federation of Labor...."[32] When the registration area for births was established in 1915, it roughly embraced 31% of the American population. By 1927, it was in use in 45 of the 48 states.

The Model Law was officially titled "A Bill to Provide for the Registration of All Births and Deaths in the State of _____." It essentially required the recording of all deaths within the State: no burials, cremations, removals, or interments were to take place without a death permit issued by the State Board of Health, and signed by the physician in last attendance[33], and if no physician was in attendance the next of kin or undertaker must notify the local health officer. The portion of the Model Law that concerned itself with birth registration began with the proviso "That the birth of each and every child born in this state shall be registered as hereinafter provided."[34] The law stated that it was the duty of the physician, midwife, or person acting as midwife, to register the birth. If there was no one acting in this capacity at the birth, then it devolved upon the father or mother of the child, or the householder or owner of the premises where the birth took place to report to the local registrar the fact of such birth within ten days of its occurrence. Upon being notified of the birth, the local registrar had the responsibility to issue a birth certificate.

The Model Law was intended to be compulsory and universal. It applied to each and every person with the geographic area of the state and the law contained penalties for failure to comply. Under Section 22 of the Model Law, failure to meet the requirements of birth and death registration became a misdemeanor, "and upon conviction thereof for the first offense be fined not less than five dollars ($5.00) nor more than fifty dollars ($50.00), and for each subsequent offense not less than ten dollars ($10.00) nor more than one hundred dollars ($100.00), or be imprisoned in the county jail not more than sixty days, or be both fined and imprisoned in the discretion of the court."[35] Although the Model Law did not explicitly endorse the idea, a footnote was inserted to the effect that "Provision may be made whereby compliance with this act shall constitute a condition of granting licenses to physicians, midwives, and embalmers."[36] This meant that, assuming people practicing these occupations were issued new licenses each year, if they were convicted of failing to meet their obligations to register all new births and deaths which they attended, they would be denied their license to practice, and if they did not cease practicing their profession, they would be liable to be convicted of "practicing without a license." Licensure denial was a very effective way of bringing about more complete birth and death registration.

It is interesting to note that as early as 1882, Dr. John Billings, the public health official who was quoted earlier in this paper, observed that:

> All registration acts which are upon a proper basis presuppose also legislation providing for the determining of those who are properly qualified physicians, and for making the names of these known to the registrar. It may be said, therefore, that the registration of vital statistics depends for its efficiency, to a very large extent, upon some system of registration of physicians and midwives.[37]

An interesting implication to draw from Billings' analysis is that unlicensed practitioners were the bane of the authorities. Unlicensed doctors (whether or not they were competent) were too difficult to track and too elusive to be certain whether they filed death certificates. In short, from the very beginning of the movement for registration of births and deaths, government authorities understood that they had to control the practitioners of the birth and death professions. If people in society at large were unwilling to conform to government dictates, the authorities realized it was much easier to enforce their regulations by focusing on a much smaller group of people, whose occupational activities could be regulated.[38] Billings follows the comments quoted above by a discussion of the obligation of physicians to report the existence of certain diseases to the public health authorities. He refers to this as "the compulsory notification of infectious diseases" and points out that if doctors are required to report infectious diseases to the public health department, there is no reason why they should not be willing to accept the compulsory reporting of deaths and the completion of death certificates.[39]

The Modern Era: The Logical Climax

In an article on "Documentary Identification and Mass Surveillance in the United States," published in 1983, the authors noted the near total acceptance of birth certificates by all Americans: "It is practically impossible for an adult to live in the United States without frequent recourse to" documents of identification, such as the birth certificate, and "Today, documentary requirements make it difficult for anyone born in the United States to do without a birth certificate; ...."[40] The government has been so successful in convincing its citizens that identification papers are necessary that even forgers and identity thieves, when they want to create a new personal identity, rely on government documents (either stolen ones or forged ones). In short, in our society the only means of proving "who you are" is by means of government paperwork. Social Security numbers and drivers license did not even exist during the 19th Century. Before the 20th Century, "the majority of births in the United States remained unrecorded with any government agency," but "[b]y 1950, census officials estimated that 97.9 percent of all births in the United States [were] being registered."[41]

The success of the United States governments, both on the federal and state level, in accomplishing the feat of legitimizing itself in the minds and bodies of its citizenry has been phenomenal. In the span of four or five generations, Americans have moved from a situation of quasi-voluntaryism (of having their lives largely unregulated by government) to one of near-total government control over all their activities (literally, from birth to death). This success is best epitomized by the comment of William Smillie, who wrote that "the child has no real legal proof of existence in the eyes of the state without a proper birth certificate."[42] Smillie's comment represents how presumptuous the government is in making government documents the starting point of a person's existence and identity. Traditionally in the United States, and in customary tribal societies, the members of the local community and social network into which a person was born stand as witness to that person's birth (and death). Such events are "a matter of public record in the minds of the people" and there is no need for the government to take note of or register such events.[43]

In the monograph *Why Should Births and Deaths Be Registered?*, the author lists numerous reasons in support of his argument. Let us examine these reasons and see if the only way to achieve them is through government birth certification.

> Such records are necessary in determining questions of parentage, heredity, legitimacy, personal identity, property rights, inheritance, and citizenship. No child labor law is of much value unless it rests on a system of birth registration and of birth certificates issued by the state by which the parent or the child can produce at any time positive proof of birth, paternity, and age. During the war [World War I], the operation of the selective draft act was greatly hampered by the fact that ... no legal evidence could be produced or existed by which the age of the individual could be positively proven.[44] [Birth certificates are also useful:] To settle disputes as to age arising out of insurance claims; ... [T]o obtain a marriage license; ... [T]o gain admission to school; ... As proof of citizenship in order to vote; ... As proof of citizenship in order to obtain a passport.[45]

In analyzing these points, it is first necessary to observe how many of them involve some government regulation or the interaction of the individual with the state. Nearly all the uses of the birth certificate evaporate if the state is removed from the picture. Child labor law enforcement; military conscription of men over a certain age; proof of citizenship for voting and passport purposes; all these reasons disappear if there is no state. The non-state reasons for having a proof of birth then become limited to questions determining property rights, legitimacy, and inheritance. How were these issues handled before the advent of state-mandated birth certificates? They were clarified, resolved, and sorted out through personal testimony, family documents, and the appearance of witnesses and friends to support one's claims. They certainly did not await settlement on the advent of state-issued birth certificates. Clearly, history is on the side of the non-state birth record, for people have lived, prospered, and died for thousands of years without such government documents.

There may be very good reasons for having records of birth and deaths, but this by no means implies that they must be maintained by the government. There are many "necessities" in life, but it does not follow that governments must provide them. For example, we all require food, shelter, and clothing, but during most of American history these necessities were provided by the free market to the extent that people could afford them and desired them. Realistically, there is no more reason for government to produce steel than there is for government to issue birth and death certificates. In a free society, a few organizations like Visa or MasterCard might evolve voluntarily to satisfy people's demands for such records. Some people might choose to maintain their family's birth and death records in an independent commercial registry; others might choose to use their family's Bible; while others might simply keep track of such details themselves by issuing their own documents of record; and those who were either too ignorant or too unconcerned would simply do nothing. The point is that no one would be forced by another person or another group of people to become documented in a way that they did not desire. Those who wanted documentation could have all the identification papers they wanted and could pay for; those who objected would not be coerced. Charities would probably arise to provide for or pay for the documentation and identification of those who could not afford it themselves.

What opponents of state-mandated birth and death certificates object to is the "means." They reject the compulsion involved in the state requiring that everyone have a birth certificate. They may or may not object to voluntarily having a birth certificate (of whatever form they or their parents chose), but they do oppose the use of coercion which would require that everyone have a *state-issued* birth certificate. Paraphrasing Robert Ringer, "I do not believe that I or any other person has the right to *force* men to be charitable [or to have state-issued birth certificates]. In other words, I am *not* against charity [or state-issued birth certificates], but I *am* against the use of force."[46]

Before the days of official birth certificates, it was standard practice in many parts of the world for strangers to carry "letters of introduction." Such documents, issued by a well-known personage, would assure the person presenting it of a much quicker reception and acceptance in a society where he was not known. Other ways of establishing one's reputation in a strange community have historically involved the use of credentials, such as educational degrees and membership certificates in professional or religious organizations. Even the credit card serves as a credential of trustworthiness and reputation.[47] Similarly, in a stateless society, private companies and organizations would probably develop a means guaranteeing a person's real or true identity. Such a procedure would be akin to the issuance of a surety bond, issued by a reputable insurance company. In transactions that merited the importance of such a guarantee, a "personal identity bond" might be demanded, so that in the event of one person masquerading as another, the party being deceived would have recourse to a reputable institution to recover his or her loss. Such a personal identity bond would be much like title insurance is today in real estate transactions. It would serve as a guarantee by an independent company that in the event of any legitimate and unexpected claim arising, the person defrauded would be reimbursed by the insurance company. The development on the internet of digital certificates, public key infrastructures, and private credentials represents a step toward a non-governmental means of identification.[48]

As with many of the services it provides, the State has done a poor job in the provision of birth-recording services. Undoubtedly, even in a free society there would be people who attempt to criminally pretend they are other than who they really are. However, under the existing state system, there is near total reliance on "self-identification." So long as a person can supply a certain amount of personal information (date of birth, mother's maiden name, father's name, place of birth, and a legitimate address) governmental authorities will issue a duplicate birth certificate to that person. As yet, there is no relatively fool-proof system of identifying the person demanding the document with the person whose birth is recorded thereon.[49] The current government attempts to use biometrics, or even the suggestions of others to fingerprint or tattoo each newborn is a way around this impasse.

When state provision of birth and death records began there was practically no thought given to where such government programs might lead. Jeremy Bentham, in the 1830s, was one of the earliest proponents of identifying everyone (by use of tattoos) in a given geographic jurisdiction. State involvement in vital statistics was justified on the perfectly innocent grounds of providing for the public's health and welfare by concentrating on the causes of death. Anyone who would have taken a principled stand on this issue in the early 1900s would have been laughed down. No one could have predicted that state-issued birth certificates would have been linked to the issuance of Social Security numbers, drivers licenses, passports, and other government documents.[50]

Effective birth registration lies at the heart of the state's governance of its people. Realizing this, governments have coercively monopolized the issuance of birth certificates by making it a criminal act for those who are responsible for a birth not to register the newborn. The classic definition of the State is that it is the only institution in society that derives its revenues from compulsory levies, known as taxation, and that it maintains a compulsory monopoly of defense services (such as the police, armed forces, and judicial system) over a given geographic area.[51] When you combine these elements with the state's success in sustaining a monopoly over the means of identification, the stage is set for a totalitarian world. Once you grant local, state, or county government a role in identifying its citizens, there is no logical stopping place until you reach the federal level of demanding complete and total identification of each person in the United States, or in the world, if you are a supporter of world government. In fact, such demands have emanated from the United Nations, both in its 1966 call for the registration of every child at its birth, and as recently as December 2001, in an effort to reduce illegal immigration.[52]

"Therefore to oppose government enumeration is not only to oppose the government's monopoly on the means of identification in modern society by opposing social security numbers, drivers licenses, biometric national ID cards, national databases, and other means now at the center of national controversy, but to oppose it at the most fundamental level, that of government-issued and-recorded birth and death certificates."[53]

Notes

1. Cressy L. Wilbur, M. D., *The Federal Registration Service of the United States: Its Development, Problems, and Defects*, Washington: Government Printing Office, 1916, p. 8.

2. John S. Billings, M.D., Appendix E: "The Registration of Vital Statistics," in *Annual Report of the [U.S.] National Board of Health*: 1882, Washington: Government Printing Office, 1883, p. 357. John Shaw Billings (1838–1913) was Director of Vital Statistics of the United States government and a "leader of the medical profession," who played an important role in the historical development of the tabulating machine, the early predecessor of the IBM computer. It was he who, in an 1880 discussion with Herman Hollerith, first suggested, "that the laborious work of hand tabulation could be replaced by mechanical devices and by the use of a card with holes punched to represent the items." Hollerith went on to develop one of the first successful mechanical tabulator/punch card readers for the Bureau of the Census in 1890. The Tabulating Machine Company, which Hollerith founded, eventually became the nucleus of the commercial organization renamed International Business Machine (IBM) in 1924. See "John Shaw Billings," II *Encyclopedia of the Social Sciences*, New York: The Macmillan Company, p. 542; James Connolly, *History of Computing in Europe*, IBM World Trade Corporation, circa 1967, pp. 5-6 and

p. 22; and Edwin Black, *IBM and the Holocaust*, New York: Crown Publishers, 2001, p. 25.

3. See Major P. Granville Edge, "Vital Registration in Europe: The Development of Official Statistics and Some Differences In Practice," 91 *Royal Statistical Society Journal* (1928), pp. 346-393, especially pp. 354-355, and p. 375, "Appendix I. The [Compulsory] Registration of Births and Deaths." Also see Billings, op. cit. p. 355.

4. Robert Rene Kuczynski, "The Registration Laws in the Colonies of Massachusetts Bay and New Plymouth," n.s. 51, *American Statistical Association*, September 1900, p. 9. Also see Wilbur, op. cit., p. 37 and Billings, op. cit., p. 356.

5. Wilbur, op. cit., p. 37.

6. Generally see Richard Shryock, "The Origins and Significance of the Public Health Movement in the United States," n.s. I, *Annals of Medical History*, 1929, pp. 645-665. For the quotation see James H. Cassedy, *Demography in Early America: Beginnings of the Statistical Mind, 1600–1800*, Cambridge: Harvard University Press, 1969, p. 211.

7. Wilson G. Smillie, *Public Health Administration in the United States*, New York: The Macmillan Company, 1947 (Third Edition), p. 13. An "English law of 1874 adopted provisions already in force in Scotland, compelling physicians to return certificates of death; ...." W. P. Prentice, *Police Powers Arising Under the Law of Overruling Necessity*, New York: Banks & Brothers, 1894, p. 156.

8. Cited in William J. Novak, *The People's Welfare: Law and Regulation in Nineteenth Century America*, Chapel Hill: University of North Carolina Press, 1996, p. 13.

9. Ibid., p. 14.

10. Robert Gutman, *Birth and Death Registration in Massachusetts 1639–1900*, New York: Milbank Memorial Fund, 1959, p. 24 and p. 10.

11. Ibid., p. 56 and p. 32.

12. Ibid. pp. 48–49.

13. Ibid., p. 60 and p. 63.

14. Ibid., p. 103.

15. Ibid., p. 106.

16. Ibid., p. 109.

17. Smillie, op. cit., p. 189.

18. *Why Should Births and Deaths Be Registered?: A Summary of the History and Present Condition of Vital Statistics Law, Including the Text of the Model Bill*, Chicago: Press of the American Medical Association, 1927, p. 8. Italics in the original.

19. Wilbur, op. cit., p. 9.

20. Billings, op. cit., p. 357.

21. Ibid.

22. W. L. Sutton, "Appendix" to the *Second Annual Report to the General Assembly of Kentucky Relating to the Registry and Returns of Births, Marriages, and Deaths, from January 1, 1853 to December 31, 1853*, Legislative Document No. 1, Frankfort: A. G. Hodges, 1854, p. 136.

23. Ibid., p. 140.

24. Billings, op. cit., p. 360.

25. Smillie, op. cit., p. 191.

26. Billings, op. cit. p. 364, and Raymond Pearl, *Introduction to Medical Biometry and Statistics*, Philadelphia: W. B. Saunders Company, Third Edition, Revised and Enlarged, 1940, p. 54.

27. "New York's First Death Certificate," *The American Cemetery* Magazine, November 1981, p. 22.

28. Smillie, op. cit., pp. 525-526.

29. Billings, op. cit., p. 365.

30. *Why Should Births and Deaths Be Registered?*, op. cit., p. 3.

31. Wilbur, op. cit., p. 17.

32. *Why Should Births and Deaths Be Registered?*, op. cit., p. 3 and 9.

33. Sec. 8, Model Law found in ibid., p. 27.

34. Ibid., Sec. 12, p. 31.

35. Ibid., Sec. 22, pp. 44–45.

36. Ibid., Sec. 22, p. 45.

37. Billings, op. cit., p. 366.

38. See Ron Hamowy, "The Early Development of Medical Licensing Laws in the United States 1875–1900," delivered at the 6th Annual Libertarian Scholar's Conference, Princeton Univ., October 1978, and which was published in 3 *Journal of Libertarian Studies* (No. 1, Spring 1979), and which can be found at http://www.libertarianstudies.org/journals/jls/pdfs/3_1/3_1_5.pdf. Also see Chapter 4, "Medical Societies and Medical Licensing," in William G. Rothstein, *American Physicians in the Nineteenth Century*, Baltimore: Johns Hopkins University Press, 1972, pp. 63–84.

39. Billings, op. cit., p. 366.

40. James Rule, Douglas McAdam, Linda Stearns, and David Uglow, "Documentary Identification and Mass Surveillance in the United States," 31 *Social Problems* (No. 2), December 1983, pp. 222–234 at p. 222 and p. 224.

41. Ibid., p. 224.

42. Smillie, op. cit., p. 191.

43. This point was made in personal correspondence from Aslam Effendi, a descendant of the Pathans in Pakistan and Afghanistan, who wrote "that in tribal society there is no bureaucratic system for recording of births" or deaths. [Email dated February 25, 2002.] Simon Cole makes a similar point in his book *Suspect Identities: A History of Fingerprinting and Criminal Identification* (Cambridge: Harvard University Press, 2001), p. 8: "In general, premodern societies already had an effective method of personal, and criminal, identification: the network of personal acquaintance through which persons were 'known' in the memories and perceptions of their neighbors [and relatives]."

44. *Why Should Births and Deaths Be Registered?*, op. cit., p. 1.

45. Ibid., pp. 5-6.

46. Robert Ringer, *Restoring the American Dream*, New York: Published by QED, 1979, p. 134 (from Chapter 4, "The Gourmet Banquet," in the next to the last paragraph of the Section headlined "The Fate of the 'Poor' in a Free Society."

47. See Steven L. Nock, *The Costs of Privacy: Surveillance and Reputation in America*, New York: Aldine de Gruyter, 1993. Nock asks, "How are reputations established among strangers?" and then answers this question by discussing the role of credentials ("credit cards, educational degrees, driver's licenses") and ordeals ("lie detector tests, drug tests, integrity tests"). Especially see pp. viii, 1-3, 14–15, 47–48, 51, 76–77, and 92–193.

48. For greater elaboration see "Private Credentials," Montreal: Zero-Knowledge Systems, Inc. (November 2000). This is a white paper available on Zero-Knowledge Systems' website.

49. For a discussion of this point see Rule, et al., op. cit., p. 227.

50. In 1998, the Social Security Administration began the "Enumeration at

Birth" program, which "allows a parent to apply for an SSN for his/her newborn as part of the State's birth registration process." This program was started to ease enforcement of the January 1, 1998 IRS requirement that tax returns must have the Social Security number of all dependents claimed as exemptions. See U. S. Department of Health and Human Services, "Unique Health Identifier for Individuals: A White Paper," at http://www.epic.org/privacy/medical/hhs-id-798.html at p. 12.

51. For a general discussion of voluntaryism and anarchism see Carl Watner, *I Must Speak Out: The Best of* The Voluntaryist *1982–1999*, San Francisco: Fox & Wilkes, 1999. Especially see p. 24 and pp. 47–48.

52. Article 24 (2) of the United Nations International Covenant on Civil and Political Rights (General Assembly Resolution 2200A (XXI) of December 16, 1966 states that "Every child shall be registered immediately after birth and shall have a name." On December 14, 2001, at a United Nations refugee meeting in Geneva, Switzerland it was proposed that "Every person in the world would be fingerprinted and registered under a universal identification scheme to fight illegal immigration and people smuggling...." Maria Hawthorne, "Refugees meeting hears proposal to register every human," at http:www/smh.com.au/breaking/2001/12/14/FFX058CU 6VC.html.

53. Thanks to Claire Wolfe for suggesting this conclusion. Also see *The Voluntaryist*, whole no. 118.

A National Fingerprint System for the United States

Pamela Sankar

*In February 1938, the American Civil Liberties Union characterized the attempts at securing voluntary fingerprints from Americans as "part of the general scheme for the compulsory regimentation of the entire population: (*Thumbs Down!: The Fingerprint Menace to Civil Liberties, *1938, p. 2). The following excerpt from* State Power and Record-Keeping: The History of Individualized Surveillance in the United States, 1790–1935 *(University of Pennsylvania, Ph.D. thesis, 1992) points out that a "national fingerprint system represents an impressive resource for state surveillance." The state is able to maintain control over its citizens over a vast geographic expanse. "With fingerprint records, and other similar individualized records, the state can enforce official identities, which [in turn] allows it to exert control over economic activities, limit geographic movement, and monitor social deviance, individual by individual. Such records constitute a critical element of the state's power base" (pp. 315–316). Read on to find out how fingerprinting evolved in its role of tracking criminals, resident aliens, and finally all civilians.*

Introduction

Bolstered by an efficient, reliable classification system, fingerprinting held great promise for enacting the wish expressed in 1889 by France's prison director, Louis Herbette, that the state "give to each human being an identity ... lasting, unchangeable, and always recognizable.[1] In theory, a well-run fingerprinting system indeed could encompass a nation's entire population with little danger of confusion. Many countries quickly embraced the concept of universal fingerprinting, notably among them, Argentina. Others, including the U.S., moved more slowly.

Suggestions for a universal U.S. fingerprint requirement were voiced as early as 1911, but did not gain popularity until after World War I.[2] This war had radically altered both public and government perceptions of the necessity of domestic surveillance and the utility of fingerprinting to enact that surveillance. Previously, officials had perceived fingerprinting narrowly as a measure to help control common criminals. During the decade following the war, however, officials began to envision fingerprinting instead as a tool of routine civil administration, in particular one which could be aimed against political dissenters.

By the early 30s, considerable progress had been made, primarily at the instigation of the FBI, toward integrating fingerprint requirements into widely varied spheres including employment and welfare eligibility, military enlistment, immigration, and registration for insurance and at maternity hospitals. By the late 1940s, the FBI's fingerprints, representing a large portion of the U.S. adult population at the time.[3]

Fingerprinting had become an acceptable, if still somewhat controversial, practice. Through the FBI collection, the U.S. government had built the capacity to individually monitor the actions and beliefs of its citizens. It was not a capacity the government used often, (at least relative to the total number of records it held), but the repressive threat that its existence implied embodied a powerful tool of domestic control.

This essay begins by reviewing the early applications of fingerprinting by both local and federal officials. It emphasizes the relatively limited sphere officials marked out for fingerprinting in the pre–World War I era. This account serves both to fill in the history of fingerprinting from its invention to its subsequent widespread dissemination, and to explore reasons why officials could not always prevail when attempting to introduce fingerprinting. This account also provides a backdrop against which to consider the changed atmosphere fostered by World War I in which fingerprinting finally did become an accepted and popular practice. The essay explores how key events of World War I encouraged these changes and goes on to describe both how the government enacted its new fingerprint policy and how the public responded.

This phase of identification history is important both for the technological advances which occurred: fingerprinting did represent a leap forward in the state's ability to easily and quickly distinguish one citizen from among millions by using a method which required no personal knowledge and could be effected across great temporal and spatial expanses, and for the social and political changes which took shape; the idea that the state has the right and the obligation to keep track of individual citizens gained a wide currency which, while often challenged and occasionally denied, indeed has never been eliminated.

Fingerprinting's Early Police Applications

During the very early 1900s, fingerprinting remained largely within the criminal identification niche created by Bertillon's anthropometry. The social trends of the mid to late 1800s that had fostered a central role for identification methods in police and penal affairs had carried on into the 1900s and assured fingerprinting an enthusiastic reception in those quarters. Urban crime continued to be a public issue and preventive policing had become the accepted response. The beliefs that linked knowledge of a criminal's identity with successful crime prevention remained strong and helped to underscore the need for an improved system of certain identification. Furthermore, police were still seeking, and to some extent had attained, professional status. Police were attracted to fingerprinting with its statistical and scientific trappings because it helped project the desired image of a modern, professional corps.

The IACP membership first heard about fingerprinting in 1904 and over the next few years witnessed several demonstrations of the new method. In 1911 the NBCI officially began to accept fingerprint cards from its members and its collection grew rapidly. Several large cities and at least one state also established independent fingerprint bureaus and during these early years built large collections as well. Although these various fingerprint bureaus often competed with one another, their administrators also understood the importance of sharing identification information and occasionally did so. Within a few years national fingerprint exchange began.[4] The first U.S. criminal conviction based solely on fingerprint evidence occurred in 1911, and it helped to assure that the fingerprint evidence being so enthusiastically collected could be usefully applied.[5]

Still, there were naysayers among the police, many of whom voiced criticisms very similar to those made of criminal anthropometry. Some rejected the statistical reasoning on which assertions of uniqueness were based, others argued that fingerprints were too easily forged to supply reliable evidence, while still others simply looked on them as unnecessarily replicating what anthropometry or collective memory already provided. None of these criticisms appear to have seriously limited fingerprintings' spread, except perhaps for the final one. Several police departments did balk at adopting yet another technology which promised to solve criminal identification problems once and for all. Still, fingerprinting's simplicity, low-cost, and reliability eventually won over even these departments.[6]

Despite its efficacy for the identification of criminals, the legality of fingerprinting did not go unchallenged. New York City police pursued one of the most aggressive fingerprint campaigns and predictably became embroiled in some of the earliest legal actions against the practice. The first appeals case decision — *Gow v. Bingham* (107 N.Y. Supp. 1011) — that spoke explicitly about police authority to fingerprint suspects was handed down in 1907. The decision rejected police arguments that the fingerprint process ought to be thought of as standard police procedure sanctioned under the ill-defined, but accepted, concept of police power. The judge harshly criticized the police for finger-printing Gow — an accused felon — at his arraignment and thus before a deter-mination of guilt. The judge characterized this fingerprinting episode as an "indignity" and "a startling invasion of personal liberty" that contravened a citizen's "natural right" to "complete immunity" and "to be let alone."[7] The judge saw no merit in the police defense that they ought to be allowed to take and keep fingerprints of any suspicious person simply on the grounds that this sort of general information provided a necessary resource in their struggle to prevent crime and protect the community.

Defying the courts' condemnation, the New York police continued to fingerprint suspects and even expanded their fingerprint operations.[8] Still, the *Gow v. Bingham* decision provides an important guidepost in tracking the vicissitudes of opinion concerning fingerprinting and official identities. Whereas by the 1930s, programs for the routine fingerprinting of employees, schoolchildren, and immigrants were legally sanctioned and rather popular among both government officials and the pubic, in the early 1900s, as *Gow v. Bingham* demonstrates, fingerprinting was still a controversial practice. Even the police could not yet clearly establish their right to fingerprint criminal suspects, traditionally a group with few rights.

Many fingerprint supporters argued that fingerprinting could be fruit-fully applied outside of police work, as well. These enthusiasts suggested that banks and employers should use fingerprints to guard against fraudulent check-cashing practices and that local governments could use fingerprints to help solve problems with voter registration and licensing applications.[9] Some went a step further and proposed a universal fingerprint program which would require all inhabitants to submit to fingerprinting. Such a system, they believed would alleviate the problems of unidentifiable dead, amnesia vic-tims, and baby-switching at maternity hospitals.[10]

But precisely because fingerprinting's initial support came from police, the dissemination of fingerprinting into other spheres was curtailed. These suggestions often met with complaints that fingerprinting was a mark of criminality and was not appropriate for routine administrative tasks. Taxi-cab drivers in both New York and Cleveland went on strike when city officials added fingerprinting to the requirements for licensing, and bank customers reportedly bridled when asked to submit to fingerprinting before being per-mitted to cash a check.[11] For some people their reaction against fingerprint-ing was so intense that they even condemned its requirement for certain criminals. For example, these critics believed that it was unfair to fingerprint young violators or people guilty of minor crimes, such as disturbing the peace. They believed that fingerprinting implied that these people were dangerous or habitual criminals, when, indeed, they were not.[12]

Police and other fingerprinting proponents repeatedly beat back these complaints, sometimes by simply asserting that fingerprints did not stigmatize people.[13] But often they launched more elaborate defenses, such as the one put forth in a 1913 *New York Times* editorial. The editorial was written in support of an article published that day in which the New York City police suggested that universal fingerprinting was a good idea. (This statement represents one of the earliest published assertions to that effect.)[14] The editorial suggested that the major reason fingerprinting had not spread more rapidly, thus far, was its association with crime. They condemned this reasoning by equating it with another belief that they considered equally illogical: that physical labor was abhorrent because of its association with slavery. Instead of concentrating on fingerprinting's ignoble past, the editorial exhorted, people should look at the advantages accruing from fingerprinting. Beyond catching criminals, it could be very useful in facilitating deportations, "the exclusion of undesirables," and the identification of unidentified dead. Indeed, fingerprinting really would be "inconvenient" only for the "evil-disposed." The editorial continued, "There should be nothing of humiliation in having prints taken," or in the "brief biographies" added to them. Instead, the fingerprint cards could be a "permanent source of pride," at least to those "who chose to lead worthy lives."

Proponents of non-criminal fingerprinting made this argument again and again in their continuing efforts to move fingerprinting out of the criminal realm. Fingerprinting, they asserted, benefited the common good and resisting fingerprinting indicated not a defensible regard for one's own privacy, but guilt.[15] However, despite strong and frequent editorializing, the association between criminality and fingerprinting remained unchanged during fingerprinting's early years and created a stigma which was difficult to overcome. Through the early 1920s attempts to move fingerprinting out from police departments and prisons into financial and bureaucratic applications largely failed and fingerprinting remained a tool of local police.

Pre–World War I Federal Interest in Fingerprinting

During fingerprinting's introductory phase, several federal agencies initiated fingerprint collections, but the government made no effort to centralize these efforts. Three offices in particular adopted fingerprinting almost immediately following its introduction into the United States. These included the criminal identification bureau housed at the federal government's Leavenworth Penitentiary which added fingerprinting to its anthropometry collection as early as 1904; the Office of Indian Affairs (in the Interior Department) which began collecting the thumbprints of Native Americans in 1908 to help deter fraudulent financial transactions; the War Department which began fingerprinting enlisted men in 1906 as a measure to prevent deserters from re-enlisting.[16] Officials in the Bureau of Immigration and the War Department also contracted with the NBCI to provide fingerprint and anthropometric information to them as needed, although these arrangements were short-lived.[17]

While these fingerprint programs demonstrate a clear interest in fingerprinting by federal officials, they represent somewhat limited applications of the new technology, especially when contrasted to other fingerprint plans being suggested at the time. In 1909, for example, Attorney General Charles J. Bonaparte tried to convince the government of the advantages of transferring the criminal identification records stored at the Leavenworth Federal Penitentiary to Washington, D.C., thus laying the foundation for a national system.[18] A few years later, IACP officials began pressing the DOJ to completely take over its NBCI collection. Little is known about the justifications for trying to move the Leavenworth bureau to Washington, but the plan to donate the NBCI collection to the DOJ is well-documented.

Believing that the NBCI offered a service which the nation desperately needed, IACP officials had been asking the federal government for support almost since the inception of the NBCI. In the mid-1910s, however, IACP officials reached the more extreme conclusion that they wanted to donate the entire collection to the federal government. They offered, as well, to help the DOJ administer what would then be a truly national identification system.

More than altruism motivated their offer, however. Although the NBCI collection had continued to grow, its support among IACP leaders was not as strong as leaders initially had hoped it would be. The identification bureau had begun to slip into decline. Ironically the introduction of fingerprinting created part of the problem.[19] The NBCI had spent many years convincing members to adopt the Bertillon system, only to decide in the early 1900s that fingerprinting offered superior dependability and efficiency. Not wanting to alienate members dedicated to criminal anthropometry, the NBCI continued to use both systems and allowed members to choose which they wanted to use. Indeed, on occasion they tried to convince members to use both systems! The burden of administering two completely different systems diminished the NBCI's quality of service. Poor service led members to withhold dues which, in turn, further compromised service. Many officials believed fervently in the NBCI and did not want to see it shut down. They hoped that its mission could be salvaged by the federal government which could use its greater resources and legislative authority to assure that the national system realized its full potential.[20]

Both the Leavenworth and IACP plans to establish a Washington-based national identification bureau called for combining records from local and national collections and for regularizing access to the collection for local, state, and federal officials. Attorney General Bonaparte — a supporter of expanding the Leavenworth collection — went as far as physically transferring the Leavenworth records to Washington in preparation for a Washington-based bureau.[21] But neither the Leavenworth plan nor the IACP plan could find sufficient Congressional backing. Several months later Bonaparte was forced to return the files to Leavenworth. Another fifteen years would pass before proponents could successfully convince the federal government of the necessity of a centralized national criminal fingerprint system.

Two factors explain this apparent disinterest at the federal level in centralized criminal fingerprinting. First the federal government itself was relatively small and its law enforcement activities narrowly focused. The DOJ itself was not established until 1870 and there was little support for the construction of a federal penitentiary until the mid-1890s. Federal crimes were limited primarily to currency and postal law violations, some tax evasion (there was no personal income tax until 1913), and a small but growing body of inter-state commerce regulations. Crime detection and prosecution were dispersed among several small forces including the Postal Inspection Service and the Treasury Department's Secret Service. In 1908, there were fewer than 2,700 federal prisoners, including several hundred offenders from the District of Columbia.[22]

The response made by Attorney General Griggs in 1900 to a bill pushed that year by the IACP to establish a federally-funded national criminal identification bureau probably remained accurate until the advent of World War I. When approached by the president of the IACP to lend his support to the bill, Griggs responded by saying that he really did not think that such a project was "so closely connected with this department [the DOJ] as to call for my official support or particular recommendation." Griggs thought that the enterprise was probably worthwhile, but of far greater utility to states and cities where the bulk of criminal prosecution took place.[23]

This attitude speaks to us from another era — one when the federal government remained within closely defined arenas of authority and was not involved, as it is today, in wide-ranging, detailed regulation of financial, cultural, and social activities. However, while the federal government's minor interest in crime accounts in large part for its refusal to act on suggestions for establishing a national criminal identification bureau, it does not provide the entire answer.

Although the debate over Attorney General Bonaparte's attempt to move the Leavenworth identification bureau to Washington apparently left no records, we do know that it took place at the same time that Bonaparte was embroiled in a debate with Congress over an even more critical issue: the establishment of a DOJ detective force, a force which eventually became the Federal Bureau of Investigation. In the early 1900s, the DOJ had no detective force of its own and had to borrow agents from Department of Treasury's

Secret Service. Several Congressmen fought vocally against giving the DOJ the right to establish its own detective bureau.

Other federal agencies had long had their own detection capabilities without creating such controversy, but these agencies differed from the DOJ's proposed detective bureau in that they had very narrow and specific law enforcement mandates. For example, the Postal Inspection Service investigated postal fraud and the DOT's Secret Service concentrated on counterfeiting. Given the broader mandate of the DOJ — to enforce all U.S. laws— a detective agency attached to it could legitimately involve itself in multifarious affairs and become very difficult to oversee. Indeed, the oversight issue was what led to the hearings about the DOJ's right to establish its own detective force in the first place. Investigators contended that the DOJ had borrowed DOT detectives to trail political opponents of then President Theodore Roosevelt.[24] Although such a practice could be outlawed on paper, legislators feared that the wide province which the DOJ rightfully could claim would make any serious enforcement impossible.[25]

Critics of the plan voiced their opposition clearly by likening a DOJ-run detective force to the political spying system purportedly strong in Tsarist Russia. Congressmen debating the issue called the plan inimical "to American ideas of government" and "opposed to our race."[26] Another critic dramatically asserted that if Anglo-Saxon civilization stood for nothing else it was the right of "the humblest citizen" to be safeguarded against secret surveillance by the government.[27]

Attorney General Bonaparte's decision to move files back to Leavenworth, which he made only a few months after the controversy over a DOJ detective force first erupted, may have been a response to these growing fears about state power.[28] As *Gow v. Bingham* also had demonstrated, such monitoring was not yet acceptable as a standard governing procedure in the U.S. Still the DOJ detective plan was passed. Starting in 1909 the DOJ established its own detective force named the Bureau of Investigation, colloquially known as "the Bureau." In the 1930s the name was changed officially to the Federal Bureau of Investigation (FBI).

German-American Alien Registration

The first time that government surveillance did gain public and congressional favor was during World War I and fingerprinting played a central role. America's 1917 declaration of war against Germany cast German-American aliens living in the U.S. as potential spies and saboteurs. Although there were few incidents to indicate that German-American aliens constituted a serious threat to the war effort, public and Congressional sentiment began to build against the group and action was demanded. Many plans were debated and various measures taken, in particular a massive registration of all German-American aliens.[29]

Starting in early 1918 all German-American aliens had to report to either their local post-office or police station. There they filled out personal information forms, supplied several photographs of themselves, and submitted to fingerprinting. They were given an ID card that featured the carrier's name, address, photograph, and thumbprint, which they were required to carry at all times. Aliens had to report to officials if they changed their address and had to acquire special certification if they needed to enter, work, or reside in or near certain war-sensitive areas, such as harbors or industrial parks.[30]

Through these measures officials sought to prevent espionage and sedition. Officials believed they could identify possibly hostile German-American aliens before they acted by reviewing ID cards of laborers or strangers. Officials then could deport or incarcerate these people, or at least keep them away from vital resources.[31] The registration process proceeded without incident and estimates based on the 1910 census indicated a near total compliance of the target population. Within a few months nearly 500,000 German-Americans had reported to registration centers.

While earlier debates over the establishment of government surveillance capabilities in the form of a DOJ detective bureau had raised strong opposition, the bill to fingerprint and monitor German-American aliens passed with only moderate criticism. Those who did have reservations made clear that only the threat of sabotage and espionage had moved them to act. Although some Congressmen favored the generalization of registration to all aliens at all times, the words of another summarized the majority position when he described the act as "purely an emergency measure." As others made clear, these restrictions would be lifted when the international conflict ended. Critics also voiced their opposition to another option, mentioned in passing: the extension of registration to the entire U.S. population.

As had been the case in the criticism of the DOJ's proposed detective force, such monitoring was perceived by some as un-American. One congressman summed up this position with the following comment: "... when people come here from other countries they have the idea that this is a free country and they do not want to feel that the police are tagging after them."[32]

World War I's alien registration requirement (and other surveillance programs discussed briefly below) netted few people who actually were guilty of sabotage or espionage. Whether this speaks to its deterrent success or its excess is unclear. Still alien registration represents a critical step in the federal government's interest in fingerprinting and in its attempt to establish fingerprinting as a routine administrative tool.

A New Kind of Surveillance

The alien registration program put into place for the first time an explicit, broad-based civilian surveillance program. It is unclear how often fingerprints were relied on to make identity checks but, for the first time, fingerprinting demonstrated its potential for individualized, routinized tracking of large populations. While fingerprinting's capacity to identify a dangerous criminal with a chance latent print was perhaps more dramatic, officials' claim that fingerprinting could oversee the monitoring of citizens during daily movements such as changing residences, finding jobs, or visiting friends signaled an even greater display of state power.

The system had at least one major flaw. Unless laws required all U.S. inhabitants to carry an ID card, failure to produce one was without clear meaning. A questionable individual could as easily be a German spy as a loyal American. Still, the flaw did not undercut completely the system's surveillance capacity. If a person detained could not produce an ID card and was later shown to be a German-American alien, he or she was automatically guilty of a crime: failure to carry an ID card. This infraction was punishable by a fine of up to $2,000 and imprisonment for up to five years, as were most registration act violations.

This rule greatly expanded the sphere of deviancy which demanded state attention and intensified surveillance by justifying constant, unpredictable intrusions: ID card checks. But providing grounds for questioning and arrest did not exhaust the functions of the ID card rule. As with other rules constituting surveillance, such as those discussed in Chapter 2 above for Walnut St. prisoners, this rule helped to generate information about the people required to follow it. In this case, the ID card rule distinguished compliant from non-compliant (and therefore potentially dangerous) German-American aliens. Although an ID card infraction might mean very little in the short-term, it could provide the grounds for opening a file about an individual and for initiating a "record." Any subsequent infraction, also entered into this record, would no longer be seen as an isolated event but as part of a pattern of resistance or deviance.

A Novel Function for Fingerprinting

Although few subsequent fingerprint programs included an ID card requirement, the link between fingerprinting and compliance introduced in the alien registration program continued. This link represents a critical transition for fingerprinting and surveillance. Previously fingerprinting had signaled only the stigma of criminality — a bodily trace taken over protest, sometimes violent protest.[33] However, under the German-American alien registration program, fingerprinting came to represent something altogether different. Virtually all German-American aliens had reported promptly and without complaint to registration centers and throughout the war they dutifully carried their thumbprint-photograph ID cards and produced them on demand. By symbolizing German-American aliens' willingness to help the U.S. government keep track of possible wrongdoers and facilitate administration of the war effort, fingerprinting took on a new connotation of conformity.

The German-American alien registration program ended with the war, but the kind of surveillance that it introduced survived and prospered. Whereas, previously fingerprinting had been limited to criminals (with some jurisdictions allowing officials to fingerprint only convicts), following the war, its non-criminal administrative applications multiplied. Starting in the mid-1920s, with the official establishment of the Bureau of Investigation's Identification Bureau (later renamed the Identification Division), the government began to extend fingerprint requirements beyond the criminal population to include military enlistees, immigrants, and federal employees. At the same time, the government started a vigorous campaign for voluntary contributions from civilians, including school children and private enterprise employees. By 1939, the Bureau's collection numbered nearly 11,000,000, representing a ten-fold increase in little more than a decade.[34] Within another ten years, the collection had swelled to over 110,000,000.[35]

As with the German-American alien program, peacetime fingerprint programs targeted individuals not because of some past criminal act, but because of their membership in broadly defined social groups: workers, immigrants, youths. These new programs also followed the principle of fingerprinting people during some common procedure, such as applying for a job. This tactic helped to establish fingerprinting as an ordinary occurrence, deserving little comment. Officials rarely offered explicit justifications for these programs. Generally, they claimed the programs were useful in weeding out criminals from the ranks of the military or from various New Deal programs, and they often characterized them as providing a "humanitarian" service by helping police identify individuals found dead or suffering from amnesia.[36] (Ironically, the Bureau's own figures do not show much success for these much-touted humanitarian applications.)[37]

While locating fugitives and aiding amnesia victims apparently sufficed as public justifications for these programs, other motivations are clear. As will be discussed below, these programs increased the state's capacity to mount ongoing surveillance of worrisome populations and to locate possible individual troublemakers (a real ability, but one which bureau cheerleaders often exaggerated). This new surveillance capacity contributed greatly to a changing face of the federal government as an authoritative and omniscient body and helped to usher in a new concept of the relationship between the state and its subjects. These programs established the expectation that *all* people —

not just criminals— should be assigned official, fixed identities that would be permanently inscribed in a centralized, national record-keeping system.

Post-war fingerprinting programs will be discussed in detail later, but beforehand it is important to examine the path by which such surveillance came to seem acceptable, even desirable, first during war and, more importantly, when the country was at peace. This examination concentrates on selected aspects of World War I which supplied not only the *model* for peacetime surveillance but the *motivation*, as well.

Notes

1. Louis Herbette, "A Speech," appended to Alphonse Bertillon, *The Identification of the Criminal Classes*, trans. E. R. Spearman. An address delivered at the International Penitentiary Congress, Rome, 1885. Reprinted in 1889, London, n.p.

2. *The New York Times*, May 26, 1912, 5:3.

3. The number of 110,000,000 prints includes duplicates and prints of foreigners. Records do not make possible a calculation of the precise number of individuals represented in the collection, but a statistician at the FBI Identification Division in Washington DC estimated that the 110,000,000 prints probably represented approximately 60,000,000 Americans. (Personal communication, April 1992.) The U.S. population in 1950 was just over 150,000,000.

4. *International Associations of Chiefs of Police, Proceedings*, 1904, pp. 91–97; 1906, p. 116; 1911, p. 86; 1911, pp. 26–27; 1904, p. 107. New York City's fingerprint collection reached 65,000 by 1911 and Chicago's reached 15,000 by 1908. *IACP Proceedings*, 1911, p. 84; 1908, pp. 117–121.

5. *IACP, Proceedings*, 1911, p. 157.

6. *The New York Times*, February 7, 1909, 5:9; Jay Hambidge, "Finger-Prints. Their Use by Police," *Century Magazine*, vol. LXXVIII, ns. LVI (May–Oct. 1909); *IACP, Proceedings*, 1907, p. 17; 1906, p. 80. See also Donald C. Dillworth, *Identification Wanted*, (Gaithersberg, Maryland, International Association of Chiefs of Police, 1977), pp. 82–88; *IACP, Proceedings*, 1906, p. 72–73.

7. *Gow v. Bingham* (107 NY Supp 1011) p. 1015, 1014.

8. Subsequent court decisions and newspaper articles reveal a continued — apparently undiminished — enthusiasm for frequent, sometimes coercive, fingerprinting of criminal suspects. *The New York Times*, February 7, 1909, 5:9. As a response to these actions, the New York state legislature passed a bill (which the governor later vetoed under pressure from local police and the IACP) to forbid police from photographing, measuring, or fingerprinting suspects before conviction. On this bill see the following *New York Times* articles: June 14, 1911, 4:4; June 14, 1911, 4:5; June 19, 1911, 8:3; June 26, 1911, 5:1; June 28, 1911, 10:3; June 29, 1911, 1:3. On controversial fingerprint practices, see the following court cases: *Bingham v. Gaynor* (126 NY Supp 353); *Hawkins v. Kuhn* (137 NY Supp 1090).

9. *The New York Times*, September 7, 1907, 5:2; October 19, 1912, 1:6; February 21, 1908, 3:5; *Journal of Criminal Law and Criminality*, vol. 1, no. 4 (November 1910) 634–636.

10. *The New York Times*, July 30, 1911, 5:12; October 25, 1913, 12:4; A. J. Renoe, "The Imperative Need of Universal Fingerprinting," ms., n.d., pp. 1–17. In A. J. Renoe Collection, FBI Academy Library, Quantico, Virginia.

11. *The New York Times*, May 24, 1920, 4:3; *Fingerprint Magazine*, vol. 2, no. 1 (July 1920): 7; *The New York Times*, June 9, 1912, pt. 3, 4:7.

12. *The New York Times* February 27, 1924, 4:5; February 28, 1924, 20:3.

13. *Journal of Criminal Law and Criminology*, vol. 4, no. 3 (September 1913): 443. See also articles in any issue of *Fingerprint Magazine*.

14. *The New York Times*, October 25, 1913, 12:4 and 12:7.

15. A later *New York Times* editorial argued, for example, that three boys, who were fingerprinted after being arrested on disorderly conduct charges for playing ball in the streets, had no justifiable complaint against the practice. As the editorial pointed out, should the boys "behave in the future" it will be "irrelevant that their fingerprints were taken" (June 16, 1916, 12:5). The same argument is made in a brief article in the *Journal of Criminal Law and Criminology*, (vol. 4, no. 3 [September 1913]: 440–443.) Between 1912 and 1923 *The New York Times* published over twenty editorials and articles supporting universal fingerprinting, a pattern which other periodicals such as *The Saturday Evening Post* and *Fingerprint Magazine* also followed.

16. According to a chart published in the Attorney General's 1910 annual report, Leavenworth Penitentiary began collecting fingerprints in 1904. [U.S. Department of Justice, *Annual Report of the Attorney General* (Washington DC, 1910), p. 255 (hereafter, *AG Report*]. Bureau of Indian Affairs, "Subject: Thumb mark signatures," Accounts Circular No. 236, September 2, 1908, RG 75, NA. See also, Records of the Bureau of Indian Affairs, entry 132, RG 75, NA; War Department, General Order No. 68, April 7, 1906, General Correspondence — Bureau of Navigation, File 5397-1; Records of the Office of the Secretary of the Interior, Central Classified Files, RG 48, NA.

17. Bureau of Immigration, Memoranda, April 16, 1903 and June 9, 1909, Box 61, 51831/49, RG 85, NA; Letter Book of the IACP Sect'y, vol. 1907–1910, July 21, 1907, RG 65, NA.

18. Attorney General Bonaparte was the nephew of Napoleon III.

19. *IACP Proceedings*, 1906, pp. 70–72.

20. Apparently difficulties encountered in law enforcement during World War I also made clear to IACP officials that the NBCI could benefit greatly from federal coordination. ("Minutes of Conference between the Attorney General of the United States and Representatives of the International Association of Police," September 21, 1925, p. 6, FBI File 62–41, FOIA request 273–451.)

21. *AG Report*, 1907, p. 44.

22. *AG Report*, 1908, p. 50.

23. Misc. Letter Book, No. 45, letter from AG Griggs to Richard Sylvester, Pres. of IACP, December 6, 1900; ex. and Cong. Letter Book, No. 45, letter from AG Griggs to Sen. George F. Hoar, April 1900, RG 60, NA. Even after Pres. McKinley's 1901 assassination by an anarchist, the reintroduction of a similar bill, which promised to weed out anarchists from the throngs of immigrants arriving daily in the U.S., failed to ignite Congressional interest in a national criminal identification system. (U.S. House of Representatives, Judiciary Appropriations Committee, *To Establish a Laboratory for the Study of Criminals, Paupers, and Defective Classes*, Hearing on Bill 14798 [Washington DC, 1901].)

24. U.S. House of Representatives, Select Committee on Appropriations for the Prevention of Fraud and Depredations Upon the Public Service, 60th Cong., 2nd Sess. (Jan. 20, 1909).

25. In fact this fear has been borne out. The Bureau of Investigation, estab-

lished in 1909 — renamed the Federal Bureau of Investigation in the 1930s — has been implicated repeatedly in illegal political surveillance scandals. For an account of these FBI activities, see Athan Theoharis, *Spying on Americans* (Philadelphia: Temple University Press, 1978).

26. Such sentiments were not isolated to the debate over the DOJ detective bureau. For the expression of a similar sentiment on a different occasion, see *IACP Proceedings*, 1903, p. 18. In his annual address, the president of the IACP called for a strong response against the growing anarchist movement in the U.S. (Pres. McKinley had been murdered by an anarchist in 1901), but still voiced a fear opposing the creation of a "centralized, secret police."

27. *Congressional Record*, House, 60th Cong., 2nd Sess. (1909), p. 671.

28. The files were moved back to Leavenworth at the close of the fiscal year 1908 (*AG Report* 1908, p. 50) and the first hearings concerning the controversy over DOJ detective practices started on April 2, 1908. For a discussion of these issues, see U.S. House of Representatives, *Congressional Record*, 60th Cong., 2nd Sess., pp. 645–684.

29. Later some of these regulations were expanded to include Austro-Hungarian aliens, as well. Committee on Immigration and Naturalization, "Registration of Aliens," HR (February 28, 1917) 64th Cong., 2nd Sess.

30. *AG Report*, 1918, pp. 25–33; "Registration of Aliens...," Exhibit 30, pp. 686–703.

31. "Registration of Aliens...," p. 21.

32. "Registration of Aliens...," p. 20.

33. A 1906 *New York Times* article relates advice from British police officers concerning the use of a newly invented thumbscrew device to help fingerprint prisoners who will not hold still. (February 5, 1906, 6:3.)

34. U.S. House of Representatives, Committee on Appropriations, *Hearings on Department of Justice Appropriation Bill for 1941* (Washington DC, 1940), p. 123.

35. Richard H. Rovere, "Letter from Washington," *The New Yorker* (May 7, 1949): 64. See footnote no. 3 above for a breakdown of the 110,000,000 figure which included many duplicate prints.

36. *Hearings ... Justice App. for 1949*, p. 237; *Hearings...Justice App. for 1951*, p. 212. Quoted in Max Lowenthal, *The Federal Bureau of Investigation* (New York: William Sloane Assoc., 1950), p. 377.

37. For example, of nearly 25,000 sets of fingerprints submitted by the New York City WPA office by January 1939, only 5 were found to belong to fugitives. *Hearings ... Justice App. 1941*, p. 129. The government never published statistics on the number of amnesia victims or unidentifiable civilian dead which its fingerprints files helped. Instead it gave only anecdotal reports, presumably because the rarity of these occurrences would have revealed an even smaller benefit from these programs.

Drivers Licenses and Vehicle Registration in Historical Perspective

Carl Watner

In this original essay, the editor of this collection examines the historical and political relationships between drivers licenses and national identification programs. Is there some imperative necessity that licenses and registrations be issued by the State or is there some other reason why government has preempted these services?

Introduction: Why?

Most of us living in the United States are accustomed to calling this country the most important bastion of the "free" world. If that is so, why is it that we now hear increased demands for national identification cards which would allow our government to number us like slaves and literally keep track of our every movement? Why do our automobiles and pickups have to be registered with our state governments, when our computers, photocopiers, television sets, power tools, and other personal property do not? Why does the government require that we pass a state test in order to operate "our" cars? Why do we have government-issued drivers licenses, rather than ones issued by our insurance companies, driver's schools, or private safety institutes? Why is the federal government now calling for standardization of state-issued drivers licenses? What is the history of these government imposed requirements and could all of this be part of a long-term pattern — deliberate or otherwise — that is leading directly to national ID? The purpose of this paper is 1) to shed some light on the history of drivers licenses and state vehicle registration; and 2) to explore the implications of government-issued drivers licenses and vehicle registration. These topics are important to understand because the calls for national identification cards would be far fewer if we did not already embrace state-issued documents certifying our birth, identity, and driving "ability." If we accept the principle that government ought to be involved in birth certificates and driver licensing, then why shouldn't it be involved in issuing national I.D.? By what principle of logic can you endorse the one and oppose the other?

Although we expect the federal and state governments to build and maintain the roads, the development of the automobile was strictly a free market phenomenon, largely spawned by individual entrepreneurs and inventors, such as Ransom Olds, James Packard, and later Henry Ford, whose ideas about mass production revolutionized car manufacturing. These backyard American tinkerers took machined steel, crafted their own internal combustion engines, and mounted them on their old farm wagons and horse-drawn buggies. The results were some of the earliest self-propelled vehicles, which they soon refined and offered for sale. From the very start of this process, government had no involvement. The steel, the wagons, the motors: all were the private property of those who built automobiles. Hence, there was no inherent necessity or reason that these new automobiles had to become subject to government regulation. In fact, "[d]uring the early years of the motor age, any person could drive an automobile or truck without restrictions.... One [was] as free to operate a motor vehicle as to drive a span of horses."[1] Private roads could have evolved without government controls, much like in the early petroleum industry, where private parties constructed their own pipelines on private property. But since the roadways had always been owned, operated, and regulated by local or state governments (federal aid did not begin until 1916), few people questioned the state's jurisdiction over the automobile and driver.

Before 1901, state governments had little to do with motoring. Most early legislation affecting the automobile and other wheeled vehicles "was the product of the cities, towns, and villages."[2] For example, in 1898 the city of Chicago had in force a law which required that the owners of "wagons, carriages, coaches, buggies, bicycles, and all other wheeled vehicles propelled by horse power or by the rider" pay an annual license fee.[3] (The law was ultimately declared unconstitutional.) A year later, Chicago passed another ordinance which "required the examination and licensing of all automobile operators" in the city.[4] At the same time, New York City had an ordinance which required that drivers of steam powered cars be licensed engineers.[5] Mitchell, South Dakota (population 10,000: a city supporting two newspapers and a university), imposed a total ban on the use of motorized vehicles!

From these humble origins, government regulation of vehicle operation and operators has evolved to the point where hundreds of millions of American adults have state drivers licenses; hundreds of millions of their vehicles carry state license tags, registration cards, and state certificates of titles. Short of issuing every adult a federal identification card, the drivers license (and its companion non-operator identification card) is the most widely government-provided and utilized means of identification in the United States. Legally, a drivers license is to be carried whenever one is operating a motor vehicle on a government road, so millions of Americans have been conditioned to use a government-issued card to prove who they are and to show that they have been granted a state privilege to operate a vehicle. It is only a small step to visualize millions of Americans carrying a federally-issued smart card programmed to serve as personal identification, drivers license, bank card, credit card, and medical history dossier. Hence, I believe it is accurate to describe state drivers licenses as the precursor of national ID cards.

Driver Licensing

Although there is no comprehensive history of the establishment of automobile drivers licenses, personal anecdotes, government legislative records, and histories of the automobile offer many details about early licenses. (By a drivers license, I refer to the requirement that motor vehicle drivers have a valid, state-issued piece of paper in order to legally drive; and by driver license examination, I mean the operator has passed a state-administered written and/or oral test about driving rules, a vision test, and a state-administered driving test proving his skills.) One thing is clear from the historical record: While the justification for government licensing of automobile operators was sometimes a safety issue, in a majority of the states, driver competency examinations were not imposed until years after the initial licensing regulations were adopted.

In the early days of motoring, every American learned to drive without any assistance from local, state, or federal government; most learned to drive safely; and most never had any government document to identify themselves or to prove that they had ever passed any government driving test. The states of Massachusetts and Missouri were the first to establish drivers licensing laws in 1903, but Missouri had no driver examination law until 1952. Massachusetts had an examination law for commercial chauffeurs in 1907, and passed its first requirement for an examination of general operators in 1920. The first state to require an examination of driver competency was Rhode Island in 1908 (it also required drivers to have state licenses as early as 1908). South Dakota was both the last state to impose drivers licenses (1954), and the last state to require driver license examinations (1959).[6] *Our contemporary belief that drivers licenses were instituted to keep incompetent drivers off the road is a false one.* The vast majority of Americans who drove already knew how to drive safely. Why the state governments demanded that they have a state-issued license and pass a government test appears to be more a matter of "control" than of public safety. Why early 20th century Americans did not resist licensure and did not see where it might lead is another question.

Personal reminiscences of many elderly Americans verify this assertion. For example, one author in *Vintage Journal* wrote that, "I remember when the first drivers licenses came out. They cost 50 cents and you didn't have to take a test."[7] Here are a few other comments located on the internet:

> In Jefferson County, Kansas "on July 8, 1947, someone from the county seat (Oskaloosa) came to Meriden to issue driver's licenses. Anyone who was 16 years or older and paid the fee was immediately issued a drivers license. No test. The date was easy to remember because I was 16 on that day and did get my drivers license."[8] [Licenses were first required in Kansas in 1931, and driving examinations in 1949.]
>
> During the 1930s in Georgia ... "you didn't have to take a test for driving. You sent for the permit by mail."[9] [There were no drivers licenses in Georgia until 1937, and no driving examination until 1939.]
>
> In Missouri the gas stations sold drivers licenses—"no test. For 25 cents, they gave you a stub — you had this until the 'real' license came in the mail."[10] [As noted, Missouri was one of the first states to require licenses (1903), but examinations were not required until 1952.]
>
> In Washington state drivers licensing was started in 1921. "Applicant must furnish signatures of two people certifying that the person is a competent driver and has no physical problems that would impair safe driving."[11] [Driving examinations were not initiated until 1937.]

James J. Flink presents a different point of view in his book *America Adopts the Automobile* (1970). In his discussion of "Licensing of Operators" (pp. 174–178) he notes that "Automobile interests were well ahead of municipal and state governments by 1902 in recognizing that the compulsory examination of all automobile operators would be desirable.... Officials of both the American Automobile Association and the Automobile Club of America publicly advocated ... that the states should certify the basic competence of all automobile operators by requiring them to pass an examination before being allowed on the road."[12] It is clear, however, that widespread public sentiment did not exist to support these proposals. It was years before all the state governments passed such laws. In summarizing, Flink concludes that

> despite the motorist's own desire to have their competence examined [an assumption which I would challenge] and certified, state governments still remained reluctant to take adequate action at the end of the first decade of the twentieth century. As of 1909, only twelve states and the District of Columbia required all automobile drivers to obtain licenses. Except for Missouri, these were all eastern states—Connecticut, Delaware, Maine, Maryland, Massachusetts, New Hampshire, New Jersey, Pennsylvania,

Rhode Island, Vermont, and West Virginia. In seven other states, only professional chauffeurs had to obtain operator's licenses— .... The application forms for operator's licenses in these nineteen states as a rule asked for little more information than the applicant's name, address, age, and the type of automobile he claimed to be competent to drive. This might have to be notarized, but in the vast majority of these states a license to drive an automobile could still be obtained by mail. In the twelve states that all operators had to be licensed, a combined total of 89,495 licenses were issued between January 1 and October 4, 1909, but only twelve applicants were rejected for incompetency or other reasons during this period — two in Rhode Island and ten in Vermont.[13]

It is simply impossible to determine how well the general population complied with these laws. Flink offers a telling statistic, however: observing that a roadcheck in Boston, Massachusetts, in 1904 revealed only 126 of the 234 motorists stopped were in compliance with Massachusetts state registration and licensing requirements.[14]

Vehicle Registration

"In the realm of government jurisdiction over traffic safety, matters at first fell to revenue collection agencies on the one hand and to law enforcement agencies on the other. Vehicles were initially licensed solely for the purpose of collecting revenue, and not for many years did the notion appear of vehicle inspection for safety purposes."[15] Although the history of vehicle registration is nearly as sketchy and incomplete as the history of drivers licensing, some limited evidence is available to back up this statement. In New York, the first state to require vehicle registration (in 1901), the law required a motorist to display a state issued number or his initials on his automobile.[16] The system in widespread use today, which encompasses a state-issued certificate of title, an annual or biennial registration fee, and state-issued license plate, was unknown in numerous states, as late as 1967.[17] When registration was imposed, in most cases it was perennial, signifying that it only had to be completed once and that it lasted as long as the owner of the vehicle owned it or lived in the county in which it was registered. By 1905, 26 states had instituted vehicle registration, but only three of the twenty-six had annual registration requirements. By 1915, every state in the union had some sort of registration law, but it was not until 1921 that annual registration was required in all states.

In *Fill 'er Up! The Story of Fifty Years of Motoring* (1952), Bellamy Partridge offers the following description of the evolution of vehicle registration in New York state:

Members of the [New York] state legislature, having officially discovered the motor vehicle, were not long in working out a method of imposing a tax on it by requiring registration. Motorists did not particularly object to [having their vehicles] registered. It gave them a feeling of importance, and many of them smiled as they read the printed instructions (which had come with the applications for registration):

"Every owner of an automobile or motor vehicle shall file in the office of the Secretary of State a statement of his name and address and a brief description of the character of such vehicle and shall pay a registration fee of $1.00. Every such automobile or motor vehicle shall have the separate initials of the owner's name placed on the back thereof in a conspicuous place. The letters of such initials shall be at least three inches in height."

Registration in New York State for the year 1901 was 954 motor vehicles…. The following year saw an increase of 128. However, the initials proved to be an unsatisfactory form of identification, since there were numerous duplications and the printed letters were not always easy to read. The suggestion was made that the motor vehicles should be named as in registration of vessels so that duplication might be avoided. But this method failed of acceptance and the state began registering the vehicles according to number. For each car registered, the state issued a numbered metal disc.[18] The disc could be carried in the pocket of the motorist, but he was required at his own expense to display the figures in Arabic numerals on the back of the vehicle where they would be plain and visible.

This brought out some fancy numerals of every color of the rainbow, and quite a few numbers from people who had not bothered to get a disc. Artistically inclined motorists painted their numbers on the body of the car, surrounded by landscapes, sunsets, or other ornamental designs. There were complaints about this, and the following year the state began to furnish number plates and raised the registration fee to $2.[19]

Vehicle registration appears to have originated for two primary reasons. The first is alluded to in the opening lines of the above quote. Registration and license fees were viewed as "a major source of revenue for highway purposes. Until 1929, these sources provided the major share of revenue derived from highway users."[20] The second reason was the need to be able to identify vehicles, both for purposes of taxation as well as for identifying those that were operated recklessly or unsafely. Flink derides the opposition to Detroit's vehicle registration law of 1904: "They claimed that the $1 fee [for registration] constituted double taxation of personal property and that the ordinance was unjust 'class legislation' because owners of horse-drawn vehicles were neither forced to carry identification tags nor deprived of the right to allow children under sixteen years of age to drive their vehicles."[21] Flink then adds:

Undoubtedly, the most important reasons for motorists' objections to numbering ordinances remained covert. Motorists generally feared that the facilitation of identification of their vehicles would increase chances of arrest, fine, imprisonment, and the payment of damage claims. Also, registration helped tax assessors identify and locate automobile owners who were evading payment of personal property taxes on their cars. To cite but one example, it was estimated that in Denver one-third of the automobiles in the city had gone untaxed prior to the adoption of a registration ordinance. Since such motives could not be expressed legitimately, motorists were forced to cloak their cases in the respectable mantle of the constitution.... Probably the last such effort worth noting was a halfhearted attempt, undertaken after a year's hesitation, by the National Association of Automobile Manufacturers to test the constitutionality of state motor vehicle registration laws in 1905. By then, however, most motorists had become convinced that "the continual wrangling with authorities was a much greater annoyance than carrying numbers."[22]

The earliest registration laws were imposed by municipalities or counties, rather than by the states, and this proliferation actually led to the demand for federal registration of vehicles as early as 1905. Motorists in 1906 found the situation in Missouri deplorable. In order to drive legally in every county in that state, a motorist had to pay $295.50 in registration fees. The law was ultimately changed so that after June 14, 1907, only a single state-wide registration of $5 was required. Such registration expired "when either the vehicle was sold or [when] the owner's county of residence changed."[23] Flink points out that national registration would have been valid in all states and would have eliminated the confusion caused by "dinky legislatures, county boards, or town trustees and supervisors."[24] Under the guise of "regulating interstate commerce," both the American Automobile Association and the National Automobile Chamber of Commerce "backed a bill in the 60th Congress [1907] that would have required Federal registration for all vehicles."[25] The bill died in committee "because legislators doubted the necessity for and the constitutionality of such an extension of power of the federal government," and by 1910 the movement was diffused by "the general adoption of interstate reciprocity provisions and a trend toward increased uniformity in the motor vehicle laws of the various states."[26]

Although there appear to have been no legal challenges to the constitutionality of requiring drivers licenses, there were a number of test cases in several states which challenged the legitimacy of the registration laws. Invariably these laws were upheld on the basis that they were a proper exercise of the police power of the state to provide for the health, safety, and comfort of the citizenry.[27] The earliest registration laws were justified by state authorities, as well as vehicle owners, by referring to "the need of identifying a vehicle with its owner as a protection against theft."[28] In order to provide this service, the states created motor vehicle administrations and state highway commissions, and these bureaucracies required funds in order to function. It was invariably held by the courts that fees collected for the registration of vehicles and for the maintenance of the highways were legitimate. In a discussion of "The Constitutionality of Motor Vehicle License Fees and the Gas Tax," published in 1924, it was noted "that the State[s] had, without any doubt, the right to regulate the use of its highways and that in doing so [they] could compel the registration and numbering of automobiles; [and] that [they] could impose fees which would compensate the State for the expenses and costs which such legislation entailed, but that such fees had to be reasonable and fair...."[29] An earlier case in New Jersey, ultimately sustained by the U.S. Supreme Court, held that "imposition of license fees for revenue purposes was clearly within the sovereign power of the State."[30] As a test case in Detroit put it, vehicle registration requirements and fees were "a justifiable exercise of the police power in the interest of the safety of the traveling public,"[31] and this new form of taxation was accepted by the American populace so long as they believed it would be applied to "securing better roads."[32]

Better Roads: Public or Private?

The extended use of the automobile increased the agitation for good roads during the first decades of the 20th Century. During those years, real and personal property taxes and other general revenues supplemented by State and local bond issues were the main source of road construction, improvement, and maintenance. At that time there were no interstates, or any well-traveled routes across the country. The first person to wage a national campaign for a transcontinental highway was Carl G. Fisher, the man who founded the Prest-O-Lite Company and inaugurated the Indianapolis 500 race in 1911. In September 1912, he publicly laid out plans for "a road across the United States," which he dubbed the Coast-to-Coast Rock Highway. He calculated that the road could be graveled for about $10 million. "This money would be used to buy only basic road-building materials; the labor and machinery, he said, would be provided by the counties, towns and cities, along ... the route," which eventually became known as the Lincoln Highway.[33]

"To fund this grand project, Fisher proposed outright donations of cash from the manufacturers of automobiles and auto accessories." He encouraged pledges of 1% of gross revenues (prorated at ⅓ of 1% for 3 years, or ⅕ of 1% for 5 years), and asked automobile owners, as well as members of the general public, to subscribe to an annual $5 membership. Frank A. Seiberling of the Goodyear Tire and Rubber Company immediately pledged $300,000. Portland cement companies all along the route made donations in kind, totaling many thousands of barrels of cement.[34] Other leading manufacturers waited to hear what Henry Ford thought of the project. If Henry Ford, with some 118,000 Model T's on the road by 1912, offered his support, so would they; but as it turned out Ford did not believe in using his money to build the Coast-to-Coast Rock Highway. Writing on behalf of Henry Ford, James Couzens, secretary and treasurer of Ford Motor Co., informed Fisher:

> Frankly the writer is not very favorably disposed to the plan, because as long as private interests are willing to build good roads for the general public, the general public will not be very much interested in building good roads for itself. I believe in spending money to educate the public to the

necessity of building good roads, and let everybody contribute their share in proper taxes.[35]

Nor would Ford change his mind: "The highways of America should be built at taxpayers' expense."[36]

Although Ford's refusal to support the private efforts of the Lincoln Highway Association stymied its attempts to build a transcontinental highway, Fisher, with the assistance of Henry B. Joy, president of Packard Motor Company, pressed on to provide marking for the entire route and to build at least one mile of experimental concrete highway in each of the states the route crossed. The test roadways were actually built in Ohio, Indiana, Illinois, Iowa, and Nebraska. The efforts of the Association, though only partially successful, gave some credence to Rose Wilder Lane's statement in her 1943 book, *Discovery of Freedom*:

> ... American government should have never interfered with highways. Americans created a free, *mutual* association, the American Automobile Association, which was dealing with all the new questions arising from the invention of automobiles. Private enterprise originated and built the first trans-Continental highway [this statement is not true if it refers to the Lincoln Highway]; free manufacturers and car-owners would have covered this country with highways, as free Americans covered it with wagon-roads. Americans wanted cars and highways; no police force was needed to take their money from them and spend it for highways. And it is injustice to the Americans who do not own cars, to compel them to pay for highways.[37]

If American roadways had been private property, another question relating to the propriety of driver licensing would have been more easily resolved. Under common law, driving a team of horses, oxen, or mules was a matter of right. Such activities were clearly not a privilege granted to the individual by the state. In one of the earliest decisions relating to registration and licensing, the Supreme Court of Illinois stated that the City of Chicago might regulate commercial activities, such as those engaged in by draymen, but "no reason exists why [licensing] should apply to the owners of private vehicles used for their own individual use exclusively, in their own business, or for their own pleasure, as a means of locomotion."

> Anything which cannot be enjoyed without legal authority would be a mere privilege, which is generally evidenced by a license. The use of the public streets of a city is not a privilege but a right.... A license, therefore, implying a privilege, cannot possibly exist with reference to something which is a right, free and open to all, as is the right of the citizen to ride and drive over the streets of the city without charge, and without toll, provided he does so in a reasonable manner.[38]

Over one hundred years have passed since this decision, and now the general legal consensus is that driving is a privilege, not a right. How we reached that point remains to be explained, but the actions of the American Bar Association's National Conference of Commissioners on Uniform State Laws should not be overlooked. Organized in 1889, as part of an effort to standardize state laws, the Commissioners developed a Uniform Motor Vehicle Operation and Chauffeur's License Act in 1926.[39] This was at a time when driving was still recognized as a common law right in at least the 8 states which issued no licenses (either operator or chauffeur). "Thus the ABA, under its self-appointed mandate to produce uniformity [of laws] among the states, labored to license every driver in America."[40]

In 1935, a debate in the Texas legislature centered on the issue of whether or not Texans had a "God-given unalienable RIGHT TO DRIVE." The Texas Senate had approved the American Bar Association's Licensure Act, which viewed driving as a privilege, rather than a right. "The Texas House knew all to [sic] well that Texans had been driving cars and trucks for … years on the roads of Texas without approval from anyone."[41] Thus the Texas' House version of the law read as follows:

> Every person in this State desiring to operate an automobile under the provisions of this law shall upon application and identification be issued an operator's license to drive by the county clerk of the county in which the motor vehicle is registered. But every person in this State over the age of fourteen (14) years and who is subject to none of the disqualifications herein- after mentioned, shall have the right to drive and/or operate a motor vehicle, as that term is now defined by law, upon the public highways and roads of this State.[42]

Although the "right to drive" language was finally incorporated in Section 17 of the Texas law of 1935, it was removed by the legislature in 1937. Nevertheless, it is apparent that some Texans recognized the unalienable right to drive was being negated by the legislation and the American Bar Association's Committee on Uniformity.

Conclusion

The end result of the ABA's efforts of "creating a country-wide trend toward uniformity" and standardization may result in a multi-use federal or state-issued drivers license and/or identification card.[43] If a federally-issued smart card were used, it could be structured in such a way that "the revocation of driving privileges would allow you to keep the card and use it to function for other purposes without actually having the issuing authority repossess the card or require you to turn it back into them."[44] A simple change in programming at the central data bureau would indicate to anyone checking the card that your driving privileges were temporarily suspended or denied, but you could use the card to draw money out of your bank account, to vote, or to identify yourself at the hospital.

Although we do not have a national identification card (yet), the drivers license of today is clearly an indication of what might occur. "Embossed with a photograph, current address, a validated signature, and (often) a social security number, the license is routinely requested by merchants when asked to accept a check, by vendors of alcohol to validate a young person's age, by voter registrars to enfranchise individuals, or by numerous others who need some reliable form of personal identification.... A drivers license is the only form of identification held by a majority of Americans and controlled and distributed by the State. In 1989, 79 percent of females and 91 percent of males (aged 16 and older) in America held drivers licenses. In all, 165 million Americans h[e]ld licenses as of 1989" and the percentages and numbers are probably higher today.[45] Such multitudinous contact with the State is not always ennobling. As the Secretary's Advisory Committee on Traffic Safety noted in February 1968:

> ... *the average adult American citizen [has] more direct dealings with government through licensing and regulation of the automobile than through any other single public activity.* Not all of these dealings [are] especially uplifting, and some [have] acquired implications all the more ominous because they so quickly came to be regarded as natural. Thus in the course of the regulation of highway traffic, the incidence of arrest [for violation of motor vehicle laws] by armed police in the United States has undoubtedly reached the highest point for any civilization, democratic or totalitarian, in recorded history. While ours is assuredly a free society, it has nonetheless become commonplace for an American citizen to be arrested by an armed officer of the law. Indeed, so frequent have such arrests become — in 1965 the California Highway Patrol alone made 1 million — that experience has ceased to be regarded for what it is at law and has come to be looked on as a rather routine accompaniment of modern life. One may well question whether the instincts of a free people will not one day be impaired by the habit of being arrested without protest; certainly the pervasiveness of automobile-related regulatory activity is a matter about which we must all agree.[46]

Drivers licensing and vehicle regulation are precursors to national ID. Both are trademarks of totalitarianism. Read the passage quoted above again if you do not believe me!

Is there not something Orwellian about the way the requirements for compulsory birth certificates and compulsory drivers licenses complement each other? Isn't this development a perfect example of how government manages to spin a web of power to ensnare unaware citizens? No one, obviously, planned the invention and development of the motorized vehicle, but notice how government has used the automobile to control its citizenry and make them submissive. First, the government "owns" the roads which it forces everyone to pay for regardless of how much they use them, or whether or not they own and drive a vehicle. Government ownership of the roads is socialism, despite the fact that most people refuse to recognize it as such. Second, the government began requiring that children have birth certificates. That demand preceded, and was, obviously, unrelated to the issuance of drivers licenses. Then the government required drivers licenses, but there was no need to show proof of who you were. Then it became a precondition to the issuance of a drivers license that one must present a government-issued birth certificate. The loss and denial of the common law right to drive (without any sort of government license) upon the state's roads only accelerated this trend toward total control.[47]

Pick any piece of government legislation that has been implemented in the last fifty years. Consider anti-bank secrecy and money laundering legislation: what started out as a requirement that banks keep microfilmed copies of customers' checks has turned into a call for electronic banking, where the use of cash in amounts larger than $3000 must be reported by both the banks and the parties receiving the cash. Look at other examples: health care; firearms regulations; the drug war; asset forfeiture programs. Practically every new piece of legislation leads to further and further government intervention. Haven't the uses for Social Security numbers expanded far beyond the wildest expectations of everyone? Won't the same hold true for national ID?

When the government has the technical ability to identify and track every person in its jurisdiction, and make an outlaw and criminal of any person who refuses to carry government "papers," then we have truly reached the situation described in Orwell's *1984*. Additionally, consider the mission creep built into these ID proposals. Not only will a national ID card keep track of who we are, they have the potential to show where we have been, what health care we have received, what we have spent our money on, where we have spent it, whether or not we have voted, and whether or not we have paid our taxes.

What is it about the operation of government that ordinarily makes it expand and expand? "How is it that everything the government does leads to greater control for it, less freedom for us?"[48] Theodore Lowi, a political scientist at Cornell University in the late 1970s and early 1980s, did a good job of explaining the reason why we always seem to get more government, rather than less. In his book *Incomplete Conquest: Governing America*, he wrote:

> Every action and every agency of contemporary government must contribute to the fulfillment of its fundamental purpose, which is to maintain conquest. Conquest manifests itself in various forms of control, but in all those forms it is the common factor tying together into one system the behavior of the courts and cops, sanitation workers and senators, bureaucrats and technocrats, generals and attorney generals, pressure groups and presidents.[49]

Although Lowi did not include them, we might add government health departments (that issue birth certificates), government motor vehicle administrations (that issue driver licenses), the Immigration and Naturalization

Service (which is responsible for keeping track of aliens residing in the U.S.), and the Office of Homeland Defense (which is responsible for waging the War on Terrorism). If and when it comes, a national ID program will be part and parcel of Lowi's description of the "fundamental purpose" of government "which is to maintain conquest."[50]

Notes

1. Richard Shelton Kirby, "Motor Vehicle Accidents," Volume XI, *Encyclopedia of the Social Sciences* (New York: Macmillan, 1933), p. 72.

2 Bellamy Partridge, *Fill 'er Up! The Story of Fifty Years of Motoring* (New York: McGraw-Hill Book Company, 1952), p. 45.

3 The City of Chicago v. Lorin C. Collins, Jr. *et al.*, 175 Illinois 445 (October 24, 1898), pp. 445–459 at p. 446.

4. James J. Flink, *America Adopts the Automobile, 1895–1910* (Cambridge: The MIT Press, 1970), p. 174.

5. Ibid.

6. "Year of First State Driver License Law and First Driver Examination," Table DL-230 (June 1977) in U.S. Department of Transportation, Federal Highway Administration, *Highway Statistics Summary to 1975* (Washington, D.C.: U. S. Government Printing Office), Report No. FHWA-HS-S75, at page 71.

7. Mary O. Stone, "Motorcycle keeps 90 year-old man going," at http://www.vintagejournal.com/VJ0701/index.cgi?template=tp100&page=motorcylcekeeps.htm

8. http://www.ku.edu/~medieval/kansas-l/1997/10/msg00007.html

9. http://www.angelfire.com/ga/GaBelle/volume1.html

10. http://genealogyinstlouois.accessgenealogy.com/memories.htm

11. http://seattletimes.nwsource.com/news/local/html98/time24m/20000724.html

12. Flink, op. cit., p. 175.

13. Ibid., pp. 177–178.

14. Ibid., p. 187.

15. *Report of the Secretary's Advisory Committee on Traffic Safety*, U.S. Department of Health Education and Welfare, February 29, 1968 (Washington, D.C.: U.S. Government Printing Office), p. 6.

16. *Highway Statistics Summary to 1975*, op. cit., p. 43: "Year In Which Motor Vehicles Were First Registered," Table MV-230.

17. *Report of the Secretary's Advisory Committee on Traffic Safety*, op. cit., p. 120.

18. The State of South Carolina at one time issued metal discs which functioned as drivers licenses. The discs were stamped with the name, address, and birth date of the driver, and often kept on the same ring as one's car keys.

19. Partridge, op. cit., pp. 46–47.

20. *Highway Statistics Summary to 1975*, op. cit., p. 42.

21. Flink, op. cit., p. 170.

22. Ibid., pp. 170–171.

23. Ibid., p. 172.

24. Ibid.

25. Partridge, op. cit., p. 197.

26. Flink, op. cit., p. 173.

27. Hendrick v. State of Maryland, 235 U.S. 610 (1915). Hendrick, a resident of the District of Columbia, was arrested for driving in Prince George's County in July 1910, without a Maryland certificate of vehicle registration. At that time, Maryland did not extend reciprocity to the residents of the District of Columbia.

28. Basil Creighton, "Motor Vehicle Administration," in Jean Labatut and Wheaton J. Jane (eds.), *Highways in Our National Life* (Princeton: Princeton University Press, 1950), p.442.

29. Henry R. Trumbower, "The Constitutionality of Motor Vehicle License Fees and the Gasoline Tax," *Public Roads* (November 1924), pp. 7–10, 14, at p. 9.

30. Ibid., p. 8 referring to Kane v. New Jersey (81 NJ 594) and affirmed by the U.S. Supreme Court (242 U.S. 160 [1916]).

31. People v. Schneider, 139 Michigan Reports 673 (April 1905) at p. 679. Schneider was convicted of operating a vehicle within the limits of the city of Detroit "without having first registered" the vehicle "and without placing thereon a number, as required by an ordinance of said city." The Michigan Supreme Court upheld his conviction.

32. Flink, op. cit., p. 174.

33. Drake Hokanson, *The Lincoln Highway: Main Street Across America* (Iowa City: University of Iowa Press, 1988), p. 6.

34. *The Lincoln Highway: The Story of a Crusade That Made Transportation History* (New York: Dodd, Mead & Company, 1935), p. 20 and p. 127. What is so interesting is that these people contributed lots of their OWN time and money to the project. They didn't immediately turn to the government for help: When Carl Fisher asked "Why can't we build a highway across the continent from New York to San Francisco?" he meant "'we' literally. He had no faith in the political system's ability to accomplish the task. If there was to be such a road, the automobile industry, which had the highest stake in the venture, would have to build it." This last quotation is from Jerry M. Fisher, *The Pacesetter: The Untold Story of Carl G. Fisher* (Fort Bragg: Lost Coast Press, 1998), p. 77.

35. Hokanson, op. cit., p. 8.

36. Ibid., p. 9.

37. Rose Wilder Lane, *The Discovery of Freedom* (New York: Arno Press & The New York Times, 1972), p. 213. This quote appears near the end of Section 7, "The Right to Vote," in Part Two, Chapter V, "The Third Attempt."

38. The City of Chicago v. Lorin C. Collins, Jr. *et al.*, 175 Ill 445 (October 24, 1898) at pp., 456–457. The Court affirmed the illegality of the Chicago "Wheel Tax" ordinance.

39. See National Conference of Commissioners, *Handbook of the National Conference of Commissioners on Uniform State Laws and Proceedings of the Thirty-Sixth Annual Meeting*, Denver, Colorado, July 6–12, 1926. See pp. 458–459, 462–463, 478–479, and 524–525. Copy of this book was obtained from the Southern Methodist University, Law School Library, Call No. KF165.A2 (1926).

40. "The Texas Driver's License Scam," a privately circulated manuscript prepared by Michael Ellis and the Ellis Family of Carrolton, TX circa 1995. See page 2.

41. Ibid., p. 3.

42. *Journal of the House of Representatives of the Second Called Session of the*

Forty-Fourth Legislature Begun and Held at the City of Austin, October 16, 1935 (Amendments offered to Senate Bill 15, p. 278).

43. Partridge, op. cit., p. 198.

44. Dee Ann Divis, "Bill would push driver's license with chip," *The Washington Times*, May 1, 2002, citing Shane Ham, a senior policy analyst at the Washington-based Progressive Policy Institute.

45. Steven L. Nock, *The Costs of Privacy: Surveillance and Reputation in America* (New York: Aldine De Gruyter, 1993), p. 59.

46. *Report of the Secretary's Advisory Committee on Traffic Safety*, op. cit., p. 3. Italics in the original.

47. It would be interesting to find out when the various states began demanding presentation of a birth certificate in order to obtain a drivers license, and how the federal government influenced this demand. No information on this topic was found during my research.

48. Claire Wolfe made this statement while critiquing this chapter for me.

49. Theodore Lowi, *Incomplete Conquest: Governing America* (New York: Holt, Rinehart and Winston, 1981, Second Edition), p. 13.

50. Simson Garfinkel in his *Wired* article of February 1994 (at http://www.wired.com/wired/archive/2.02/dmv.html), "Nobody Fucks with the DMV: The government is using your driver's license to play Big Brother," points out that "Oregon has 109 different offenses that can result in the temporary suspension of a driver's license; 50 of them have nothing at all to do with driving." As a means of enforcing other government laws, our defacto national ID — the drivers license — already acts as lever to exert governmental control over the driving populace in most of the states. Imagine how much more control could be induced by means of a national ID. Also see *The Voluntaryist*, whole no. 119.

The Russian Card:
The Propiska
Nicolas Werth

Practically all socialist and communist countries embrace national ID for the simple reason that it is much easier to control people if they are required to have a state-issued document that not only identifies them and their place of residence, but which they must have in order to move about, work, and obtain goods and services. In the former USSR the essence of police power "lay in the passport and registration system administered by the militia.... Police controls affected every aspect of Soviet citizens' daily lives: individuals could not move, take a vacation, travel abroad, register their cars or obtain a driver's license without authorization from the police" and without their internal passport.[1] This excerpt, taken from The Black Book of Communism, *examines the Russian propiska (which functioned as an internal passport and residence permit). Nicholas Werth is a researcher at the Institut d'Historie du Temps Present (France).*

Reprinted by permission of the publisher from The Black Book of Communism *by Stephane Courtois, Nicolas Werth, Jean-Louis Panne, Andrzej Paczkowski, Karel Bartousek, and Jean-Louis Margolin, translated by Jonathan Murphy and Mark Kramer, pp. 174–177, Cambridge, Mass.: Harvard University Press, Copyright © 1999 by the President and Fellows of Harvard College.*

By destroying social structures and traditional rural ways of life, the forced collectivization of the countryside and the accelerated program of industrialization spurred the migration of an enormous number of peasants to the towns. Peasant Russia became filled with vagabonds, the *Rusbrodyashchaya*. From late 1928 until late 1932, Soviet cities were flooded by an influx of peasants—12 million by official estimates—fleeing collectivization and dekulakization. The regions surrounding Moscow and Leningrad alone were swollen by more than 3.5 million migrants. Among these were a number of enterprising peasants who had preferred to flee their villages, even at the price of being classified as kulaks, rather than enter a *kolkhoz*. In 1930–1931 the huge public works programs absorbed these peasants without too many difficulties. But in 1932 the authorities began to worry about the massive and uncontrolled movements of a vagabond population that threatened to destabilize the urban areas. Their presence also threatened to jeopardize the rationing system that had been carefully structured since 1929; the claimants for ration cards increased from 26 million in 1929 to nearly 40 million in late 1932. Migrants often forced the authorities to transform factories into huge refugee camps. Gradually the migrants were considered responsible for an increasing range of negative phenomena, such as absenteeism, lapses in discipline at work, hooliganism, poor quality of work, alcoholism, and criminality, all of which had a long-term destabilizing effect on industrial production.

To combat this *stikhia*—a blanket term used to describe natural disasters, anarchy, or any sort of disorder — the authorities enacted a series of repressive measures in October 1932, ranging from harsh new employment laws to purges of "socially foreign elements." The law of 15 November 1932 severely punished absenteeism at work by immediate dismissal, confiscation of cards, and even eviction. Its affirmed intention was to unmask "pseudo-workers." The decree of 4 December 1932, which gave employers responsibility for issuing ration cards, aimed chiefly at the removal of all "dead souls" and "parasites" who were wrongfully included on some of the less tightly controlled municipal rationing lists.

The keystone of the new legislation was the introduction of the internal passport on 27 December 1932. The "passportization" of the population addressed several carefully defined objectives, as the preamble to the decree explained: it was intended "to eliminate all social parasitism," to prevent "infiltration" by kulaks into city centers and markets, to limit the rural exodus, and to safeguard the social purity of the towns. All adult townspeople over age sixteen who had not yet been deprived of their rights, such as railway workers, permanent workers on construction sites, and agricultural workers on state farms, automatically received a passport from the police. The passport was valid only after it received an official stamp (*propiska*) showing the legal residence of the citizen in question. The status of the individual depended on his or her *propiska* and could determine whether an individual received a ration card, a social security card, or the right to a home. All towns were categorized as either "open" or "closed." The closed cities— initially Moscow, Leningrad, Kyiv, Odessa, Minsk, Kharkiv, Rostov-on-Don, and Vladivostok — were those that had been awarded a privileged status and were better supplied. Right of residence in a closed city was obtainable only through family ties, marriage, or a specific job that officially entitled the worker to a *propiska*. In the open cities, a *propiska* was much easier to obtain.

The passportization operations lasted a whole year, and by the end of

1933, 27 million passports had been issued. The first effect was to allow the authorities to purge the cities of undesirable elements. Begun in Moscow on 5 January 1933, within the first week passportization "discovered" 3,450 "ex-White Guards, ex-kulaks, and other criminal elements." Nearly 385,000 people were refused passports in the closed cities and forced to vacate their homes within ten days. Moreover, they were prohibited from residing in any other city, even an open one. The chief of the passport department of the NKVD noted in his report of 13 August 1934 that "to that figure should be added all those who preferred to leave the towns of their own accord when passportization was first announced, knowing that they would in any case be refused a passport. In Magnitogorsk for example, nearly 35,000 immediately left the town.... In Moscow, during the first two months of the operation, the population fell by 60,000. In Leningrad, in a single month, 54,000 people vanished back into the countryside." Some 420,000 people were expelled from the open cities.

Police raids and spot-checks for papers resulted in the exile of hundreds of thousands of people. In December 1933 Genrikh Yagoda ordered his men to "clean up" the railway stations and the markets in the closed cities every week. In the first eight months of 1934 more than 630,000 people in the closed cities were stopped for violations of the passport laws. Of these, 65,661 were imprisoned and then usually deported as socially undesirable elements with the status of "special displaced." Some 3,596 were tried in court, and 175,627 were sent into exile without any status; the others escaped with a fine.

The most spectacular operations took place in 1933. From 28 June to 3 July, 5,470 Gypsies from Moscow were arrested and deported to Siberian "work villages," from 8 to 12 July, 4,750 "socially undesirable elements" were arrested and deported from Kyiv; in April, June, and July, three waves of police activity in Moscow and Leningrad resulted in the deportation of 18,000 people. The first of those contingents was sent to the island of Nazino, with the results described earlier. More than two-thirds of the deportees died within a month.

A Party instructor in Narym, in the report quoted earlier, commented on the identity of "socially undesirable elements" who had been deported as the result of a simple police raid:

> There are many such examples of totally unjustified deportations. Unfortunately, all these people, many of whom were Party members or workers, are now dead. They were precisely the people who were least adapted to the situation. For example, Vladimir Novozhilov from Moscow was a driver in the steamroller factory in Moscow who had been decorated three times and was married with a child. He tried to go to the cinema with his wife, and while she was getting ready he went out without his papers to buy cigarettes. He was then stopped by the police in the street and picked up. Another example was [K.] Vinogradova, a collective farm worker. She was going to visit her brother, the chief of police in the eighth sector in Moscow, when

she got picked up by the police after getting off the train at the wrong station. She was deported. Or Nikolai Vasilievich Voikin, who had been a member of the Komsomol since 1929, and was a worker in the Serpukhov Red Textile factory, having been decorated three times. He was on his way to a soccer game one Sunday and had forgotten his papers. He was arrested and deported. Or I. M. Matveev, a builder on the construction site of the new No. 9 bakery. He had a seasonal worker's passport, valid until December 1933, and was picked up with that passport. He reported that no one had even wanted to look at his papers.

Notes

1. For further discussion see "The Militia and Daily Life," Chapter 7 of Louise I. Shelley, *Policing Soviet Society* (New York: Routledge, 1996), pp. 128–142.

Population Registers in the Netherlands During World War II

Bob Moore

Government tracking — without the use of computers — probably reached its apogee in Sweden and Holland before World War II. Based upon the traditional ledgers which were kept by the public authorities in most European municipalities to track every "birth, marriage, … death, and migration into or out of the community," Dutch statisticians J. L. Lentz and H. W. Methorst, in the early 1930s, developed and implemented a personal registration card "to be made out at birth, to follow the individual to every community of residence until his emigration or death." Several aspects of such a program of population registration are to be noted. First: "Since civil rights, duties, and benefits are determined on the basis of registration as a resident, a person who evades registration is considered to have no such rights or benefits." Second: People who disappeared or refused to cooperate were listed in a special "Register of the Non-Existent." Third: Lentz "makes an excellent case for the use of the [registration] system in a planned social economy." As the following excerpt illustrates, the Nazis also took advantage of the Dutch administrative system of population registration to locate and roundup most of the Jews in Holland during the early 1940s. Bob Moore is a senior lecturer in modern history at Manchester Metropolitan University, and author of Victims and Survivors: The Nazi Persecution of the Jews in the Netherlands 1940–1945 *(London: Arnold, 1997). The excerpt reprinted here is found at pages 195–199 of his book. Reproduced by permission of Arnold.*

While the majority of Dutch civil servants could have little or no real effect on the ability of the German occupiers to achieve their administrative or ideological aims, one specific aspect of the Dutch bureaucracy looms large in the history of the Holocaust in the Netherlands and requires further detailed analysis. This was the system of population registration which formed an integral part of the Dutch state machinery. Innocent enough in peacetime, this system became an 'unfavorable factor' peculiar to the Netherlands in its comprehensiveness. Neither Belgium nor France had such a complete registration. Moreover, the Dutch system was long established with its own specialist bureaucracy. Where the Germans attempted to have lists made up, for example the Tulard list for the Jews of Paris,[1] anyone suspecting the motives for the registration could try and evade enumeration. The Jews in the Netherlands, habitually registered alongside the rest of the Dutch population, would have had no such qualms in the 1930s. Only in the case of 'foreign' Jews was there some degree of parity with Belgium and France. Police registers of resident foreigners were used by the Germans in all three countries. While far from complete or accurate, they often provided a good deal of detailed information. Thus in Belgium, where over 90 per cent of the Jews did not hold Belgian nationality, and in France, where their numbers were also substantial, these particular police records had a greater impact than in the Netherlands where the number of foreign Jews was proportionally smaller.

There is no question that the population registers in the Netherlands assisted the German occupiers in a number of important respects. For example, their use as the basis for the introduction of increasingly sophisticated personal identity cards provided a major headache for all those underground and/or working illegally. However, it is the role they played in the persecution of the Jews which concerns us here. As has already been shown, the registers were used to compile and to check lists for arrests and deportation. In addition, their existence often convinced Jews that there was little point in trying to evade later censuses on the grounds that the authorities already had the information to hand. Moreover, this particular issue also demonstrates how a specific individual in the right (or wrong) place could become an 'unfavourable factor' almost in his own right. The man in question was Jacob Lentz, who had risen from humble beginnings to become the head of the *Rijksinspectie van de Bevolkingsregisters* (State Inspectorate of Population Registers). In 1936 he had instituted rules to standardize the population registers and their compilation throughout the country. For this he was decorated by the crown. However, his ambition was to create a complete registration system which would include identity cards. The idea of such a card was discussed by the government in 1939, but mainly in relation to the possibility of war and the need for an effective rationing system. The resulting *distributiestamkaart* (ration card) did not begin to fulfill Lentz's wishes. It did not carry a photograph, and a government commission report in March 1940 noted that the introduction of a compulsory identity card, with the implication that every citizen was a potential criminal, was contrary to Dutch tradition.[2] The arrival of the Germans gave renewed impetus to Lentz's ambitions. In the aftermath of the surrender, the College of Secretaries-General had accepted that some form of identity card was advisable in order to control any social unrest. In the interim, this involved the use of passports and appending photographs to existing *stamkaarten*. In the meantime Lentz set about creating the ideal identity card. Using watermarked paper and special inks, the document included personal details about the owner as well as his or her photograph and fingerprint. He was so successful that his new cards were deemed by the Germans as better and more secure than their own *Kennkarte*.[3]

The introduction of these cards took time and was not completed until the end of 1941.[4] Once in place, it allowed the Germans to carry out regular checks on cards in public places, thus greatly increasing the risks for people without valid papers when venturing on to public transport, or even on to the street. All the details on the identity cards were kept in a huge card index, thus making it possible to check if a card had been falsified in some way, or was being used by a third party. The use made of this register by the SD is testimony to its importance. Lentz later defended himself by saying that the same information could have been found in the normal population registers, but the depth of information, the photographs, fingerprints and signatures, as well as the ease of access, all militate against this defense. A compliment to the thoroughness of Lentz's work came from a leader of the LO who claimed that it had never been possible to create a false identity card which would have escaped detection by anything but the most cursory of checks. The fact that people could survive and travel with false papers was because most checks were superficial, or carried out rapidly by officials with no desire to ask too many questions.[5] Mainly because the resistance had no other choice, attempts continued to beat the system and produce accurate forgeries. Things became even more pressing when Jews began to be rounded up, and the "J" stamped in their genuine identity cards would betray them immediately. One of leading members of the resistance, Gerrit-Jan van der Veen, spent two years trying to perfect a way of reproducing Lentz's card, yet had to send out imperfect versions as the need became greater.[6] His *persoonsbewijzencentrale* (center for identity cards) produced between 60,000 and 70,000 blank cards before the printers were arrested in June 1944.

The extent of the population registration and the apparent inviolability of the identity card system were undoubtedly a factor unique to the Netherlands in relation to other German occupied territories, and provided a major hindrance for any type of illegal work. Lentz, however, also took a particular interest in the German desire to identify the Jews in the Netherlands. The Germans had decided in September 1940 that there should be a separate registration of the Jews. Their intention had been to use the existing population registers, even though Lentz had informed them that they were far from complete. He set to work compiling detailed instruction for the local authorities to carry out the registration of Jews decreed on 10 January 1941. The information gained from this registration was then transferred to the existing population registers and the cards were marked with a special stamp. He also made a special study of Jewish surnames which was ultimately used to investigate people with such names who might not have registered as Jews. Lentz did, however, make the mistake of presenting a copy of his study to *Generalkommissar* Wimmer, who was less than impressed to find his own family name mentioned in the list.[7] Lentz was also involved in the German scheme to introduce a new system of ration cards which would only be issued to holders of valid identity cards and in person. Begun in the middle of 1943 and designed primarily to force *onderduikers* out into the open, the link between identity cards and ration cards was abandoned as the resistance was increasingly successful in acquiring genuine blank identity cards and the necessary stamps to validate them.[8] Thus by 1944 the Germans were losing the battle to control the population through Lentz's cards and indexes, but they remained a hindrance to all illegal work until the end of the occupation.

In many respects, Lentz was the ideal servant for the Germans. Uncommitted to National Socialism although undoubtedly pro-German[9] (perhaps because of their supposed efficiency in all things), he immersed himself in his work to the exclusion of everything else, including his marriage. His aim and motivation was bureaucratic perfection, apparently without concern for the practical effects of his work. One of his officials intimated that he had no love for the Jews, perceiving them as attempting to undermine the smooth running of his registration system, but whether this was the product of an ingrained anti-Semitism or just the perfectionist railing at those who would upset his quest for perfection remains uncertain. If this is the only evidence for an anti-Semitic stance, the fact that he did not join the NSB or any other known anti-Semitic group, either before or during the occupation, suggests that he was that strange animal, the bureaucrat who was always anxious to please his masters and for whom perfect organization was everything. However, Lentz cannot be seen merely as a cipher, happy to please by carrying out the orders of others. The arrival of the Germans gave him the chance to carry out his dream of complete population registration without being hampered by the restraints of democratic government. In his mind, the uses which the Germans might make of his work were only of secondary importance. Even in 1943, he could not understand it when someone suggested whether it might not be better if all the population registers were destroyed. Certainly others thought this was true. In March 1943 the resistance attempted to burn down the population register in Amsterdam, and on 11 April they arranged an RAF raid to bomb the headquarters of Lentz's *Rijksinspectie* at Kleykamp, in The Hague. Neither raid was completely successful, but the damage done was substantial.[10] Lentz became worried when he was attacked as a scoundrel (*schurk*) in the underground press, and even more nervous when he received death-threats through the post. The Germans gave him a bodyguard but refused to let him resign. He was absent from his office the day it was bombed and returned to work afterwards, but this may have been the final straw. A few weeks later, he gave up altogether, a mental wreck.[11] After the war, he was sentenced to a mere three years in jail, yet his struggle for perfection and his unswerving dedication to this work undoubtedly contributed to the arrests and therefore the deaths of many thousands of Jews and non-Jews at the hands of the Germans. If nothing else, here was a case where the traditional Dutch civil service ethos of obedience and order had shown itself capable of implication in the most heinous crimes when all moral and legal controls were removed.

Notes

1. Michael Marrus and Robert Paxton, *Vichy et les Juifs* (Paris: Calmann-Lévy, 1981), p. 99. S. Klarsfeld, *Vichy-Auschwitz: Le Rôle de Vichy dans la Solution Finale de la Question Juive en France*, 1942 (Paris: Fayard, 1983), p. 20.

2. L. R. de Jong, *Het Koninkrijk der Nederlanden in de Tweede Wereldoorlog*, 14 vols. (The Hague: Staatsuitgeverij, 1969–1992), V, pp. 446–448. L. R. de Jong, "Help to People in Hiding," *Delta* VIII (Spring 1965), pp. 41–42.

3. De Jong, *Het Koninkrijk* V, pp. 451–452; VI, pp. 95–96. De Jong, "Help to People in Hiding," pp. 42–44.

4. De Jong, *Het Koninkrijk* V, pp. 452–453. By 31 December 1941 some 7,177,504 identity cards had been issued. By this stage, registration of the entire population was all but complete.

5. De Jong, *Het Koninkrijk* V, pp. 454–455. De Jong, "Help to People in Hiding," p. 46.

6. De Jong, "Help to People in Hiding," pp. 46–47. For details of the specific problems of falsifying identity cards, see De Jong, *Het Koninkrijk* VII, pp. 715–716.

7. De Jong, *Het Koninkrijk* V, pp. 532–534.

8. Warmbrunn, *German Occupation*, pp. 52–53.

9. De Jong, *Het Koninkrijk* V, p. 456.

10. De Jong, *Het Koninkrijk* VI, pp. 714–736; VII, pp. 797–804.

11. De Jong, *Het Koninkrijk* VII, p. 803.

The English Identity Cards

C. H. Rolph

What has been the English experience with identity cards? In the United Kingdom, the National Registration Act of 1939 required that all residents carry an identity card for the duration of the war "emergency." Like other government regulations, it remained in force long after its alleged purposes (tracking people for the military draft and rationing) had been served. In 1950, Clarence Willcock decided to challenge the legality of the Act, which was to expire at the conclusion of World War II. This excerpt is taken from Chapter II of Personal Identity *(London: Michael Joseph, 1957), pp. 20–29. C. H. Rolph was the pseudonym of Cecil Rolph Hewitt, who was chief inspector in the City of London Police, member of the editorial staff of the* New Statesman, *and broadcaster and scriptwriter for the BBC.*

One November evening in 1950 Mr. Clarence Henry Willcock, the general manager of a French dry-cleaning company, was sitting in a cab with his solicitor, Mr. Lucien Fior. They were on their way to an election meeting at Uxbridge, where the Liberal Party were inviting the electors to have Mr. Fior as their M.P., and Willcock, a lifelong Liberal, was to tell them why. "You know," said Willcock suddenly, "I don't believe in identity cards."

"Neither do I," said Mr. Fior. "Nor Income Tax. Still, there they both are."

"I think we could get rid of identity cards," persisted Willcock. He thought it was an imposition that an entire population should be required to carry in its pockets and handbags this prescribed evidence of separate personality; he saw it as a challenge to the principles of individual freedom and integrity. To him, as to many other sturdy individualists, an identity card was an affront to human dignity, comparable to the brand on the flank of a sheep.

The war had been over for five years. The National Registration Act, 1939, had served its purpose. That purpose had been understood to be the compilation of a list of all our names and addresses, to facilitate the National

Service call-up and the rationing of consumer goods and to make life difficult for the Fifth Column. No one minded much in September 1939. The immediate outlook was so much like the end of the world that people saw hope in every new display of planning and authority. If they felt that their identities were getting lost in a vast uniformity of cardboard gas-mask boxes and Anderson shelters, they were also comforted to have their individuality reaffirmed with an official document on which one's number, at least, was different from anyone else's. And to make the scheme work, it was essential for Parliament to enact that anyone who failed or refused to produce his identity card to the police should be prosecuted and fined. The police were not empowered to arrest him, and it rather looked as though the power to do so had been deliberately withheld from them, for reasons still dimly associated with the liberty of the subject and the size of police stations. They did arrest, of course, whenever they thought it was a good idea; but when they did, if the episode leading to the arrest had seemed to have no other basis than the failure to show an identity card, it was surprising how often a further basis turned up.

Once the people had been allowed to get used to this new edict that they must not only be and stay one person, but prove if required that they were doing so, the screw was tightened considerably. A person who failed to produce his card was still guilty of an offense, though he could cure it (and would not be prosecuted) if he produced it at a police station, which he could name to suit his own convenience, within two days; but he was now made liable, by way of a Defense Regulation, to further penalties if he refused to tell the policeman his sex, age, nationality, occupation, and whether he was married or single. Resentment grew.

In December 1947, Mr. W. S. Morrison, M.P., moved the annulment of the Regulation that required all this additional frankness in conversation with the police, and although that would still have left the original burden of identity cards intact, it was a way of forcing a debate about what he called "these troublesome documents."

"The main argument for them," he said, "is that as long as rationing persists they are necessary. I do not believe it. We were told in the House the other day that there are 20,000 deserters still at large. How have those 20,000 persons contrived to equip themselves with food and clothing? *Ex hypothesi* they cannot be possessed of valid identity cards, but that has not prevented them from sustaining themselves with food and clothing themselves with raiment. As a deterrent to the evasion of the rationing arrangements the case is proved: they are of little value." At about the same time Sir William Darling told a London audience what he thought about identity cards. "We should throw them on to the bonfire," he said, "and announce to the world that we have done so. We have become," he added, "a docile, dumb people, a nation of subservient cattle."

A number of cattle wrote to the newspapers to say that they didn't really mind about identity cards. They pointed out that a lost pocket-wallet containing an identity card was more likely to find its way back to the owner; that tradesmen were more willing to accept a cheque if you showed your identity card; that the Post Office like to see it when you pushed your bank-book under the grille; that people found unconscious in the street or suffering from loss of memory could by reason of their identity cards be more quickly identified and returned to their friends. What was all the fuss about, asked one letter in *The Times*? "To some," it said, "they seem to be one of the few wartime measures worth retaining.... I foresee many citizens voluntarily carrying these cards, just as the foreign traveler used to provide himself with a passport when one was not required by law. In many ways they will be a safeguard to the individual as well as a valuable administrative adjunct."

The adjuncts survived it all; and the police, who had by now got used to the exhilarating new belief that they could get anyone's name and address for the asking, went on calling for their production with increasing frequency. If you picked up a fountain pen in the street and handed it to a constable, he would ask to see your identity card in order that he might record your name as that of an honest citizen. You seldom carried it; and this meant that he had to give you a little penciled slip requiring you to produce it at a police station within two days. You chose any police station you liked.

A man came out of a cinema one evening with a lady who was not his wife, and was stopped by a youth who wanted a match to light his cigarette. "I'm sorry," said the man, "I'm a non-smoker." The youth had been drinking. He raised his voice about non-smokers and people who don't like to be spoken to; the man became angry and a little frightened; a couple of blows were exchanged, and two policemen took the youth into custody for being drunk and disorderly. "Can you come to the police station, sir?" one of them asked the man. "Oh no, thanks." (Don't want to be mixed up in anything tonight of all nights.) "Well, perhaps you'll give me your name and address, please?" No, he wouldn't do that either; he wanted nothing more to do with it; goodnight. "Just a moment sir: I'm afraid I'll have to see your identity card." He hadn't got his card in his pocket. "Then I shall have to serve this notice on you to produce it within a couple of days." No, he wasn't going to produce it at all, anywhere.

Now, the policeman at this point must either let the man go unscathed, thus incurring the anathema of his colleague (who wanted a witness) and the displeasure of his superior officers, or he must take him into custody. What for? Assaulting the youth? Insulting behaviour? Disorderly conduct? There must be something. He took him. At the police station, not knowing whether the alternative was going to be a night in the cells, the man gave his name and address at long last, and was allowed to go home. A week later he was summoned before a magistrate and fined ten shillings for refusing his name and address to the constable, having first failed to produce his identity card.

Clarence Henry Willcock thought this kind of thing was an outrage.

"If I get myself prosecuted for not producing my identity card to a policeman," he said to his solicitor in the cab, "will you defend me?"

"Certainly," said Mr. Fior, and launched a cause célèbre.

A fortnight later, on the evening of December 7, 1950, Willcock was driving home to Barnet along Ballard's Lane, Finchley, at a speed which exceeded the thirty miles an hour permitted in built-up areas. He was stopped by P.C. Harold Muckle, and the formalities began. Car numbers, Road Fund license, driving license, certificate of insurance. Thank you sir. Identity card, please?

"No," said Willcock firmly.

"You haven't got it with you?" said the constable.

"I didn't say so. I mean that I'm not going to produce it to you."

Another constable came round the car. They both looked at him: you get all kinds, but they were not to know that this kind was the personification of liberalism with a small 'L' and a strenuous exemplar of what it is that keeps the fires burning so obstinately in Liberalism with a large one. A small man, Willcock was a great Liberal: he is remembered by a large number of people with affection and respect, to which, in the case of the London Liberal Party, there is added pride and the sense that he was peculiarly its property.

"Well, then," said the constable, as he pulled a little wad of forms out of his notebook case, "no doubt you'll produce it at a police station within the next forty-eight hours." He began writing, on one of the forms, the name and address he had taken from the driving license.

"I will not," said Willcock.

The constable may have winced slightly, but he went on writing.

"What police station?" he asked.

"No police station."

"Now listen, sir —"

"You listen to me. I've got no complaint about you; no doubt you're simply obeying instructions. I'm fed up with these identity cards and the way you people are exploiting an Act that ought to be dead and buried. I'm determined —"

"I'll make it out for Finchley Station, sir. It's at 193, Ballard's Lane, just up the road."

"I tell you I'm not —"

"Maybe you'll be back this way in the morning? You could drop it in then. Here you are, sir."

Willcock took the form, screwed it up, and ceremoniously tossed it into the road. The other constable tenderly retrieved it, smoothed it out, and put it in the car. And after a further exchange of prophecies about the identity card, Willcock drove away.

Mr. Lucien Fior received the summons a few days later. The Middlesex Justices, sitting at Hornsey, were to try the charge brought by Police Constable Harold Muckle that Clarence Henry Willcock did fail to produce his National Registration Identity card upon the demand of the said Harold Muckle, a police constable in uniform.

Now Willcock and Mr. Fior were old acquaintances; old enough for the latter to be quite sure, when Willcock had asked him if he would undertake the defense in such a case, that the occasion was imminent. How could it be fought? The facts were indisputable, they proclaimed themselves. If you fail to produce a document which the law requires you to produce, a constable's allegation to that effect throws the onus of proof upon you. It is thus with a driving license or a certificate of insurance (neither of which, by the way, has ever seemed to arouse the ire of liberalism; the identity card system, by licensing a man merely to be himself, perhaps went just too far). Willcock was accepting no onus of proving that he did produce his identity card: he wanted a fuss made about the mere fact that he was required to do it at all.

The National Registration Act, 1939, was to endure "for the period of the present emergency," i.e., the Second World War. The Defense Regulation that had sharpened it up and made it a bit more irksome, by enabling the police to ask you which sex you belonged to and whether you had ever got married, was being renewed every year by an annual Emergency Laws (Transitional Provisions) Bill. But if it could be shown that "the period of the present emergency" had come to an end, then so had the Defense Regulation, which must die with it, and so had identity cards.

Now it happened that another important Act, the Courts (Emergency Powers) Act, which had authorized a large number of war-time aberrations in the administration of justice, had recently been "terminated by Order in Council." This Order declared that "the emergency which was the occasion of the passing of this Act" had come to an end. In other words, the war was over. If, thought Mr. Fior, it was over for one purpose, it was over for all. It was the same war, the same emergency. Therefore the National Registration Act was dead, and with it had died the obligation of the citizenry to own and carry identity cards, and the powers of the police to call for their production.

All this Mr. Fior confidently urged upon the Magistrates, concluding with the submission that the summons against Clarence Henry Willcock was "misconceived and disclosed no offense." The Bench decided against him and convicted Willcock, but gave him what is called an "absolute discharge" and agreed to "state a case" for the consideration of the High Court. In the King's Bench Division, the appeal case of *Willcock v. Muckle* (1951, 49 L.G.R. 584), after a preliminary skirmish before a court of three Judges, was adjourned for argument by the Attorney General before a full court of seven Judges because of the unexpected magnitude of the issue it raised.

That issue was not merely the life or death of identity cards, which had by now become a minor matter. If Mr. Fior's suggestion was right, and the "end of the present emergency" for the purposes of the Courts (Emergency

Powers) Act was also the end of the purposes of the National Registration Act, then the same must be true of a large number of other war-time statutes. They had all died together — about thirty of them — and the effect on the administration and commerce of the country would be chaotic. Five of the Judges decided that the Courts (Emergency Powers) Act had died alone — a decision, in effect, that in thirty different Acts the words "period of the present emergency" could have thirty different meanings and the war thirty different durations. That was the way it seemed to Lord Goddard (the Lord Chief Justice), Lord Justice Jenkins, Lord Justice Somervell, Mr. Justice Hilbery, and Mr. Justice Lynskey. The remaining two Judges— Lord Evershed (Master of the Rolls) and Mr. Justice Devlin — thought otherwise. The majority thus upheld Willcock's conviction; but it is interesting that to this day there is a large body of opinion among lawyers that Lord Evershed and Mr. Justice Devlin were right, that the issue was wrongly decided; and when the case is discussed you will sometimes hear it said that if some general statute, designed to clear up the legislative debris of the war by scheduling thirty-odd Acts of Parliament for repeal *en bloc*, had inadvertently missed one out, the Judge might well have found that the intention to repeal it must be presumed.

But Willcock's case was not to end like this. The Lord Chief Justice made it the occasion of one of his common sense broadsides, using language that transported all identity card haters with joy; and in this, at any rate, every one of the other Judges agreed with him. "This Court," he said, "wishes to express its emphatic approval of the way in which the Magistrates dealt with this case by granting the defendant an absolute discharge. Because the police have powers, it does not follow that they ought to exercise them on all occasions or as a matter of routine" (which was roughly what they were doing about identity cards). "From what we have been told it is obvious that the police now, as a matter of routine, demand the production of National Registration Cards whenever they stop or interrogate a motorist for whatever cause.... This Act was passed for security purposes: it was never intended for the purposes for which it is now being used."

There followed almost at once a letter from the Home Secretary to Chief Constables, reciting Lord Goddard's remarks and resulting in this injunction to the police: "In future, the police will demand the production of identity cards only when it is absolutely necessary; for example, in cases where there is reason to suspect serious crime, or when the person concerned is suspected of being a deserter or absentee without leave from H.M. Forces." The fact that this instruction to the police seemed to have general public approval, coupled with the expectation that food rationing would remain for some years and National Insurance for ever, gave identity cards a new but restricted lease of life. They went on being mildly useful without really being much of a nuisance; but whereas no one wept when, a few months later, the National Registration Act was repealed altogether, most of the M.P.s who congratulated the Government on its decision took the opportunity to give the identity card a parting kick, and there were, in fact, a few of the bonfires for which Sir William Darling had been longing. There was for a month or two some official pretense that people were remembering their identity numbers just *in case* one of the Ministries might forget who somebody was, but this soon took its place alongside the contemporary fiction that, just in case, everyone was carefully preserving his gas-mask.

Two years later Willcock, now nationally famous as "the man who got rid of identity cards," was addressing a Liberal meeting in London when suddenly, saying "Mr. Chairman, I don't think I can go on," he sat down and died. He was fifty-eight, and apparently in full vigour. Many such men have changed the course of English law: they have been prisoners, jurors, judges, writers, contenders in many guises for the freedoms that have seemed at the time the most dear because the most in danger. Among them all, we could remember Clarence Henry Willcock as the patron saint of anonymity.

A History of the Census

Carl Watner

The United State decennial census is another tool in the arsenal of government controls. What is the history of the census in this country and other parts of the world? Have people always willingly stood up to be counted or have governments encountered resistance in their efforts to "number" their people? These and other questions about the census are answered in this article which was first published in The Voluntaryist *(whole no. 107), December 2002. A short bibliographic addendum to the article has been prepared for this anthology.*

History detectives unite! What is the common element in these episodes in American history?

> ... On his march through Georgia, near the end of the Civil War, General William T. Sherman used a map annotated with county-by-county livestock and crop information "to help his troops 'live off the land'";
> ... During World War I, the Justice Department prosecuted men who did not register for the draft. Government records helped them determine the names and ages of evaders [Bohme and Pemberton, p. 1];
> ... During World War II, the Army used information regarding how many Japanese-Americans were living on the West Coast, and how many lived in any given neighborhood; and then used that data to help round them up and intern them;
> ... In 1983, the IRS attempted to determine the names of those not filing federal income tax returns by comparing names in government records to the names in privately purchased mailing lists [Bovard].

Any guesses? How did General Sherman, the Justice Department, the Army, and the IRS get that information? If you guessed "the census," you were right!

Voluntaryism and the Census

The impetus for this essay was James Scott's book, *Seeing Like the State* (New Haven: Yale University Press, 1998). One of Scott's main themes is concerned with what he describes as "legibility." How much does the State know about its citizens and how visible are they and their activities to the State? Historically, how did the State "gradually get a handle on its subjects and their environment?" He answers this question in the following manner: "Much of early modern European statecraft," such as "the creation of permanent last names, the standardization of weights and measures, the establishment of cadastral [land] surveys and population registers, the invention of freehold tenure, the standardization of language and legal discourse, the design of cities, and the organization of transportation" permitted not only "a more finely tuned system of taxation and conscription but also greatly enhanced" the state's ability to intervene in society (pp. 2–3). The use of survey maps, census returns, state-designated names, addresses, and identifiers all increased the state's capacity to rule. On the other hand, as Scott writes: "If we imagine a state that has no reliable means of enumerating and locating its population, gauging its wealth, and mapping its land, resources, and settlements, we are imagining a state whose interventions in that society are necessarily crude.... An illegible society, then, is a hindrance to any effective intervention by the state..." (pp. 77–78).

One of the most interesting sections of Scott's book deals with "The Creation of Surnames." He explains that "universal last names are a fairly recent historical phenomenon," and that until sometime during the 1300s few Europeans used permanent last names (pp. 65–71). It is his contention that

> Some of the categories that we most take for granted and with which we now routinely apprehend the social world had their origin in state projects of standardization and legibility. Consider, for example, something as fundamental as permanent surnames.... Tax and tithe rolls, property rolls, conscription lists, censuses, and property deeds recognized in law were inconceivable without some means of fixing an individual's identity and linking him or her to a kin group. Campaigns to assign permanent patronyms have typically taken place ... in the context of a state's exertions to put its fiscal system on a sounder and more lucrative footing. Fearing ... that an effort to enumerate and register them could be a prelude to some new tax burden or conscription, ... population[s] ... often resisted such campaigns [pp. 64–65].

Most historians of English surnames and naming practices agree with Scott's interpretation. For example, C. M. Matthews (in his book *English Surnames*, 1967, p. 44) points out that the English Poll Tax of 1381, not only precipitated the Peasant's Revolt, but gave added impetus to the use of hereditary surnames. People who had already paid their poll tax once did not want to have to pay it a second time because state officials could not accurately identify them or verify that they had previously paid.

It was Scott's mention of the census that made me curious about the history of governments' attempts at counting its people. Intuitively, it would seem that a State's ability to keep tabs on its population — to know how many potential soldiers it has available, to know how many factories may be converted to military uses, to know the amount of revenue it might possibly collect, all these and other aspects of the census — would be critical to those engaged in the exercise of State power. Historically, this is certainly true. One of government's earliest activities was enumerating its citizens and their resources. From the Biblical story of the sin of David, when King David's choice to number his people resulted in a pestilence that felled seventy thousand Hebrews, to the Roman censors who counted the Joseph, Mary, and Jesus in Bethlehem; from the decennial censuses provided for in the United States Constitution of 1789, to the 21st century penalties and punishments for those who refuse to cooperate with federal census-takers — history is replete with examples of making the citizen more knowable to the State. Thus the purpose of this article is to survey the efforts of the State to use the census to maintain its conquest and control over its subject population.

However before that story is related, let me state my fundamental opposition to State censuses and the collection of information by the State. As long-time readers of this newsletter probably realize, my objection to State censuses is not so much directed at the collection of information, but rather at the coercive nature of the institution that gathers it. If some private organization chooses to solicit information from me, I may or may not respond. But regardless of my choice, I will suffer no criminal penalties if I refuse to cooperate. When the State collects information about the people and their affairs there are possible fines, penalties, or imprisonment for those who will not answer. As we shall see, this was true when the United States Congress passed its first census legislation in 1790, and is still true today. So even though I am spending a great deal of time and effort outlining the history of government censuses, I want to state that I am unalterably opposed to State censuses of any kind; that I advocate complete and total civil disobedience to State laws that provide for censuses; and that it is my belief that State collection of information about its people and their resources represents the complete antithesis of a free and voluntaryist society. So with that said, let us delve into the history of the census.

Early Censuses

The word "census" is commonly defined as an official enumeration of people, houses, firms, or other important items in a country. "The term itself comes from the Latin 'censure' which means 'to tax'." Most early censuses involved the counting of males of military age, of heads of households and their valuables, or of landowners. Such inventories were primarily made for the purpose of determining who should be taxed or conscripted into the military or forced to labor for the state. Such pre-modern censuses tended to be inaccurate for the simple reason that the individuals involved were disposed to appear invisible to the state. It was not in an individual's interest to be counted or give correct information. Unlike contemporary population censuses, these early enumerations did not seek to count all the people in a given politically defined area ("Census," p.22).

Surveys of military-age population and wealth occurred in ancient Babylonia, Persia, Israel, China, and Rome. The Hebrews repeatedly counted the number of their fighting men after their exodus from Egypt. A census taken in 1017 B.C. was commanded by King David. Accounts are found in the 24th chapter of Samuel II, and in chapters 21, 23, and 27 of Chronicles I. "Satan stood up against Israel and provoked David to number Israel." In response to the "sin" committed by King David, the Lord gave him three choices: three years of famine, defeat in battle, or three days of pestilence. David chose the later, during which some 70,000 Hebrews fell dead of illness. Sir George H. Knibbs (1858–1929), who organized the first census in Australia, was of the opinion that the story of King David's census made many people feel "that the Lord's wrath was an indication of his displeasure with counting people." He believed that this attitude "had the effect of delaying the adoption of the census by Christian Europe for many years" (Alterman, p. 26).

The Roman censor was an important public official charged, not only with the guardianship of the public morals, but with the official registration of all citizens, the valuation of their property, and the collection of revenue. Augustus, the first Roman emperor (27 B.C.–A.D. 14), conducted a census to determine the military resources, population and wealth of his empire. Later emperors recognized the public role of the censor and the census, but with the fall of Rome in the fifth century, there was no public authority with enough power to resume the practice until the emergence of modern nation-states in the 15th and 16th centuries. The main exception was the inquest of William the Conqueror of England, known as the Domesday Book begun on Christmas Day of 1085. Its primary goal was to determine the extent and value of his newly conquered lands and to identify his tenants.

The modern, state-conducted population census did not emerge all at once. Efforts were made in New France (Quebec) and Acadia (Nova Scotia), where sixteen enumerations were made between 1665 and 1754. In 1749, the Swedish government obtained lists of parishioners, long kept by the clergy, in an effort to determine the populations of Sweden and Finland. In 1753, "An Act for Taking and Registering an Annual Account of the Total Number of People..." in Great Britain was proposed in Parliament. William Thornton, who opposed the bill in the House of Commons, found nothing but ill in the proposal.

He could find no advantage in knowing our numbers. 'Can it be pretended, that by knowledge of our number, or our wealth, either can be increased?' He thus inferred that the result of the project would be increased tyranny at home,.... It was 'totally subversive of the last remains of English liberty.' If it became law, he would oppose its execution, and if any official came to collect information regarding the 'number and circumstances of my family, I would refuse it; and, if he persisted in the affront, I would order my servants to give him the discipline of the horse pond....' If necessary he would spend his remaining days in some other country rather than be a spectator of the ruin he could not prevent [Glass, pp. 19-20].

Thornton's opposition was successful, and it was not until late 1800 that a census bill was actually passed by Parliament. The enumeration took place on March 10, 1801, nearly a decade after the first federal census in the United States.

Census Guidelines

The United Nations has taken an instrumental part in conducting world population surveys by offering technical assistance in the planning and conduct of censuses by its member nations. In the decade after World War II "at least 150 nations or areas took censuses collecting individual data on more than two billion persons" and "when China reported a census in 1953, the last large part of the world was removed from demographic darkness" ("Census," p. 22). The statement of a Nigerian statistician, pretty much sums up the unofficial attitude of United Nations bureaucrats: "Without an accurate census you cannot plan" (Scott, p. 24). According to the United Nations a population census must have six key features. They are:

1. National Sponsorship: Only a government has the resources to conduct a thorough census, and only a government has the power to compel its citizens to participate in the process.
2. Defined Territory: The geographic coverage must be defined precisely, and boundary changes from one census to the next must be clearly identified.
3. Universality: All persons residing within the defined territory must be counted with no duplications or omissions.
4. Simultaneity: The census must take place on a fixed date [(known as the census moment). The tally must be made in one of two ways—people must be counted according to their regular or legal residence or according to the place where they spend the night of the day enumerated]. As nearly as possible, persons should be counted at the same, well-defined point in time. Individuals born after the reference date, or who die before that date are excluded from the count.

5. Individual Enumeration: Data should be collected separately for each individual.... [T]he individual person remains the basic unit of enumeration.

6. Publication: A census is not complete until results have been compiled and published (Lavin, p. 6).

These United Nations guidelines offer one means of establishing a population count, but there is at least one other method that has been used in modern times. The population register has been used in China by the political authorities to both keep track of individual citizens, as well as a means of establishing a population count. Such a system must be "permanent, compulsory, and continuously updated" (Lavin, p. 4). A file is opened on each citizen as he or she is born. Important developments are recorded in the file as they occur. For example, when a person moved or married entries would be made; when he or she died, the name would be removed from the registry. Under such a system, a population count would simply consist of counting the number of current entries in the register. In the communist bloc countries, where such registers were popular, periodic censuses were still conducted in order to check their accuracy. While only a few nations maintain such universal population registers today (Taiwan being one), many others have specialized directories for recording special events. In the United States, for example, such registers consist of birth and death records maintained by state departments of health and vital statistics, voting records (lists of those who are qualified and registered to vote in political elections), registers of motorists holding drivers licenses, and lists of retirees applying for and receiving Social Security benefits.

Censuses in the Early United States

The North American colonists were no strangers to censuses. "From the settlement of Jamestown, Virginia, in 1607 to the first national census in 1790, there were at least thirty-eight counts of population in some American colony" (Alterman, pp. 164–165). Many of these numberings were instigated by the British Board of Trade, in order to obtain information that would be of value to its administration of colonial affairs. Before 1790, there were eleven enumerations in New York, seven in Rhode Island, and four each in New Hampshire and Connecticut. A total of 27 of these 38 censuses were taken before the Continental Congress met in 1774. Only the people in Pennsylvania, Delaware, North Carolina, and Georgia had never been counted until the first federal census in 1790.

The census played a pivotal role in the history of the United States, from the very inception of the revolution against Great Britain. The reason was simple. There had to be some acceptable way for the members of the Continental Congress and the Congress of the Articles of Confederation to assess and collect revenue for the government. The original version of the Articles of Confederation, which was introduced as early as 1776, provided for a triennial enumeration of the population as the basis for apportioning the charges of war and other expenditures. During the Revolutionary War, when the American government issued bills of credit, it became the obligation of each colony to redeem its share in proportion to the number of its inhabitants of all ages, including mulattos and negroes. When the final version of the Articles of Confederation was adopted in 1781, the value of land was actually used as the basis of apportioning contributions from each state to the federal government. However, Congress was authorized to make requisitions for fighting men according to the white population of the several states. Consequently in November 1781, Congress considered a resolution urging the several states to make an enumeration of their white inhabitants, pursuant to the ninth article of the Articles. Although the resolution failed to pass, the Articles of Confederation "unquestionably contemplated a national census to include both a valuation of land and an enumeration of population" (Cummings, p. 670).

When the details of the federal Constitution were under discussion, in Philadelphia in 1787, delegates had to consider the fact that for years the Continental Congress had asked the states to conduct censuses for purposes of apportioning expenses and manpower. The states had either refused to comply, or, in those that did, there was no consistently-applied method of conducting the census and counting the people. The delegates were also faced with the difficult question of how to balance representation in the new government with responsibility for sharing in its expenses. A federally-conducted census was the linchpin as to how to link taxation and representation. As Margo Anderson, in her book *The American Census* explained: "Such a coupling was one of the classic checks and balances of the Constitution. Large states would receive more House representation but would pay more taxes. And the coupling would guard against fraud in the taking of the census. Areas that might wish to overestimate their population to gain representation would pay the penalty by raising their tax burden. Likewise, areas that tried to evade taxes through undercounting their population would also lose representation in Congress. The census was intended to solve the [hitherto] intractable problem of defining the basis of representation and taxation — by balancing gains from representation against the penalties of taxation for a state or local area" (Anderson, p. 10).

The First Federal Census

When the legislation for conducting the census was discussed in the House and Senate of the first Congress, James Madison become the foremost advocate of expanding the census count beyond the simple constitutional stipulation to determine the number of free and enslaved persons in the country. Madison was a member of the committee responsible for drawing up the "enumeration bill." In it, he proposed "classifying the population into five categories—free white males, subdivided into those over and under the age of sixteen, free white females, free blacks, and slaves—and for identifying each working person by occupation" (Cohen, p. 159). The question was immediately raised as to whether or not this transcended Congress' "constitutional powers in authorizing purely statistical inquiries other than those for the single purpose of apportioning representatives and direct taxes" (North, p. 42). The only essential required by the Constitution, as we have seen, was to distinguish free persons from the slaves, since slaves were only to be counted as three-fifths of a person for purposes of representation. Further distinctions, such as "distinguishing free blacks from whites, females from males, and boys from men, as Madison proposed, had the effect of identifying and isolating the group that most mattered, the free white adult males—in other words, the workers, voters, and soldiers of the [new] nation" (Cohen, p. 159).

Madison's proposal for identifying each working person by occupation was opposed in the House by Samuel Livermore of New Hampshire. Livermore claimed that it would be difficult to assign to each person one single occupation. "His constituents, for example, often had two or three [occupations] depending on the season." He also noted that attempting to determine their occupation "would excite the jealousy of the people; they would suspect that the government was so particular, in order to learn of their ability to bear the burthen of direct or other taxes," and hence "they would refuse to cooperate" with the census takers. The House eventually passed Madison's proposal, but "the Senate approved only the five basic categories of sex and race as legitimate objects of inquiry" (Cohen, p. 160).

It was not until the census of 1840 that a concerted effort was made to expand the statistical scope of the census beyond Madison's basic enumeration. Men of the new American republic, beginning in the early 1790s, made it a point to collect information about the new country, including details about population, wealth, trade, industry, occupations, and both civil and religious institutions. Prominent men, like Noah Webster of dictionary fame, and Timothy Dwight of Yale University, collected and edited statistical gazetteers, commercial reference works, statistical manuals, and almanacs to record and disseminate a wide potpourri of facts relating to American society and its new government. Works of this genre included *A View of the United States of America* (Philadelphia: 1794), *A Geographical, Commercial, and Philosophical View of the Present Situation of the United States* (New York: 1795), and *Facts and Calculations Respecting the Population and Territory of the United States* (Boston: 1799). Since the compiling of statistical information by the federal government was limited largely to the population census, the task of "broad fact-finding missions" was "first taken up by private individuals" who published state and local gazetteers and regional guidebooks (Cohen, p. 151). Joseph Worcester, editor of *The American Almanac and Repository of Useful Knowledge* (1831) agitated for an increased role of the federal government in collecting statistics in the 1840 census. "His own experience with the *Almanac* had made it clear to him that data collection on" the scale he envisioned "was beyond the capacities of individuals or even private associations." He recommended that the federal government makes its decennial census an all encompassing survey of America (Cohen, p. 179).

Although the census was not expanded until fifty years after its beginning, it is clear that the Founding Fathers saw the census as an important tool of the federal government. The United States was the first country in the history of the world to mandate a census in its constitution (Lavin, p. 24). Found in Article I, Section 2, Paragraph 3 is the requirement that "The actual Enumeration shall be made within three Years after the first Meeting of the Congress of the United States, and within every subsequent Term of ten Years, in such Manner as they shall by Law direct." The members of the first congress considered this a serious part of their governing agenda. Not only would the federal censuses eventually determine how many of them would be chosen from each state, but they probably hoped that the first federal census would have "a unifying effect upon the country" (Alterman, p. 207). Certainly there must have been some residents of the United States who had never heard of the adoption of the new constitution or who, for whatever reasons, did not consider themselves citizens or subjects to be ruled by the new government. Many of the self-reliant and independent Americans on the frontier "did not [always] take kindly to [political] authority, which inevitably to them meant order, limitations on freedom of action, mutual obligations, and, worst of all taxes" (Nelson, pp. 42-43). The census taker was probably the first representative of the new federal government that many of these "ungovernables" met.

Resistance to the First Census

The legislation implementing the federal census is found in *The Public Statutes at Large of the United States*, First Congress, Session II, Chapter 2. In Section 6 of "An Act providing for the enumeration of the Inhabitants of the United States," approved March 1, 1790, Congress made sure that those counting the American people for the very first time — as Americans— would have something with which to threaten possible recalcitrants:

> That each and every person more than sixteen years of age ... shall be, and hereby is, obliged to render to such [marshal's] assistant [the actual census taker], a true account, if required, to the best of his or her knowledge, of all and every person ... on pain of forfeiting twenty dollars, to be sued for

and recovered by such assistant, the one half for his own use, and the other half for the use of the United States.

And, indeed, those census takers did meet with some resistance! "One difficulty encountered by the enumerators in certain sections of the country was the unwillingness of the people" to cooperate. [North, p. 45] Heretofore, some of the people had never been counted. Others were superstitious, remembering an early colonial enumeration in New York that had been followed by much sickness. "But a very much more potent factor in arousing opposition to the enumeration was the belief that the census was in some way connected with taxation" (North, p. 46). This is confirmed by at least one contemporary source. On July 28, 1791 George Washington wrote a letter to Gouverneur Morris regarding the census. In it he noted that

> the real number [of people] will greatly exceed the official return, because, from religious scruples, some would not give in their lists; from an apprehension that it was intended as the foundation of a tax, others concealed or diminished theirs; and from the indolence of the mass and want of activity in many of the deputy enumerators, numbers were omitted [Bohme and Dailey, p. 424].

Federal enumerators, appointed by the marshals in each judicial district, began their work on August 2, 1790. They had a tremendous amount of territory to cover, and often met with difficult travel conditions, as well as suspicion from the populace. Nevertheless, the census schedules were completed on time — by October 1791—for every state but South Carolina. By an act passed on November 8, 1791, the time for completing the census in that state was extended from the end of April 1791 to March 1, 1792. The delay in South Carolina partially resulted from the fact that the federal marshall experienced difficulty in getting assistants at the lawful rate of pay. Another potent reason for the delay was that the enumeration met with some opposition from the people. On September 26, 1791, it was reported in the *State Gazette* of South Carolina, published in Charleston, that the grand jury of the Federal District for Charleston, made the following presentment a week earlier:

> That they have examined the several returns of the marshal of the said district, and find them accurate and correct for every part of the state, except that part of Charleston district.... We present on the information of Hezekia Roberts, one of the assistants to the marshal, William Reynolds of St. Helena Island, in Beaufort district, for refusing to render an account of his family, pursuant to the directions of the aforesaid act. We present on the information of Jacob Fitzpatrick, another of the marshal's assistants, William Russell, Jacob Vanzant, Benjamin Ingram, Ragnal Williams, and James Hayes, all of Orangeburg..., for refusing to render an account of their respective families....

Subsequent issues of the paper do not indicate what disposition was made of these cases. Nor does a check of surviving federal archives indicate whether any of these resistants were punished.

Should There Even Be a Census?

In 1996, author Michael Lavin in his book *Understanding the Census* raised the question: "Can the government force people to answer the Census?" His answer is revealing:

> Under Title 13 [of the United States Code], all residents are obligated to answer Census questions completely and truthfully. This has been a feature of Census law since 1790. Failure to comply can result in fines and/or imprisonment. In practice, however, few people have been prosecuted for refusing to answer the Census. The success of each decennial census depends largely on public cooperation [p. 11].

Actually, Mr. Lavin does not answer the question he raises. The government cannot force people to answer the Census; all it can do is punish them if they do not. That is what the government threatened to do in late 1791 to resisters to its first census; and that is all it could do to resisters in the Year 2000 Census. But what makes his question so interesting is that over the years the nature of the census and people's attitudes about it have changed.

Originally, early U.S. census schedules were posted publicly to enable residents to be sure that they were counted and to allow them to correct any erroneous information. Until 1840, each enumerator was to have a copy of his census schedule posted at two of the most important public places in his jurisdiction so that they could be inspected by the public. "From 1840 through 1870, census takers were instructed to keep their records confidential, but no legal restrictions were imposed. Beginning in 1880, and continuing to this day, all Census employees have taken an oath of confidentiality, and since 1890, penalties have been established for breaking that oath. In 1910, William Howard Taft issued the first Presidential Proclamation on Census confidentiality, a tradition which has been followed in every subsequent Census" (Lavin, p. 11). Taft's Proclamation stated that the Census was to be only used to generate statistical information. As President Taft declared

> The census has nothing to do with taxation, with army or jury service, with the compulsion of school attendance, with the regulation of immigration, or with the enforcement of any national, State, or local law or ordinance, nor can any person be harmed in any way furnishing the information required. There need be no fear that any disclosure will be made regarding any individual person or his affairs ["Proclamation for Thirteenth Decennial Census," March 15, 1910 cited in Bohme and Pemberton, p. 8].

Yet there has never been a law that has prevented other agencies of the government from using census data to their advantage. One way is the "use of census information to detect illegal two-family dwellings." Many local jurisdictions responsible for building code enforcement take census data applicable to their area and analyze it "to check compliance with zoning regulations" [Bovard].

Despite the fact that Social Security numbers are not recorded during the decennial censuses, and that the Freedom of Information Act does not apply to individual census records, some small "percentage of the U.S. population has always chosen to evade" the census-taker [U.S. General Accounting Office, p. 32]. Even the most ardent proponent of the census recognizes that some people will be missed — either because of they refuse to be counted because of their conscientious objections or because of simple technical errors in collecting data. But the fact remains that a successful census is based upon the individual's willingness to respond — in short, any national census depends upon the willing cooperation of the public. It is imperative that the questions raised on the census schedules be acceptable to the majority of people; otherwise their failure to answer or their offering of false answers will invalidate the efforts of even the best-intentioned government.

Probably no other government collects and publishes as much information about its people as the American polity. "Every conceivable aspect of our society is measured and analyzed, but one of the most frequently examined is the demographic information — statistics on the number, distribution, and character of people." The federal and state governments use this information to allocate over $100 billion in federal funds annually for community programs and services including education, housing, health care, job training, and welfare. "The unquestioned mother lode of United States demographic data is the decennial Census, known officially as the Census of Population and Housing. The reason for this is simple: no one except the federal government could attempt to collect information about every man, woman, and child in the country on a systematic basis" (Lavin, p. 3).

But hardly ever is the basic question raised: Should this information be collected at all? Is there any justification for knowing how many people are in our society? The only reason for our rulers to collect this information is that it aids them in exerting control and power over us. They count what is to be controlled and manipulated. In short, the census is another tool in the government's arsenal of conquest over us.

The census has always been and continues to be a political football in every country. The worst census story is that of Stalin's 1937 Census in the Soviet Union. The famine and Great Purges of the 1930s left the Soviet population greatly reduced. "Because population totals from the Soviet Union's 1937 Census would chillingly document the effect of this crushing oppression, Stalin suppressed the results and ordered census workers shot. Another census, containing significantly doctored data, was published in 1939" [Lavin, p. 5]. Another census story involves the government of Turkey, which in December 1997 concluded its latest quinquennial census. The entire population of Turkey was counted manually in one day over a 14-hour period. "Citizens were required to stay at home and be counted under threat of punishment if found in public without special permission" (U.S. General

Accounting Office, p. 24). Even in the United States the federal census has been used for political purposes. Draft boards often compare the number of males in certain age groups by census tract with its registration for the same area in order to detect how many men have not been registered (Bohme and Pemberton, p. 13).

There is no question that the collection of data is an onerous and time-consuming task, but so are most jobs and services on the free market. How would population and other demographic statistics be gathered in a free society? First of all, that question assumes that some people think there is a need to collect them at all. So, assuming there is a sufficient demand for such information, it would be collected just like every other statistic is collected in a free society: by those willing to pay the price for the collection of the information — by those willing to voluntarily supply the information (either for a price or as a freebie) — and by those voluntarily doing the collection and compilation of the information. As we have seen, this was how the collection of demographic statistics started out in the early American republic. If some wished not to participate in the process, they would be no more penalized or criminalized than those who refused to buy General Motor products or Ford products. That is to say, they would not be punished at all, except as other participants in the market chose to shame or ostracize them for their non-participation. So until such time as the gathering of public statistics is organized in a free market fashion and while our coercive political governing institutions are responsible for the Census, I want nothing to do with it or the census-taker. So please: Count Me Out!

Short Bibliography

Alterman, Hyman. *Counting People: The Census in History*. New York: Harcourt, Brace & World, Inc., 1969.

Anderson, Margo J. *The American Census: A Social History*. New Haven: Yale University Press, 1988.

Bohme, Frederick G., and George Dailey. "1990 Census: the 21st Count of 'We the People'." *Social Education*, vol. 53, no. 7, November/December 1989, pp. 421–426.

Bohme, Frederick G., and David M. Pemberton. "Privacy and Confidentiality in the U.S. Census— A History," Bureau of Census, 1991, and presented at the American Statistical Association annual meeting, August 18–22, 1991, in Atlanta, GA.

Bovard, James. "Honesty May Not Be Your Best Census Policy." *The Wall Street Journal*, August 8, 1989, p. A10.

"Census." Entry in Volume 3 of *The New Encyclopaedia Britannica*, 15th Edition, Chicago: 1992, pp. 22–23.

Cohen, Patricia Cline. *A Calculating People: The Spread of Numeracy in Early America*. Chicago: University of Chicago Press, 1982.

Cummings, John. "Statistical Work of the Federal Government of the United States," in John Koren (ed.), *The History of Statistics.* New York: Macmillan, 1913.

Glass, D. V. *Numbering the People: The 18th-century Population Controversy and the Development of Census and Vital Statistics in Britain.* Farnborough: Saxon House, 1973.

Lavin, Michael R. *Understanding the Census.* Kenmore: Epoch Books, 1996.

Nelson, William E., and Robert C. Palmer. *Liberty and Community: Constitution and Rights in the Early American Republic.* New York: Oceana Publications, 1987.

North, S. N. D., Director. *A Century of Population Growth from the First Census of the United States to The Twelfth 1790–1900.* Washington: Government Printing Office, 1909.

Scott, Ann Herbert. *Census, U.S.A.* New York: Seabury Press, 1968.

United States General Accounting Office. *Decennial Census: Overview of Historical Census Issues.* Washington: 1998, SuDoc No. GA1.13: GGD–98–103.

Although I refer to the census as "one of the tools in the government's arsenal of conquest," I failed to mention the horrible genocidal potential of national statistical systems. Evidence for this claim is found in the history of Nazi Germany (1933–1945), and, more recently, of Rwanda (1994). Two articles and one book stand out in the literature discussing the census and Nazi Germany. They are:

Black, Edwin. *IBM and the Holocaust.* New York: Crown Publishers, 2001.

Luebke, David Martin, and Sybil Milton. "Locating the Victim: An Overview of Census-Taking, Tabulation Technology, and Persecution in Nazi Germany." *16 IEEE Annals of the History of Computing* (1994), pp. 25–39. (For a contra point of view, see Friedrich W. Kistermann, "Locating the Victims: The Nonrole of Punched Card Technology and Census Work," *19 IEEE Annals of the History of Computing,* 1997, pp. 31–45.)

Seltzer, William. "Population Statistics, the Holocaust , and the Nuremberg Trials." *24 Population and Development Review* (1998), pp. 511–552.

In his discussion of population statistics and the Holocaust, William Seltzer points out that "Most of the countries of Europe ... had well developed national statistical systems.... The basic routine sources of population and related statistics in Europe ... [pre–World War II] were: population censuses, birth and death registration systems, administrative reporting systems under the jurisdiction of the education, labor, health, and similar ministries and, in a few of the countries, population registers" (p. 513). The Nazis undertook comprehensive censuses in 1933 and 1939, and as Luebke and Milton put it, "a strong continuity existed between the Nazi censuses and their predecessors" of 1925, 1910 and the earliest all-German census of 1871 (p. 26). The Reich Registration Law of January 6, 1938, required that all inhabitants of Germany (including foreigners) register and provide their local police with their domicile data. Failure to comply was punishable with six weeks imprisonment, and present-day Germans still have to do this. "The explicit purpose of resident registration was social control," and this "enabled the government to keep tabs on the physical location of all Germans" (Luebke, pp. 28–29).

Edwin Black's book, *IBM and the Holocaust,* relates the history of punch card technology and censuses in the United States and Europe. Not only did the Nazis count people, in some of the conquered territories they undertook censuses of mules and horses. Unfortunately, there is no index entry "Census" in Black's book (only an entry for the "Census Bureau" of the United States). However, references to censuses in various European countries are found at pp. 139–141 (Austrian and German censuses), pp. 169–171 (German census of 1939), p. 194 (Polish horse and mule census of 1940), p. 197 (Czech census of 1939), p. 206 (Polish horse census), pp. 293–332 (an extensive discussion of the administrative and statistical apparatus in "France and Holland"), pp. 345–346 (the United States census of 1940 and the Census Bureau's effort to assist in locating Japanese-Americans for internment), and p. 424 (the 1946 German occupation census: "People counting was what [IBM Germany] did best.")

Systematic Federal Surveillance of Ordinary Americans

Charlotte Twight

Federal data collection of information about citizens probably began with the first federal census in 1790. This article examines how various government programs track and retain information about every American. The author describes these programs as "the government's most critical" method for "institutionalizing government control" over us. This chapter is reprinted with permission of the publisher from The Independent Review: A Journal of Political Economy *(Fall 1999, vol. 4, no. 2), © 1999 The Independent Institute, 100 Swan Way, Oakland CA 94621-1428; http://www.independent.org. Charlotte Twight is a professor of economics at Boise State University. She is author of* Dependent on D.C.: The Rise of Federal Control Over the Lives of Ordinary Americans *(New York: Palgrave for St. Martin's Press, 2001).*

Imagine for a moment a nation whose central government mandated ongoing collection of detailed personal information — individually identified — recording each citizen's employment, income, childhood and subsequent educational experiences, medical history (including doctors' subjective impressions), financial transactions (including copies of personal checks written), ancestry, living conditions (including bathroom, kitchen, and bedroom facilities), rent or mortgage payment, household expenses, roommates and their characteristics, in-home telephone service, automobile ownership, household heating and sewage systems, number of stillbirths, language capability — and periodically even demanded to know what time each person in the household usually left home to go to work during the previous week. Imagine further that such a government assigned every citizen a central government identification number at birth and mandated its use in reporting the information just listed. Suppose the same government were actively considering mandatory nationwide use of a "biometric identifier" (such as finger-prints or retinal scans) along with a new counterfeit-proof permanent gov-ernment identification card incorporating the individual's government-issued number and other personal information, through magnetic strips and embed-ded computer chips capable of holding up to sixteen hundred pages of infor-mation about the individual. If a contemporary novelist were to portray the emergence of such a government in America, his novel undoubtedly would be regarded as futuristic fiction in the same vein as George Orwell's *1984*.

Yet this national portrait is no longer fiction. The model for the forego-ing description is a government that now wields exactly those awesome pow-ers over the citizenry — America's federal government in 1999. In this article I substantiate each of the preceding statements and provide citations to the laws, regulations, and working papers establishing and designing such intel-ligence systems. The logical outgrowth of such all-encompassing federal col-lection of personal information has increased government power and concomitant individual dependence on government.

Governments have long recognized the capacity of information collec-tion to erode individual autonomy by fostering deep personal uncertainty about the uses to which the information might be put. Paul Schwartz (1992) has described the linkage clearly:

> Personal information can be shared to develop a basis for trust, but the mandatory disclosure of personal information can have a destructive effect on human independence... Totalitarian regimes have already demonstrated the fragility of the human capacity for autonomy. The effectiveness of these regimes in rendering adults as helpless as children is in large part a prod-uct of the uncertainty that they instill regarding their use of personal infor-mation [1363–1364].

With respect to U.S. government data collection in the 1990s, he added:

> Americans no longer know how their personal information will be applied, who will gain access to it, and what decisions will be made with it. The resulting uncertainty increases pressure for conformity. Individuals whose personal data are shared, processed and stored by a mysterious, incalcula-ble bureaucracy will be more likely to act as the government wishes them to behave [1374].

With extensive federal data collection creating ever-greater incentives to behave as government wishes us to behave, the societal result is metasta-sizing government control. Indeed, Schwartz views the computer's ability to digitize personal information as offering "the state and society a powerful way to control the behavior of individuals" (1343). The result — and often the purpose — is a profound erosion of individual autonomy.

In this article, I focus on central government data-collection programs that share one defining characteristic: they compel production, retention, and dissemination of personal information about every American citizen.[1] Their target is ordinary American citizens carrying out ordinary day-to-day activities. Although these programs by no means constitute the whole universe of federal data collection, they are today the government's most critical informational levers for institutionalizing government control, individual dependence, and unprecedented threats to American liberties. Even within this circumscribed sphere, the immense volume of federal data collection defies brief summary. Accordingly, I confine the present inquiry to government development and recent expansion of

• Databases keyed to Social Security numbers—examining unchecked use of those numbers as a fulcrum for government data collection about individuals, and probing current legislative efforts to establish a national identification card;
• Labor databases—revealing new statutory provisions aimed at building a federal database of all American workers and requiring employers to obtain the central government's approval before hiring employees;
• Medical databases—assessing creation of the "unique health identifier" and implementation of the national electronic database of personal medical information mandated by the 1996 Health Insurance Portability and Accountability Act;
• Education databases—revealing federal databases mandated by the 1994 Goals 2000 Act, Improving America's Schools Act, and related legislation that establish detailed national records of children's educational experiences and socioeconomic status;
• Financial databases—describing provisions of federal statutory law requiring banks and other financial institutions to create permanent, readily retrievable records of each individual's checks, deposits, and other financial activities.

Largely linked through an individual's Social Security number, these databases now empower the federal government to obtain an astonishingly detailed portrait of any person: the checks he writes, the types of causes he supports, what he says "privately" to his doctor.

Of course, federal officials always provide an appealing reason for such governmental intrusion into our private lives, however inadequate the reason or unconstitutional the intrusion. In this case, as in others, backers of these measures, in their effort to minimize resistance, predictably use political transaction-cost manipulation to that end, increasing the transaction costs to private individuals of perceiving—and taking collective action to resist—governmental encroachments (Twight 1988, 1994). There is always an asserted benefit to be obtained, a plausible cover story.

The ostensible reasons have been diverse. With the spread of government-mandated use of Social Security numbers for database after electronic database, we have been told that it will reduce fraud — tax fraud, welfare fraud, the usual litany. With government assertion of the power to require businesses to contact the government for approval before hiring anyone, we have been told that it will help in cracking down on illegal immigration. With regard to government mandates for private physicians to record what we say to them in confidence, we have been told that it will reduce health-care fraud, promote efficiency, allow better emergency treatment, make it easier for the patient to keep track of his medical records, and the like. To rationalize government assertion of power to track what public school teachers record concerning our children, we have been told that it will assist in students' selection of a "career major," enhance assessment of school courses, and facilitate identification of students needing help. With government assertion of power to require banks to keep microfilm of all the checks we write, we have been told that it is to "reduce white-collar crime" and "inhibit money laundering." Who could oppose such worthy goals unless he had something to hide?

The immense powers now exercised by the federal government have made these rationales inevitable. Having empowered the federal government to exert centralized control over far-flung human endeavors, most Americans want government officials to administer the programs effectively and responsibly. But administering them effectively and responsibly necessitates functions such as "reducing fraud" and "promoting efficiency" in the programs, legitimate objectives that often become chameleonic rationales that ultimately are invoked in the service of illegitimate ends. The pattern is unmistakable. With vast federal power comes vast federal surveillance, providing plausible cover for those seeking to extend the central government's purview even further.

Political transaction-cost manipulation has framed the issue in other ways besides these appealing rationales. In some cases discussed later, the database maneuvers were deliberately obscured from public view by means of what Claire Wolfe (1997) calls "land-mine legislation" that people don't notice until they step on it. In other cases Americans were encouraged to view new proposals piecemeal, a strategy that forestalled public perception of the confluent streams of nationwide government-mandated data centralization and their likely eventual result. Incrementalism again served activist policy making. Information-law scholar Simon Davies (1994) judged the public's "greater acceptance of privacy-invasive schemes" to be in part a result of "proposals ... being brought forward in a more careful and piecemeal fashion" that may be "lulling the public into a false sense of security."

Given that piecemeal progression, legislators and members of the popular press today seldom discuss the likely cost of government data centralization in terms of lost liberty. Perhaps "liberty" does not resonate so strongly or create so powerful an image for most people as "cracking down on illegal immigration" or "reducing health-care fraud." Liberty, after all, is an abstraction whose concrete reality often is not appreciated until its opposite is experienced firsthand. Yet we ignore at our peril the long-cited "use of personal information systems by Nazi Germany to enable the identification and location of a target race" (Davies 1994). Less than sixty years ago, race-based government roundups of law-abiding citizens also occurred in America, similarly facilitated by government data collection. As Solveig Singleton (1998a) and others have reported, "In the U.S., census data were used to find Japanese-Americans and force them into camps," a historical reality that gives fresh meaning to a 1990 U.S. Census instruction stating that "it is as important to get information about people and their houses as it is to count them."[2] By 1998, however, the events of the 1940s have become only a "vague memory"—and, except for the elderly, not a living memory at all (Davies 1994).

So today Congress proceeds apace. Having exposed most areas of our lives to ongoing government scrutiny and recording, Congress is now working to expand and universalize federal tracking of law-abiding citizens' private lives. Concurrently, new developments in biometry are producing technologies that most observers concede "imperil individual autonomy" and pose "real threats to the fabric of contemporary society" (Davies 1994). The next generation awaits the full flowering of those technologies and their availability to governments. Our privacy, our personal identity, our independence, and our freedom hang in the balance.

Linking Personal Records: A "De Facto National Identification Number"[3]

The Social Security number (SSN) has become the key to detailed government portraiture of our private lives. Even the Secretary of Health and Human Services (HHS) now describes American Social Security numbers as a "de facto personal identifier" (U.S. Dept. of HHS 1998, Section III[A][1]). Kristin Davis, senior associate editor for *Kiplinger's Personal Finance Magazine*, recently described "the growing use of social security numbers as an all-purpose ID" as the "single biggest threat to protecting our financial identities" (quoted in Miller 1998). Since the Social Security program's inception in the 1930s, when officials slighted public fears that identification of citizens for Social Security purposes implied regimentation, that reality has relentlessly emerged.

Federal officials long denied that Social Security numbers would function as national identification numbers. They were supposed to be mere "account numbers" denoting an individual's "old-age insurance account" in which his "contributions" were set aside in a federal "trust fund" for his retirement. But expansion of SSN use came quickly, much of it ordered by the federal government. President Franklin D. Roosevelt (1943) began the process with his executive order that subsequently, whenever the head of any federal department or agency found "it advisable to establish a new system of permanent account numbers pertaining to individual persons," the department or agency "shall ... utilize exclusively the Social Security Act account numbers" assigned pursuant to that act.

The full impact of Roosevelt's order was not felt until computers became available. Gradual computerization made SSN-based record systems increasingly appealing throughout the 1960s. In 1961 the Civil Service Commission first ordered the use of SSNs to identify all federal employees. The Internal Revenue Service (IRS) began using SSNs as taxpayer identification numbers in 1962. Department of Defense military personnel records were identified by SSN beginning in 1967. The SSN became the Medicare identifier in the 1960s. Thereafter, SSN use spread unabated:

> By the 1970s, the SSN floodgates had opened fully. Congress in 1972 amended the Social Security Act to require the use of SSNs for identifying legally admitted aliens and anyone applying for federal benefits. In following years, additional legislation required the SSN for the identification of those eligible to receive Medicaid, Aid to Families with Dependent Children ("AFDC") benefits, food stamps, school lunch program benefits, and federal loans [Minor 1995, 262–263; footnotes omitted].[4]

Moreover, the 1970 Bank Secrecy Act, discussed later in this article, required all financial institutions to identify customers by SSN and to preserve detailed records of their customers' personal checks and other financial transactions.

The Privacy Act of 1974 did not stop the flood.[5] Although purporting to restrict federal dissemination of SSNs, not only did it exempt existing federal SSN use previously authorized by statute or regulation, but it also created a massive exemption allowing disclosure of personal information obtained by federal officials if the disclosure involved a "routine use" of the data. Two years later, utterly countermanding any notion of restricting SSN use and dissemination, Congress included in the 1976 tax reform act a provision that gave states free rein to use SSNs. It stated:

> It is the policy of the United States that any State (or political subdivision thereof) may, in the administration of any tax, general public assistance, driver's license, or motor vehicle registration law within its jurisdiction, utilize the social security account numbers issued by the Secretary for the purpose of establishing the identification of individuals affected by such law, and may require any individual who is or appears to be so affected to furnish to such State (or political subdivision thereof) or any agency thereof having administrative responsibility for the law involved, the social security account number ... issued to him by the Secretary.[6]

On top of the far-reaching use of SSNs thus authorized, Congress continued to press for more.

Incrementalist policies continued to advance SSN use, as illustrated by the gradual introduction of requirements that Social Security numbers be obtained for young children. For approximately the first fifty years of the Social Security program, one did not acquire an SSN until beginning one's first job, usually at about age sixteen. Today every child must acquire an SSN at birth or shortly thereafter. How did policy makers accomplish such a radical change? Much as one conditions dogs: a bit at a time, and always with a reward attached. First, members of Congress required by statute in 1986 that every child claimed as a dependent on federal tax forms have an SSN by age 5. Then in 1988 Congress reduced the requirement by statute to age 2; in 1990 to age 1. Finally, in 1996, Congress passed a global requirement that an SSN must be presented for anyone of any age claimed on federal tax forms as a "dependent." No SSN, no federal tax exemption. The Department of HHS reported that "beginning with tax returns filed 1/1/98 or later, the SSNs of all dependents claimed by a taxpayer must be included on the tax return" (U.S. Dept. of HHS 1998, Section III[A][3]). In general, to obtain any federal benefit, tax-related or otherwise, today one must present the Social Security numbers of all parties affected.[7] To facilitate assignment of SSNs at birth, the federal government has financed state programs to secure issuance of the numbers as part of the birth-certificate registration process, an enticement that has enabled the Social Security Administration to secure adoption of its "Enumeration at Birth" process in all fifty states.

A coordinated government effort now under way to require even greater use of SSNs will further centralize federal monitoring of all American citizens. Its elements include

- federal mandates governing state driver's licenses and birth certificates;
- federal "work authorization" databases covering all working Americans and keyed to SSNs;
- federal development of a "unique health identifier" for each American in implementing a national electronic database of private medical histories;
- federal implementation of education databases; and
- federal development and issuance of new "tamper-resistant" Social Security cards, perhaps with biometric identifiers, viewed by many as precursor of the long-feared "national identity card."

The education, medical history, and work authorization databases are later discussed separately. First I consider the driver's license, birth certificate, and tamper-resistant Social Security card provisions.

The unprecedented federal assertion of control over state-issued drivers' licenses is buried in an omnibus bill, the 749-page Omnibus Consolidated Appropriations Act of 1997, which includes the "Illegal Immigration

Reform and Immigrant Responsibility Act of 1996" (the "Immigration Reform Act"), the statute containing the relevant language.[8] The key provisions begin on page 716, sandwiched between a section entitled "Sense of Congress on Discriminatory Application of New Brunswick Provincial Sales Tax" and another entitled "Border Patrol Museum." So well concealed, the provisions are difficult to spot even when you already know they are there.

Section 656(b) of the Immigration Reform Act deals with "State-Issued Drivers Licenses and Comparable Identification Documents." Cleverly conceived, it specifies that a "Federal agency may not accept for any identification-related purpose a driver's license or other comparable identification document, issued by a State, unless the license or document satisfies" federal requirements. The language thus makes compliance mandatory without saying so. Instead of telling the states "you must," it makes it nearly impossible for state residents to interact with the federal government if the state does not comply. The charade of voluntariness is buttressed by hard cash — grants to states "to assist them in issuing driver's licenses and other comparable identification documents that satisfy the requirements" promulgated by the federal government.

Compliance requires the states to follow federal Department of Transportation regulations specifying both the form of the license and what constitutes federally acceptable "evidence of identity" in issuing the license. Raising the specter of biometric identifiers, it requires "security features" intended to "limit tampering, counterfeiting, photocopying, or otherwise duplicating, the license or document for fraudulent purposes and to limit use of the license or document by imposters." In addition, the statute mandates that in general "the license or document shall contain a social security account number that can be read visually or by electronic means." States can avoid including the SSN on the license only by requiring "every applicant for a driver's license ... to submit the applicant's social security account number" and "verify[ing] with the Social Security Administration that such account number is valid." Either way, the SSN is readily at hand, mandated by the federal government — and easily linked electronically to any alternative identifier a state may adopt. Proposed federal Department of Transportation rules implementing these provisions already have been published.[9]

The other prong of the new federal control over state-issued identification documents entails regulation of the states' issuance of birth certificates. The tactic is the same, requiring that a "Federal agency may not accept for any official purpose a certificate of birth" unless the birth certificate complies with federal regulations specifying "appropriate standards for birth certificates."[10] Bribes follow in the form of "grants to States to assist them in issuing birth certificates that conform to the standards set forth in the regulation." Federal grants also are authorized for states "to assist them in developing the capability to match birth and death records" and to finance demonstration projects showing the feasibility of mandatory reports to "establish the fact of death of every individual dying in the State within 24 hours of acquiring the information." An explicit objective is to "note the fact of death on the birth certificates of deceased persons." However fleeting, the sole federal concession is to "not require a single design to which birth certificates issued by all States must conform" and to "accommodate the differences between the States in the manner and form in which birth records are stored and birth certificates are produced from such records." The substance is another matter.

Perhaps the most ominous of Congress's innocuously titled "Improvements in Identification-Related Documents" requires the development of "prototypes" of a "counterfeit-resistant Social Security card."[11] Congress specifically mandated that the prototype card "shall employ technologies that provide security features, such as magnetic stripes, holograms, and integrated circuits." Integrated circuits? Integrated circuits open the door to biometric identifiers and the storage of vast amounts of personal data on each person's government-required Social Security card, a theme that recurs in government discussions of the "unique health identifier" for medical records.[12] And these changes are aimed not just at people newly entering the Social Security system. The statute requires the Social Security Commissioner and the Comptroller General to study the "cost and work load implications of issuing a counterfeit-resistant social security card for all individuals over a 3, 5, and 10 year period" (1996 Immigration Reform Act, sec. 657). The new cards "shall be developed so as to provide individuals with reliable proof of citizenship or legal alien status." Proof of citizenship? Federal officials have claimed that such a document is not a "national identification card" because — note well — we will not be required to carry it around with us at all times.[13] Not yet, anyway.

Despite all such protestations, the SSN is now at the heart of a vast array of government databases, and linkage of those separate databases occurs despite periodic statutory lip service to individual privacy. One example is the Social Security Administration (SSA) itself. Its own regulations state that SSA officials "disclose information when a law specifically requires it," including

> Disclosures to the SSA Office of Inspector General, the Federal Parent Locator Service, and to States pursuant to an arrangement regarding use of the Blood Donor Locator Service. Also, there are other laws which require that we furnish other agencies information which they need for their programs. These agencies include the Department of Veterans Affairs..., the Immigration and Naturalization Service..., the Railroad Retirement Board..., and to Federal, State, and local agencies administering Aid to Families with Dependent Children, Medicaid, unemployment compensation, food stamps, and other programs.[14]

And, of course, the IRS. "Information" is defined to mean "information about an individual" that "includes, but is not limited to"

> Vital statistics; race, sec, or other physical characteristics; earnings information; professional fees paid to an individual and other financial information; benefit data or other claims information; the social security number, employer identification number, or other individual identifier; address; phone number; medical information, including psychological or psychiatric information or lay information used in a medical determination; and information about marital and family relationships and other personal relationships.[15]

Even without the Social Security Administration's much-reviled on-line dissemination in 1997 of the agency's database of "Personal Earnings and Benefit Estimate Statement" information on Americans, making the data electronically accessible via the Internet to third parties without the subject individual's knowledge or consent, the SSA's broad regulatory power to transmit personal information to other government agencies seriously compromises individual privacy.

Concrete examples of the data linkages across government agencies are provided by the Aid to Families with Dependent Children (AFDC) program — now called Temporary Assistance to Needy Families (TANF) — and the Child Support Enforcement (CSE) program. In describing the effects of computerization of federal records, Schwartz (1992) states that AFDC has progressed from midnight searches of the welfare beneficiary's home to continuous searches of the beneficiary's personal data." Explaining "the enormous amount of information to which AFDC offices have access" and the "extensive data bases that are manipulated in administering the AFDC program," Schwartz adds:

> From the Social Security Administration, AFDC receives access to the BEN-DEX [Beneficiary Data System] and SDX [Medicare eligibility and Supplemental Security Income payment] data systems. From the Internal Revenue Service, AFDC receives data relating to the tax interception and parent locator programs. Within state government, AFDC receives information from the Employment Security Division (worker's compensation and employment) and the Child Support Enforcement Unit (child support payments). AFDC offices also receive information about unemployment payments from other states [1357].

Over time the program's broad reach predictably spawned increasingly intrusive data collection and data sharing in the name of curtailing welfare fraud.

A similar pattern is evident in the federal Child Support Enforcement program. As Schwartz has recounted, after the program's creation in 1974, officials were granted access to ever more government databases of personal information. Use of the SSN passkey was authorized in 1976, when "Congress explicitly authorized the use of social security numbers in searches of federal and state data banks for information leading to the location of these delinquent parents of AFDC families" (1367). Thereafter they gained access to IRS records and expanded the data-matching and tax interception with the IRS." Schwartz quotes a state director of Child Support Enforcement as saying, "Some people would say that's Big Brotherism. Well, it is."[16] Every child-support enforcement unit (CSEU) has access to all the AFDC data just listed as well as the Federal Parent Locator database. The Federal Parent Locator database in turn contains information from "the Social Security Administration; the Department of Defense; the Veterans Administration; the Motor Vehicle Bureau of the state in which the CSEU is located; the IRS, including 1099 forms; and commercial credit bureaus. The parent locator also allows searches of state databases, three states at a time" (Schwartz 1992, 1369, footnotes omitted).

Pervasive government extraction of personal data that are stored and linked via compulsory use of SSNs is today's reality. As we move toward the equivalent of a national identity card tied to the ubiquitous SSN, the threat to privacy is clear. Although it will not be labeled a "national identity card," Stephen Moore (1997) correctly stated in his testimony on a related bill, if it "looks like a duck, … quacks like a duck, … walks like a duck … it's a duck."

Tracking (and Preventing) Your Employment: Illegal Aliens and Other Excuses

A key aspect of the federal government's ongoing effort to establish the equivalent of a national identity card is its quest to obtain current, continually updated, detailed electronic data about where and for whom each individual in America is working. To overcome resistance to such federal surveillance, Congress has used several rationales. Recurrent excuses for increasing federal surveillance of every working American are controlling illegal immigration, locating absent parents who owe child-support payments, preventing welfare fraud, and supporting workforce investment. These purported rationales have become ritual incantations: once they are uttered, Congress expects a mesmerized citizenry to grant whatever liberty-curtailing federal powers Congress demands. So far the strategy has worked.

During the 1990s, federal authority to collect labor-related data skyrocketed. The federal government's desires were particularly evident in a 1992 amendment to the Job Training Partnership Act that ordered the U.S. Commissioner of Labor Statistics, cooperating with state governments, to "determine appropriate procedures for establishing a nationwide database containing information on the quarterly earnings, establishment and industry affiliation, and geographic location of employment, for all individuals for whom such information is collected by the States," including "appropriate procedures for maintaining such information in a longitudinal manner."[17]

Four years later, further statutory changes supported these ends. The first was part of the "Personal Responsibility and Work Opportunity Reconciliation Act of 1996," the 1996 welfare reform act (P. L. 104–193).[18] For the stated purposes of preventing welfare fraud and enforcing child-support obligations, the law established an electronic database called a Directory of New Hires at both the state and the national level, simultaneously authorizing pervasive new data sharing among federal and state agencies. Despite the law's welfare motif, neither the State Directory of New Hires nor the National Directory of New Hires is limited in any way to individuals receiving public assistance or to individuals paying or receiving child support. Instead, the new databases cover every working individual in America who enters the workforce or changes jobs.[19] The journalist Robert Pear (1997) has called it "one of the largest, most up-to-date files of personal information kept by the government," whose size and scope "have raised concerns about the potential for intrusions on privacy."

The 1996 law (P.L. 104–193, sec. 313[b]) specifies that each state must establish a State Directory of New Hires that "shall contain information supplied ... by employers on each newly hired employee." Each employer is mandated to turn over to state officials "a report that contains the name, address, and social security number of the employee, and the name and address of, and identifying number assigned under ... the Internal Revenue Code [to] the employer." State officials then must give this information, along with wage and unemployment data on individuals, to the federal government for inclusion in its National Directory of New Hires. Within each state, the State Directory of New Hires must be "matched" against a mandatory "state case registry" containing "standardized data elements for both parents (such as names, social security numbers and other uniform identification numbers, dates of birth, and case identification numbers), and ... such other information ... as the Secretary may require" (P.L. 104–193, sec. 311).

SSNs provide the key link between the electronic databases. State agencies are required to "conduct automated comparisons of the social security numbers reported by employers ... and the social security numbers appearing in the records of the State case registry" to allow state agencies to enforce child-support obligations by mandatory wage withholding. States also are ordered to require SSNs of applicants for any "professional license, commercial driver's license, occupational license, or marriage license" and to include SSNs on certain court orders and on death certificates. Broad information sharing with other state and federal agencies and "information comparison services" is mandated. Access to the new hires database is explicitly granted to the Secretary of the Treasury (IRS), and the Social Security Administration is to receive "all information" in the National Directory. The statute instructs the Secretary of HHS and the Secretary of Labor to "work jointly" to find "efficient methods of accessing the information" in the state and federal directories of new hires (P.L. 104–193, secs. 311, 316, 317).

Other major changes in 1996 came via the "Illegal Immigration Reform and Immigrant Responsibility Act of 1996" (P.L. 104–208). Although its most ominous provisions are cast as "pilot programs," their scope and structure clearly indicate the direction of things to come. Using the rationale of controlling illegal immigration, this 1996 statute establishes pilot programs requiring employers to seek the central government's certification of a person's "work authorization" before making final an offer of employment. And the manner in which the federal government's approval is to be sought substantially overlaps the pressure for SSN-based national identification cards and enhanced SSN-based state drivers' licenses discussed earlier.

Congress created three "pilot programs for employment eligibility confirmation": the "basic" pilot program, the "citizen attestation" pilot program, and the "machine-readable-document pilot program. Underlying all three is Congress's mandate that the U.S. Attorney General establish a pilot "employment eligibility confirmation system," keyed to information provided by the Social Security Administration and the Immigration and Naturalization Service (INS). The idea is to create a federal database capable of confirming any individual's SSN and his INS-decreed work eligibility before an employer hires that person. As John J. Miller and Stephen Moore (1995) described such proposals prior to passage of the pilot-program law, "In other words, the government would, for the first time in history, require employers to submit all of their hiring decisions for approval to a federal bureaucrat." Although individual firms' election to participate is at present voluntary, the reward for participating is protection from both criminal and civil liability for "any action taken in good faith reliance on information provided through the confirmation system" (P.L. 104–208, sec. 403).

The three pilot programs reflect increasing proximity to a national identification card system. The "basic" program requires the Attorney General to secure participation by at least "5 of the 7 states with the highest estimated population of aliens who are not lawfully present in the United States" (P.L. 104–208, sec. 401). When hiring, recruiting, or referring any individual, participating firms must obtain the potential employee's SSN (or INS identification number for aliens) and require presentation of specified identification documents. The firms then must use the government's "confirmation system" to get federal approval for the hiring decision. The statute requires that, within three working days after hiring a person, the employer "shall make an inquiry ... using the confirmation system to seek confirmation of the identity and employment eligibility of any individual" [P.L. 104–208, sec. 403(a)]. If the firm continues to employ the individual after a "final nonconfirmation" of work eligibility through the federal electronic database system, the statute creates a rebuttable presumption that the firm has violated a provision of immigration law that carries civil penalties of as much as $2,000 per unauthorized hire on the first offense and as much as $5,000 or $10,000 for subsequent offenses.[20]

With the "Citizen Attestation Pilot Program," linkages with other facets of the coordinated federal data expansion effort become apparent. While extending the approach of the "basis" pilot program, the idea here is to waive the requirement for work-eligibility confirmation in certain circumstances if the job applicant claims to be a U.S. citizen — but only if the state in which a participating firm is located has adjusted its drivers' licenses to include "security" features such as those described in the previous section. The statutory language is almost identical, requiring each state driver's license to contain both a photograph and "security features" that render it "resistant to counterfeiting, tampering, and fraudulent use."[21] If a state has complied with the federally desired format and application process for state drivers' licenses, then participating firms can avoid mandatory use of the federal work-eligibility confirmation system by inspecting the job applicant's state driver's license.

The "Machine-Readable-Document Pilot Program" comes even closer to a national-identity-card approach. With one major exception, it follows the basic pilot program. To participate in the machine-readable document pilot program, a state must have adopted a driver's license format that includes a "machine-readable social security account number." Participating firms "must make an inquiry through the confirmation system by using a machine-readable feature of such document" to obtain confirmation from the federal government of the work eligibility of new employees (P.L. 104–208, sec. 403[c]). The potential for future linkage of such procedures to the new skill-certificate programs called for by the 1994 School-to-Work Opportunities Act is all too evident.

After establishing the infrastructure for a national identification card, the 1996 immigration reform act, like other recent statutes, includes a provision headed "No National Identification Card" that proclaims that "nothing in this subtitle shall be construed to authorize, directly or indirectly, the issuance or use of national identification cards or the establishment of a national identification card" (P.L. 104–208, sec. 404[h]). Such provisions, appearing ever more frequently in federal legislation, merely highlight the clear and present danger of exactly the type of system disavowed.

A bill introduced in 1997, H.R. 231, reflected the continuing congressional pressure to move the nation closer to a national-identification-card system. Like the pilot-program legislation, H.R. 231 prominently displayed a provision entitled "Not A National Identification Card." Further embracing the spirit of political transaction-cost manipulation, H.R. 231 was appealingly labeled as a bill "To improve the integrity of the Social Security card and to provide for criminal penalties for fraud and related activity involving work authorization documents for purposes of the Immigration and Nationality Act." Testifying before congress on the bill, Stephen Moore (1997, 2–3) described it as a dangerous extension of pilot work-authorization programs that had already created "an insidious national computer registry system with the federal government centralizing work authorization data on every one of the 120 million Americans in the workforce." Moore told the House Judiciary Committee's Subcommittee on Immigration and Claims:

> The centralized computer registry system is dangerous enough. But to add to that a photo ID card issued to every citizen that matches up with the computer database is to put in place the entire infrastructure of a national ID card system. All that is missing is the nomenclature. As someone once put it: this is about as ill fated as giving a teenager a bottle [of] booze and keys to a motorcycle, but getting him to promise that he won't drink and drive. You're just asking for trouble.

We have already asked for trouble. With laws now on the books, we do have a national-ID-card system; the open question is how much additional personal information we will pour into it.

Vastly more was poured into it in 1998. The Workforce Investment Act specifically authorized the Secretary of Labor to "oversee the development, maintenance, and continuous improvement of a nationwide employment statistics system" intended to "enumerate, estimate, and project employment opportunities and conditions at national, State, and local levels in a timely manner." Designed to include information on all of us and our employment, the system is to document the "employment and unemployment status of national, State, and local populations" and incorporate "employment and earnings information maintained in a longitudinal manner." Despite requirements for the data's "wide dissemination," the statute reassures us that this vast array of information will remain "confidential."[22]

Behind nomenclature that continues to conceal more than it reveals to ordinary Americans, government pressure thus persists for an ever-increasing repository of personal information to fatten and consolidate national employment databases and identification systems. The Workforce Investment Act and the federal pilot work-authorization program move in that direction, taking steps likely to be validated regardless of their actual effects. As Moore remarked regarding the work-authorization program, "it is almost a certainty that no matter how big a failure this new system proves to be, within ten years the registry will be applied to all workers in the nation" (1997, 2).[23] The objectives of controlling illegal immigration, enforcing child-support obligations, and supporting workforce investment continue to provide fertile ground for rationalizing increased government surveillance of the employment and whereabouts of every person in America.

Tracking Your Personal Medical History: The "Unique Health Identifier"

Further jeopardizing our privacy and individual autonomy is the new federal mandate for a unique nationwide health identifier for each individ-

ual, to be used in a national electronic database of personal medical information. People familiar with the proposed encroachments find few words
strong enough to impart the magnitude of the threat to personal privacy.
Although the federal government already has access to millions of medical
records through Medicare, Medicaid, and the newly authorized federal subsidies for State Children's Health Insurance Programs, the national electronic
database of health information authorized by the Health Insurance Portability
and Accountability Act of 1996[24] (HIPAA, P.L. 104–191) involves the government in everyone's health care, whether or not they receive federal subsidies
(Twight 1998). Steve Forbes (1997) has described it as a "breathtaking assault
on the sanctity of your medical records." Ellyn Spragins and Mary Hager
(1997) noted the "big, ugly fact" that under the 1996 act "every detail of your
medical profile may well land in this new system without your consent,"
explaining that the new national databank will allow "anyone who knows
your special health-care number" to become "privy to some of your most
closely guarded secrets."

Despite such occasional outcries, even today neither the public nor the
media have fully awakened to the scope of the 1996 law. In fact, when the *New
York Times* on July 20, 1998, ran a front-page story entitled "Health Identifier
for All Americans Runs into Hurdles," the nearly two-year-old fact that such
a unique health identifier was mandated by statutory law was described elsewhere in the media as "breaking news" (Stolberg 1998a). Depicting the Clinton administration as "quietly laying plans to assign every American a 'unique
health identifier,'" the *Times* described the identifier as a "computer code
that could be used to create a national database that would track every citizen's medical history from cradle to grave." Yet, for two years hardly anyone
had paid heed to those provisions of statutory law.

Meanwhile the federal bureaucracy proceeded systematically to carry
out its statutory duty to select a health identifier. On July 2, 1998, the U.S.
Department of Health and Human Services released a lengthy White Paper
entitled "Unique Health Identifier for Individuals." In that chilling document, HHS calmly discussed exactly what Orwellian form the "unique health
identifier" will take, what degree of encroachment on individual privacy will
be compelled. HHS considered six alternatives as "candidate identifiers":
"Social Security Number (SSN), including the proposal of the Computer-
based Personal Record Institute (CPRI); Biometric Identifiers; Directory Service; Personal Immutable Properties; Patient Identification System based on
existing Medical Record Number and Practitioner Prefix; and Public Key-
Private Key Cryptography Method." As HHS stated, "many of the proposals
involve either the SSN, SSA's enumeration process [including its "Enumeration at Birth" process], or both." The federal drive to link birth and death
records with SSNs seen elsewhere in the push to expand government data collection recurred here, augmented in this case by linkage to the health

identifier. Noting that all SSN-dependent proposals would "benefit from further improvements in the process for issuing and maintaining both SSNs and birth certificates," the HHS document suggested that an "improved process could begin with a newborn patient in the birth hospital" where "at once the proper authorities would assign a birth certificate number, assign an SSN, and assign the health identifier" (U.S. Dept. of HHS 1998, sec. III[A]). That goal echoes throughout today's multifaceted federal data-collection efforts.

In considering SSN-based health identifiers, HHS listed as a positive aspect of the unenhanced SSN that it "is the current de facto identifier" and that people "are accustomed to using their SSN as an identifier" and "would not be required to adjust to change." One alternative proposal would add to the SSN a "check digit" for fraud control. Another would "use the SSN as the health identifier for those individuals to whom it is acceptable, but offer an alternative identifier to others." From the perspective of political transaction-cost manipulation, that proposal holds appeal, for it would give the appearance of individual control without the reality. (Does anyone think that there would not be a data table linking the SSN and the "alternative" identifier?) Amazingly, listed among potential negative aspects of this proposal was the fact that a "potential stigma could be attached to the alternate identifier" because "a request for the identifier might be interpreted to mean that the individual has something to hide"! HHS also was troubled by the proposal because of the department's "anticipat[ion] that, given the choice, significant numbers of individuals would request the alternate identifier" (U.S. Dept. of HHS 1998, secs. III[B][1]–III[B][3]).

Equally stunning are proposals to require biometric identifiers as the unique health identifier. The HHS White Paper describes biometric identifiers as "based on unique physical attributes, including fingerprints, retinal pattern analysis, iris scan, voice pattern identification, and DNA analysis." Listed negative aspects of this alternative are chiefly mechanical obstacles—that "no infrastructure" now exists to support such identifiers, that the necessary "special equipment" would "add to the cost" of this alternative, and the like (U.S. Dept. of HHS 1998, sec. III[c][2]). Cost and equipment issues thus were set against the benefit of "uniqueness" that this alternative would provide. Only the fact that biometric identifiers are already used in law enforcement and judicial proceedings prompted HHS to state that their usage in health care might make it "difficult to prevent linkages that would be punitive or would compromise patient privacy." No mention was made of loss of liberty or threat of a police state, unless those issues inhered in the reference to "linkages that would be punitive."

Another alternative presented was a "civil registration system." Such a system would "use records established in the current system of civil registration as the basis to assign a unique, unchanging 16-position randomly-generated (in base 10 or base 16) identifier for each individual." The identifier "would link the lifetime records of an individual's human services and medical records" and "track these and other encounters with the civil system," including "state birth files," visas, "SSA records and military identification," and "library card and membership in civil organizations, etc." (U.S. Dept. of HHS 1998, sec. III[C][4]). HHS noted that although such a system "meets the requirement of HIPAA for a standard, unique health identifier for each individual," it "would be likely to raise very strong privacy objections." Evidently, from HHS's perspective, the public's "strong privacy objections" are the only barrier to police state methods.

One proposal that elicited strong HHS support was a hybrid proposal called "Universal Healthcare Identifier/Social Security Administration" (UHID/SSA). The UHID is an identifier as many as twenty-nine characters long involving a sixteen-digit sequential number, some check digits, and an "encryption scheme identifier." HHS noted that the UHID/SSA proposal, by selecting the SSA as a "trusted authority" to maintain the system, "echoes the call for improvements to the birth certificate process to ensure reliable issuance of SSNs and UHIDs at birth." The SSA would issue the UHID with each new SSN, and those without SSNs "would be issued UHIDs as they generate their first encounter with the health system." Although the UHID would not appear on the Social Security card, the "SSA would maintain the database linking the SSN with the health identifier for its internal verification process, but other unauthorized users would be prohibited from linking the two numbers." In conjunction with the UHID/SSA proposal, HHS praised the SSA as an "experienced public program with a national identification system that includes most U.S. citizens and with the infrastructure necessary to issue and maintain the health care identifier." HHS stated that selecting the SSA "as the responsible authority for assignment the health care identifier builds on the present infrastructure for issuing SSNs" and would allow us to "restrict the identifier to health care uses that can be protected with legislation or regulation" (U.S. Dept. of HHS 1998, sec. III[E][1]).

There is more, including some less intrusive measures, but these excerpts convey the spirit of this shocking document. Although HHS "welcome[s] comments" on the alternative health identifiers, absent congressional reversal of the underlying statutory mandate the die is largely cast. However, as implementation approaches, greater efforts will be made to soothe the public. Such efforts were apparent in HHS's disingenuous reference to consumers' "confidentiality right"—a "right to communicate with health care providers in confidence and to have the confidentiality of the individually identifiable health care information protected"—proclaimed in November 1997 by the President's Quality Commission. No one knowledgeable of the electronic-database provisions of the 1996 Health Insurance Portability and Accountability Act has objective grounds for believing such rights to be secure any longer under existing statutory law. Indeed, the HHS White Paper itself stated that the President's Quality Commission and the HHS secretary already had "recognized that we must take care not to draw the boundaries of the health care system and permissible uses of the unique identifier too narrowly" (U.S. Dept. of HHS 1998, secs. II[B], II[C]). Given the predilections of federal officials and the proposals at hand, the problem is quite the opposite.

Yet the effort to soothe continues. In late July 1998, after the *New York Times* had publicized the issue, federal officials took steps to distance themselves from the unique health identifier. It was a remarkable display, given that the very language of the statutory provisions involved — including the lack of privacy restrictions — was a Clinton administration creation first unveiled in the reviled 1993 Health Security Act. Nonetheless, on July 31 Vice President Al Gore ceremoniously proclaimed a new White House commitment to a multifaceted "Electronic Bill of Rights" supposed to include, among many other things, restrictions on dissemination of people's medical records. Bowing to public pressure, the vice president said that the administration would not proceed with the unique health identifier until Congress passed appropriate privacy legislation (White House Press Release 1998).[25]

However, if Congress does not pass privacy measures by August 21, 1999, HHS is statutorily bound to proceed. The 1996 legislation stated:

> If legislation governing standards with respect to the privacy of individually identifiable health information ... is not enacted by the date that is 36 months after the date of the enactment of this Act, the Secretary of Health and Human Services shall promulgate final regulations containing such standards not later than the date that is 42 months after the date of the enactment of this Act [P.L. 104–191, sec. 264(c)(1)].

The language mandating unique health identifiers was equally unequivocal, stating that the "Secretary shall adopt standards providing for a standard unique health identifier for each individual ... for use in the health care system" and "shall adopt security standards" and standards to enable electronic exchange of health information (P.L. 104–191, sec. 262[a], sec. 1173). Unless statutory provisions now mandating the national electronic database and "unique health identifiers" are repealed, both will become realities, regardless of the source or efficacy of privacy restrictions and despite predictable political posturing.

Once the medical information is assembled, its likely uses and constituencies will multiply. As early as June 1997, Spragins and Hager reported that "organizations clamoring for unfettered access to the databank include insurers, self-insured employers, health plans, drugstores, biotech companies and law-enforcement agencies." Moreover, as with the U.S. Census, pressure will materialize to expand the scope of the centralized information. Already the National Committee on Vital and Health Statistics has "tentatively recommended that this mother lode of medical information be further augmented by specifics on living arrangements, schooling, gender and race."

The issue is not just privacy; it is government power. Assessing the impact of the new national database and unique health identifiers, Dr. Richard Sobel of Harvard Law School understood that aspect clearly: "What ID numbers do is centralize power, and in a time when knowledge is power, then centralized information is centralized power. I think people have a gut sense that this is not a good idea" (quoted in Stolberg 1998a, A13). Whether that "gut sense" will find effective political voice is the troublesome question.

Tracking Your Child's Education: The National Center for Education Statistics

If centralized information is centralized power, the information now being collected about children's educational performance is especially disturbing. Today federal data collection permeates our educational system, its scope expanded by the 1994 legislation mentioned earlier. As with medical and employment information, in the education system individually identified information is being centralized in linked national electronic databases, and we are again being asked to trust that it will not be misused.

Recent experience in Fairfax County, Virginia, suggests what such legislation has spawned. In January 1997 several Fairfax County school board members "challeng[ed] a planned $11 million computer database that would let schools compile electronic profiles of students, including hundreds of pieces of information on their personal and academic backgrounds." The database would "be used to track students from pre-kindergarten through high school" and "could include information such as medical and dental histories, records of behavioral problems, family income and learning disabilities." The *Washington Post* reported that Fairfax was "considering providing some of the data to a nationwide student information network run by the U.S. Department of Education," possibly making the database "compatible with a nationwide data-exchange program, organized by the Department of Education, that makes student information available to other schools, universities, government agencies and potential employers" (Robberson 1997).

That nationwide data-exchange network — orchestrated by the federal government and extended through the 1994 Goals 2000: Educate America Act; the Educational Research, Development, Dissemination, and Improvement Act; the School-to-Work Opportunities Act; and the Improving America's Schools Act — is now the lifeblood of centralized data collection about American students and preschoolers, creating vast and potentially ill-protected computerized records about children and families throughout America. The data-exchange pathways are (perhaps intentionally) complex, largely connected via the Office of Educational Research and Improvement within the U.S. Department of Education.

That office, administered by the Assistant Secretary for Educational Research and Improvement, stands at the apex of the data-centralization hierarchy, broadly empowered to "collect, analyze, and disseminate data related to education" and charged with "monitoring the state of education" in America.[26] Included within the Office of Educational Research and Improvement are the National Center for Education Statistics, five "national research institutes,"[27] the Office of Reform Assistance and Dissemination, the National Educational Research Policy and Priorities Board, and "such other units as the Secretary [of Education] deems appropriate."[28] Horizontal data linkages between subordinate units in this hierarchy are made explicit by a statutory requirement that the Office of Reform Assistance and Dissemination create an "electronic network" linking most education-related federal offices as well as "entities engaged in research, development, dissemination, and technical assistance" through grants, contracts, or cooperative agreements with the U.S. Department of Education.

The federal education network is further required to be linked with and accessible to other users such as state and local education agencies, providing file transfer services and allowing the Education Department to disseminate, among other things, "data published by the National Center for Education Statistics," a directory of "education-related electronic networks and databases," and "such other information and resources" as the Department of Education "considers useful and appropriate." Sixteen regional "educational resources information center clearinghouses" support the data dissemination, along with the National Library of Education intended to serve as a "one-stop information and referral service" for all education-related information produced by the federal government.[29] Through the School-to-Work Opportunities Act the Labor Department also participates in the data endeavor, its Secretary required to act jointly with the Secretary of Education to "collect and disseminate information" on topics that include "research and evaluation conducted concerning school-to-work activities" and "skill certificates, skill standards, and related assessment technologies."[30]

A spider web of data exchange is the planned outcome. But central to the entire process is the National Center for Education Statistics (the "National Center"), the federal entity most directly and extensively involved in receiving individually identifiable information about American children and their education.

The National Center has statutory authority to "collect, analyze, and disseminate statistics and other information relating to education" in the United States and elsewhere.[31] It is specifically authorized to collect data on such subjects as "student achievement," the "incidence, frequency, seriousness, and nature of violence affecting students" and, still more intrusively, "the social and economic status of children." The clear implication is that schools will be required to obtain information from children and their families on such topics. In addition, to carry out the "National Assessment of Educational Progress" (NAEP), the Commissioner of Education Statistics is authorized to "collect and report data ... at least once every two years, on students at ages 9, 13, and 17 and in grades 4, 8, and 12 in public and private schools" (P.L. 103–382).[32] States participating in the NAEP testing process thus generate additional individually identified student information for the federal government.

Making education data from diverse sources dovetail at the national level is an explicit federal objective. The Commissioner of Education Statistics is authorized to gather information from "States, local educational agencies, public and private schools, preschools, institutions of higher education, libraries, administrators, teachers, students, the general public," and anyone else the commissioner "may consider appropriate"—including other offices within the Department of Education and "other Federal departments, agencies, and instrumentalities" (the IRS, SSA, and federal health-care database authorities come to mind). To facilitate centralization of the data, the commissioner is empowered to establish "national cooperative education statistics systems" with the states to produce and maintain "comparable and uniform information and data on elementary and secondary education, postsecondary education, and libraries" throughout America.[33]

The scope of these databases is so large and their information so personal that even Congress understood the need to genuflect toward privacy and confidentiality. Indeed, the education statutes purport to protect individually identifiable information, directing the federal bureaucracy to "develop and enforce" standards to "protect the confidentiality of persons" in its data collection and publication process. Individually identifiable information is said to be restricted to use for statistical purposes only. In addition, the NAEP provisions prohibit the Commissioner of Education Statistics from collecting data "not directly related to the appraisal of educational performance, achievement, and traditional demographic reporting viables," admonishing the commissioner to insure that "all personally identifiable information about students, their educational performance, and their families" will remain "confidential" (P.L. 103–382, sec. 408). Moreover, the National Center's records—"including information identifying individuals"—are made accessible to a bevy of federal officials and their designees, including the U.S. Comptroller General, the Director of the Congressional Budget Office, and the Librarian of Congress as well as the Secretary of Education, again with the boilerplate admonition that individually identifiable information is to be used only for statistical purposes (P.L. 103–382, sec. 408[b][7]). Separate Department of Education privacy regulations also countenance myriad disclosures without the consent of the subject individuals, among them disclosures made for "routine uses" (one of the major loopholes in the 1974 federal Privacy Act discussed earlier) and those made to another government agency "for a civil or criminal law enforcement activity" authorized by law, and to either house of Congress or to "any committee or subcommittee thereof" with relevant subject-matter jurisdiction.[34]

The family educational Rights and Privacy Act (FERPA) similarly fails to protect individuals effectively against disclosure of student information to the federal government. Although FERPA's rules in general prevent educational agencies and institutions from disclosing personal information about students without their consent, FERPA explicitly permits release of such information to authorized representatives of the U.S. Comptroller General, the Secretary of Education, and state educational authorities whenever individually identifiable records are "necessary in connection with the audit and evaluation of Federally-supported education program[s], or in connection with the enforcement of the Federal legal requirements" related to such programs. In other words, FERPA simply does not protect us against disclosure of student records to the federal government. Again federal bureaucrats are admonished that, unless "collection of personally identifiable information is specifically authorized" by federal law, "any data collected by such officials shall be protected in a manner which will not permit the personal identification of students and their parents by other than those officials, and such personally identifiable data shall be destroyed when no longer needed" for the above purposes.[35] How such destruction could be enforced and electronic copies prevented are unanswered — and unanswerable — questions. The officials themselves have unquestioned access to such personally identified information, without the subject individual's consent. That much the lawmakers intended.

But disclosures beyond those intended by lawmakers are inevitable. Together the statutes have spawned huge databases containing individually identifiable personal and educational information, widely distributed, whose use is supposed to be confined to "statistical" endeavors. The laws don't block the government's collection of individually identifiable information, only its use. The risk analogy cited earlier comes to mind again: giving a teenager keys to a motorcycle, handing him a bottle of liquor, and admonishing him not to drink and drive. Once again we're asking for trouble. Even criminal penalties authorized for individuals convicted of violating confidentiality provisions of the laws do little to assuage legitimate privacy concerns.

Nonetheless, although on one level the shell of protection around this reservoir of personal information is extremely porous, on another level it is dangerously tight. With respect to administrative and judicial review, legislators have built a statutory firewall around the information and its collection — a provision seemingly designed to block ordinary legal oversight while giving nearly total discretion to the Commissioner of Education Statics. The statute states:

> No collection of information or data acquisition activity undertaken by the Center shall be subject to any review, coordination, or approval procedure except as required by the Director of the Office of Management and Budget ... except such collection of information or data acquisition activity may be subject to such review or coordination if the Commissioner determines that such review or coordination is beneficial.[36]

By placing vast discretion regarding collection and distribution of personal information in the hands of a single individual, and by largely preventing citizens from blocking transfer of such information to the central government, these laws again subordinate privacy to the imperative of federal prying into people's private lives. As Electronic Privacy Information Center director Marc Rotenberg remarked concerning compilation of databases on students such as those proposed in Fairfax County, "The Privacy concerns are really extraordinary" (quoted in Robberson 1997).

Tracking Your Bank Account: The Bank Secrecy Act and Its Progeny

Privacy in America is further jeopardized by federal statutory law now requiring banks and other financial institutions to create permanent records of each individual's checks, deposits, and other banking activities. Along with the FDIC's ill-fated proposal in December 1998 to require banks to scrutinize every customer's banking records for evidence of "unusual" transactions—which in effect would have mandated warrantless searches of private financial records—the legislation authorizing those intrusions and the U.S. Supreme Court cases upholding them illuminate the tenuous status of privacy in America today.

The pivotal legislation was the Bank Secrecy Act of 1970 (P.L. 91–508).[37] In the name of assembling banking records with "a high degree of usefulness in criminal, tax, and regulatory investigations and proceedings," Congress empowered the Secretary of the Treasury to require every federally insured bank to create

(1) a microfilm of other reproduction of each check, draft, or similar instrument drawn on it and presented to it for payment; and

(2) a record of each check, draft, or similar instrument received by it for deposit or collection, together with an identification of the party for whose account it is to be deposited or collected ... (P.L. 91–508, sec. 101).

That requirement entailed microfilm records of every detail of every customer's bank account — each check, each deposit — with each account identified by the holder's Social Security number.[38] The statute authorized similar record-keeping to be required of uninsured institutions, including even credit-card companies (P.L. 91–508, sec. 123). Putting further discretionary power in the hands of the Treasury secretary, a simultaneously passed "Currency and Foreign Transactions Reporting Act" required individuals and financial institutions to report the "payment, receipt, or transfer of United States currency, or such other monetary instruments as the Secretary may specify, in such amounts, denominations, or both, or under such circumstances, as the Secretary shall by regulation prescribe."[39] What could not be learned about an individual from such records?

Court challenges quickly arose. In 1974 the U.S. Supreme Court in *California Bankers Association v. Shultz* upheld the constitutionality of the record-keeping requirements of the Bank Secrecy Act against challenges grounded in the First, Fourth, and Fifth Amendments to the U.S. Constitution.[40] Although the Court stated that the act did not abridge any Fourth Amendment interest of the banks against unreasonable searches and seizures, the Court explicitly reserved the question of the Fourth Amendment rights of banks' customers if the banks' records were disclosed to the government as evidence through compulsory legal process. The Court stated that "claims of depositors against the compulsion by lawful process of bank records involving the depositors' own transactions must wait until such process issues" (416 U.S. 51–52). Dissenting, Justice Marshall stated:

> The plain fact of the matter is that the Act's record-keeping requirement feeds into a system of widespread informal access to bank records by Government agencies and law enforcement personnel. If these customers' Fourth Amendment claims cannot be raised now, they cannot be raised at all, for once recorded, their checks will be readily accessible, without judicial process and without any showing of probable cause, to any of the several agencies that presently have informal access to bank records [416 U.S. 96–97].

Justice Marshall added that it was

> Ironic that although the majority deems the bank customers' Fourth Amendment claims premature, it also intimates that once the bank has made copies of a customer's checks, the customer no longer has standing to invoke his Fourth Amendment rights when a demand is made on the bank by the Government for the records,

calling the majority's decision a "hollow charade whereby Fourth Amendment claims are to be labeled premature until such time as they can be deemed too late" (416 U.S. 97).

Justice Marshall's "hollow charade" assessment was vindicated two years later by the Court's 1976 decision of *United States v. Miller*.[41] Stating flatly that depositors have "no legitimate 'expectation of privacy'" in their bank records, the Court held that the "depositor takes the risk, in revealing his affairs to another, that the information will be conveyed by that person to the Government," a conclusion not altered by the fact that the Bank Secrecy Act mandated creation of the records (425 U.S. 442–443). Accordingly, the Court held that a depositor's Fourth Amendment rights were not abridged by the government's acquisition of account records from his banks as part of a criminal prosecution, even if the subpoena for the documents was defective.

The case was too much for even Congress to stomach. In response to *U.S. v. Miller*, Congress in 1978 passed the Right to Financial Privacy Act ("Financial Privacy Act"), attempting to restore some protection of personal financial records in the wake of the Bank Secrecy Act's forced disclosures.[42] The central idea of the Financial Privacy Act was to prevent federal government authorities from obtaining personal financial records held by banking institutions unless either the customer authorized the disclosure or the bank was responding to a properly issued subpoena, administrative summons, search warrant, or "formal written request" by a government authority.[43]

In broad outline, the act prohibits banks from disclosing personal financial records maintained pursuant to the Bank Secrecy Act unless the federal authority seeking those records "certifies in writing to the financial institution that it has complied" with the Financial Privacy Act.[44] That certification may be based on any of the listed rationales, including a federal official's "formal written request," the lenient prerequisites for which potentially undermine the statute's core objectives. Such a request requires mere government assertion that "there is reason to believe that the records sought are relevant to a legitimate law enforcement inquiry," accompanied by government notification of the bank customer at his last known address.

But "law enforcement inquiry" is used as a term of art in the statute. Defining it to include any "official proceeding" inquiring into a failure to comply with a "criminal or civil statute or any regulation, rule, or order issued pursuant thereto," the statute explicitly includes the broad sweep of federal regulatory matters and thereby radically expands the bank records that can be targeted and disclosed in the name of "law enforcement inquiry." Moreover, the notification requirement can be met simply by mailing a copy of the request to the targeted bank customer "on or before the date on which the request was made to the financial institution." Unless the individual then takes specific steps to resist the disclosure by filing and substantiating a motion with a U.S. District Court within fourteen days from the date when the request was mailed, the bank is permitted to give the government the records it wants. Once obtained by federal authorities, the bank records can be shared with other federal agencies or departments if the transferring entity certifies in writing that there is "reason to believe that the records are relevant to a legitimate law enforcement inquiry within the jurisdiction of the receiving agency or department."[45] In light of such procedural impediments to private resistance and the magic words "law enforcement activity" that allow countless channels of federal access to personal bank records, it is clear in whose favor the deck is stacked.

Besides the looseness evident in these statutory provisions, two other major problems pervade the Financial Privacy Act: its specific exclusions and, more generally, the unreliability of Congress as protector of financial privacy. Sixteen listed "exceptions" to the Financial Privacy Act allow government authorities to avoid its provisions in a wide variety of circumstances.[46] In addition, the act allows government authorities to obtain emergency access to financial records from banks and other financial institutions if they declare that "delay in obtaining access to such records would create imminent danger of —(A) physical injury to any person; (B) serious property damage; or (C) flight to avoid prosecution," provided that the government authority subsequently files in court a sworn statement by a supervisory official and provides notification as specified in the act.[47]

These exceptions, along with the porosity of the statute's strictures, make the Financial Privacy Act weak grounds for protection from unwarranted federal scrutiny of personal bank transactions. No surprise. Surely we cannot expect federal officials who still claim power to order third-party microfilming of our personal banking records to always show delicate restraint in using them. Yet we continue to rely on Congress— the very source of the initial privacy breach — to formulate laws supposed to protect our financial privacy. As obliging Congresses cobble together loose statutes such as the Right to Financial Privacy Act, we now know that even such porous protections can be withdrawn, our financial privacy utterly destroyed, without constitutional objection from the U.S. Supreme Court. In such circumstances, congressional architects of the nationwide structure of bank records now threatening our financial privacy are unlikely to provide reliable protection.

Government as Privacy Protector?

In 1974 Congress passed the omnibus Privacy Act, cited earlier in this article, to regulate disclosure of personal information by federal agencies. Even that long ago, Congress recognized the damage that federal record-keeping and disclosure could do, as lawmakers made explicit in the following "findings" accompanying the act:

(1) the privacy of an individual is directly affected by the collection, maintenance, use, and dissemination of personal information by Federal agencies;

(2) the increasing use of computers and sophisticated information technology, while essential to the efficient operations of the Government, has greatly magnified the harm to individual privacy that can occur from any collection, maintenance, use, or dissemination of personal information;

(3) the opportunities for an individual to secure employment, insurance, and credit, and his right to due process, and other legal protections are endangered by the misuse of certain information systems;

(4) the right to privacy is a personal and fundamental right protected by the Constitution of the United States; and

(5) in order to protect the privacy of individuals identified in information systems maintained by Federal agencies, it is necessary and proper for the Congress to regulate the collection, maintenance, use, and dissemination of information by such agencies.[48]

Despite that clear acknowledgment of the federal threat to personal privacy, the 1974 Privacy Act — riddled with exceptions and counterbalanced by disclosure mandates in the Freedom of Information Act[49] —failed to fulfill the promise these declarations seemed to hold. The Electronic Frontier Foundation was unequivocal in its 1994 assessment, stating that in meritorious cases "it is extremely difficult for individuals to obtain relief under the ... Privacy Act" and calling the act's bias in favor of government record keepers "one of the most ugly faces of privacy" (quoted in Prowda 1995, 749–50).

No stronger proof of the act's failure could be given than the fact that all of the privacy-destroying measures discussed in this article were initiated or sustained after the Privacy Act's adoption and are deemed compatible with its mandates. The federally required expansion of use of Social Security numbers, the federal databases of "new hires," the employment-authorization databases, the federal mandates for a national electronic database of personal health information and "unique health identifiers," the expanded federal collection of individually identified educational information, the continued federal requirement that financial institutions microfilm our checks and deposits in case the federal government desires to examine them — all of these intrusions now coexist with a law ostensibly assuring our privacy vis-à-vis the federal government's "collection, maintenance, use, and dissemination" of personal information.

In 1988, as people became increasingly alarmed about government centralization of personal information, Congress sought to strengthen the Privacy Act by adding the "Computer Matching and Privacy Protection Act."[50] Again, however, the statutory privacy protections amounted to less than met the eye, creating procedural hurdles rather than firm obstacles to database matching. The 1988 act continued to allow such matching provided that a "computer matching program" was "pursuant to a written agreement between the source agency and the recipient agency" that met specified procedural requirements. Recent federal database matching activities through the "new hires" database, pilot programs for work authorization, child-support enforcement programs, and other programs confirm that the 1988 act provided scant impediment to the ongoing federal data quest.

Today, federally required databases of personal information continue to proliferate. One measure of their current scope is that, in the Code of Federal Regulations, the index entry under the heading "Reporting and record-keeping requirements" is itself sixty-two pages long! Information on such a scale would not be collected unless federal officials planned to use it to change private behavior — social behavior, economic behavior, political behavior. Far from innocuous, this data collection and the intensity of its pursuit reveal the enormous value placed on such intelligence by federal officials. Representative Jim McDermott (D., Washington), one of the few members of Congress who actively resisted the 1996 authorization of a national electronic database for health care, recently stated, "There is no privacy anymore," adding that "it has been eroded in so many ways that you can find out almost anything about anybody if you know how to work the computer well enough" (quoted in Stolberg 1998a, A13).

Legislation aside, the personal behavior of government officials offers little hope that they can be trusted to behave ethically with respect to the personal data now at their fingertips. Republicans and Democrats alike succumb to temptation when the stakes are perceived to be high enough. Republican President Richard Nixon in 1971 expressed his intention to select an IRS commissioner who "is a ruthless son of a bitch, that he will do what he's told, that every income tax return I want to see I see, that he will go after our enemies and not go after our friends" (quoted by Wall Street Journal Board of Editors 1997). It has been widely reported that Democratic President Bill Clinton, for similar reasons, apparently sanctioned illegal transfer of nine hundred or more FBI files to the White House. And, ironically, federal agencies such as the IRS have routinely used privacy legislation to shield evidence of their own misdeeds (Davis 1997, 164–168). Does anyone contemplating today's ubiquitous federal collection of personal data still imagine that political leaders cannot and will not abuse this system for their own ends? Each passing administration demonstrates anew Sobel's succinct observation that "centralized information is centralized power" (Stolberg 1998a, A13).

The converse is also true: with today's technology, centralized power is centralized information. Substantive powers of government spawn correlative record-keeping powers; as federal power grows, so does related data collection. Personal freedom accordingly gives ever more ground to expanding government responsibility. Given these inevitable tendencies, Solveig Singleton (1998a) proposed a better way to protect privacy:

> The better model for preserving privacy rights and other freedoms in the United States is to restrict the growth of government power. As the federal

government becomes more entangled in the business of health care, for example, it demands greater access to medical records. As tax rates grow higher and the tax code more complex, the Internal Revenue Service claims more power to conduct intrusive audits and trace customer transactions. Only holding back the power of government across the board will safeguard privacy — and without any loss of Americans' freedom.

Of course, the Founders tried to hold back the power of government through the U.S. Constitution. As H. L. Mencken (]1940] 1990) explained:

[Government] could do what it was specifically authorized to do, but nothing else. The Constitution was simply a record specifying its bounds. The fathers, taught by their own long debates, knew that efforts would be made, from time to time, to change the Constitution as they had framed it, so they made the process as difficult as possible, and hoped that they had prevented frequent resort to it. Unhappily, they did not foresee the possibility of making changes, not by formal act, but by mere political intimidation — not by recasting its terms, but by distorting its meaning. If they were alive today, they would be painfully aware of their oversight [350].

As I have shown elsewhere (Twight 1988, 1994), that avoidance of the formal amendment process has been an integral part of the political transaction-cost manipulation undergirding the twentieth-century expansion of federal authority and the corresponding erosion of individual liberty.

Though fiercely concerned about privacy, for decades Americans have allowed the juggernaut of federal data collection to roll on, unmindful of Albert J. Nock's ([1939] 1991) insight that "whatever power you give the State to do things for you carries with it the equivalent power to do things to you" (274). Public passivity on this issue reflects the usual politico-economic forces, central among them high costs of resistance exacerbated by federal officials' manipulation of political transaction costs. As we have seen, in repeated instances privacy-jeopardizing provisions have been hidden in omnibus bills hundreds of pages long, making it difficult for lawmakers, let alone citizens, to see them and react before they become law. Misinformation has also helped, especially when uncritically repeated by the media — the appealing justifications, the ignored data-collection authority. In the case of the 1996 Health Insurance Portability and Accountability Act, despite outspoken efforts in 1996 by Representative McDermott and several other legislators to publicize the extraordinary threat to privacy contained in the provisions for a national electronic database, neither Congress nor the media spread the story. Although some didn't know, some definitely did. Yet, two years later, face-saving untruths or careless reporting further obscured the events of 1996. When the "unique health identifier" story was reported in 1998 as breaking news, the Associated Press, for instance, uncritically reiterated statements attributed to an unnamed "Republican congressional aide" claiming that "members of Congress did not recognize the privacy implications of what they had done until media reports about the issue came out this week" (Associated Press 1998).

So easily assuaged, so vulnerable to political transaction-cost manipulation, individuals who prize liberty and privacy even now are celebrating a spurious victory regarding the unique health identifier, apparently comforted by Vice President Gore's commitment to an "Electronic Privacy Act." But Gore's own press release, though it notes a raft of new controls the administration would like to place on private businesses' use of personal information, is nearly silent regarding *government* use of personal information, stating only an intention to "launch a 'privacy dialogue' with state and local governments" that will include "considering the appropriate balance between the privacy of personal information collected by governments, the right of individuals to access public records, and First Amendment values" (White House Press Release 1998). With existing statutes and regulations usurping personal privacy more aggressively with each passing day, it is much too late for a bureaucratically mired "privacy dialogue."

Those invasive statutes and regulations are today's reality. The government data collection they now authorize would have seemed unimaginable in an America whose citizens once boldly, meaningfully proclaimed individual freedom. Indeed, what important personal information is *not* now at the fingertips of curious federal officials? Centralized power is centralized information, and centralized information is centralized power. The usual consequences are well known: "As history has shown, the collection of information can have a negative effect on the human ability to make free choices about personal and political self-governance. Totalitarian regimes have already demonstrated how individuals can be rendered helpless by uncertainty about official use of personal information" (Schwartz 1995, 307; footnote omitted).

Reducing central government power is the only alternative to such helpless dependence. Whether that alternative can be realized is a more complex question. As government data-collection mandates proliferate and encryption issues loom larger, those who cling to government as privacy's bulwark might well reflect on John Perry Barlow's statement that "trusting the government with your privacy is like having a peeping Tom install your window blinds."[51] As Bernadine Healy (1998) wrote regarding unique health identifiers and the national medical record database, the "Government does a lot of things well, but keeping secrets is not one of them."

References

Associated Press. 1998. Congress Won't Delay Medical Identification Law. Posted by Cable News Network ( ), July 23.

Bovard, James. 1997. The Dangerous Expansion of Forfeiture Laws. *Wall Street Journal*, December 29, p. A11.

Brinkley, Joel. 1998. Gore Outlines Privacy Measures, but Their Impact is Small. *The New York Times* on the web, August 1.

Davies, Simon G. 1994. Touching Big Brother: How Biometric Technology Will Fuse Flesh and Machine. *Information Technology & People 7* (4).

Davis, Shelley L. 1997. *Unbridled Power: Inside the Secret Culture of the IRS.* New York: HarperCollins.

Forbes, Steve. 1997. Malpractice Bill. *Forbes*, October 6, p. 27.

Gupte, Pranay, and Bonner R. Cohen. 1997. Carol Browner, Master of Mission Creep. *Forbes*, October 20, pp. 170-77.

Healy, Bernadine. 1998. Hippocrates vs. Big Brother. *New York Times*, July 24, p. A21.

Mencken, H. L. 1940. The Suicide of Democracy. In *The Gist of Mencken: Quotations from America's Critic*, edited by Mayo DuBasky. Metuchen, N.J.: Scarecrow Press, 1990.

Miller, John J., and Stephen Moore. 1995. A National ID System: Big Brother's Solution to Illegal Immigration. *Cato Policy Analysis* no. 237 (September 7). Washington, D.C.: Cato Institute (http://www.cato.org).

Miller, Theodore J. 1998. Look Who's Got Your Numbers. *Kiplinger's Personal Finance Magazine*, July, p. 8.

Minor, William H. 1995. Identity Cards and Databases in Health Care: The Need for Federal Privacy Protections. *Columbia Journal of Law and Social Problems* 28 (2): 253-96.

Moore, Stephen. 1997. A National Identification System. Testimony before the U.S. House of Representatives, Subcommittee on Immigration and Claims, Judiciary Committee, May 13. (Available on the Internet at http://www.cato.org/testimony/ct-sm051397.html).

Nock, Albert Jay. March 1939. The Criminality of the State. In *The State of the Union: Essays in Social Criticism*, edited by Charles H. Hamilton. Indianapolis, Ind.: Liberty Fund, 1991.

Pear, Robert. 1997. Government to Use Vast Database to Track Deadbeat Parents. The New York Times on the Web, September 22.

_____. 1998. Not for Identification Purposes. (Just Kidding.) The New York Times on the Web, July 26.

Pilon, Roger. 1998. High Court Reins in Overweening Government. *Wall Street Journal*, June 23, p. A20.

Prowda, Judith Beth. 1995. Privacy and Security of Data. *Fordham Law Review* 64:738-69.

Robberson, Tod. 1997. Plan for Student Database Sparks Fears in Fairfax. *Washington Post*, January 9, p. A01 (www.washingtonpost.com)

Roosevelt, Franklin D. 1943. Executive Order 9397: Numbering System for Federal Accounts Relating to Individual Persons. *Code of Federal Regulations*, Title 3, pp. 283-84. November 22.

Schwartz, Paul. 1992. Data Processing and Government Administration: The Failure of the American Legal Response to the Computer. *Hastings Law Journal* 43 (part 2): 1321-89.

_____. 1995. The Protection of Privacy in Health Care Reform. *Vanderbilt Law Review* 48 (2): 295-347.

Simons, John. 1998. Gore to Propose Consumer-Privacy Initiative. *Wall Street Journal*, July 31, p. A12.

Singleton, Solveig. 1998a. Don't Sacrifice Freedom for "Privacy." *Wall Street Journal*, June 24, p. A18.

_____. 1998b. Privacy as Censorship: A Skeptical View of Proposals to Regulate Privacy in the Private Sector. *Policy Analysis* no. 295 (January 22). Washington, D.C.: Cato Institute.

Spragins, Ellyn E., and Mary Hager. 1997. Naked before the World: Will Your Medical Secrets Be Safe in a New National Databank? *Newsweek*, June 30, p. 84.

Srodes, James A. 1998. Protect Us from Environmental Protection. *World Trade*, July, pp. 14-15.

Stolberg, Sheryl Gay. 1998a. Health Identifier for All Americans Runs Into Hurdles. *New York Times*, July 20, pp. A1, A13.

_____. 1998b. Privacy Concerns Delay Medical ID's. The New York Times on the Web, August 1.

Twight, Charlotte, 1988. Government Manipulation of Constitutional-Level Transaction Costs: A General Theory of Transaction-Cost Augmentation and the Growth of Government. *Public Choice* 56: 131-52.

_____. 1994. Political Transaction-Cost Manipulation: An Integrating Theory. *Journal of Theoretical Politics* 6(2): 189-216.

_____. 1998. Medicare's Progeny: The 1996 Health Care Legislation. *Independent Review* 2(3): 373-99.

U.S. Department of Health and Human Services. 1998. Unique Health Identifier for Individuals: A White Paper. Washington, D.C.: U.s. Government Printing Office, July 2.

U.S. Department of Transportation, National Highway Traffic Safety Administration. 1998. State-Issued Driver's Licenses and comparable Identification Documents; Proposed Rule. *Federal Register* 63 (116), June 17, pp. 33219-33225; *Code of Federal Regulations*, Title 23, Part 1331.

Wall Street Journal Board of Editors. 1997. Politics and the IRS. *Wall Street Journal*, January 9, p. A10.

White House Press Release. 1998. Vice President Gore Announces New Steps toward an Electronic Bill of Rights. July 31.

Wolfe, Claire. 1997. Land-Mine Legislation. Posted by America-Collins, http://www.america-collins.com (Internet); america-collins@america-collins.com (E-mail); 5736 Highway 42 North, Forsyth, Georgia 31029, 912-994-4064 (office).

Notes

1. Government collection of trade data and business information is not discussed here. Those important aspects of government data collection were highlighted recently by the Environmental Protection Agency's expansion of its "Toxic Release Inventory" to require businesses to report production data so detailed that Kline and Co. (a member of the Society of Competitive Intelligence Professionals) judged its impact as "the equivalent of having the U.S. voluntarily turn over its code book to its enemies" in wartime (quoted in Gupte and Cohen 1997, 176). Posting the information on its Internet Web site, the EPA "overrode heated industry protests and made it easy for corporate trade secret thieves to make off with billions of dollars' worth of America's most proprietary trade secrets" (Srodes 1998, 14). See also 15 U.S.C. sec. 4901–4911 (1998); 15 U.S.C. secs 175–176, 178, 182 (1997).

2. See also Singleton (1998b). The 1990 U.S. Census form required respondents to answer questions about their ancestry, living conditions (including bathroom, kitchen, and bedroom facilities), rent or mortgage payment, household expenses, roommates and their characteristics, in-home telephone service, automobile owner-ship, household heating and sewage systems, number of stillbirths, language capabil-ity, and what time each person in the household usually left home to go to work during the previous week. The form stated that "By law [Title 13, U.S. Code], you're required to answer the census questions to the best of your knowledge," adding that the infor-mation requested "enable[s] government, business, and industry to plan more effectively." Nowhere did it state that, in sec. 221, Title 13 of the U.S. Code also specifies a maximum penalty of $100 for someone who chooses not to answer. See U.S. Dept. of Commerce, Bureau of the Census (1990), Form D-2 (OMB No. 0607–0628).

3. Schwartz 1992, 1356, n. 165.

4. See also Pear 1998. Some people seemed reluctant to admit what was being done with SSNs. When I wrote to complain about usage of my SSN as my "account number" on my federally insured student loan, a "loan servicing representative" from Academic Financial Services Association (AFSA) replied: "Your AFSA account number is not your social security number since it begins with a portfolio num-ber SM 799 B followed by 10 digits"—despite the fact that my Social Security num-ber constituted the next nine of those digits (letter of June 11, 1986).

5. *Privacy Act of 1974*, Public Law 93–579 (December 31, 1974), 88 Stat. 1896. Codified to 5 U.S. Code sec. 552a (1996).

6. *Tax Reform Act of 1976*, Public Law 94–455 (October 4, 1976), 90 Stat. 1525, at 90 Stat. 1711–1712. This law also made mandatory use of the SSN for fed-eral tax purposes a matter of statutory law rather than IRS regulation. See Minor (1995, 264–265) on this point.

7. See, for example, Public Law 105-34 (August 5, 1997), Title X, sec. 1090(a)(2), 111 Stat. 961, 962, which amended the statute governing the Federal Par-ent Locator Service to provide that "Beginning not later than October 1, 1999, the information referred to in paragraph (1) [42 U.S.C. sec. 653(b)(1), governing "Dis-closure of information to authorized persons"] shall include the *"names and social security numbers of the children of such individuals"* and further that the *"Secretary of the Treasury shall have access to the information* described in paragraph (2) [42 U.S.C. sec. 653(b)(2)] for the purpose of administering those sections of Title 26 which grant tax benefits based on support or residence of children" (emphasis added). See also 42 U.S.C. secs. 651–652 for relevant AFDC provisions.

8. *Omnibus Consolidated Appropriations Act, 1997*, Public Law 104–208 (Sep-tember 30, 1996), 110 Stat. 3009; *Illegal Immigration Reform and Immigrant Respon-sibility Act of 1996*, Public Law 104–208, Division C (September 30, 1996), 110 Stat. 3009–546 ff.

9. U.S. Department of Transportation (1998). In a passage that would make the Framers' blood boil, the Department of Transportation's explanation of the pro-posed rule notes that "States must *demonstrate compliance* with the requirements of the regulation by submitting a certification to the National Highway Traffic Safety Administration" (emphasis added).

10. *Illegal Immigration Reform and Immigrant Responsibility Act of 1996* [here-after 1996 Immigration Reform Act], Public Law 104–208, Division C (September 30, 1996), 110 Stat. 3009–546 ff., at 110 Stat. 3009–716, sec. 656(a).

11. *Ibid.*, sec. 657. Virtually identical language was included in Public Law 104–193 (August 22, 1996), section 111, 110 Stat. 2105 ff.

12. Miller and Moore (1995) reported that Drexler Technology Corporation recently had patented an "optically readable ID card ... [that] can hold a picture ID and 1,600 pages of text," cards that could be mass-produced for less than five dollars each.

13. H.R. 231 (January 7, 1997), 105th Congress, 1st Session, a proposed bill "To improve the integrity of the Social Security card and to provide for criminal penalties for fraud and related activity involving work authorization documents for purposes of the Immigration and Nationality Act." Section 1(c) of the bill states: "NOT A NATIONAL IDENTIFICATION CARD — Cards issued pursuant to this section shall not be required to be carried upon one's person, and nothing in this section shall be construed as authorizing the establishment of a national identification card."

14. *Code of Federal Regulations*, Title 20, Chap. III, Subpart C, sec. 401.120 (April 1, 1997).

15. *Ibid.*, sec. 401.25.

16. Schwartz 1992, 1367, 1369. Schwartz cites Jerrold Brockmyre, Director, Michigan Office of Child Support Enforcement, as quoted in Nancy Herndon, "Garnish: Dad," *Christian Science Monitor*, November 28, 1988, p. 25.

17. *Job Training Partnership Act*, Public Law 97–300 (October 13, 1982), 96 Stat. 1322; Public Law 102–367, sec. 405(a) (September 7, 1992), 106 Stat. 1085.

18. *Personal Responsibility and Work Opportunity Reconciliation Act of 1996*, Public Law 104–193 (August 22, 1996), 110 Stat. 2105.

19. Although it contains information about all working individuals, the National Directory of New Hires is housed within the federal government's "Federal Parent Locator Service."

20. P.L. 104–208, at 110 Stat. 3009–662, referencing *U.S. Code*, Title 8, sec. 1324a(a)(1)(A). See also *U.S. Code*, Title 8, sec. 1324a(e)(4).

21. P.L. 104–208, sec. 403(b), 110 Stat. 3009–662 ff. See also sec. 656(b) of the same act, 110 Stat. 3009–718, discussed earlier ("state-issued drivers licenses and comparable identification documents").

22. *Workforce Investment Act of 1998*, Public Law 105–220 (August 7, 1998), 112 Stat. 936 ff., at sec. 309, 112 Stat. 1082–1083; emphasis added.

23. Moore added: "I have worked in Washington for fifteen years mainly covering the federal budget, and I have never encountered a government program that didn't work — no matter how overwhelming the evidence to the contrary."

24. *Health Insurance Portability and Accountability Act of 1996*, Public Law 104–191 (August 21, 1996), 110 Stat. 1936 ff.

25. See also Simons (1998); Stolberg (1998b); Brinkley (1998).

26. *Educational Research, Development, Dissemination, and Improvement Act of 1994*, Public Law 103–227, Title IX (March 31, 1994), 108 Stat. 212 ff., sec. 912.

27. These include the National Institute on Student Achievement, Curriculum, and Assessment; the National Institute on the Education of At-Risk Students; the National Institute on Educational Governance, Finance, Policy-Making, and Management; the National Institute on Early Childhood Development and Education; and the National Institute on Postsecondary Education, Libraries, and Lifelong Education. See *ibid.*, sec. 931.

28. *Ibid.*, sec. 912.

29. *Ibid.*, sec. 941(f) (clearinghouses); sec. 951(d) (national library of education). The statute also amended federal vocational education legislation to require state boards of higher education to provide data on graduation rates, job placement

rates, licensing rates, and high school graduate equivalency diploma (GED) awards, to be "integrated into the occupational information system" developed under federal law. *Ibid.*, sec. 991.

30. *School-to-Work Opportunities Act of 1994*, Public Law 103–239 (May 4, 1994), 108 Stat. 568 ff., sec., 404.

31. The functions of the National Center for Education Statistics were amended by the *Improving America's Schools Act*, Public Law 103–382, Title IV (October 20, 1994), 108 Stat. 4029 ff., sec. 401 ff., at sec. 403. Title IV of the *Improving America's Schools Act* was entitled the *National Education Statistics Act*.

32. *National Education Statistics Act of 1994*, Public Law 103–382, Title IV (October 20, 1994), 108 Stat. 4029 ff., sec. 404 ("violence"), sec. 411 ("grades 4, 8, and 12").

33. *Ibid.*, sec. 405 ("may consider appropriate"), sec. 410 ("uniform information").

34. *Code of Federal Regulations*, Title 34, Subtitle A (July 1, 1997), sec. 5b.9.

35. *Family Educational Rights and Privacy Act*, Public Law 93–380, Title V, sec. 513 (August 21, 1974), 88 Stat. 571, as amended. Codified as *U.S. Code*, Title 20, sec. 1232g (1998). See 20 U.S.C. sec. 1232g(b)(3) and sec. 1232g(b)(1)(C).

36. *National Education Statistics Act of 1994*, Public Law 103–382, Title IV (October 20, 1974), 108 Stat. 4029 ff., sec. 408(b)(4). See also sec. 408(a)(1), which states "No person may ... permit anyone other than the individuals authorized by the Commissioner to examine the individual reports."

37. Public Law 91–508, Title I (October 26, 1970), 84 Stat. 1114. The FDIC's notice of proposed rulemaking may be found in *Federal Register*, Vol. 63, No. 234 (December 7, 1998), pp. 67529–67536. Withdrawal of that notice by the FDIC was announced in: *Federal Register*, Vol. 64, No. 59 (March 29, 1999), p. 14845. The FDIC received 254,394 comments on the proposed mandate for "Know Your Customer" programs, of which only 105 favored the proposed rule.

38. Although the Bank Secrecy Act's power extended to microfilming all checks and deposits, early on the Secretary of the Treasury decided to mandate microfilming of checks and deposits of $100 or more.

39. The *Currency and Foreign Transactions Reporting Act* constituted Title II of the same statute: Public Law 91–508, Title II (October 26, 1970), 84 Stat. 1118 (see sec. 221, sec. 222). The act also required detailed reporting regarding monetary instruments of $5,000 or more received from or sent to individuals in places outside the United States. Regarding the federal government's exuberance in applying forfeiture penalties under this statute, see Pilon 1998 and Bovard 1997.

40. *California Bankers Association v. Shultz*, 416 U.S. 21, 39 L.Ed.2d 812, 94 S.Ct. 1494 (April 1, 1974).

41. 425 U.S. 435, 48 L.Ed.2d 71, 96 S.Ct. 1619 (April 21, 1976).

42. *Right to Financial Privacy Act*, Public Law 95–630, Title XI (November 10, 1978), 92 Stat. 3697 ff., codified to *U.S. Code*, Title 12, sec. 3401 ff.

43. *Ibid.*, sec. 3402.

44. The Act also permits financial institutions to notify government authorities of information "which may be relevant to a possible violation of any statute or regulation," but such information is confined to identifying information concerning the account and the "nature of any suspected illegal activity." *Ibid.*, sec. 3403.

45. *Ibid.*, sec. 3401 ("law enforcement inquiry"), sec. 3408 (notification by mail), sec. 3412 (sharing records with other agencies).

46. *Ibid.*, sec. 3413. These include, inter alia, disclosure to the IRS pursuant to the Internal Revenue Code; disclosure pursuant to "legitimate law enforcement inquiry respecting name, address, account number, and type of account of particular customers;" disclosure pursuant to "Federal statute or rule promulgated thereunder;" disclosures pursuant to "consideration or administration" of Government loans or loan guarantees; disclosure sought to implement withholding taxes on Federal Old-Age, Survivors, and Disability Insurance Benefits; and disclosure to the Federal Housing Finance Board or Federal home loan banks.

47. *Ibid.*, sec. 3414(b). Moreover, the Financial Privacy Act does not apply to state or local government attempts to gain access to these records. See *U.S. v. Zimmerman*, N.D. W.Va., 957 F. Supp. 94 (1997).

48. *Privacy Act of 1974*, Public Law 93–579 (December 31, 1974), 88 Stat. 1897, sec. 2(a). Codified to *U.S. Code*, Title 5, sec. 552a (1998).

49. Public Law 89–554 (September 6, 1966), 80 Stat. 383, as amended. Codified to *U.S. Code*, Title 5, sec. 552 (1998).

50. Public Law 100–503 (October 18, 1988), 102 Stat. 2507–2514, sec. 2. Codified at *U.S. Code*, Title 5, sec. 552a(o).

51. John Perry Barlow, co-founder of the Electronic Frontier Foundation, is quoted in Prowda 1995 (765, citing Jeff Rose, "Right to E-mail Privacy Would Seem Self-Evident, *San Diego Union Tribune*, March 1, 1994 [Computerlink], p. 3, as the source of the Barlow quotation).

National ID: Our Line in the Sand

Claire Wolfe

Should the American people draw a line in the sand? Should they say to their government: "This far, no more"? In this article, a column originally written for the online edition of Backwoods Home Magazine *(November 2001), writer Claire Wolfe argues that if the American people accept national ID, they will have unwittingly destroyed their liberty. Her most recently published book was co-authored with Aaron Zelman and is titled* The State vs. The People *(Hartford: Mazel Freedom Press, Inc., 2001). The original article can be found online at http://www.backwoodshome.com/columns/wolfe0111.html.*

"If you don't have anything to hide, it's not a problem."
"It'll help stop terrorism and illegal immigration."
If you hold either of those views about national ID, for the sake of your own future I hope you'll reconsider.
"Sure it's obnoxious. But get real; we already have a national ID system. It's called our driver's license. Or Social Security. What they're talking about now is just a technical refinement."
If you hold that view, you're right — as far as it goes. But things are going to go a lot farther.
If we accept national ID, we'll all have a problem. We won't be one bit safer from violence. And we will have crossed a crucial line that forever divides the free from the unfree.

What They're Proposing

National ID isn't a new idea. American politicians and bureaucrats have been proposing it since the Great Depression. "Infallible" national ID has been proposed over the years as a means of fighting communism, illegal immigration, crime, census undercounting, terrorism, welfare fraud, voting fraud, and a variety of other disasters du jour.

Until now, Americans have always said no to being forced to show "Your papers, please!" on demand. But since the catastrophe of September 11, polls say as many as 87 percent of us may be willing to submit to a nationwide, biometric ID system.

Larry Ellison, CEO of the giant database company Oracle, has been the chief cheerleader for the proposed system, which would require us to carry a card containing a scannable "smart chip," and would identify us through a combination of our Social Security number, fingerprint, and retinal pattern or facial-recognition scan (this is called biometrics— measuring of our biological characteristics). Ellison admits that from its inception the accompanying federal ID database would give government agencies, and anyone else with access, instant information on our "places of work, amounts and sources of income, assets, purchases, travel destinations, and more."[1]

President Bush is reported as not favoring national ID. But statements coming out of the White House have been non-committal — of the "we're keeping all options open" variety. Dozens of high-level government officials, including Sen. Dianne Feinstein and Attorney General John Ashcroft, do favor the scheme.

At first the cards wouldn't be mandatory — at least not in Ellison's plan. But even in the "voluntary" system, anyone who "chose" not to present a national ID card and submit to biometric scans on demand would be subject to invasive body searches at airports and extensive, humiliating, time-consuming questioning at checkpoints about his identity, plans, motives, and activities. Everyone without approved ID would, in short, be treated as a criminal suspect.

If the system became legally mandatory, those refusing to cooperate could also be arrested, jailed and fined.

There's an alternative plan in the works. The American Association of Motor Vehicle Administrators (AAMVA) has been striving for years to get biometric national ID implemented by stealth — by having states, under federal mandate, convert their own IDs and drivers licenses to biometric form, then linking all 50 state databases into a nationwide system. They have partially succeeded by getting congressional leaders to plant small, hidden "landmines" in large bills passed by Congress since 1996.

The AAMVA announced in November 2001 that it was "working closely" with the new Office of Homeland Security to implement a mandatory biometric system through state licensing agencies. And this system would be mandatory.

Why Is This a Problem?

Well, so what? The United States isn't Nazi Germany — which used a computerized national ID system to round up Jews and other "undesirables" and send them to slave labor and death. (This "civilized" bureaucratic process behind the Nazi slaughter is icily documented in Edwin Black's 2000 book, *IBM and the Holocaust.*) So what's the big deal?

The *very* big deal is "mission creep." When Social Security numbers were introduced in the 1930s, the system was "voluntary." Citizens who worried about the biblical number of the Beast (Rev. 13: 16-18) or more mundane forms of tyranny were assured that, by law, the number would never — ever — be used for ID.

In the tradition of nearly every limited, temporary, or voluntary government program our Social Security number eventually became our universal identifier. No law requires you to get a Social Security number, even today. But try functioning in the everyday world of work, banking, credit, schooling, home-buying, or even video rental without one.

If national ID becomes U.S. law, five years from now you won't be able to do any of these things without submitting to various biometric scans. But that's barely the beginning.

The new, more high-tech national ID system would enable the federal government and its contractors to follow and electronically analyze your activities in real-time — to pinpoint your location, check your purchases, view records of your medical condition, and monitor your bank deposits and withdrawals as you make them, for instance. Worse yet, it ultimately gives government the ability to *control* your activities — to (accidentally or deliberately) freeze your bank account, shut down your credit cards, deny you access to public transportation, forbid you entry into such public places as county courthouses, deny you health care, even deny you entrance to your job once your employer has (in the name of standardization, and possibly with the spur of federal subsidies or regulations) adopted the federal system. All at the click of a computer key, somewhere in Washington, D.C.

Does this sound too much like something out of the movie "Enemy of the State"?

But remember, you're dealing with a federal government that already forbids professional licenses, drivers licenses, and even fishing licenses not to known terrorists, criminals, or illegals — but to ordinary parents who get behind in child support. Just think what it could do to with the *instant* ability to monitor and cut off access to transportation or services for a variety of disobedient or "questionable" people.

It could happen to you if you're a "deadbeat dad," if you've neglected some traffic tickets, if you fit the "profile" of a drug user or a gun owner, if you've stated too many controversial opinions on the Internet, if your activities appear "suspicious" by any mysterious standard, if you've made political enemies— or even if there's a glitch in the system. And have you ever tried to straighten out even a little glitch with a government agency? Good luck to you.

This is still only the beginning. Shortly (after too many people have misplaced their cards, and too many criminals continued to get useable ID), the card-borne "smart chip" would be replaced by an implanted chip — one of which, Digital Angel, is already on the market.[2] Periodic scanning could then be augmented by 24-hour-a-day, satellite-based tracking. People in the U.S. will be watched and controlled far more thoroughly than Winston Smith was controlled by Big Brother in *1984* — and for the very same reasons; to impose some social manager's ideal of order.

The second big deal is self-ownership. Maybe you don't believe the scenario I just spelled out. You know the U.S. government is judicious and benevolent, and that it would only monitor, not control us.

Before you say, "It's no problem if you have nothing to hide," consider this:

If you catch your neighbor peeking through a knothole in the fence, you're offended — even if your neighbor merely sees you drinking a glass of iced tea. If you came home and found that same neighbor going through your bank statements, credit card records, school transcripts, medical records, and travel itineraries in your desk, you'd be livid, and you'd probably call the cops— again, even if your financial and personal life was pure as new snow. Why? Because your neighbor has stepped over a line; he has violated the psychic and physical territory that belongs only to you.

Where did the government acquire the authority to freely inspect your life? What legitimate law enforcement or security purpose is served by surveiling the innocent?

The question isn't what do you have to hide but why is the government so persistently determined to find out everything about you.

The third big deal is that national ID violates your rights

When you have to prove your identity to government agents on demand, you're being treated as a criminal — and your Fifth and Sixth Amendment rights are being trashed.

When you have to produce identity papers on demand, you're being searched illegally. If you're "detained" until you prove your identity, you're being seized illegally. Both are violations of the Fourth Amendment.

If you must give information that could get you prosecuted (for instance, the information that you're not carrying your national ID), you're being forced to provide evidence against yourself— a Fifth Amendment violation.

If your religion forbids universal numbering, your First Amendment rights are being broken by national ID.

And by extending its authority into areas forbidden to it by the Constitution, the federal government violates the Ninth and Tenth Amendments.

Is it worth it to you, to gain national ID and lose all these historic protections?

Worse. Your loss of freedom won't do *anything* to make you safe

Random surveillance may help criminals and terrorists. Even before the September 11 attacks, commentators such as Daniel Pipes of the Middle East Forum and former CIA operative Reuel Marc Gerecht had warned that reliance on mass electronic surveillance and neglect of hard, culturally aware field work, was causing U.S. intelligence agencies to overlook years of extensive planning by terrorists.[3]

Mass surveillance catches the unwary — ordinary people who may engage in unpopular political activities, have innocently "suspicious" patterns of behavior, or who accidentally violate obscure technical provisions of law. Mass surveillance might also catch petty larcenous (and not very bright) criminals. But serious criminals — and that includes international terrorists — take precautions against random spying. Thus, they get away with planning murder while the National Security Agency is overloaded, scanning your e-mails for "dangerous" words and while the FBI's Carnivore gobbles up millions of useless records of worldwide Web surfing habits.

National ID — with its on-the-spot links to vast databases of material covering your financial activities, skills, travels, and interests — is simply more of the same, only with faster, more detailed, more widespread reporting. It targets YOU without protecting you from them.

Criminals, terrorists, and illegal immigrants will still get useable fake ID. We're supposed to believe that when we present that card and subject ourselves to the accompanying biometric scans, we're proving beyond all doubt that we're who we say we are.

Well, we're not doing that.

And even if we were, so what?

Anybody who wants it badly enough and is able to pay the price will still get fake ID — even biometric national ID.

Want proof? When the AAMVA succeeded in getting its last round of "foolproof" ID imposed via state drivers licensing agencies in the mid-1990s, an entire industry developed in which employees of government licensing agencies sold "real" ID to illegal immigrants and criminals — complete with scannable, verifiable database entries, real fingerprints, real digitized photos, and plausible but non-existent Social Security numbers.

Social Security employees have also been caught selling "real" SSNs, complete with "real" database entries, to illegal immigrants, including at least one terrorism suspect.

Exactly that same thing will happen with *any* ID system — no matter how sophisticated or allegedly secure it is. (Naturally fake ID will always be available. How do you think the CIA, FBI, DEA, IRS, et al. manage to provide "cover" identities for their secret agents? Well-heeled criminals will simply imitate the methods originated by government intelligence agencies.)

Terrorists will still get *genuine* ID. Thousands of foreign agents (and potential suicide attackers) will continue to get *real* U.S. ID — as at least 13 of the 19 September 11 hijackers did. A well-funded terrorist organization or foreign government with long-term plans to harm the U.S. would simply insert into this country, entirely "clean" agents — idealistic students, legitimate contractors or diplomats, all with unobjectionable records — who would be fully qualified to obtain genuine U.S. national ID. Once possessing "foolproof" biometric ID, such people would lay low, live their lives peaceably, and pass any ID scan — until the day they set off their backpack nukes or released their smallpox infections upon the populace.

National ID? It won't stop a determined enemy for a moment. But future failures of the "foolproof" national ID system will be the justification for the implanted subcutaneous chip and perpetual satellite tracking — which in turn will be compromised by criminals, terrorists, and rogue governments.

Violence will actually increase. One day, Americans will wake up to discover that all their freedoms have been destroyed in the name of "saving freedom." They're going to be furious.

But by then national ID and all its noxious consequences will be firmly entrenched. No pragmatic Congress is going to repeal them. No chronically insecure security agency is going to give up its newfound centralized control. No giant corporation is going to say, "Oh, we'll gladly dismantle our multi-billion-dollar money-making surveillance systems."

After all, if it took nearly 30 years to get rid of our National Tea Tasting Board after Richard Nixon singled it out in the media as a prime example of stupid waste, who's going to get rid of anything as "useful" to bureaucrats, enforcers, statisticians, and social managers as national ID — even if it's completely ineffective in making us safe?

Eventually, frustrated, fed-up, angry Americans will strike back — violently and with the fury of people who have nothing left to lose. And they, too, can do that while bearing their nationalized identities — real or fake — when they are serious and desperate enough.

Why it's going to be so hard to draw the line

How do we stop this? There are too few influential people listening and too many actively on the other side.

In all probability, the ID system will be imposed gradually — either one state at a time under quiet federal mandate, or nationally but "voluntarily."

That way, Congresspeople can more easily say, "National ID? Don't be silly; we don't have national ID! We're just 'enhancing identity protection' to make America safe."

And millions of Americans will simply yawn and change the channel.

There's a broad, indefinite line that separates a free nation from a police state. On one side of that line, the people control the government. On the other, the government controls the people. We've been veering toward that line and into it for decades now. But with national ID we'll have crossed it decisively.

So what do you do about it?

Freedom lovers labor under a handicap. We are almost unfailingly burdened with a sense of civic responsibility that — given the ruthlessness and machinations of our opponents— is laughable. We practice the methods of American Government 101— polite letters to uncaring congresspeople, labors wasted on the campaigns of craven oath breakers— while they vote at midnight for bills they haven't read and trade our freedom for the momentary pleasure and power of the deal. Faceless bureaucrats write the laws, implement, interpret, and enforce them while elected officials posture, preen, and pretend to be the representatives they long ago ceased to be.

Believing we can politely influence such power seekers is rather like believing we can reason with men who fly airplanes into buildings.

But what's the alternative?

Certainly, we must educate ourselves and anyone else who will listen that national ID is a problem, and potentially the most dangerous one Americans will ever face. We need numbers, informed brains, and determined spirits.

We must still try to tell our *soi disant* leaders that we forbid national ID. The way to do this is not to beg them or our freedom, but to warn them of the consequences of stealing our freedom. To whatever extent we communicate with our alleged representatives (and it's best to do this in public forums and in the media, where others who care might hear), we should make it absolutely clear that this is a line-in-the-sand issue — that we won't tolerate the standard political trickery or typical dodges ("Oh, goodness, I had no idea *that* was hidden in that must-pass appropriations bill"). First, we must warn them that any vote for national ID is a vote that could get them thrown out of office, regardless of anything else in their record. (Then we have to back that, which is the hard part.) We must make it clear — in a responsible way — that rebellion and resistance will follow if national ID is imposed. Don't make specific threats to commit illegal activity and don't recommend specific illegal activities to others unless you're willing to bear the legal consequences; focus in the abstract on American's historic refusal to accept tyranny.

Prepare to resist — and prepare for the consequences of resistance. It will be the job of truly patriotic — not just flag-waving patriotic — Americans to break any national ID system thrust upon us.

If national ID and tracking is imposed, people who value freedom will need to ensure that the databases are full of such garbage that the system can't function usefully and that the scanners are constantly non-operative. The more flamboyant among us will need to stage public confrontations (anything from sit-down strikes to surround the scanners, to wearing of Groucho glasses and chemical defacing of fingerprints, to playful acts of public-protest theater, as many groups now perform in front of streetside facial-recognition cameras).

Ultimately, millions will need to refuse to accept the card — even if it means loss of jobs, travel restrictions, jail, or worse. Right now, few have that will. If enough understand the long-term consequences of national ID, we might — it's our only hope — develop the courage that comes from understanding.

It isn't nice. It isn't safe. But if you want to see something really ugly and really dangerous — stand by and give the federal government the means to control your daily life.

And have a nice *1984*.

Notes

1. Ellison, Larry. "Smart Cards: Digital IDs Can Help Prevent Terrorism." *WSJ.com Opinion Journal*, October 18, 2001. (Originally appeared in the *Wall Street Journal*, October 8, 2001) Found at http://www.opinionjournal.com/extra/?id=95001336. NOTE: By early 2002, the George W. Bush administration had shot down the Ellison ID plan. However, by the summer of 2002, the administration (via its Homeland Security plan), the American Association of Motor Vehicle Administrators, and the Department of Transportation (via a stunning advancement in its CAPPS passenger profiling system) were already in the process of implementing a system similar to the Ellison proposal. For instance, CAPPS, which has profiled airline passengers since 1998, has been expanded to the point where it can check your credit records and purchasing habits to learn whether you meet the profile of a terrorist. According to the government's analysis and algorithms, doing something as innocent as purchasing a pizza and paying for it by credit card is evidence that you may be a terrorist.

2. Since the original publication of this article, Digital Angel, a tracking chip, has been joined by the VeriChip. The VeriChip is specifically designed to be implanted under your skin. Although at present it holds only ID, it was created to carry medical records and other fairly extensive data on your life.

3. See Pipes, Daniel. "Mistakes Made the Catastrophe Possible." *Wall Street Journal*, September 12, 2001. Found at http://interactive.wsj.com/articles/SB1000270817760286077.htm. And Gerecht, Reuel Marc. "The Counterterrorist Myth." *The Atlantic*, July/August 2001. Found at http://www.theatlantic.com/issues/2001/07/gerecht.htm.

The Australia Card:
Campaign of Opposition
Simon Davies

Proposals for identity (ID) cards have provoked public outrage and polit-
ical division in several countries. In this essay Simon Davies analyzes the key
elements of public opposition to ID Card schemes, and profiles the massive 1987
Australian campaign against a national ID card. Simon Davies is founder of
Privacy International, and author of numerous books and articles on privacy
and surveillance issues. This essay is found on the website of Privacy Interna-
tional at: http://www.privacyinternational.org/issues/idcard/campaigns/html.

Following the announcement of an official identity card scheme, there
is inevitably a public debate. Such debate often occurs as a three-stage process:

During the first stage of the debate, a popular view is usually expressed
that identification, per se, is not an issue related to individual rights. When
an identity card is proposed, the public discussion is initially focused on the
possession and use of the card itself. At this level of debate, the perceived
benefits of ID dominate discussion. People often cannot see past the idea of
a card being used strictly for purposes of verification of identity (banks, public transport, travel etc.). Invariably, at this early stage of awareness, support
for ID cards is high. The device is perceived as an instrument to streamline
dealings with authority.

The second stage of public debate is marked by a growing awareness of
the hidden threats of an identity card: function creep, the potential for abuse
by authorities, the problems arising from losing your card. Technical and
organizational questions often arise at this level of discussion. As for the
question of abuse by authorities (i.e. routine ID checks by police) a common
response is still "I have nothing to hide, so I have nothing to fear."

The final level of discussion involves more complex questions about rights and responsibilities. At this stage, the significance of the computer back-up and the numbering system come into the picture.

Most public opposition to administration strategies such as numbering systems, identity cards or the census are structured around an organized campaign of negative imagery (Big Brother) and a more systematic process of public education. In the Netherlands and German anti-census movements, and in the campaign against the Australia Card, hostile imagery sat comfortably alongside a strong intellectual foundation of opposition.

To the organizers of a campaign, the imagery is important. No government assurances can counteract hysteria. The intangible arguments against national ID cards often include:

• A fear that the card will be used against the individual
• A fear that the card will increase the power of authorities
• A feeling that the card is in some way a hostile symbol
• A concern that a national ID card is the mechanism foretold in Revelations (the Mark of the Beast)
• A fear that people will be reduced to numbers— a dehumanizing effect
• A rejection of the card on the principle of individual rights
• A sense that the government is passing the buck for bad management to the citizen

The tangible concerns that tend to create a more powerful long-term campaign focus are:

• Any card system needs rules. How many laws must be passed to force the citizenry to use and respect the card?
• A card or numbering system may lead to a situation where government policy becomes "technology driven" and will occur increasingly through the will of bureaucrats, rather than through law or public process
• Practical and administrative problems that will arise from lost, stolen or damaged cards (estimated at up to several hundred thousand per year)
• Will the system create enough savings to justify its construction? If the system fails, can it be disassembled?
• To what extent will the system entrench fraud and criminality? What new opportunities for criminality will the system create?
• What are the broader questions of social change that relate to this proposal? How will it affect my children?

Concerns over the potential abuse of ID cards by authorities are supported by the experience of countries which have such cards. Complaints of harassment, discrimination and denial of service are, in some countries, quite common.

The issue of privacy, which is central to concern about ID cards, tends to embrace all political philosophies. Concern over identity cards is as strong on the right as it is on the left. Libertarians and Conservatives believing that a card will increase the power of government, tend to dislike the notion. The left is often split on the issue, but contains a significant number who fear card systems on the basis of human rights.

It is, of course, true that a large number of people will support an ID card in the belief that it will solve many problems of fraud and criminality. Whether a Parliament accepts the notion is another matter. In Australia and New Zealand, MPs have crossed the floor and resigned from their party over this issue. And even when only a minority of the public opposes the card, they do so with vehemence.

It cannot be taken for granted that the public will automatically support the ID card concept. The Australian public took almost two years to protest against the card proposal. Within two months of the New Zealand announcement, hundreds of people were protesting in public. The reaction cannot be predicted.

The United States has always viewed the introduction of ID cards as a fundamental attack on the relationship between authorities and the citizen, and therefore, a proposal that is politically unsustainable.

The government of Ireland recently abandoned plans to establish a national numbering system and ID card.[1] The Data Protection Commissioner for Ireland, Donal Linehan, objected vehemently to the proposal. While acknowledging the importance of controlling fraud, the Commissioner observed that the proposal posed "very serious privacy implications for everybody."[2]

Anatomy of an Anti-ID Card Campaign — The Australian Experience

ID card systems are often made appealing to the public by being marketed as "service cards," offering access to a range of facilities and benefits. The cards are also often marketed as voluntary instruments, thus neutralizing perhaps the key plank of any potential campaign of opposition.

These factors have contributed to the dearth of opposition in recent years to card systems. The specter of an Orwellian Big Brother society has also diminished since the fateful year 1984, and apocalyptic scenarios of information brutality by an information-bloated State have also been treated with more skepticism than in the past. Information Technology has been absorbed by the public.

Over the past ten years, opposition of ID cards has been confined to a handful of countries. French authorities have encountered opposition to their efforts to make cards machine-readable. German authorities have run up against public and constitutional barriers in establishing a national numbering system for the German ID card. The Philippine ID card ran aground in 1991 because of cost factors which were made public through a campaign of opposition by human rights groups. The New Zealand public also opposed the Kiwi Card.

The campaign which stands out, however, is the one which stopped the proposed Australia Card. This movement, the largest in recent Australian history, forced a dissolution of the parliament, a general election, and unprecedented divisions within the Labour government. The issues which were raised in this campaign provide important insights into the range of concerns related to ID cards in every country.

THE AUSTRALIA CARD

To the older generation of Australians, the idea of a national identity card was not novel. Australians were given an identity card during the Second World War. This scheme, similar to the British identity card, relied on the imposition of rations as an incentive for registration and production of the card, and it was dropped soon after the hostilities had ended.[3]

Thirty years passed before the idea of a national identity card was again raised. Three government reports[4] suggested that the efficiency of the Commonwealth Government could be increased, and fraud better detected, through the use of an ID card system. Two Cabinet Ministers of the Fraser Government were reported as viewing such a proposal as politically unworkable, and the idea went no further.[5]

The Australia Card's genesis can be traced to the early 1980s, with widespread concern about tax evasion and tax avoidance. Coupled with concerns over the extent of welfare fraud, there was a belief expressed in some quarters that an identity card or national registration procedure might assist the government's administration processes. Fears over the extent of illegal immigration added fuel to these suggestions.

The identity card idea was then raised at the national Tax Summit in 1985 (initially by Labor MP David Simmons and later by the chief executive of the Australian Taxpayers Association[6]) and found its way into legislation the following year. Playing on patriotism, the government called it the "Australia Card" (it later became widely known as the "UnAustralia Card and the Aush-tralia Card).

The Australia Card was to be carried by all Australian citizens and permanent residents (separately marked cards would be issued to temporary residents and visitors). They would contain a photograph, name, unique number, signature and period of validity, and would have been used to establish the right to employment. It would be necessary for the operation of a bank account, provision of government benefits, provision of health benefits, and for immigration and passport control purposes.

The plan consisted of six components:

• REGISTER: A central register containing information about every member of the population, to be maintained by the Health Insurance Commission (HIC).

• CODE: A unique numerical identifier to be given to every member of the population, and assigned by the HIC.

• CARD: An obligatory, multi-purpose identification card to be issued by the HIC to every member of the population.

• OBLIGATIONS: The law would require all individuals to produce the card for a variety of reasons, and would require organizations to demand the card, apply sanctions to people who refused to do so, and to report the data to the government.

• USE: The number and the Australia Card register were to be used by a variety of agencies and organizations as their administrative basis.

• CROSS NOTIFICATION: Agencies using the system would be required to notify each other of changes to a person's details.[7]

Despite the extraordinary change that the plan was likely to prompt in the relationships within the Australian Community, the proposal caused hardly a ripple of concern. Early opinion polls showed a seventy percent public support for the scheme.

Not everyone was enthusiastic about the plan. A handful of journalists ran occasional stories raising questions about the proposal. The parliamentary opposition opposed the plan. Most significantly, a small number of committed academics and advocates worked to provide a critical analysis of the scheme and its implications.

As early as July 1985, the Privacy Committee of NSW, a government agency, devoted a special issue of its "Privacy Bulletin" to the ID card, warning that the proposal encompassed grave dangers for liberty in Australia. The Committee's view was that this proposal was more than a mere identification procedure. It was, said the Committee, a tool for the centralization of power and authority within the government.

Legal centers, civil liberties councils, academics and advocates joined the opposition to the ID card plan. Over the next two years, a strong intellectual foundation was developed.

In one of the earliest critiques of the ID card proposal (January 1986) Professor Geoffrey de Q Walker, now dean of law at Queensland University, observed:

One of the fundamental contrasts between free democratic societies and totalitarian systems is that the totalitarian government relies on secrecy for the regime but high surveillance and disclosure for all other groups, whereas in the civic culture of liberal democracy, the position is approximately the reverse.[8]

Australian data protection expert Graham Greenleaf, one of the pioneers of the anti ID card push, warned:

Is it realistic to believe that the production of identity cards by children to adults in authority to prove their age will be "purely voluntary?" The next generation of children may be accustomed to always carrying their cards, to get a bus or movie concession, or to prove they are old enough to drink, so that in adult life they will regard production of an ID card as a routine aspect of most transactions.[9]

As the Australia Card Bill was subjected to increasing scrutiny, the surveillance nature of the scheme received more attention. Greenleaf described the components of the Australia Card as "the building blocks of surveillance." The most obvious of those building blocks were the card, the unique number, the Australia Card Register (containing all the information and acting as an information exchange) and the telecommunications links between different agencies and arms of the Card scheme.

Not so obvious, however, were the extensive reporting obligations throughout the government and the community, the automatic exchange of information throughout the government, weak data protection, the ease of legislative expansion of the system, and the effective encouragement of the private sector and state governments to make use of the card's number.

Advocates pointed out that whilst it is true that some civil law countries (Spain, France etc.) have an ID card, none would have been as intrusive or dangerous as the one proposed by the Australian Government. The Australia Card would have gone much further than the mere identification purpose of ID cards in other countries. It would have created a central information register that would touch many aspects of a person's life.

At the end of 1985, the Opposition controlled Senate forced the appointment of a Joint Select Committee to investigate the proposal. The Committee raised a wide spectrum of concerns that eventually came to haunt the government. The majority of the Committee, including one government member, came down against the proposal, warning that the scheme was speculative and rubbery, and that all common law countries had rejected such proposals.[10] The fact that no common law country has accepted an ID was crucial to the whole debate over the Australia Card.

Rather than supporting the Australia card option, the Committee's report recommended a number of reforms to Departmental practices and information management. The government ignored the findings of the Select Committee, and proceeded with its proposal.

A self-proclaimed "unholy alliance" was formed in Victoria between such figures as the Builders Labourers Federation, Norm Gallagher, Western

Mining Corporation chief Hugh Morgan, civil liberties leader Ron Castan and popular singer Peter Garrett, and had placed advertisements in National publications. Several organizations also publicly opposed the Card, including the libertarian Adam Smith Club and Centre 2000, the NSW and Victorian Councils for Civil Liberties, the NSW branch of the Australian Computer Society, and a number of left wing trade unions. Three academics, Roger Clarke, Professor Geoffery de Q Walker and Graham Greenleaf, provided powerful and persuasive analysis of the government's proposals. The arguments against the card were seldom reported by media, who appear to have generally been persuaded by the government's revenue arguments.

The committee's report formed the basis of the Parliamentary Opposition's rejection of the scheme. On two occasions the Government presented the legislation to the Senate, where it does not have a majority, only to see the bill rejected. After the second rejection by the Senate, the Government used the issue as the trigger to employ its constitutional right to call an election on the ID card legislation, and to call a joint sitting of parliament, where it would have had a majority.

As things turned out, the election campaign of July 1987 contained almost no reference to the ID card issue. In the opinion of the media, the ID card was simply not on the agenda.[11] The government was re-elected and promptly re-submitted the ID card legislation.

Until then, few Australians had taken any notice of the proposal. A rally in Sydney's Martin Place convened by Democrat Senator Paul McLean, succeeded in attracting less than a hundred people.[12] People held concerns privately, but were reluctant to express these fears lest they be branded "friends of tax cheats" (as the government had already labeled the parliamentary opposition).

Three weeks after the election, the fortunes of the Australia Card were reversed. On 28th July 1987, seventeen people from wildly different edges of the political spectrum met to plot the card's demise. The meeting involved well-known libertarians, communists, mainstream political party leaders, media figures, and business, farming and community leaders.[13]

The meeting established a trust (later to be called the Australian Privacy Foundation) and resolved to form a campaign as a last ditch effort to fight the card. The almost complete absence of media interest demanded a publicity stunt, and the group decided to launch its campaign in the Ballroom of Sydney's plush Sebel Town House.[14]

The key element in the campaign launch was the diversity of speakers. Right wing broadcaster Alan Jones, Democrat leader Janine Haines, America's Cup hero Ben Lexcen and rock singer Peter Garrett provided an unprecedented mix of famous talent, and the launch enjoyed saturation coverage. Ben Lexcen threatened to leave Australia forever if the scheme proceeded. Peter Garrett called it "the greatest threat Australia has ever faced."[15]

Once these well known figures had stated their opinion, other highly respected Australians rapidly joined the condemnation of the scheme. Former Westpac Bank chairman Sir Noel Foley stunned his colleagues with the blunt assessment that the card would pose "a serious threat to the privacy, liberty and safety of every citizen." Australian Medical Association president Dr. Bruce Shepherd went as far as to predict, "It's going to turn Australian against Australian. But given the horrific impact the card will have on Australia, its defeat would almost be worth fighting a civil war for." Fuelled by the unique alliance, newspapers and talk-back shows recorded a logarithmic increase in public concern.

More Australians joined the Privacy Foundation to voice protest at the scheme. Right wing academic Professor Lauchlan Chipman, communist author Frank Hardy, former Whitlam Government minister Jim McClelland, and left wing economist Professor Ted Wheelwright all linked arms with their ideological foe to fight the scheme.

Within weeks, a huge and well-organized movement was underway. Rallies were organized on almost a daily basis. Although these were described as "education nights" the reality was that most were hotbeds of hostility rather than well ordered information giving sessions.

The strength of public feeling was never more clear than on the night of September 14, when 4,000 angry people crammed the AMOCO hall in the central New South Wales town of Orange. One in eight of the cities population attended the meeting. Other towns responded in a similar way.

The massive wave of public outrage was generated by scores of ad-hoc local and regional committees from coast to coast. Rallies formed on a daily basis, culminating in a gathering of 30,000 outside Western Australia's Parliament House. The Australian Privacy Foundation, which had organized the campaign, had planned rallies in Sydney and Melbourne that were tipped to have sealed off the Central Business District.

The passion of those weeks reached the point of open civil disobedience. The Labor caucus came close to violence on one occasion,[16] while public demonstrations against the ID card began to turn nasty.[17]

The letters pages of most newspapers reflected the strong feelings of Australians. "We won't be numbers!" was a typical letters page headline, with others such as "I have no intention of applying," "An alternative is the ball and chain," "Biggest con job in our history," "Overtones of nazi Germany," "I will leave the country" and "Passive resistance gets my vote."[18] The cartoonists contributed to the strong feelings, with some constantly portraying then Prime Minister Robert Hawke in Nazi uniform.

Historian Geoffrey Blainey compared the extraordinary protest to the Eureka Stockade. "The destruction of the licenses at Ballarat, and the stand at Eureka Stockade was a rebellion against the erosion of personal liberty associated with the Australia Card of that era."[19] The card had touched a nerve in the national psyche by cutting across what many saw as the national character.

A major national opinion poll conducted in the closing days of the campaign by the Channel Nine television network resulted in a ninety percent opposition to the card. The normally staid *Australian Financial Review* produced a scathing editorial which concluded "It is simply obscene to use revenue arguments ('We can make more money out of the Australia Card') as support for authoritarian impositions rather than take the road of broadening national freedoms."[20]

Within weeks of its commencement, the campaign had galvanized Australia against the Card. Despite elements of hysteria, the average Australian came to understand that the introduction of such a scheme would reduce freedoms and increase the power of authorities. Indeed, "freedom" would come to mean the freedoms granted by the card. As the *Financial Review* had so eloquently observed, Australia's rights and freedoms are far more fragile than those of older counterparts. A government should be committed to strengthening those freedoms.

As news of the specifics of the ID card legislation spread, the campaign strengthened. If you were in employment without an ID card, it would be an offense for your employer to pay you (penalty $20,000). If you were then forced to resign, you could not get a new job, as the law would make it a offense for an employer to hire a cardless person (penalty $20,000). A person without an ID card would be denied access to a pre-existing bank account, and could not cash in investments, cannot give money to or receive money from a solicitor, or could not receive money in unit, property or a cash management trust.

Cardless people could not buy or rent their own home or land (penalty $5,000), nor would benefits be paid to the unemployed, widows, supporting parents, the aged, the invalid or the sick.

If your card is destroyed for any reason than cannot be proven as accidental, the penalty would be $5,000 or two years imprisonment or both. A $500 penalty would be imposed if you lost your card and failed to report the loss within twenty-one days. Failure to attend a compulsory conference if ordered to by the ID card agency would result in a penalty of $1,000 or six months' gaol. Failure to produce your ID card on demand to the Tax Office would invoke a penalty of $20,000.

By this time, the Card's architect, the Health Insurance Commission was well and truly on the nose. Talk back radio hosts had become fond of quoting a paragraph of an HIC planning document on the Australia Card:

"It will be important to minimize any adverse public reaction to implementation of the system. One possibility would be to use a staged approach for implementation, whereby only less sensitive data are held in the system initially with the facility to input additional data at a later stage when public acceptance may be forthcoming more readily."[21]

The campaign organizers stressed the pseudo-voluntary nature of the card. Whilst it was not technically compulsory for a person to actually obtain a card, it would have been extremely difficult to live in society without it. Indeed, the government actually coined the term "pseudo-voluntariness" to describe its aspirations.

By mid-September, the government was facing an internal crisis. The left of the party had broken ranks to oppose the card[22] while right wing members (particularly those in marginal seats) were expressing concern within caucus.[23] Deputy Prime Minister Lionel Bowen urged the Party to tread with caution, and suggested that a re-think may be necessary.[24]

Within weeks, in the face of mass public protests, a party revolt and civil disobedience, the government scrapped the ID card proposal. It was provided with the convenient face-saver of a technical flaw in the legislation revealed by opposition senator John Stone. The government had the option of re-introducing the legislation, but did not do so. Journalists reported that the government was overwhelmed with joy that the flaw had been discovered.

The Hawke Government made several key mistakes in its preparations for the Australia Card scheme. First, it had made assumptions about the right of government that simply did not match community expectations. People felt that the government did not have a mandate to do as it pleased. Second, the resort to patriotism (calling this the Australia Card) was resented hotly. Finally, and perhaps most important, the government was simply not able to establish that it and its law enforcement agencies could be trusted with the mechanism.

The sophistication of public debate was highly developed. Letters to the newspapers and calls to radio stations put the argument that with the implementation of the card, the onus of proof in day-to-day transactions would be reversed. Trust within society would be replaced by the demand for formal identification. The government appeared unable to understand people's concern that there would emerge a shift in the balance of power in the relationships between citizen and the state. According to academic experts and privacy advocates leading the campaign, the card would suffer "function creep" and would find its way into many aspects of life. These were fears that could never be countered by government assurances.

There can be little doubt that, in addition to the problems listed above, several very substantial privacy and data protection fears were established. These included matters of data security, function creep, incursions related to data matching, improper use and disclosure of data, erroneous data, the establishment of central control and tracking, and the possible development of an "internal passport." Coupled with the government's inability to establish that the system would actually tackle major problems such as the underground economy, even the most conservative government supporters became skeptical.

There was a very real fear in the Australian community in 1987 that the fundamental balance of power was shifting. Justice Michael Kirby, President of the New South Wales Court of Appeal, observed, "If there is an identity card, then people in authority will want to put it to use.... What is at stake is nothing less than the nature of our society and the power and authority of the state over the individual."[25]

Notes

1. Announced in the 1989–1993 *Programme For Government* document.

2. *Commissioner's Annual Report*, 1991, p.2, 42.

3. James Rule, *Private Lives and Public Surveillance; Social Control in the Computer Age*, Schocken Books, 1974. Supra note 3.

4. Asprey, Australian Government Publishing Service (AGPS) *Report of the Taxation Review Committee* (1975), Mathews (AGPS) *Report on Inflation and Taxation* (1975), Campbell (AGPS) *Report on the Australian Financial Systems*, (1975).

5. Peter Graham, "The Australian Card: A Technology Driven Policy?" 45, (1990). Unpublished M. Phil thesis. Griffith University, Brisbane.

6. Roger Clarke, "The Resistible Rise of the National Personal Data System," *Software Law Journal*, Chicago, February 1992, p. 36.

7. *Ibid.*, p. 38.

8. Geoffrey de Q Walker, "Information as Power," CIS Policy Forum (Centre for Independent Studies) January 22, 1986.

9. *Law Society Journal*, Sydney, October 1987.

10. *Report of the Joint Select Committee on an Australia Card*, AGPS, Canberra, 1986.

11. Neither the government nor the opposition raised the ID card as a key issue during the election campaign.

12. June 1987.

13. An account of this meeting was published in the *Sydney Morning Herald* on October 5, 1987.

14. The launch took place on August 28, 1987.

15. These comments were published in an Australian Privacy Foundation booklet entitled "Why the ID Card Must Be Stopped NOW."

16. *The Australian*, September 23, 1987.

17. *The Australian*, September 24, 1987, reported that a car carrying the Western Australian Premier was attacked by demonstrators in Perth, and required police assistance.

18. *West Australian*, September 12, 1987.

19. *Daily Sun*, Brisbane, September 8, 1987.

20. *The Australian Financial Review*, August 28, 1987.

21. Health Insurance Commission, *Planning Report of the Health Insurance Commission*, February 26, 1987.

22. *Daily Telegraph*, Sydney, September 8, 1987.

23. *The Sun Herald*, Sydney, September 13, 1987.

24. *Daily Telegraph*, Sydney, September 19, 1987.

25. In evidence to the Joint Select Committee on an Australia Card, 1986.

The Social Security Number in America: 1935–2000

Robert Ellis Smith

This chapter documents the six-decade trend towards a national identify-ing number. It tells the story of the history of the Social Security number and of the attempts to create a national ID document. Robert Ellis Smith is a lawyer, journalist, and publisher, since 1974, of Privacy Journal *newsletter. He is also an "advocate for increased privacy protection, and an expert in credit report-ing, electronic surveillance, medical confidentiality, and all aspects of personal property." This essay is taken from his book* Ben Franklin's Web Site: Privacy and Curiosity from Plymouth Rock to the Internet *(Providence: Privacy Jour-nal, 2000), pp. 284–308. Footnotes have been deleted.*

From the beginning, most Americans have been vigilant about the dan-gers of being enumerated by their government. The mounting demands for enu-meration since 1936 perhaps prove only that they have not been vigilant enough.

The possibility of a national enumeration system arose seriously for the first time with enactment in August 1935 of a nationwide government pen-sion program, to take effect the next year. This would involve deducting taxes from workers' regular paychecks, depositing the funds in Washington, and then dispersing monthly pension checks to retirees. To make the system work, everybody would have to be issued a number. Or so it was assumed at the time.

Recent immigrants were the ones most concerned; those from Europe were well aware of the latent dangers of a system of enumerating or regis-tering all citizens. The Nazi regime, after all, had located targets of their ter-ror by using various registration systems already in place in the nations they occupied. An Italian immigrant to America told his children, "They are going to require a number for all of us. There goes our family name, it will no longer be important."

"The invention of permanent, inherited patronyms ["last names"] was the last step in establishing the necessary preconditions of modern statecraft.... Fearing, with good reason, that an effort to enumerate and register them could be a prelude to some new tax burden or conscription, local officials and the population at large often resisted such campaigns." Yale University scholar James C. Scott, in *Seeing like a State: How Certain Schemes to Improve the Human Condition Have Failed*," 1998.

In addition, there was simply something in the American spirit that abhorred being known as a number. It was dehumanizing and impersonal, regimented. Many religious fundamentalists feared national registration because of the Biblical threats that pestilence and plague might follow.

The United Mine Workers and the United Steelworkers both expressed a different fear: that Social Security account numbers could be used by companies to blacklist pro-union men and women involved in the labor strife at the time. The unions, in fact, persuaded friendly officials in Franklin D. Roosevelt's New Deal Administration to include in the Social Security Act of 1935 a provision allowing an individual to replace an existing Social Security number with a second one when "showing good reasons for a change," a provision that remains in the law.

The new pension system marked the first time in the United States that a government agency would be required to collect and use personal information from most of the population. This would be unlike the data collection by the Bureau of the Census, which aggregates its individual data once it collects it and makes no decisions based on the information that affect individuals. For the first time, Americans would be asked to register with their government. No wonder there was such unease among the public.

It was unlike previous military conscription programs, as well, which had affected only men in their twenties, and only in wartime. It is true that thousands of rioters in New York City objected to the military draft of 1863 because a man could pay $300 to avoid it or could pay someone to go to war in his place. The bloody riots were a reaction to the unfairness of the system and the racist overtones of the way that it was administered. They were not a reaction to the idea of conscription itself. America's first military registration requirement in "peacetime" was to come in 1940.

In the election year of 1936, Congressional Democrats defended their government-run innovation, and Republicans stressed the disadvantages of the idea — that it would mean lower take-home pay. A week before the election the Republican National Committee flooded employers with millions of official-looking inserts for pay envelopes warning of the deduction to come in the first paycheck of the New Year.

But it became clear that the trickiest part of the task of implementing a radical pension program would not be assuring the public about the new payroll deduction, but persuading Americans to register.

And so the bureaucrats never mentioned the word. "The process was called 'assignment of social security account numbers' instead of 'registration,'" recalled Arthur J. Altmeyer, who was FDR's acting chair of the Social Security Board at the time of creation. "The use of the word 'registration' was avoided because it might connote regimentation. An analogy was drawn between the issuance of a social security account card and the issuance of a department store credit card, which was the only form of credit card in common use at the time."

The notion of a government-run registration was so abhorrent that Altmeyer, with Roosevelt's approval, asked the Postmaster General to assume the responsibility of assignment numbers for Social Security purposes. More Americans apparently trusted the local post office than the new Social Security Board. "He agreed to do so and in a few weeks plans were completed for carrying out this gigantic task through the 45,000 post offices, beginning November 16, 1936," Altmeyer recalled in a memoir. "I had urged that the assignment of account numbers should not begin until then in order to avoid becoming involved in the Presidential campaign of that year." In September Republican candidate Alfred M. Landon denounced the "old-age insurance system," saying "To call it 'social security' is a fraud on the working man."

On the day before the election William Randolph Hearst's *New York Journal-American* published a front-page attack on the pension system accompanied by a drawing of a man with his identity masked, stripped to the waist, wearing a dog tag with an identifying number. It was labeled "Snooping and Tagging." The caption stated, "Each worker would be required to have one for the privilege of suffering a pay cut under the Social Security Act, which is branded as a 'cruel hoax.'" (Alf Landon had used that term in his campaign.) The illustration was not far-fetched. The Addressograph Corp. had tried to sell the Social Security Board on the idea of issuing metal nameplates to all registrants. Altmeyer said he kept Addressograph's prototype nametag as a souvenir of these negotiations.

Some press reports said that the new program would require a person's religion, union affiliation, criminal record, medical history, and other personal data. The *Boston American* wrote, "Your personal life will be laid bare, your religion and the church you attend will be listed. Your physical defects will go down in black and white ... your union affiliation will be stated.... Even your divorce, if you have one, will be included." In fact, an applicant needed to provide only name, date of birth, and parents' names. Each file would include only earnings information.

The Social Security Board retaliated against the Republicans' negative envelope stuffers with 50 million leaflets of its own that were distributed at factory gates. The brochures explained the process for *assigning* Social Security numbers (not *registering* for Social Security). One of the government's explanatory films to soothe citizens' fears was run continuously in Times Square on the last day of the election campaign, as well as elsewhere throughout the country.

The 1935 law assigned to the Bureau of Internal Revenue in the Department of Treasury the task of collecting the taxes from both employees and employers. The bureau waited until two days after the election to issue a regulation creating "an account number." Each person was to apply at a post office and be assigned a number and then provide it to his or her employer. The regulation also provided that a person could change his or her number "showing good reason."

Despite misgivings and despite the fact that the Social Security Act had not yet been declared constitutional, most of the 26 million application forms were returned through post offices during the first three weeks of registration. By June of 1937, 30 million persons had applied for numbers. Not bad, in a nation of 50 million employed adults. No one wanted to miss out on a government pension, of course, and there was no need to show any proof of identity in order to register. At the time, there seemed little incentive to get an SSN under an assumed name or to get more than one because that might actually reduce one's later benefits. This remained true so long as the SSN was used for no other purpose. Thus, for many years later, no proof of identity was required to get a Social Security number.

In 1936 the board twice issued statements promising confidentiality and it issued a regulation — Social Security Board Regulation No. 1 dated June 15, 1937 — requiring that no employee "shall disclose to any person or before any tribunal, directly or indirectly" any account information, even in response to a subpoena.

Altmeyer said that this regulation was violated only in a few cases involving persons suspected of espionage and other crimes. But there were other close calls. Every attorney general "at the urging of the Federal Bureau of Investigation," requested access to Social Security information during the 19 years in which Altmeyer was in office. J. Edgar Hoover's persistence paid off, and in 1939, President Roosevelt issued an executive order authorizing FBI access to Social Security files in any criminal investigation.

The information on accounts was intended to stay confidential, but it did not stay that way for long. By 1997, an official publication of the Social Security Administration admitted euphemistically, "The next two decades saw a gentle evolution in SSA's disclosure policies with changes made to respond to changing social needs, additional program responsibilities and other material interests." In other words, in the computer age, the floodgates were opened.

The implied promise that Social Security *numbers* would be used solely for administering the insurance program was a separate issue. That pledge lasted less than a year — and the Social Security Board itself broke it. It directed that the Social Security number also be used in state unemployment insurance programs, which were funded by the 1935 act. This meant that many more employees not covered by the Social Security program — railroad employees, laid-off federal employees, and others— had to get numbers as well. Still, in a time when most families had only one wage earner and when there was little out-of-home employment for women, a majority of Americans still did not have — and did not need — SSNs.

For many years, the 3-by-2-inch Social Security card bearing a person's number had the legend "NOT FOR IDENTIFICATION" printed on its face. This has led many citizens to this day to believe that a law or regulation prohibited the use of the number for purposes other than Social Security. But that was never the case. (Partial restrictions on government agencies *collecting* the numbers were enacted in 1974.) The purpose of the legend, the Social Security officials would say, was merely to notify anyone to whom a card might be presented that it should not be relied upon as evidence of identity. After all, no proof of identity was required then to get a Social Security card. To this day, persons in places of authority nonetheless demand and accept it as evidence of identity.

In the first year of the program, the Social Security Board turned to large insurance companies for advice in creating a central record system to keep track of the millions of accounts, in a time of primitive counting machines. The board was shocked to discover that no company had a records system that could serve as a prototype for the massive information collection that the government insurance program would require. The board was building the largest database in the world, and there was no model to emulate. An expert in private-sector data systems told members of the board that it couldn't be done, that the board's only hope of managing the massive amount of data was to create separate regional organizations. This would have required an amendment to the legislation that created the pension system. And it wouldn't work, in a nation where up to a fifth of the citizens move from one community to another in a year.

Instead the board established 12 units organized by geographical regions, but centralized them in the nation's capital and linked them with a single universal index. The index of 30 million names was organized by a phonetic translation of last names, not by numbers, showing that large personal data systems need not be organized by numbers. That was true then and it is true today. The system was good enough to locate a file within a few seconds.

Americans' suspicions of enumeration became clear after World War II when vital statistics officials throughout the country proposed a national Birth Certificate Number, to be affixed to each new birth certificate. This would assign a unique identifying number for a person's lifetime, something the Social Security number was not. Officials in nearly half of the states declined to participate in the program and the idea was dropped.

A number is a number is a number, but Social Security account number 078-05-1120 was one of several numbers that took on lives of their own. It first appeared on a sample Social Security card inserted in wallets sold in 1938. It simply showed a person what the little plastic pocket in the wallet was for. But many purchasers naively assumed that the made-up number was to be their own account number 078-05-1120. The year 1943 was the peak, when 5755 wage earners were listed under that number. Even in the 1970s, 39 older persons filed tax returns under 078-05-1120. In the 1970s the Social Security Administration said that it was still processing multiple accounts for persons using what the bureaucrats called "pocket-book numbers."

President Franklin D. Roosevelt signed Executive Order 9397 in 1943 requiring federal agencies to use the Social Security number for identifying individuals in any new "system of accounts." The Civil Service Commission, which managed federal personnel, had asked for the authority. It had decided that it needed a numerical system for keeping track of payroll records of federal civil-service workers, who at that time did not participate in the Social Security program. The order, which is still in effect, directed the Social Security Board to assign an account number to any person required by a federal agency to have one, whether the purpose was for pensions or not. And it directed that, "The Social Security Board and each federal agency shall maintain the confidential character of information relating to individuals obtained pursuant to the provisions of this order." The order also required that the federal agency requiring an account number pay for the enumeration process. The Civil Service Commission always said that it lacked the funds to do this, and so for 18 years civil service employees simply went without SSNs. There was apparently no pressing need for them to have them.

Thus, Roosevelt's executive order had no practical impact at all for many years, until federal agencies resurrected it with the coming of computer systems. Executive Order 9397 is an example of a governmental action that profoundly affected citizens' rights but turned out not to be necessary at all at the time.

In 1961, the Civil Service Commission finally decided to issue SSNs to federal employees. As it began to use computer systems for processing tax returns, the Internal Revenue Service decided to use the Social Security number as an individual taxpayer identification number. This was authorized by an amendment to the tax code in 1961. Until the 1980s the IRS was fairly casual about this requirement, imposing only a $5 penalty for failure to comply.

Use of the number as a taxpayer ID opened the floodgates. Soon state tax authorities began to use it. The U.S. Treasury Department began to use it as an identifier for holders of U.S. securities, including savings bonds.

In 1964, the Commissioner of Social Security approved the issuance of Social Security numbers to school pupils in the ninth grade and above, if a school requests this. Pupils in the public schools of Baltimore, where the Social Security Administration was now located, became the leading guinea pigs. Social Security officers set up tables at high schools registering students. Of course, the program was voluntary, but there was no way for pupils *to know* that. Everything done in school seems required.

Issuing SSNs in schools was more cost effective and more convenient than having young people register one by one when they entered the job market. That was one of the stated reasons for issuing them in schools.

There was another purpose, according to the Social Security Administration manual in the 1960s: It was to accommodate requests from school systems "desiring to use the SSN for both automated data processing and control purposes, so that the progress of pupils could be traced throughout their school lives across district, county, and state lines." This was one of the first articulations of the reason behind the many demands for personal information in the Sixties and Seventies: "The computer needs it."

This was a breach of a key principle of privacy protection (one that was not drafted and circulated until a decade later, however). The principle is that information gathered for one purpose ought not to be used for an incompatible purpose without consent of the individual. Pupils thought that they were securing Social Security numbers to make it easier for them when they applied for work. They did not realize that they were also providing a means for school authorities to link records about them.

"The assignment of a number to an individual, I suspect, is going to go out of existence pretty much. The computer can recognize a name as well as a number." Yale Professor of Economics Richard Ruggles, expert on statistics and computers, in 1968.

And if high school students were being issued Social Security numbers en masse, why shouldn't colleges use them as student ID numbers? This is exactly what happened.

With the coming of the federal Medicare and state Medicaid supplemental health insurance programs in the early Sixties, thousands of Americans who had reached retirement age without ever needing a Social Security number — including many post–World War II newcomers — now had to be issued identifying numbers. If Medicaid and Medicare used SSNs, why not state elderly assistance programs? This is exactly what happened in 1965.

If state elderly programs used SSNs, why not the Indian Health Program? And that is what happened in 1966. In the same year, the Veterans Administration used the numbers for hospital admissions and other accounting purposes. If the Veterans Administration used the numbers, why shouldn't the Pentagon use them as service numbers for all military personnel? And this is what happened in 1967.

A new banking law that Congress passed in 1970 required banks and other financial institutions to get Social Security numbers for all customers, whether the accounts produced taxable income or not. This was an obligation on the bank, not the individual, but most customers did not know this or did not care. Just as we think that most things we are asked to do in school are mandatory, we think that most things we are asked to do in a bank are mandatory. People offered up their Social Security numbers. As a consequence of this requirement, many banks urged customers to have their Social Security numbers printed on the face of their checks, or banks simply went ahead and did so. This, of course, was not required by the law, but it was a natural consequence of it.

There is nothing private about a Social Security number printed on the face of a bank check. Checkout clerks in a grocery story, retail sales personnel, payments processors, the guy who fixes the car, personal friends— everybody gets to see it. Nor is a number printed on an Army dog tag or on thousands of military documents very private.

In fact, a prisoner named George Turner at a federal facility in Missouri did well for himself exactly ten years after the military converted to SSNs as service numbers. His job was to sort old Army fatigues from Fort Leonard Wood, the nearby Army training base. It took Turner less than a week — after all, he was serving time for tax fraud — to figure out that he could use the discarded clothing to continue his schemes. On each piece of clothing was a soldier's name and Social Security number. Turner requested blank tax forms by mail and filed phony returns and requests for refunds, using the names and Social Security numbers (which now was *both* taxpayer ID *and* military ID) on the different forms. George Turner generated more than 200 refund checks this way. The Internal Revenue Service after a while detected the fraud, but the Army continued to send discarded clothing to the prison with service member's names and Social Security numbers.

Oddly, while the Social Security number was becoming more and more a public piece of information, as George Turner demonstrated, people in places of authority were treating it as *an authenticator of a person's real identity*, as if it were a secret identifier known only to the individual. This practice had the effect of allowing impostors or perpetrators of fraud to use someone else's Social Security number as a means of "proving identity" with any clerk or bureaucrat in the land.

An advisory committee appointed by the Secretary of Health, Education, and Welfare in 1972 to study the proliferating uses of numerical identifiers and the implications of personal databanks noticed the irony. To attend a weekend meeting in a government building, the members were required to give names and Social Security numbers to a guard at the main entrance. The guard had earlier been given a list of members and their numbers. The committee's final report said:

Given the wide dissemination of SSNs, we were impressed by how easily someone could have impersonated any one of us to gain admittance to the building.

This was not a theoretical concern. It was going on all over the country in the 1970s— people enlisting in the Army, applying for a job, getting a birth certificate or driver's license, getting welfare assistance — while using a stranger's Social Security number *to verify their own identities*. This reached epidemic proportions in the nineties, when it became known as "theft of identity." Still, no one in Congress or the Executive Branch realized the irony and sought to remedy it. There were selected members of Congress who raised concerns about the proliferation of SSN uses, as a dehumanizing trend or threat to privacy, but no one mentioned the misplaced reliance upon the number to authenticate identity.

George Turner, the prisoner in Missouri, was simply ahead of his time. By the 1990s, criminal impostors were victimizing thousands of Americans with schemes similar to Turner's. It was called "identity theft." A stranger would secure the victim's Social Security number —from payroll records, by pretext over the telephone, in trashcans, or at World Wide Web sites— and then pose as that person to get a duplicate birth certificate, driver's license, or job. In a more common variation, the imposter would access the individual's credit report — using the Social Security number to verify identity — and discover the retail credit accounts the person had and the account numbers. Then the stranger would ask the retailers to change the address on the account to the imposter's or to a bogus address set up for this purpose. Or the impostor would simply use the victim's Social Security number to apply for a new account. The victim would be unaware that a stranger was using the accounts to order products and services — dunning notices for overdue accounts would be sent to the impostor's new address, not to the true account holder's address. But notices about the delinquent accounts would be sent regularly to the major credit bureaus. Only when the individual was rejected on a new credit application or had credit cards canceled would he or she become aware of the fraud.

But then reclaiming a clean credit report became impossible. A credit bureau would dutifully erase the bad information as required by the federal Fair Credit Reporting Act of 1971, but in the next 45 days, when retailers and credit-card issuers would make their next automated reports to the credit bureau, the fraud-produced information would reappear on the victim's credit report. Only after Congress tightened the law in 1996 and the credit bureaus faced several lawsuits did they take partial steps to prevent this from happening over and over. Further, because retailers accepted the losses as a cost of doing business, they didn't bother to change their practices so that the fraud could be curbed. They didn't bother to alter their systems so that Social Security numbers were unnecessary to retrieve data about an individual.

A prime source of other person' Social Security numbers is the identifying information at the top of a credit report, what the credit bureaus call "header" or "above-the-line" information, including phone numbers, addresses, mother's maiden names, and Social Security numbers. Because most people provide their telephone numbers on credit applications whether or not their numbers are "unlisted," credit bureaus include listed and unlisted phone numbers "above-the-line." The Federal Trade Commission, which regulates credit bureaus, ruled in a non-public negotiation in 1993 that credit bureaus are free to rent "header" information all they want. That is when identity fraud became a nationwide epidemic.

This means that "information brokers," which buy personal information from large vendors and resell it to individuals and small businesses, could easily purchase Social Security numbers and unlisted telephone numbers. Many of these brokers sold the data on the World Wide Web sites.

The Federal Trade Commission has compounded the problem by encouraging credit bureaus to use Social Security numbers to verify the identity of a consumer who seeks to get a copy of his or her credit report, as permitted by law. A Social Security number does not provide much verification of a person's identity if a stranger can get it easily.

"It wouldn't bother me in the slightest to be numbered in every file that was kept on me by the same number. I can see no negatives."
Thomas J. Watson, Jr., retired chair of IBM Corp., in 1975.

A task force created within the Social Security Administration in the early 1970s took a long look at the burgeoning use of the Social Security number. Its study focused on the function of the number as the key component for linking records about a single individual in disparate and remote computer systems.

One reason organizations were collecting Social Security numbers was precisely to link records; they wanted to be able in the future to allow for pooling or merging records about an individual from different systems. Data files were not then linked by telephone or any other telecommunications. Even "batch processing," by which a file or list from one computer file was loaded on to another system to merge data, was just beginning. Data managers, however, certainly anticipated that automated matching and merging of files would soon be routine. If each individual record could be retrieved by a single ID number, then the process of matching files, for whatever reason, would be feasible. Insurance companies, for instance, discovered that if they used separate policy numbers of their own, processing Medicare and Medicaid information was slow and awkward. Using a common number created the possibility of linking records with data systems outside the organization.

The Social Security number was simply a convenient number, one that most people had memorized or had access to. It was widely believed that a common numerical identifier was essential for merging files or even for managing large data systems. The discovery of alternative techniques since that time has made that belief outdated.

The Social Security task force issued a report in 1971 that questioned the desirability of "*any* kind of universal identification system in terms of its psychological impact on the individual citizen." The reason for this "psychological impact" was apparently not the dehumanizing aspect of enumeration, but the loss of control that would come from linking data:

> It is clear that if the SSN became the single number around which all or most of an individual's interactions were structured ... the individual's opportunity to control the circumstances under which information about himself is collected and disclosed would be greatly circumscribed.

President Nixon's Secretary of Health, Education and Welfare, Elliott L. Richardson, decided to appoint an Advisory Committee on Automated Personal Data Systems to study the larger questions posed by increased use of computers to collect information on individuals. Just a few months after the Social Security Administration task force issued its report, the Secretary's Advisory Committee took a new look at the increasing uses of Social Security numbers.

The HEW committee — the one whose members gave up their Social Security numbers at the front door — issued a well-received report on *Records Computers and the Rights of Citizens* in 1972, saying, "The federal government itself has been in the forefront of expanding the use of the SSN." It concluded:

> We recommend against the adoption of any nationwide, standard, personal identification format, with or without the SSN, that would enhance the likelihood of arbitrary or uncontrolled linkage of records about people, particularly between government or government-supported automated personal data systems.

The committee recommended that use of the number be limited to requirements imposed by federal agencies, and only pursuant to authority from Congress. And "Congress should be sparing in mandating use of the SSN." Further, "when the SSN is used in instances that do not conform to the three foregoing principles," it should be totally voluntary.

Both the HEW advisory committee and the Social Security Administration task force were created partly in reaction to a standard developed by the American National Standards Institute in 1969 for a uniform identifier for each American, incorporating a person's Social Security number and additional elements. As with the earlier proposal for a mandatory Birth Certificate Number, the public and the press met the idea with immediate opposition. The organization was forced to withdraw the proposed standard.

Congress took the HEW recommendations seriously and in drafting a comprehensive privacy-protection proposal in 1974 moved towards making the recommendations part of the law. Senators Sam J. Ervin, Jr., Charles H. Percy, and Barry M. Goldwater were especially vigorous about this. But support for making the privacy protections apply to private businesses faded in both houses of Congress. What emerged in the late fall was the Privacy Act of 1974, which seeks to protect personal information gathered *by the federal government*, but not information collected by private businesses like banks, credit-card companies, employers, and health-care providers. Congress included in the Privacy Act a modest provision on Social Security numbers that applied to state, local, and federal levels of government only; it did not extend to the private sector. In essence, it authorized current uses of Social Security numbers, but no more. The provision in the Privacy Act says that government benefits may not be denied an individual for declining to provide a Social Security number unless there was an existing federal or state law or regulation specifically authorizing this. (In 1976 Congress amended the law to exempt tax, motor-vehicle, and welfare offices in state government from its limitations. This meant that these agencies could continue to require Social Security numbers.)

Since 1974, agencies at all levels of government have justified their demands for Social Security numbers by pointing to general authorizations in laws predating the Privacy Act that simply allow the agencies to conduct some function or to collect information to conduct their functions. That is not at all what members of Congress had in mind in the fall of 1974, but the practices are only occasionally challenged successfully.

The lasting effect of the HEW report was in its creation of a Code of Fair Information Practice governing computer databases, not in its warnings about Social Security numbers.

Meanwhile, private businesses began insisting on the Social Security number, often using it as a customer or account number. If the Medicare and Medicaid programs used it, why wouldn't it be convenient for insurance companies to use it as a policy number? And that is what many insurance companies began to do. Newspapers sponsoring sweepstakes for their readers often made the Social Security number the basis for entering the contests (although the HEW report strongly condemned this). This only accustomed millions of persons to disclosing their numbers for non–Social Security purposes and non-tax purposes without thinking of the consequences. It also motivated some people to get more than one Social Security number or to use more than one — to have a better chance of winning.

A man in Cleveland, Ohio, was surprised when his two children, aged seven and five, received notices to pay overdue taxes. Then the father recalled that to enter the children in the *Cleveland Press* sweepstakes in 1976 he had applied for new Social Security numbers for them. The Social Security Administration routinely put the children and their numbers on lists it regularly sends to local tax agencies. The local agency had no record of the two paying taxes and sent the delinquency notices.

A Native American father descended from the Abenaki Tribe had the opposite approach. Stephen J. Roy of Pennsylvania regarded Social Security numbers as part of "a great evil" used by computers to rob people's spirits. This, he said, is what non-Indians would call *dehumanization.* He based his spiritual belief on what he called the legend of Katahdin, the mountain that overlooks a settlement of the Abenaki Tribe in the state of Maine. He did not want his daughter, Little Bird of the Snow, to be enumerated in this way, and insisted that she decide for herself when she was older about having a Social Security number.

But the family received state Aid to Dependent Children, food stamps, and state medical assistance. The state and federal governments insisted that the family provide a Social Security number for four-year-old Little Bird of the Snow. When the state reduced the family's public assistance in the 1980s, the father filed a lawsuit in federal court. He found a sympathetic federal judge. In fact, the judge, Malcolm Muir, said that he himself converts numbers into words as a personal way of remembering digits. The judge nick-named the chief judge on his court "Philippino Overpot," for instance, simply as a way of remembering his colleague's telephone number. Using his personal system, the judge figured that the little girl's name would translate into the number 515-94-1802. Would the government accept this number as an alternative? A government witness thought that the bureaucracy could handle this, even if the first three digits would indicate that the number had been issued in Kansas and the judge's fabricated number would be 30,000 numbers ahead of Social Security numbers in use at the time. The Social Security Administration's computers would reject "impossible" account numbers, and so some accommodation would be necessary. Would the father accept it, the judge asked. The father liked the idea a little bit, but was unwilling to accept it as an alternative because it would be a unique identifier. Only at the end of the trial was it revealed that Little Bird of the Snow had had an SSN assigned to her at birth, the parents had returned it and asked that it be revoked. That was not relevant to Judge Muir. He ruled that the SSN requirements in the welfare and food stamp programs were an unconstitutional infringement on religious beliefs. He enjoined the agencies from denying benefits to the family.

The federal government said that it would appeal the ruling to the U.S. Supreme Court and argue that its inability to get Social Security numbers on everybody would hamper its plans to match computer lists in different state and federal agencies and thereby uncover fraud and "double-dipping."

Department of Justice lawyers were busy that fall with two vexing challenges from individuals concerned about their personal privacy. A woman who wanted to apply for a driver's license without providing a photograph of herself had succeeded in getting the Eighth Circuit Court of Appeals to agree with her argument. Because of the injunction in the Ten Commandments, "Thou shalt not make unto thee any graven image," Frances Quaring did not want to be photographed. Lawyers in the U.S. Department of Justice were preparing to persuade the U.S. Supreme Court to overturn the opinion by the court of appeals that the state of Nebraska had to accommodate the religious objections of Ms. Quaring.

When the Supreme Court heard the Nebraska case, Warren E. Burger, then chief justice of the U.S. and a man renowned for objecting to any and all photographs of himself, immediately asked the attorney for the woman what would happen if press photographers snapped her picture at the Supreme Court. It won't happen, the man responded; she had stayed home on that important day in her life precisely to make sure that did not happen. Associate Justice Sandra Day O'Connor noted aloud that the Court's decision in the photograph case would surely have an effect on its ruling in the government's anticipated appeal in Little Bird's case.

On June 17, 1985, the Court announced that it was deadlocked 4-4 whether the government had to accommodate a religious objection to providing a photograph. Justice Powell was hospitalized and did not participate. Whenever there is a tie on the high court, the opinion of the lower court stands, meaning that the Eighth Circuit's ruling that a person has a constitutional right not to provide a photograph for a driver's license is the governing law to this day. On the same day, the court agreed to hear the government's appeal in the case of "Little Bird vs. Big Government."

A few weeks later, the Missouri Supreme Court expressly rejected the Eighth Circuit's opinion and ruled that the state *could* deny a driver's license to someone who refused to provide a Social Security number (not a photograph this time) because of that person's "sincerely held" religious belief against being assigned a number.

In contrast to the photograph-driver's license issue, the Supreme Court had little difficulty on the issue of Social Security numbers and government benefits. In 1986, it voted 8-1 in Little Bird of the Snow's case that the government's demand for a Social Security number does not itself impair a person's freedom to exercise religion, guaranteed in the First Amendment to the Constitution.

"The harm that can be inflicted from the disclosure of a SSN to an unscrupulous individual is alarming and potentially financially ruinous."
U.S. Court of Appeals, Fourth Circuit, 1993.

By the late eighties, Americans were now being asked for Social Security numbers in order to rent an apartment, to get a fishing license, to order a cable TV connection, to begin telephone service, to donate blood, to make funeral arrangements, to get medical treatment. At different times, people have been asked for Social Security numbers to rent a room at a Holiday Inn, to use credit cards at gasoline stations, and, in Virginia, to register to vote.

The trend towards constant demands for a Social Security number for any transaction, which gave rise to a citizens group in Massachusetts called PANIC, People Against National Identity Cards was clear — the Social Security number (with all its imperfections was becoming a de facto national ID number. The nation was inexorably moving towards what had once been unthinkable: requiring every man, woman, and child to have a government-issued identity number and to carry proof of it on one's person at all times.

This was no idle Orwellian fear. The Director of the Passport Office in the Department of State, Frances G. Knight, actually advocated the issuance of an identity card, with fingerprints, to every citizen. This was in 1975. Knight, who held her job for 22 years before retiring in 1977, was the female equivalent of J. Edgar Hoover, an entrenched, expert bureaucrat whom no politician cared to cross. But on this one, Frances G. Knight stood alone. No one wanted to side with Ms. Knight on a national ID card. By coincidence, at the time, a diverse committee appointed by the Attorney General was studying the use of false IDs to commit crimes. The law enforcement and vital statistics officials on the committee said that they were tempted to recommend creation of a national identity card; they were sure that this would solve all problems related to fraud. But they wouldn't say so publicly, because they were aware that the public reaction would be immediately negative. And so the pro-law enforcement group voted down a proposal to create a national ID number.

Instead in subsequent years, officials and politicians created, one by one, discreet new demands for proof of identity that led in the same direction. But no one else would endorse a national identity card itself.

There was evidence of this in the debates of a Select Commission on Immigration and Refugee Policy established in 1980 to find a way to prevent employers from hiring illegal immigrants and to ration the flow of newcomers to America. The Rev. Theodore M. Hesburgh, then president of the University of Notre Dame, chaired the panel, which included Senators Alan K. Simpson and Edward M. Kennedy, as well as the Secretary of State and Secretary of Labor at the time. Hesburgh could find nothing objectionable about a mandatory ID card in order to hold a job. After returning from Asia, he told the press, "If I can walk into a restaurant in Bangkok and just hand them a card to charge $100, it shouldn't be that difficult to establish some method to establish legal status in the U.S. You wouldn't have to carry it always. If you wanted to use it for other purposes you could do so."

At a meeting in December 1980, after the election of Ronald Reagan as President and a Republican majority in the Senate for the first time in 26 years, Hesburgh asked for a vote on tightening current identity requirements. A majority agreed. Then he asked for a vote on a new "more certain" document that each worker would have to present before getting hired. A slim majority including Kennedy voted *against* that. But Hesburgh said then that he would poll the three members of the panel who were absent. He tried, but the chair could not garner the votes to make such a recommendation.

In the end, the commission's final report avoided recommending a national ID card or a mandatory work card. Instead, Congress tossed around various proposals for requiring existing ID documents for employment, even though none of them, except a passport, verifies citizenship or legal immigrant status. A bipartisan bill in 1982 would have required workers to present one of four different Ids before getting hired. (Strangely, only one of the required documents has a photograph.) The bill also would have required the Reagan Administration to develop a plan for "secure identification" within six months. Congress could not reach agreement on an immigration-reform bill that year, and so the ID proposal died.

A year later, Senator Robert J. Dole convened a three-day hearing on moving towards a national ID scheme. But members of Congress were not willing to endorse such an idea; instead they tossed the issue to the Executive Branch and insisted that it develop a plan for a national identifier.

Witnesses before Dole's committee said that government agencies were relying more and more on the mere presentation of a Social Security number — as proof of identity — and also discovering that their files were full of erroneous and duplicate SSNs. The Department of Defense alone found at least 1000 persons in its systems using numbers also being used by others.

The issue was not resolved in the 1980s — nor was the issue of controlling immigration. In 1990 Congress appointed a bipartisan Commission on Immigration Reform to resolve the impasse. In July of 1994, the chair, former Representative Barbara Jordan of Texas, let float a trial balloon. It's the Washington way. She seemed to endorse the idea of a mandatory work card with photograph, or a plastic national ID card, or at least a "tamper-proof" Social Security card.

Because of her advocacy during the nationally televised impeachment hearing about President Nixon in 1974, Jordan enjoyed a reputation as a defender of the Constitution and a liberal. "I would not be a party to any system I felt was an unwarranted intrusion into private lives," she said.

When it came time to testify before a Senate committee the next month, Jordan merely endorsed the idea of a "more secure" worker ID document and a computerized system for employers to verify the identity and citizenship status of any applicant. She seemed to be backing off her original proposal for a national identity card. Senator Alan K. Simpson of Wyoming, then chair of the immigration subcommittee and primary advocate of the verification system, said:

> Does this mean we are creating a "national ID card"? Not at all. I have always provided in my legislation, as the commission has in its recommendation, that no one would be required to carry a card, should one be used, or to present it to law enforcement officials for routine identification purposes. The card, if there is to be one, would be presented *only* at the time of new-hire employment, or at the time of application for federally funded benefits, including health card.

Simpson's proposed card, then, would be required to get a job and to get health care. His insistence that this would not evolve into an all-purpose card was reminiscent of assurances from the Social Security Board in the 1930s. Anyone familiar with the 40-year erosion of the Social Security number as an exclusive, single-purpose identifier would, of course, view Simpson's assurances with great skepticism.

Simpson had disparaged the fear of a national ID number earlier in 1991, at the only Congressional hearing ever held exclusively to study the trend. Representative Andy Jacobs, Jr., of Indiana, convened a hearing of his Ways and Means Subcommittee on Social Security and heard groups representing immigrants discourage use of mandatory identity numbers. Representatives of credit bureaus said for the first time publicly that they were highly dependent on Social Security numbers to keep straight the 450 million credit reports they issue yearly.

Robert Ellis Smith, publisher of *Privacy Journal* newsletter, said in his testimony, "It is ironic that less than one year after we Americans rejoiced in the liberation of peoples in Eastern Europe we are seriously considering a means of social control that Eastern Europeans rejected soundly. One year after we rejoiced in the liberation of Nelson Mandela, we are considering a 'domestic passport' similar to that in South Africa."

In the end, Simpson and other immigration reformers settled for a law enacted by the new Republican Congress in 1996 establishing a computerized system of verifying the citizenship status and the accuracy of Social Security numbers of new hires— but only as a pilot project in the immigration-intensive states of California, New York, Texas, Florida, and Illinois. By a vote of 221-191, the House of Representatives narrowly rejected a requirement for a "tamper-proof" Social Security card or a mandatory worker ID document. The law that was passed required the Social Security Administration to evaluate options for a "tamper-proof" card. In a report issued in 1997, the agency said that to issue new cards to every American would cost from $3,898 to $9,231 million. The plan is feasible, the report said, "However, the issuance of an enhanced card raises policy issues about privacy and the potential for the card to be used as a national identification card." In its report, the agency noted with enthusiasm that at least 75 percent of all newborn infants are now being assigned Social Security numbers before they leave the hospital, as part of the Enumeration at Birth program.

> "Would government be able to resist the temptation gradually to expand
> this new system, to track people, or to store more and more information
> on them? The answer depends on your view of government."
> Representative Steve Chabot of Ohio, in debates
> about creating a database of new hires, in 1995.

It turned out that 1996, not George Orwell's 1984, was the disastrous year for government attempts to monitor individuals by assigning them an ID number. Congress included in the immigration reform law passed that year the following requirement effective October 2000:

> A federal agency may not accept for any identification related purposes a driver's license, or other comparable identification document, issued by a state, unless the license or document satisfies the requirements [of displaying the person's Social Security number on the face of the license itself or imbedding it in the document in electronic form].

Very few people even noticed this new requirement. But when the U.S. Department of Transportation in 1998 proposed regulations to implement the Congressional mandate, thousands of citizens did take notice and registered their objections. Most of the objectors were conservative Americans, many of them reflecting the Biblical injunction against enumeration that had motivated fears among Puritan New Englanders two and one-half centuries earlier. Pushed by a bizarre alliance of the conservative Eagle Forum and the libertarian American Civil Liberties Union, conservative members of Congress took up the cause and successfully repealed the requirement, in a law passed in October 1999. Many Senators and representatives who had voted for the 1996 legislation now voted to repeal it.

But there was more in 1996. The welfare reform law that year created a duplicative National Directory of New Hires, which requires employers to report immediately to Washington the name, Social Security number, and birth date of every person newly hired in the private and public sectors. This time the intention was to catch errant parents who owed child support and should have it deducted from their paychecks. The Department of Labor was assigned to create the system, which would operate nationwide. By contrast, Senator Simpson's immigration system to detect undocumented immigrants seeking employment was created as an experiment involving only five major states.

The solemn assurance from Senator Simpson and others that these two verification system for screening new hires would be used only for the one discreet purpose of catching illegal immigrants or deadbeat parents was not worth much. After the senator retired from the Senate, members of the House of Representatives in 1999 — oblivious to all the pledges — approved overwhelmingly two new uses for the Department of Labor database: to track down persons who have defaulted on higher education student loans and to catch persons who may be collecting state unemployment compensation and holding a job at the same time. The Senate approved the second use, but not the first. It was a safe bet that members of Congress would try to approve new uses for the database in the future, thereby creating an all-purpose screening system for everyone in the nation.

There is still more. The welfare reform law also required all states to collect Social Security numbers when renewing or issuing licenses of *any kind*, including occupational licenses, marriage licenses, and commercial drivers' licenses. Before enacting this rule in the summer of 1996, Congress heard objections similar to those registered over the immigration measure on drivers' licenses. In the end, it deleted non-commercial drivers' licenses from the welfare-reform requirement. But the end result is that each state must now require Social Security numbers on a marriage license.

By means of a cruel joke by a Congressional paper-pusher or of an incredible coincidence, the new provision was indexed in the federal statutes as Section 666(a)(13) of Chapter 42! Fundamentalists who believe that the "mark of the beast" condemns anyone who is enumerated see red when they see the number 666. The Book of Revelation in the Bible says that the number 666 *is* the mark of the beast. By another bit of serendipity, the privacy protection organization Electronic Privacy Information Center happened to locate its office in Washington at 666 Pennsylvania Avenue, S.E.

But there is still more. Also in 1996, Congress, in a law allowing employees to transfer their health-insurance benefits, included a provision for "administrative simplification" of payments for health care. In the process, Congress ordered that an identifying number be issued to every doctor and medical facility and *to every patient*, whether or not the patient was paying for the health care himself or herself. It assigned to the federal Department of Health and Human Services the task of deciding whether the health-care identifier should be a person's Social Security number, a totally new number, or a combination of the SSN and additional digits. There was such sharp disagreement within the department over the patient ID number and the objections from the public were so great that Congress in 1998 — mostly the same elected representatives who had approved the original idea — passed a moratorium on this issue as well.

In the previous decade, Congress had required parents to provide their own Social Security numbers on any application for a birth certificate and, beginning in 1997, any application for a Social Security number for a child. Of course parents felt compelled to get Social Security numbers for their newborns, because a 1986 federal law now requires a Social Security number be listed for any dependent child claimed on a federal tax return. The Internal Revenue Service claimed that in the first year after it began requiring Social Security numbers on all dependents, the number of claimed dependents dropped by seven million. The IRS assumed that taxpayers were no longer claiming these seven million persons as dependents because they were not entitled to do so in the first place and feared that they would get caught, through matching of Social Security numbers.

All of this abetted the drift towards a de facto national ID document, as did a secret directive by the Federal Aviation Administration that airlines must ask passengers to present a government-issued photo identification document. The order was issued in 1995 after an anonymous threat to blow up planes at Los Angeles Airport. There was also concern about security at the upcoming 1996 Olympics in Atlanta and concern about the trial of persons suspected of bombing the World Trade Center in New York City. The FAA refused to release the text of the directive. The agency told the public that it did not directly require identification as a condition of boarding an airplane. Airlines were directed to take alternative security precautions if a person declined to present identification.

"From whatever part of the globe a person comes, he may visit all the ports and principal towns of the United States, stay there as long as he pleases, and travel in any part of the country without ever being interrupted by a public officer."
French visitor François Andre Michaus, in 1802,
marveling at his freedom in the U.S.

Airlines discovered immediately, however, that the government's directive about asking for ID, though it was secret and confusing, allowed them to detect travelers using the return portion of someone else's discounted round-trip ticket, in violation of airline rules. In fact, they could do this *because the directive was kept secret from the traveling public.* Thus, most of the airlines used the directive to deny passage to anyone not presenting an ID. This was for revenue purposes, not for security purposes. After all the connection between assuring the true identification of a passenger and assuring that luggage was free of bombs, weapons, or contraband was tenuous.

At any rate, the directive — combined with the airlines' enthusiasm to interpret it as authority to deny passage to passengers without government-issued ID — served to force most Americans to carry identification whenever they traveled by airplane, without regard to the long-recognized Constitutional right to travel without undue restrictions. Only a few Americans objected, for fear that they would be regarded as callous to airline security.

Americans seemed hardly haunted by the specter of being required to carry identity papers. A national public opinion survey in 1995 asked a cross-section of adults, "Is not having a national government identification number extremely important or not?" In response, 24 percent rated it extremely important, 30 percent said somewhat important, 20 percent said not very important, 20 percent said not at all important. Five percent were not sure.

Americans' level of concern was twice as high for getting access to their own credit reports, for having food properly labeled, or for protecting the confidentiality of their personal information. It was three times as high for controlling false advertising, reducing insurance fraud, avoiding excessive debt, or controlling health-care costs.

By the end of the Twentieth Century, the strong coercion to carry photo identification, along with the multiplying demands for Social Security numbers, had created a de facto requirement that every American have his or her "papers in order" at all times. The regimentation anticipated in 1935 was complete.

My National I.D. Card Is a Threat to Your Civil Liberties

Gregory Dicum

This essay shows that there already exists a national identification card program for the millions of foreigners who legally and permanently work and live in the United States. It explains the "what, why, and how." The presumption behind such a system for resident aliens is that one's presence in the United States must be authorized by the federal government. Such a presumption also lies behind any national I.D. program for all natural-born Americans. A people who are "issued" a national identification card by their government are no longer a free people because the tables have been turned. Rather than the people authorizing and limiting the acts of government, the government grants them permission to live and exist. Parts of this article first appeared in Harper's Magazine *of February 2002 (pp. 48–49). Gregory Dicum is a Canadian living in the United States, and the co-author of* The Coffee Book: Anatomy of an Industry from Crop to the Last Drop. *Copyright © 2002 by Harper's Magazine. All rights reserved. Reproduced from the February issue by special permission.*

I

In the aftermath of the September 11 attacks, as the death and destruction began to be tallied, it was clear from the outset that civil liberties were going to be one of the casualties. Within days the President had floated the idea of a National Identity Card — the first time that a president had dared to even suggest an assault on this sacred cow. The proposal has since stalled, but for roughly 13 million of U.S. who are permanent legal immigrants its underlying premise is our daily reality. At all times, I am required by law to carry this, my Alien Registration Receipt Card (or "Green Card"). Unlike a

224

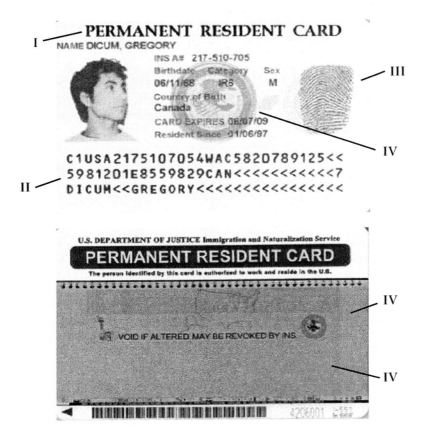

driver's license, this Green Card does not allow me simply to engage in some specific activity; rather, my possession of it is a precondition for my mere presence in the country. As would be the case with a national I.D., the card's purpose is quite explicitly to monitor me, and it serves, furthermore, as a visible badge of the constriction of my civil liberties. If you are curious to know what your rights may come to look like in twenty-first-century America, ask me; in many respects, I already live there.

II

For over 160 years, until World War II, foreigners in the United States were not even tracked in any sort of national registry. Even then, the first registrations were casual affairs undertaken at post offices, and registration was not required for employment. Not until the anti-Communist Internal Security Act of 1952 were immigrants required to carry these cards (which were, at the time, green). Today my own card offers a bewildering wealth of detail, including this machine-readable text, which serves as a database key to my I.N.S. file. Complete with detailed financial and work information, health records, address history, family and educational history, and job history and status, this file is as near a complete dossier on my life as exists anywhere in government annals (I hope). And that's not all; the Green Card serves as a visible affidavit for all of the things I swore were true and complete in the application process: that I am not a terrorist, Nazi, communist, prostitute, dope fiend, spy, smuggler, draft dodger, polygamist, kidnapper or purveyor of genocide, vice, or moral turpitude, and that my fingerprints have been successfully screened through the FBI databases. In this way, the card becomes shorthand for my compliance with a host of regulations, the violation of which threatens my very livelihood.

The mere existence of a national ID card — one that is required for all interaction with government services, for all airline travel, and for financial transactions — would create a situation in which running afoul of the issuing authority would be tantamount to immediate loss of liberty. Once in place, a national ID card would present an irresistibly tempting tool for the would-be despot bent on forcing compliance to any social program. This is how, for example, the federal government was able to cast a dragnet for Arab men so quickly and easily. Imagine the ramifications of a similar system applied to citizens: any group–social, economic, racial, or political–could be singled out and its members monitored and rounded up effortlessly. They could be identified by any official, and could be systematically extracted from the population at large. Black, Native, and Japanese Americans, union members, social change activists and others have all faced this kind of persecution in the past, but a modern national I.D. system would put in place a capability of chilling and highly tunable efficacy that would enable the instant targeting of unprecedentedly narrow groups.

III

Under a national I.D. system, your fingerprint might reside in a central database, just as mine does today. The database would also store a picture of your face, which could prove useful: at least two U.S. airports are now testing face-scanning technology (already widely used by Las Vegas casinos) to identify undesirables, and more airports — as well as other official checkpoints — may soon join them. Federal agencies are making an effort to link their criminal databases, and such integration would certainly benefit a national I.D. system. Given the amorphousness of the terrorist threat, the F.B.I.'s DNA database, which currently stores genetic material from over 600,000 felons, might make room for you, and in so doing append your "biological fingerprint" to your I.D. file. And surely ECHELON — the cross-governmental surveillance network, led by our National Security Agency, that intercepts a wide range of communications from satellite feeds — has happened across some of your e-mails by now; these, too, could be added to your file.

IV

This category, "IR6," means that I obtained my Green Card by marrying a U.S. citizen. My wife and I may be equal partners in matrimony, but we are decidedly unequal in the eyes of U.S. law. Even before September 11, under the Foreign Intelligence Surveillance Act, warrants to search my property could have been issued in secret. When questioned, I would have had a right to a lawyer, but none would have been provided for me. I could have been detained for two days without cause. Today, of course, a run-in with the law could prove far more perilous. I could be investigated merely for making — or having made — statements in support of "terrorist organizations" — statements that would be considered protected speech were they to come from the mouth of a citizen. Were I a candidate for military tribunal, I could be detained indefinitely; my trial (and all evidence in it) could be kept secret, as could my deportation — even my execution. To put it in a more personal perspective, now that you know my name, you can call up the I.N.S. and denounce me because you don't like where I'm going with this article (please don't do this!). Then, federal agents might investigate me and possibly imprison me indefinitely without me ever finding out what the basis for the investigation is. The proceedings will be kept secret, and I may never have legal representation throughout the ordeal leading to my execution. But at least I might die in good company: although the Bush administration has assured the nation that military tribunals would apply only to foreign nationals, the Supreme Court decision it cites to justify the constitutionality of such tribunals explicitly condones them for citizens as well. (See Ex Parte Quirin, 317 U.S. 1 at 38-39.)

V

While not (yet) a "smart" card of the sort promoted by Oracle CEO Larry Ellison, since 1998 the Green Card has been one of the must sophisticated documents produced by the U.S. government. Into this metallic field, festooned with microscopic portraits of the Presidents, information about me has been laser-etched. Green Cards are designed to frustrate forgers, yet counterfeit Green Cards abound; in Tijuana, one can be had for $500, little more than is required to obtain a real one. Fraud also bedevils Social Security numbers (six of the Sept. 11 hijackers had fraudulent ones) and driver's licenses (four had them), and would surely plague a national I.D. too. Thus the I.D. would fail, in the end, to allay our fears, just as this card failed to defuse anti-Communist fears during the Cold War. Given that John Ashcroft wants to allow the F.B.I. once again to spy on U.S. groups, his recent warning to Congress — that our enemies have been trained "to use America's freedom as a weapon against us" — is an ominous echo of 1947, when J. Edgar Hoover cautioned that "American progress ... is being adopted as window dressing by the Communists to conceal their true aims." Hoover later used this logic to justify surveillance of such traitors as Albert Einstein and Martin Luther King, Jr.

VI

That a person would need a card to "authorize" him or her to work and reside in the United States would have seemed odd to our nation's founders, but today this fact is, for the most part, accepted. More disturbing, though, is the alacrity with which our government has taken to representing itself, even to citizens, as a granter of the people's rights rather than as a repository of their will — as in Tom Ridge's remark that "Liberty is the most precious gift we offer our citizens." While I've long been used to the Constitution not applying in full to me, this is something that the rest of you are going to have to get used to, pronto. Although the move for a national ID card has stalled, much more important abridgements of rights have been proceeding at a furious pace. Ironically this all lends further support to ID card booster Larry Ellison's central argument: "[With a national I.D. card,] all you have to give up is your illusions, not any of your privacy."

How Computers Are a Menace to Liberty

Hans Sherrer

In the last few years, much has been written about the glories of the computer revolution. Computers and the Internet have been touted as mankind's salvation. Is it possible, however, that such technology is not really a boon, but rather a threat to human freedom? How and why were computers developed? What was their original purpose? Who was the original and primary consumer of computers and the services they provide? Hans Sherrer, in this original essay, argues the contrarian's case against computers. Hans lives in the Pacific Northwest. He first wrote about the dangers of computerization to liberty in "The Double Edge of Computers" (The Voluntaryist, Whole No. 87, August 1997).

> "the right to be let alone — [is] the most comprehensive of rights and the right most valued by civilized men."
>
> Justice Louis D. Brandeis dissenting in *Olmstead v. U.S.* (1928)

Computers are the greatest menace to human liberty yet created by man. Conceived as a device for the federal government to efficiently compile, analyze and store data about Americans, the very nature of the computer is to impair a person's liberty by undermining their "right to be let alone." As Justice Brandeis lucidly stated in 1928, liberty is directly related to being "let alone."[1] The more the government knows about people the easier it is for it to interfere with their lives by controlling, regulating and taxing them.

The menace of computers to liberty is traceable to its conception and development by a U.S. Census Bureau employee who patented the world's first electro-mechanical computer in 1884. Specifically designed to efficiently compile and analyze information about Americans, that computer's resounding success at processing the 1890 federal census created a demand for its use by governments around the world. In the intervening 100+ years governments have relied on computers to compile detailed dossiers on many hundreds of millions of people. The computer has proven to be such a versatile device that governments have expanded their uses to include such diverse tasks as administering the economy, monitoring the distribution of social services and waging war more efficiently.

Reflecting the computer's origin as a child of the government's desire to count, sort, catalog and keep tabs on Americans, the federal government has been a driving force behind its development up to the present. The government's nurturing of the computer has resulted in its evolvement into a near perfect instrument for interfering with a person's "right to be let alone," and hence undermining their liberty.

The Menace of the Electro-Mechanical Computer

Governments have long hungered to accumulate information about people living within their geographical confines. That desire is even embodied in the census provision of the U.S. Constitution.[2] Until the 19th Century, however, the gathering of information by governments was limited, slow, and once compiled it was largely inaccessible. Those physical limitations on the government's ability to invade the privacy of people served as an effective check on its ability to limit their liberty.

The critical event that led to obliteration of technological limitations on the government's invasion of privacy occurred in 1879. During dinner with nineteen year-old Census Bureau worker Herman Hollerith, the federal government's Director of Vital Statistics planted a subconscious seed in Hollerith's mind when he made the comment: "There ought to be a machine for doing the purely mechanical work of tabulating population and similar statistics."[3]

A year later Hollerith had a brilliant insight triggered by seeing a train conductor punching tickets in a manner that recorded specific physical characteristics of a passenger. Hollerith's vision was that a card could be punched with standardized holes representing information, such as an individual's occupational, personal and ethnic characteristics. Hollerith figured the holes in the card would create a *punched photograph* of a person's life readable by a spring mechanism using electrical brush contacts to sense the holes. As the cards were processed, they could be sorted into stacks based on data-specific holes.[4]

Hollerith's groundbreaking idea was to transform punch cards from their then static uses of merely instructing cloth machines to weave a particular pattern or a piano to play a particular tune, into a dynamic means of recording data about an individual person that could be used to identify and differentiate information about that person from information about any and every other person. Hollerith's idea for a mechanical brain was much more expansive in its concept and possible applications than the few working mechanical devices that had been invented prior to 1879 to perform mathematical calculations.[5]

Several thousand dollars borrowed from a German friend enabled Herman Hollerith to patent and manufacture a working prototype of his idea by 1884. Its initial test, which it passed with flying colors, was a count of the dead for the local health departments in Maryland, New York, and New Jersey. The electro-mechanical punch card computer proved successful at keeping track of details and analyzing data hundreds of times faster than was possible by hand. However, his device was considered somewhat of a novelty and he didn't produce any for sale. That changed when Hollerith won a contest sponsored by the U.S. Census Bureau for the best device to automate the 1890 Census.[6] The resulting government contract enabled him to manufacture his first machines.

Hollerith's electro-mechanical computer had an immediate impact on the ability of the federal government to collect information about the American population. In 1890, census takers were able to ask 235 *specific* questions: *4,700%* more than in 1870 when they only asked 5 *general* questions. Hollerith's device made it possible for federal officials to view the country's population on punch cards, and to isolate a particular racial, ethnic or religious group. After his success with the 1890 census, Hollerith was hired by Czar Nicholas II in 1895 to provide the same technology for Russia to conduct its first census.[7]

Hollerith's success with the U.S. census and the Russian census proved his revolutionary tabulating device was the key governments around the world had been waiting for to unlock Pandora's Box of accumulating a practically unlimited amount of useful information about people under their control. That capability soon attracted government statisticians in many other countries, including England, France, Austria, and Germany.[8]

It was apropos that Hollerith named his company the Tabulating Machine Company (TMC) when he incorporated it in 1896.[9] It is noted in *Psychological Principles in System Development* that Hollerith's innovations—of using punch cards as a memory device to store information for future use and to instruct a computer how data will be processed — were the most important developments in the computer's history. Today's most sophisticated electronic computers continue to use variations of Hollerith's storage and programming ideas.[10]

In 1911, Hollerith sold out to industrialist Charles Flint who combined TMC with his other business enterprises. The evolution of Hollerith's original punch card computer into a sophisticated data-manipulation device was reflected in the new company's name: Computing-Tabulating-Recording Company (CTR).[11] Revenue from being the leading data-services provider to governments around the world helped fuel the company's growth, and in 1922 it was renamed International Business Machines (IBM).[12]

The world-wide depression that began in late 1929 escalated the demand for government welfare services in every country in the world. The computers of the day were the only means available to do such things as count the number of unemployed, to determine the size of their families, and to determine the amount of their benefits.

Within weeks after Hitler came to power in January 1933, for example, IBM began investing millions of Reichsmarks to expand the manufacturing capacity of its German division (Dehomag). The company considered it a safe bet since it anticipated a significant growth in business due to the Nazi's well-publicized desire to increase monitoring of the German people.[13] IBM handsomely profited by modifying its equipment so it would be more useful to the Nazi government's data compilation and analysis objectives, and from selling it the more than 4 *million* punch cards it used daily.[14]

Mirroring the growth in computer services in Germany was the dramatically increased demand in the U.S. following President Roosevelt's inauguration in January 1933. He pushed for the creation of numerous government programs, such as the National Recovery Act of 1933 that resulted in a huge increase in demand for computer equipment and supplies.[15] The collection of data on Americans again increased with the passage of the Social Security Act of 1935 and the initial assignment of a federal identity number to over twenty-six million of Americans. To handle the workload generated by Congress' creation of the world's most extensive real-time monitoring of a nation's citizens, IBM developed a special high-speed electro-mechanical computer known as the 077.[16] The computer made possible the creation of a single centralized registry of names and numbers required by the Social Security Administration.

A person's name became superfluous to the government after their assignment of a unique Social Security number. The *practical* reason for assignment of a number is that while 100 people may be named William Smith Jones, none would share the same government identifier. The *psychological* reason for assignment of a number is the dehumanizing effect it has on the human psyche.

Only eleven years after Yevgeny Zamyatin's futuristic 1920 novel *We* was first published in English, the Social Security Act brought to life Zamyatin's vision of a world in which a person's identity was embodied in their government-assigned identifier.[17] Reflecting the American people's new status of being identifiable as a number in a database, the first Social Security benefit checks *were* punch cards, and even today government checks have numbers at the bottom that are reminiscent in appearance of the punch card holes they replaced.[18]

The ability of the electro-mechanical computer to efficiently tabulate and analyze census data and other information about tens of millions of people was the crucial means enabling the German and U.S. governments to dramatically increase privacy invasions and physical intrusions into the lives of their respective populations beginning in the 1930s.

The Nazi's use of computer-analyzed census data to enforce military conscription and round up Jews and other undesirables was reflected by Roosevelt's similar use of 1940 census data to organize the military draft and the round up of Japanese-Americans for confinement in concentration camps after Pearl Harbor.[19] Computers also aided the war effort of both the Allies and Axis powers by breaking military codes and calculating artillery trajectories.[20]

The Menace of the Electronic Computer

Just as the federal government's *need* to compile information about Americans drove the commercial development of the electro-mechanical punch card computer, the federal government's growing and continuing *need* to compile information about Americans drove the development of the first commercial electronic computer. In April 1946, the Census Bureau gave a $300,000 deposit to two members of the ENIAC research computer team to begin development of a commercial electronic computer to handle compilation of detailed information about the burgeoning population in the U.S.[21] Named UNIVAC (UNIVersal Automatic Computer), the world's first commercial electronic computer was delivered to the Census Bureau on March 31, 1951.[22]

The public first became aware of the electronic computer's awesome ability to analyze large amounts of data when UNIVAC correctly predicted that Dwight D. Eisenhower would win the 1952 Presidential Election over Adlai Stevenson.[23] That demonstration provided solid evidence to thoughtful observers that the dynamic analytical capabilities of an electronic computer were a quantum leap beyond those of an electro-mechanical computer. There was not, however, a widely perceived need for electronic computers beyond their function of tracking people. By 1956 there were less than two-dozen in use throughout the world.

The ways in which the electronic computer has enabled government agencies to compile, readily access, and analyze the most personal information about Americans is so well-known that it is redundant to recount more than a few of them. Since 1935 the Social Security number has become a near universal personal identification number (PIN) for contacts between Americans and the government, banks and utility companies; the FBI has credit, law enforcement contact, and other information about literally all adult Americans in its NCIC (national criminal) database; and all state-issued drivers licenses must comply with federal standards. There are also thousands of specialized databases that federal, state, county and state agencies maintain on the Americans who have contact with them.

The following are just a few of the innumerable examples that illustrate how computerized databases are fulfilling the omnipresent threat computers have long posed to the obliteration of privacy and liberty. Government monitored cameras panning public area use face recognition software melded to a government database to search for hits between a photographed person and a particular person or someone that fits a profile. Digital cameras tied to state DMV databases photograph the license plates of vehicles approaching the border so Customs agents know the registered owner when the vehicle arrives at the checkpoint. People coming into or leaving the country are computer analyzed against a preconceived profile of a person who might be a security threat or involved in drug trafficking or some other unapproved activity. Portable computers in police cars enable law enforcement officers to instantly find out vehicle information and run a criminal background check on the occupants of a car. In addition, since the late 1980s the five Western governments involved in ECHELON have been using computer technology developed by the NSA to monitor a significant percentage of the world's telephone calls, facsimiles, telexes, and email messages transmitted by satellite.[24]

These and other surveillance activities are enhanced by federal and state agencies sharing their proprietary information databases.[25] A revolution in privacy invasions is also related to the digitization of enormous quantities of federal and state public records that makes them more readily available and easily transportable to casual observers.[26] The people named in those records have until now been able to maintain a modicum of privacy because the records were only available in either paper or magnetic tape form to people interested enough in their content to track them down. There is almost no end to the possible examples of privacy invasion that could be cited – and they are escalating as rapidly as the processing power of the computer is increasing. The gravity of the situation is indicated by the estimate that by 2006 the federal government will be spending $62 billion annually on surveillance and recording the private activities of Americans.[27]

However, as great as the invasive presence of the government's computerized monitoring of American's is, the menace of the electronic computer is being enhanced many times over by the joining of its information with private databases to create an all-encompassing surveillance capability. Concepts such as "data mining" and "predictive profiling" are being used to analyze the innumerable public and private electronic tracks that people leave. The FBI, for example, has purchased data from a national credit reporting agency and mailing list brokers to augment the information in its NCIC database, and it also used that information to create new federal criminal records for tens of millions of Americans. Another example is that after the events of September 11, 2001, a major national supermarket chain voluntarily and covertly turned over to the FBI its database of customers who have a discount club card, and the purchases they had made with their card.[28]

Those events also caused the head of Oracle, the world's largest database software company, to offer to set-up a "national database" that would be linked to an array of public and private information sources.[29] That data would be intertwined with iris scans, thumbprints and other personal biometric information, all of which would be accessible through a federally issued digital ID card. That card would make state driver's licenses and social security cards obsolete. What wasn't disclosed in news reports about this proposed database linked national ID card is that Oracle "was founded to assist the CIA with a database project code-named Oracle, and a quarter of its licensing revenue still comes from federal contracts."[30] So under the guise of performing a magnanimous civic duty, the head of the world's leading computer database company–that has close financial ties to the federal government — offered to be a central participant in the establishment of a national ID system.

The ominous menace to privacy posed by the melding of government and private computer resources is also indicated by the FAA's intention to implement a system that will analyze every airplane passenger's financial history, travel history, criminal history, family history, living arrangements and location, and other bits of personal data. The information will be used to build a real time "predictive profile" of the passenger's probability of causing problems, that will then be compared to a standardized "threat index" to determine if the passenger needs to be targeted for a search and questioning.[31]

Another grave menace to privacy is the computerized monitoring of products. It is apropos that the original concept of bar coding and computerizing product information was inspired by Herman Hollerith's use of punch cards to record individualized personal data. Described by its two graduate student inventors in their 1949 patent application as a *Classifying Apparatus and Method*, the bar code was barely used for several decades.[32] In 1972 one of the bar code's inventors expanded on his original concept while working for IBM, by co-inventing the Uniform Product Code (UPC). Although the UPC fulfilled the initial promise of the bar code as a product cataloguing and tracking tool, it was a market failure. Duplicating the computer's history, there was no rush by private industry to use the UPC. As with the computer, it was the federal government's need for UPC technology that is directly responsible for its ubiquitousness throughout society. On September 1, 1981 the Department of Defense mandated that a UPC had to be on every product purchased by the U.S. military.[33] That mandate effectively meant every common consumer product from chewing gum to televisions to dog food had to be marked with a UPC.

The threat to privacy by the universal branding of products with a computer code became crystal clear with the advent of Auto-ID technology. Developed at MIT, a significant recipient of federal intelligence agency funding, Auto-ID supersedes the UPC code with what is known as the Electronic Product Code (ePC). Auto-ID relies on sophisticated computer technology to brand each individual item – such as the cans in a case of pop – with a unique ePC identifier. This branding is accomplished by imbedding a very low cost microchip transmitter, presently the size of a piece of glitter, in each item. The item can be identified by a scanning device — similar to a UPC reader – or its location can be known at any given time by the transmitter's communication of the items identifying ePC to satellites.[34] The identification feature of *Auto-ID* works optimally when a product is purchased by a method linking it to its purchaser. This occurs when a credit, debit or customer discount card is used. That would also occur if as it has been suggested, a digitized national ID card is designed so it could be used as a universal product purchase card.

However, the grand daddy of all surveillance programs was established by the Department of Defense's Advanced Research Project Agency (DARPA) in early 2002. DARPA created the Information Assurance Office to oversee various surveillance projects, one of which is the Total Information Awareness (TIA). That program is intended to collect, store, extract and analyze every known piece of electronic data on all Americans, and selected people in countries around the world.[35] It is planned for TIA to do that through the multi-pronged approach of processing information and communications electronically and biometrically, in multiple languages, and by using predictive modeling of behavior and probable responses. TIA is envisioned to create an electronic DNA body print of the hundreds of millions of people under its surveillance net.

Initially funded by Congress with a $120 million appropriation authorized at the same time the Homeland Security Act was passed on November 20, 2002, the TIA program is a manifestation of that Act's *Information Analysis and Infrastructure Protection* provision. The processing of many thousands of bits of information in real-time related to each of the hundreds of millions of people the TIA will have under constant surveillance is the most demanding data processing project ever undertaken. Technology developed by IBM as a result of its $290 million dollar contract with the federal government for two supercomputers could satisfy the TIA's need for processing power. Announced the day before the Homeland Security Act was passed by Congress, the first of those computers will be 10 times faster than any previous computer, and capable of 360 *trillion* mathematical operations a second.[36]

It should be obvious by now that the computer was not invented so that word processing could replace typing a letter with a typewriter, or so a company's sales could be analyzed with a spreadsheet instead of on graph paper, or so customer information could be compiled in a database instead of keeping track of them with index cards, or so people could email messages instead of making telephone calls. As Jerry Mander observed *In the Absence of the Sacred,* it is arguable that the glamorization and consumerization of the computer has aided the public's acceptance of technology that is fundamentally repugnant to mankind in its purpose. The computer's repugnancy is inherent in its *form* of collecting, storing, analyzing and distributing detailed personal information that fulfills its *function* of being an efficient tool for the government to more thoroughly invade the privacy of individual human beings.

The Menace of the Internet

Although the Internet is generally hailed as a communication and research "wunderkind," the truth is far more disturbing.

For untold millions of people the Internet is considered nearly synonymous with the use of computers. That status makes its origin as a child of the federal government particularly relevant to the tidal wave of privacy invasions occurring in this country and throughout the world. As disturbing as it is that the electro-mechanical and the electronic computer were developed as commercial products to track Americans, it is perhaps more disquieting that the Internet is a child of the military's desire to have a bomb-proof reliable communications network between critical locations during and after a nuclear war.[37]

Development of what evolved into the Internet was begun by the Department of Defense's ARPA in late 1962 (renamed DARPA in 1996).[38] Years of developmental work paid off when data was successfully transmitted by the project in 1969. Initially known as ARPANET — a combination of ARPA and NETwork — the term Internet wasn't used to describe the computerized transmission system until 1982.[39]

The Internet's conception and design as a tool to make nuclear war practical was consistent with the first use of the federally funded ENIAC electronic computer after its completion in December 1945: the design of more efficient nuclear weapons.[40] As previously noted, two of the ENIAC's developers contracted with the Census Bureau to develop UNIVAC, that in 1951 became the first commercial electronic computer.

The probable destruction of telephone lines and intermediate sites during a nuclear war is what led to development of the Internet's unique capability to route information through its network of connections by alternate lines if the most direct route is unavailable. If Omaha and St. Louis are nuked, for example, then data could be routed through Minneapolis, New Orleans, or another routing equipment location. So that aspect of the Internet's form followed its function of making nuclear war a viable military option worthy of serious consideration. The Internet was intended to make the lunacy of the government's policy of Mutual Assured Destruction (MAD) possible. Coincidentally, shortly after the Cuban missile crisis in October 1962 brought the U.S. and Russia to the brink of nuclear war, production began on Stanley Kubrick's Dr. Strangelove or: How I Learned to Stop Worrying and Love the Bomb, and the military began development of the Internet.[41]

In addition, since it was designed as a method of transmitting highly classified military information that needed to be authenticated by the receiving party, the capability of ascertaining the source of all messages was incorporated into the Internet's design. That means a backdoor method for monitoring all Internet traffic is a feature of the system. Consequently the Internet's form also follows its function of needing to compromise the privacy of those who use the system.

The success of the military's ARPA networking project is unknown to the vast majority of people, who simply think of the Internet as a recreational vehicle, a business, shopping, dating or research aid, or an easier or cheaper way to communicate for pleasure or profit. Those benefits are merely incidental to the Internet's purpose of facilitating reliable military and other government communications in a time of great tumult and crisis. Although the military relies on the Internet for well over 50% of its communication, that primary function of the system is outside the public's consciousness due to the government's use of technology inaccessible to the civilian population.[42]

The structure of the Internet also makes it possible for the government to impair the privacy of its users. The government regularly and frequently uses subpoenas, search warrants and intimidation to acquire email logs and messages from Internet service providers, such as AOL. Those companies retain such records even after a person has deleted them from their own hard drive and made them inaccessible to their own email software. Such invasions of privacy are only one aspect of the surveillance made possible by the Internet's extension of the electronic computer's innate qualities, and the melding of private and government databases to create a covertly supra personal information resource.

The Computer's Menace to Privacy and Liberty

Different aspects of the computer's menace to privacy and human liberty have been explored in various forums. Three of those significant threats are graphically illustrated in a book, a movie and a television series episode that are all more than 30 years old. They reflect the concern expressed by learned people about the possible negative impact of computers to humankind: a concern that seemed to largely evaporate after the 1960s.

Year of Consent, a 1954 novella by Kendell Foster Crossen, presents a remarkably accurate vision of the menace electronic computer's pose for the obliteration of human privacy and the submergence of liberty to the whims of rulers exercising near absolute power masked by a public facade of governmental benevolence and concern for carrying out their Constitutional mandates to protect the public's welfare and ensure national security. Crossen's vision includes an extremely powerful central computer that uses predictive software and an enormous database of personal information to electro-biometrically analyze images captured by cameras placed in all public and many private areas to determine who may be thinking thoughts that could threaten the rule of the government. As it is envisioned the Department of Defense's TIA program will bring Crossen's prophecy into the realm of reality.

The 1969 movie *Colossus: The Forbin Project*, based on D. F. Jones' 1966 book, extended the concept of computer-monitored surveillance to encompass the entire world. It is so intensely real and its vision of the future so disturbing that its release to theaters was delayed until 1970: a year after it was completed. In *Colossus* the catastrophe mankind suffered originated with the government carrying out its mission to provide national security. *Colossus* portrays with crystal clarity how easy it is for the use of electronic devices developed by the government for outwardly benign and beneficently-intentioned purposes to rapidly spin out of control. Multiple aspects of human life were invaded and profoundly affected by the hydra-headed surveillance monster *Colossus* became, and that were unrelated to the stated reasons for its development and deployment.

First broadcast in November 1963, *O.B.I.T.* was an episode of The Outer Limits television series that clearly showed the profoundly negative psychological impact of surveillance systems both on the people being monitored, *and* on the people involved in the monitoring. A murder investigation at a top-secret defense facility uncovers the existence of an electronic device called the Outer Bank Individuated Teletracer (O.B.I.T.). O.B.I.T. is capable of spying on anyone at anytime, anywhere, and it is used at the defense facility to help ensure national security. It is learned during the course of the investigation, however, that O.B.I.T. machines have been distributed throughout government agencies and private businesses by aliens who understand the demoralizing impact that spying and being spied on has on the human psyche. O.B.I.T. may have been a prophetic foretelling of the psychological consequences of the escalating level of computerized monitoring and diminishment of privacy in the U.S. and other westernized nations. It also served as a dire warning that pervasive electronic monitoring of human beings is an *unnatural* "alien" process that negatively and perhaps permanently alters the consciousness of the watcher *and* the watched.

Driven by the needs of the federal government, the electronic computer is the vehicle that has enabled the theory and fears of pervasive surveillance to be translated into real life. Reminiscent of O.B.I.T.'s distribution process, the Department of Defense's secretive and mysterious ARPA funnels its technological breakthroughs involving surveillance of Americans into the "private" sector for mass manufacture and distribution.[43]

Proponents of privacy invasions are fond of flippantly asserting that if you have nothing to hide you have nothing to fear from government surveillance and data collection. Yet it is doubtful any of those people believes what they are saying. Their hypocrisy can easily be revealed by proposing that multiple video cameras broadcasting a picture and sound live over the Internet be installed in every room of their home. The cameras would be strategically aimed so people all over the world would be able to view and hear what goes on in every nook and cranny of their home at all times. A person claiming to have nothing to hide would be watched by people all over the world as he or she used the toilet, took a shower or bath, changed their clothes, brushed their teeth, as well as everything else they did in their home. People worldwide would know what brand of breakfast cereal the person ate, whether they chewed with their mouth open, what brand of deodorant they used, how often they changed their underwear, and whether they snored.

Portable cameras broadcasting live over the Internet could continue the monitoring of the person's life whenever he or she left their home. People around the world could watch and hear them as they shopped at the supermarket, serviced their car, worked at their job, went to a movie, visited family or friends, or went to a restaurant for Sunday brunch. Is their any doubt every person claiming they have nothing to hide would recoil in horror when faced with having *every* moment of their life watched 24-hours a day by Peeping Toms, government agents and other voyeurs over the Internet?

The technology exists for a person to live a real life O.B.I.T. situation that would have profound psychic effects on not just that person's mind and behavior, but on the watchers as well. It may even be the case that living inside an all-pervasive surveillance prison 24-hours a day can be more psychologically debilitating than confinement in a physical prison where moments of privacy may be found occasionally.[44]

Humanity thus faces ever-increasing privacy invasions that are indicative of the computer's continuing fulfillment of its function and purpose for being. From whatever perspective one looks at Herman Hollerith's invention, his success at creating a comprehensive instrument of human monitoring makes him the Godfather of the modern surveillance state.

There is a German word describing what Hollerith hath wrought on mankind: *Karteimensch*, which loosely means a person who is living a punch card existence. Every person in a society dominated by computers has a digital representation of their life stored in multiple databases. Insofar as those who rely on those databases for information about the person are concerned, the person's existence is not defined by who they are as a person, but by how they are categorized in those databases. So the more a society relies on computers, the more the people in that society can be considered to live "a punch card existence."

Compounding moral and philosophical issues related to replacing the evaluation of a person based on who they actually are with a numerical representation of them that exists only in an inanimate database, is the consideration that it is known computer databases have a high degree of erroneous and stale data.[45] So any computer based punch card representation of a person is likely to be seriously flawed.

Given the current extent of data collection and surveillance, considerations of a national ID card in the U.S. are more symbolic than substantive. The national ID card would be a front-end for accessing information already accumulated by a multitude of current data-collection methods. However, a national ID card would also endanger people by providing more ready access to that information. In 1890, a far-seeing person could have likely predicted that some form of national ID card would one day be a reality. Such an ID card is simply an extension of the surveillance capabilities of Hollerith's original electro-mechanical computer.[46]

The all-pervasive presence in our society is the direct result of the federal government's Constitutional mandate to use the Census Bureau to spy on American's every 10 years. If the federal government had not spurred its invention, commercial marketing and continued development, the computer as we know it today would not exist.[47] In many cases private users have taken advantage of the computer's integrated spy capabilities to mimic the government's use of them as an invasive personal data resource. However, if perchance the computer had been invented under alternate circumstances for private uses unrelated to invading privacy, it would be at a different stage of development and its form would likely be radically different. It is even less likely the Internet would exist in the absence of the federal government's need for its creation, since there is no need in the private world corresponding to the military's push for its development to ensure reliable and secure communications during a nuclear war.

This means the benign uses of computers by individuals and businesses are only incidental to their central function of *spying* on people, and those relatively innocuous uses obfuscate reality by creating the illusion that the *spying* is the incidental activity. The perceived and trumpeted advantages of using the computer and its child — the Internet — misdirect attention away from the deviousness underlying it — like a Siren's song luring enchanted mariners to their deaths on hidden rocks.

The multitude of invasive purposes computers are being used for today does not stem from the misuse of a neutral technology. Quite to the contrary, those *nefarious* uses are the most perfect expression of the technology underlying the conception and design of computers. That emphasizes a great unresolved issue facing humanity: How is it to deal with the fundamental nature of the computer as a device created for the efficient destruction of privacy, and concomitantly, human liberty?

Conclusion

Our liberty has been subverted by the avalanche of privacy invasions that have followed in the wake of the computer's invention as a means of turning the census into a gold mine of detailed information about Americans.

The degree to which our liberty has evaporated in the face of seemingly beneficent public and private computerization is not surprising to those who understand its relationship to privacy. One hundred and twenty-seven years before Herman Hollerith had his "ah ha" moment of conceiving the computer that changed the world, William Thornton expressed his fears to the House of Commons about the consequences of surveilling the British people with a census: "I hold this project to be totally subversive of the last remains of English liberty."[48]

In his 1851 book *Idée Générale de la Révolution au XIX Siècle*, Pierre-Joseph Proudhon gave voice to what Thornton left unspoken: A census is destructive to liberty because it contributes to a person being, "... noted, registered, enumerated, accounted for, stamped, measured, classified, audited, patented, licensed, authorized, ... in every operation, every transaction, every movement."[49] Those are the very activities the computer has enabled to be done to a degree that was only imaginable before its creation.

The proclamation of the lead character in the 1967-68 television series *The Prisoner*, who was imprisoned in a remote village, designated as Number 6, and subjected to omnipresent electronic and human surveillance may prove to be an anthem for those of the 21st Century that cherish liberty: "I am not a number. I am a free man! I will not be pushed, filed, indexed, debriefed, or numbered!"[50]

That emphatic statement sums up the intertwining relationship between privacy and liberty: the former is a prerequisite for the latter. Envisioned and designed to obliterate privacy, the computer is doing the same to liberty. Man is now left to ponder how to deal with the consequences of what Herman Hollerith loosened upon the world: a grave menace to human liberty.[51]

It is not a problem that can be ignored except at our peril, because whether one's life is scrutinized and cataloged under the guise of a census, a bank account number, a social security number, a supermarket discount card, or a national identification card, the result is the same: one's liberty is undermined and its exercise impaired.

Notes

1. Justice Brandeis dissented in *Olmstead v. U.S.*, 277 U.S. 438, 479 (1928). That was the first case in which the Supreme Court gave its stamp of approval to the wire tapping of private telephone conversations by government agents. Justice Brandeis wrote: "The makers of our Constitution undertook to secure conditions favorable to the pursuit of happiness. They recognized the significance of man's spiritual nature, of his feelings and of his intellect. They knew that only a part of the pain, pleasure and satisfactions of life are to be found in material things. They sought to protect Americans in their beliefs, their thoughts, their emotions and their sensations. They conferred, as against the Government, *the right to be let alone — the most comprehensive of rights and the right most valued by civilized men*" (emphasis added).

2. *Article I, Section 2*. One of the two specific purposes of the census provision was to facilitate tax collection.

3. Edwin Black, *IBM and the Holocaust* (New York: Crown Publishers, 2001), 25.

4. Robert Sober, *IBM: Colossus in Transition* (New York: Truman Talley Books, 1981), 14, cited in *IBM and the Holocaust* at 25 fn.5.

5. One of these was the Schertz calculating machine, circa 1855.

6. Emerson W. Pugh, *Building IBM: Shaping an Industry and Its Technology* (Cambridge: MIT Press, 1995), 12–13, cited in *IBM and the Holocaust*, 26 fn. 10.

7. *IBM and the Holocaust*, 26, 28. The next census in Russia wasn't performed until 1926.

8. *Id.* at 27

9. *Id.* at 26

10. Robert M. Gagne et al., *Psychological Principles in System Development* (New York: Holt, Rinehart and Winston, 1966), 78. It is also noted in the book that the punch cards were referred to as Hollerith cards after their inventor.

11. *IBM and the Holocaust* at 31.

12. *Id.* at 40

13. *Id.* at 50. IBM was able to increase its investment in Germany in near secrecy because the name of its German subsidiary, Dehomag, didn't imply any connection with IBM. For the same reason, IBM was able to export American computer technology to Germany that the company profited from by servicing the needs of the Nazis.

Dehomag was founded in Germany in 1910 to market Hollerith's machines in exchange for a share of its business and royalties on his patents. *Id.* at 30. IBM assumed 90% ownership of Dehomag in 1922 when it became an IBM subsidiary. *Id.* at 43.

IBM's aiding of the Nazis in their cause without any moral compunction dated back to the precedent Hollerith set in the mid 1890s when his fledging company performed a census of Russia that could have provided information to be used by Czar Nicholas II to strengthen his rule. *Id.* at 46–47.

IBM's moral neutrality about the use of its technology was very financially rewarding. In 1933 its German subsidiary, Dehomag, generated over 50% of the profits of IBM's 70+ foreign subsidiaries. *Id.* at 43–44. Dehomag has been known as IBM Germany since 1971.

14. *Id.* at 22

15. *Id.* at 46

16. William Moseley, Ph.D., *Some Computer History*, Interdisciplinary 15, UC Santa Barbara, April 3, 2002, p. 18 at: http://www.ic.ucsb.edu/~int15/lectures/lecture2_s02.pdf.

17. It is noteworthy that Zamyatin intuitively recognized the relationship between a government assigned number and the utter obliteration of privacy. The two central features of his futuristic vision was the universal use of a government assigned number that replaced the use of personal names in daily activities, and homes that had glass walls so a person was constantly under surveillance by neighbors and passersby. Augmenting the lack of privacy was the inculcation in people from an early age that it was their civic duty to report suspicious activity by strangers, or odd behavior by someone they knew, to the police.

18. *Id.*

19. *IBM and the Holocaust* at 344–346. In a radio address encouraging participation in the 1940 census, Eleanor Roosevelt described it as "the greatest assemblage of facts ever collected by any people about the things that affect their welfare" at 345. That information was subsequently used to ghettoize Japanese-American undesirables in concentration camps who also had their wealth confiscated — just as the Nazi's did to Jews, Gypsies, communists and other groups.

20. *Id.* at 120. IBM received so many lucrative contracts from the United States government ("from the Department of Labor to the War Department") that "[t]he company became [a] quasi-governmental" entity.

21. Mary Bellis, *The History of the UNIVAC Computer — Inventors Presper Eckert and John Machly*, in *Inventors of the Modern Computer*, at http://inventors.about.com/library/weekly/aa062398.htm. The ENIAC was a federally funded research computer that when completed in December 1945, was first used to design nuclear weapons and calculate artillery trajectories. Source: Museum of Computer History, RE-PC, Seattle, WA.

22. *Id.* The Census Bureau placed a $400,000 ceiling on the project when the computers design and contract was finalized in 1948. Remington Rand, Inc. bailed out Drs. Eckert and Machly when they ran out of money in 1950. The computer was completed by the UNIVAC Division of Remington Rand. A total of forty-six UNIVACs were sold to government and large businesses.

23. *Id.*

24. The transmissions are scanned for the presence of predetermined keywords that could indicate involvement in some covert activity. See e.g., Nicky Hager, *Secret Power: New Zealand's Role in the International Spy Network*, (Craig Potton Publishing, PO Box 555, Nelson, New Zealand, 1996). See an excerpt from the book in Covert Action Quarterly at: mediafilter.org/caq/echelon/

25. "Government Exchange and Merger of Citizens' Personal Data Called 'Systematic and Routine'," privacilla.org, March 12, 2001. Available at: http://www.privacilla.org/releases/press005.html

26. See, e.g., "The End of Practical Obscurity," privacilla.org, June 15, 2001. Available at: http://www.privacilla.org/government/practicalobscurity.html

27. Jeffrey Rosen, "Silicon Valley's Spy Game," *New York Times Magazine*, April

14, 2002. Available at: http://www.nytimes.com/2002/04/14/magazine/14TECHNO. html

28. Kelley Beaucar Vlahos, "Store Customer Cards a Source for FBI?" Fox News, August 1, 2002. See also CASPIAN's website at www.nocards.com.

29. As of September 20, 2002, Oracle's annual revenues were $10.8 *billion*. Source: http://www.oracle.com/corporate/index.html

30. Brendan I. Koerner, "The Security Traders: As Washington prepares to spend tens of billions on Homeland Security, companies are gearing up for the biggest government bonanza since the Cold War," *Mother Jones*, October 2002 (6), pp. 46–47.

31. Jeffrey Rosen, "Silicon Valley's Spy Game," *New York Times Magazine*, April 14, 2002.

32. Russ Adams, *Bar Code 1*, http://adams1.com/pub/russadam/history.html and, *History of Bar Codes*, Tony Seideman, American Heritage of Invention and Technology, reprinted at: http://www.swlamall.com/WebTronics/barcodeHostory.htm

33. *Id.*

34. See the official MIT Auto-ID website at: http://autoidcenter.org/main.asp

35. For an excellent explanation of the implications of the TIA project, see, William Safire, "You Are a Suspect," *The New York Times*, Nov. 14, 2002; and Audrey Hudson, "A Supersnoop's Dream," *The Washington Times*, Nov. 15, 2002. Mr. Safire didn't mention that state drivers licenses can easily be turned into de facto national I.D. cards by linking them to the TIA databases, and any other database collection and analysis system authorized under Homeland Security's Title II's.

36. John Markoff (staff), "I.B.M. Plans a Computer That Will Set Power Record," *The New York Times*, Technology Section, November 19, 2002. The computer is code named Blue Gene/L. The publicly announced purpose of the supercomputers is to do simulations related to nuclear war and nuclear waste. However, just as the development of the ENIAC computer in 1945 that was used for nuclear weapons related research, led to development of the UNIVAC for the Census Bureau, the technology underlying the Blue Gene/L will enable a level of data processing that was inconceivable prior to its development.

37. Walt Howe, "A Brief History of the Internet," April 21, 2002. Available at: http://www.walthowe.com/navnet/history.html.

38. Robert H Zakon, *Hobbes' Internet Timeline v5.6*, April 1, 2002. Available at: http://www.zakon.org/robert/internet/timeline/. The Defense Department formed ARPA in 1958 after the Russian's launched the Sputnik satellite, to ensure the U.S. would have the lead in militarily useful science and technology. DARPA is independent from other military R&D agencies and it reports directly to senior DoD officials.

39. Walt Howe, "A Brief History of the Internet," April 21, 2002. Available at: http://www.walthowe.com/navnet/history.html. ARPA (also known as DARPA) is still the central military research organization. See: www.darpa.mil.

40. *The History of the UNIVAC Computer*, supra. The ENIAC was a federally funded research computer that when completed in December 1945, was first used to design nuclear weapons and calculate artillery trajectories. Source: Museum of Computer History, RE-PC, Seattle, WA.

41. Source: http://www.teachwithmovies.org/guides/dr-strangelove.html

42. Professor Peter Kirstein, "The ARAPANET," June 26, 1998. Available at: http://www.funet.fi/index/FUNET/history/internet/en/1980.html. This technology includes sophisticated encryption technology.

43. See, e.g., A summary of DARPA's mission and accomplishments on its website at: www.darpa.mil/body/pdf/transition.pdf.

44. O.B.I.T.'s all-pervasive monitoring is an extension of Jeremy Bentham's idea of a Panoptical Prison constructed so that all prisoners would be subjected to near constant surveillance.

45. See e.g., *The Justice Juggernaut: Fighting Street Crime, Controlling Citizens* (New Brunswick, N.J.: Rutgers University Press, 1991), pp. 70–75.

46. The ghost of Herman Hollerith lives on in IBM's recent development of a computer storage device code named Millipede that stores information by punching tiny holes in a plastic surface. Resembling a tiny punch-card system, Millipede stores data at a density 20 times more than the most advanced magnetic or electronic devices. Millipedes indentations can be erased and rewritten hundreds of thousands of times, and its nanotechnology can pack 3 billion bits of information into a hole the size of that used to store a single bit of information in the Hollerith's original computer. That translates into the storage of 25 million pages of data on a surface the size of a postage stamp. Source: David Legard (IDG News Service), "IBM Updates Punch-Card Storage," *PC World*, June 11, 2002.

47. An excellent indicator that private investors and companies would not have funded the production and marketing of the computer in the absence of the government's involvement is that they *didn't*. Herman Hollerith successfully demonstrated the computer he developed in 1884 to a number of companies, *none* of which purchased a single one. The same computer those companies didn't purchase was the one that the U.S. Census Bureau chose to use for the 1890 census. It was the money from that contract that enabled Hollerith to begin manufacturing his computers. Furthermore, five years after the UNIVAC computer became commercially available, less than *two-dozen* were sold worldwide.

Another indicator of why the computer would not have developed as it has in the absence of the government's involvement is that there wasn't, and may still not be, a discernable need for them apart from its indisputable ability to compile, store and analyze enormous amounts of data about people. Articles in the *Atlantic Monthly* have raised the spectre that the computer does not contribute to the productivity of businesses (Alan S. Blinder and Richard E. Quandt, "The Computer and the Economy; will information technology ever produce the productivity gains that were predicted?" Dec. 1997, v280, n6, p26(6)), and it may even retard the learning of children (Todd Oppenheimer, "The Computer Delusion," July 1997, v280, n1, p45(14)).

48. In his 1753 address William Thornton said: "I was never more astonished and alarmed since I had the honour to sit in this House.... And what purpose will it answer to know where the kingdom is crowded ... except we are to be driven ... as graziers do cattle? As to myself, I hold this project to be totally subversive of the last remains of English liberty." Kevin Ashley, "Process re-engineering: a brief history of Government computing," *NDAD Newsletter* #8, June 2000. Available at: http://ndad.ulcc.ac.uk/events/newsletters/news008/adros.html

49. Jane Caplan and John Torpey, eds., *Documenting Individual Identity*, (Princeton, N.J.: Princeton University Press, 2001), cited at p. 1. A more complete quote is: "To be governed is to be under surveillance, inspected, spied on, superintended, regulated, restrained, indoctrinated, preached at, controlled, appraised, assessed, censored, commanded. To be governed is to be noted, registered, enumerated, accounted for, stamped, measured, classified, audited, patented, licensed, authorized, ... in every operation, every transaction, every movement."

50. Apropos to this essay's theme that a punch card society has been systematically and deliberately created by the federal government is the following question by The Prisoner's lead character, and the response by his captors: "What do you want?," to which they respond, "We want information, and by hook or by crook we will get it!"

51. This begs a disturbing question to be asked and the answer needs to be faced clearly. Since it was known by learned people at the time the Constitution was written that one of the most destructive acts the government could take to undermine human liberty was a census, why was the Constitution written to mandate a national census every 10 years? In other words, the "founding fathers" specifically included the obliteration of privacy and the accompanying destruction of liberty is a built-in feature of the Constitution. For that reason alone the Constitution cannot be viewed as a document promoting human liberty. It was left to Herman Hollerith to create the technology that enabled the effects of the census mandate, which can be referred to as the "liberty destruction provision," to be fully realized.

Why I Oppose
Government Enumeration
Carl Watner

This essay, an original contribution to this anthology, was written to question the assumptions (1) that governments should coercively collect information about their citizens, and (2) that coercive governments can legitimately serve as the proper organizations in a free society to identify and document people for legal purposes. The author is editor of this anthology.

> ... as I was cold and wet I sat down at a good fire in the bar room to dry my great coat and saddlebags.... There presently came in, one after another half a dozen ... substantial yeomen of the neighborhood, who sitting down to the fire after lighting their pipes, began a lively conversation upon politics [circa 1773]. As I believed I was unknown to all of them, I sat in total silence to hear them. One said, "The people of Boston are distracted." Another answered, "No wonder the people of Boston are distracted; oppression will make wise men mad." A third said, "What would you say if a fellow should come to your house and tell you he was come to take a list of your cattle that Parliament might tax them for you for so much a head?" And how should you feel if he should go out and break open your barn, to take down your oxen, cows, horses, and sheep?" "What would I say," replied the first, "I would knock him in the head." "Well," said a fourth, "if Parliament can take away Mr. Hancock's wharf and Mr. Row's wharf, they can take away your barn and my house." After much more reasoning in this style, a fifth who had as yet been silent, broke out, "Well it is high time for us to rebel. We must rebel sometime or other: and we had better rebel now than at any time to come: if we put it off for ten or twenty years, and let them go on as they have begun, they will get a strong party among us, and plague us a great deal more than they can now. As yet they have but a small party on their side."
>
> — John Adams, "Old Family Letters," p. 140 cited
> in David McCullough, John Adams
> (New York: Simon & Schuster), 2001, pp. 74–75.

The purpose of this essay is to question the assumption that we need a government program that produces national ID (and by implication observe that resistance should be based on principle not pragmatism). From the Biblical story of King David (who caused a plague by counting his people), to the Roman censors who counted Joseph, Mary and Jesus in Bethlehem, to Parliament's attempt to list colonial cattle, to today's call for national identification cards the essential purpose behind government data gathering has always been the same: to enhance government's control over its subject population. The only difference between "breaking down barn doors" to count your animals, or forcibly implanting their offspring or our newborn children with a subdermal micro-chip is the advance of technology. Government identification programs, whether they are based upon a birth certificate, a wallet card (like the Social Security card), a smart card (with a programmable microchip), an implanted micro-chip, or some other form of biometric recognition are all based upon the same principle: that the government has the right and necessity to track, monitor, and control the people and property within its geographic boundaries.[1] As one commentator has pointed out, "there is no difference in principle between being forced to carry a microchip in a plastic card in your wallet or in a little pellet in your arm."[2] The question is not whether one technology is better or worse than another; the question is whether we endorse the argument that some sort of government enumeration is necessary.

Whether what we call "national ID" would be administered at the state or federal level, each and every person in the United States would be issued a government identification, and would be required to use it in order to participate in numerous activities. A true national identification card would necessarily be universal (if not issued to every newborn it would be issued to children upon reaching a certain age) and compulsory (it would become a crime, punishable by fine or imprisonment, to refuse to accept or use such a document). It would also be a violation of the law to have more than one card, to use the card of another person, or to hold a card in the name of an alias. In short, a national ID would act as a domestic passport. In many countries around the world, where such cards actually exist, they are needed to rent an apartment, to buy a house, apply for a job, pay one's utility and telephone bills, withdraw books from the library, or to access health care services. They could act as a surrogate drivers license, passport, voter registration card, and hunting/fishing license.[3] With micro-chip technology, such a card would act as a complete medical, financial, tax, and travel dossier, documenting where you have been, how you got there, and how you paid for the services you purchased. In conjunction with other income data reported to the Internal Revenue Service, it could be used to generate an income tax return for you every year. The chips could be linked "directly to all government agencies so the card could be used to verify that the holder has no delinquencies on taxes or child support," no overdue library books, no parking fines, no bounced checks, and no unpaid traffic violations. They would also "have the capability to be disabled from a central location at the discretion of any government agency, instantly rendering its holder unable to travel or function in society."[4] In short, government identification would be a "license to live," based on the idea that "living is a government privilege, not a right."[5] It would be an attack on every person's right to exist upon the surface of the earth without being seized by the authorities for violating the laws governing personal identification.

Most readers picking this book up for the first time would want to know if I am opposed to *all* government enumeration. "Don't censuses and other government surveys, etc., serve many useful social purposes? Aren't the various forms of government data gathering simply like other tools and technologies that are capable of doing both good and harm?" the reader might ask. Nonetheless, "Yes," *I* am really opposed to *all* forms of government enumeration. My objection to government enumeration and data gathering is not to the collection and registration of information *per se*, but rather to the coercive nature of the institution that gathers it. If some private organization chooses to solicit information from me, I may or may not respond. However, I will suffer no criminal penalties if I refuse to cooperate. When the State demands we conform to its identification procedures or collects information about us and our affairs, there are usually fines, penalties, or imprisonment for those who do not cooperate.

There is a definite ethical question involved in justifying government data gathering. Is it morally proper to coerce those who refuse to participate in enumeration programs or provide information demanded by the government? Do the ends justify the means? I don't necessarily object to the ends (such as improved public health or security) but I do object to the means, and question whether improper means can bring about beneficial ends for everybody.[6] In many countries if one steadfastly refuses to cooperate (e.g., in refusing to register the birth of one's children with the government, or in refusing to carry a government ID card), one will be arrested; and if one resists arrest, one will be ultimately dragged off to jail. Or if one acts in self-defense to protect one's self from arrest one will be killed for resisting an officer of the law. By using violence or the threat of violence against the non-cooperator, governments are ultimately violating the moral commandment not to kill or molest peaceful people.

Many times throughout history, government collection of seemingly innocent data (such as tribal or ethnic or racial affiliation) has resulted in horrible and deplorable genocide. The uses (and the abuses which are ultimately inherent in government administration) of government information in identifying and locating the civilian victims of the Nazis during World War II, or of the blacks in South Africa, or of the Tutsis in Rwanda, would, by themselves, be reason enough to question and then demand the cessation of government enumeration. The numbering and internment in the United States of over 100,000 American citizens of Japanese descent during World War II should be sufficient to prove my point.[7] But even if it could be proven that government data collection benefits society in other ways (thus using the ends to justify the means), I would still be opposed because government necessarily has to act coercively in the manner in which it collects such information. I believe this to be wrong from an ethical perspective, and believe its sets the stage for the sorts of human right abuses that we have experienced under every species of government, whether democratic or totalitarian. As Robert Nisbet once noted, "With all respect to differences among types of government, there is not, in strict theory, any difference between the powers available to the democratic and to the totalitarian State."[8]

The best example of a voluntary ID system that I can offer is that presented by the credit card companies, such as Visa, MasterCard, Discover, and American Express. These companies have managed "to make their cards acceptable in all civilized countries."[9] Although they each might like to attain a coercive monopoly over the credit card market, unlike national governments, none of these organizations has the right to compel people to use their credit cards. Compare credit cards to national identification cards: no one is forced to have a credit card; some people may have more than one credit card from the same company, or even have multiple credit cards from different companies. Most people pay their bills because they want to maintain their credit rating and want to take advantage of the benefits and conveniences derived from using credit cards. But no one is put in jail: neither those who do not use credit cards, nor those merchants who refuse to accept credit cards in their businesses. In short, the absence of coercion and the existence of a "variety of legal choices does not mean chaos." As the ruminations at the end of my essay on the history of the state birth certificate, and the discussion in Sunni Maravillosa's essay, "ID Without Big Brother," both point out, there are many noninvasive methods which might be used to identify people in the absence of a government monopoly.

No one can really know for sure whether the September 11th terrorist attacks would have been prevented by the existence of a national ID card, or if ways could have been found to circumvent the system. Beside the moral question, there are all sorts of pragmatic problems associated with the issuance of a national ID card. Fake identity documents are to be found in every country of the world.[10] If cards were issued to some 280 million Americans in the course of a year, that means that more than a million cards would have to be issued every work day, or at least 125,000 per hour. And more importantly, what sort of document will a citizen have to show to secure such a card? There is still no fool-proof system in existence in the United States for affirming legitimate birth certificates or other proofs of identity. If you question this, then how did some 3000 dead people vote in one Florida county in the 2000 Presidential election, or why do statistics show that there are many millions more drivers licenses issued nation-wide than there are adults who drive? The point is there are extreme problems with the integrity of data in existing systems, so how will a new system function effectively?[11] Certainly, national ID programs in such countries as Spain, France, and Italy have not stopped terrorists, and even if it could somehow be proved that a national ID program would have prevented the September 11th hijackings, the point is that national ID is not really an issue about technology or its practical implementation.[12]

The decision whether or not to adopt national I.D. is really a moral and philosophical issue that we have to face: do our rights emanate from the State or do individual rights inhere in the individual? Is everyone "endowed by their Creator with certain inalienable rights," as the Declaration of Independence puts it, or do we need to be registered and identified by government in order to be assured that we receive whatever privileges and benefits it (the government) grants us? While there certainly are dangers living in a free world, the principle behind national ID leads straight to a totalitarian society. With national I.D. there is no logical stopping point short of totalitarian control. Do we want to embrace that prospect? As "Harvey Silverglate, a criminal defense lawyer in Boston who specializes in civil liberties issues," put it

> Individuals, groups, gangs— the damage that they have done pales in significance when compared to the damage done by governments out of control. There is no example of a privately caused Holocaust in history.... I would prefer to live in a world where governments are more circumscribed than in a world that gives governments enormous, unlimited powers [such as a national I.D. program] to keep private terrorism circumscribed. I would rather live with a certain amount of private terrorism than with government totalitarianism.[13]

The evidence in this book lends credence to the conclusion that national ID cards are a "trademark of totalitarianism" and that no totalitarian government operates without such a system.[14]

Notes

1. My references to "national ID cards," government enumeration, government identification, and government data gathering are all-inclusive. They refer to both "card-type" and "card-less" governmental systems, past, present, or future which track, identify, and monitor people within the space boundaries which governments monopolize. It is even possible that we might have a card-less system given the advance of biometrics technology. Using biometric features, such as iris-scan, voice recognition, and/or fingerprints each person's features could be fed into a database and identification verified by scanners (thus obviating the need for each

person to carry around their own I.D. card). Another card-less possibility would make use of the ability of surveillance cameras to match faces of people with centrally-stored digital images.

2. Peter Lalonde and Paul Lalonde, *Racing Toward the Mark of the Beast* (Eugene: Harvest House Publishers, 1994), p.18, quoting Martin Anderson from *The Washington Times*, October 13, 1993.

3. Ching-Yi Liu, "How Smart Is the IC Card?: The Proposed National Smart Card ...," http:www/isoc.org/inet99/posters/439/ paragraph 6. ID cards are already used for these purposes in Taiwan and Singapore.

4. This point was made in a forwarded e-mail message of March 9, 2002, from John Utley [jbutley@earthlink.net].

5. See Robert Ellis Smith's monograph, "A National ID Card: A License to Live," Providence: *Privacy Journal*, 2002, p. 44, footnote 1. Fred Woodworth of *The Match* in Tucson, also developed this theme in personal correspondence (December 28, 2001) with the author. Also see Duncan Frissell, "What's Our National Identity?" *The Sierra Times*, December 6, 2001 at http://sierratimes.com/archive/files/dec/06/eddf120601.htm

6. See Murray N. Rothbard, "Toward a Reconstruction of Utility and Welfare Economics," in Mary Sennholz, editor, *On Freedom and Free Enterprise* (New York: D. Van Nostrand Company, 1956), pp. 224-262. See the discussion of the unanimity principle and "The Role of the State," pp. 244-253.

7. On the numbering of Japanese-Americans see Mine Okubo, *Citizen 13660* (Seattle: University of Washington Press, 1946). Ms. Okubo's family number and internment number was 13660. In the second printing (1989) of the reprint edition of 1983, see her drawings and commentary on pages 19 and 22. In Maisie and Richard Conrat, *Executive Order 9066: The Interment of 110,000 Japanese Americans* (Los Angeles: California Historical Society, 1972), see the photos of numbering tags on the frontispiece and page 50. In Lawson Fusao Inada (editor), *Only What They Could Carry: The Japanese American Internment Experience* (Berkeley: Heyday Books, 2000) see the photo of Hiro Niwa's evacuation tag # 13664, at p. 57.

8. Robert Nisbet, "The State" in D. J. Enright, editor, *Fair of Speech* (Oxford: Oxford University Press, 1985), pp. 185-202 at p. 186.

9. See Edward Stringham, "Market Chosen Law," 14 *Journal of Libertarian Studies* (Winter 1998-1999), pp. 53-77 at pp. 62-63.

10. See the interesting article by Kitty Oviedo, "Only We Can Make Ourselves Safe: Personal Protection, Not Government Protection," *The Voluntaryist* whole number 117 (2nd Quarter 2003), p. 8, in which this observation is made.

11. "Technology Problems with the National ID Card" were raised by Jason Kosorec of Eaglecheck, Ltd., Cleveland, OH, in personal e-mail of February 18, 2002.

12. See Julia Scheeres, "ID Cards Are *De Rigueur* Worldwide," at http://www.wired.com/news/conflict/0,2100,47073,00.html, paragraph 14.

13. Josh Gewolb, Assistant to Harvey Silverglate, approved use of this quote in an e-mail of April 10, 2002, to the author. The original version of this quote appears in Simson Garfinkel, *Database Nation* (Sebastopol: O'Reilly & Associates, 2000), at p. 239.

14. For the expression "trademark of totalitarianism," see Congressman Ron Paul, "Statement for the Government Reform Committee Hearing on National ID Card Proposals," November 16, 2001 at http://www.house.gov/paul/congrec/con-grec2001/cr111601.htm. For the assertion that "no totalitarian government operates

without such a system" of ID see the 1986 reference to Analise Anderson, by Annie I. Anton, "National Identification Cards," PUBP 8100s—Information Policy, December 17, 1996, at http://www.cc.gatech.edu/computing/SW_Eng/people/Phd/id. html, next to last paragraph of Sec. IV, Summary.

Gandhi's Story in South Africa
Calvin Kytle

On August 22, 1906, the South African government of the Transvaal pub-lished a draft ordinance under which all Indians (men, women, and children 8 or older) were required to register and receive a certificate of registration from the Registrar of Asiatics. Such certificate was to be carried at all times, was to be produced for any police officer upon demand, and was to be required to con-duct any official business. An Englishman who lived in the Transvaal called the registration "the fastening of the dog's collar" around the neck of the Indians. This story recounts Gandhi's leadership of the resistance to the registration law. It showed him that "truth force" (satyagraha) or nonviolent resistance and civil disobedience were both a moral and practical way to protest unjust laws. Calvin Kytle, as acting director of a federal conciliation agency, 1964-1965, "saw first-hand the enormous impact of the Mahatma's teaching on the civil-rights move-ment in the South [U.S.A.]." Excerpted from Gandhi: Soldier of Nonviolence: An Introduction, *by permission of the author, Calvin Kytle. Second Edition, 1982, Seven Lock Press, Santa Ana, CA, pp. 89–103.*

He was soon summoned to Johannesburg. The Transvaal legislature, it was reported, was ready to pass a bill that would require every Indian over eight years old to be fingerprinted and registered, presumably as a means of preventing further migration of Indians into the province.

When the full text of the bill was published in the *Transvaal Gazette*, Gandhi was stunned. An Indian could be challenged to produce his regis-tration card at any time, at any place; police officers could enter an Indian's home to examine permits; failure to register was to be punishable by impris-onment, heavy fines, or deportation. Such stringent terms could only mean that the government was determined to drive all Indians out of the Trans-vaal. If the bill became law, if the Indians submitted to it, it would spell "absolute ruin." It had to be resisted. Gandhi called a mass meeting for September 11 at the Empire Theater in Johannesburg. Three thousand Indians showed up.

As the main agenda item, he had prepared a resolution condemning the bill as a violation of basic civil rights and announcing the unanimous intent of the Indian community not to comply with its provisions should it pass. It was a strong statement and he was uneasy for fear it might boomerang. Unless the community was prepared to back words with action, it would be worse than no statement at all. And what assurance did he have, really, that these people — most of them poor and easily cowed — would hold fast and move together when the time came for follow-through? Was he guilty of asking more commitment than they were able to give? If so, how else could the authorities read the resolution but as an admission of impotence?

He was sitting on the stage, agonized by doubt, when all of a sudden he was jolted to hear one of the warm-up speakers declare that "in the name of G___" he would never submit to the law. From this impromptu reference to a solemn oath, there now exploded in Gandhi's mind an entire strategy. A feeling surged through him like nothing he had ever experienced before. Where he had been tense and anxious, he was now exhilarated, confident, firmly calm. When he rose to address the crowd, it was as if everything he had been through during the past twelve years, up to and including his recent vow of *bramacharya*, had prepared him for this moment.

"The government," he said, "has taken leave of all sense of decency.... There is only one course open — to die rather than submit." The struggle would be long, he warned. It meant the risk of imprisonment, starvation, flogging, even death. "But I can boldly declare, and with certainty, that so long as there is even a handful of men true to their pledge there can be only one end to the struggle — and that is victory."

He then called on everyone in the audience to join him in a pledge of resistance till death. He did not specify the form of resistance; he only made it clear that it was to be nonviolent. On cue, his fellow Indians rose, raised their hands, and vowed, "with God as our witness," not to submit to the ordinance if it became law. On that resounding note, the meeting adjourned.

He now had the strategy — nonviolent resistance to an unjust law, carried out by the masses sworn to God and psychologically prepared for imprisonment or death. But he had no name for it. He rejected the phrase, "passive resistance." There was to be nothing passive about his movement. Moreover, in a meeting with Europeans, he was told that the term was commonly associated with English suffragettes, that it was sometimes characterized by hatred, and that it often manifested itself as violence. At a loss, he offered a nominal prize through *Indian Opinion* to the reader who came up with the best suggestion. The winner was his cousin, Maganlal, who coined a word, "*Sadagraha*"—*sad* meaning truth and *agraha* meaning firmness or insistence. For the sake of clarity, Gandhi changed it to *Satyagraha*. In Gujarati *satya* means both truth and love and both are attributes of the soul. *Satyagraha* is thus variously translated as "soul force" or "insistence on truth." Thereafter, Gandhi's organization was known as the *Satyagraha* Association and its members — the warriors of truth and love — as *Satyagrahis*.

For Gandhi, and in time the entire civilized world, *Satyagraha* was more a process than a strategy. It was not so much a philosophical statement but a slogan — a kind of convenient shorthand for describing either one particular way, or all the various ways, in which he would apply politically the things he kept learning from his "experiments with truth." But at the personal level its emergence in 1906 represented something quite distinct — the final, victorious resolution of seemingly irreconcilable emotional conflicts. For with the crystallization of *Satyagraha* he had found a way to see beyond the world of chaos into a universe of order; to stay sane in an insane society; to live inwardly at peace in the midst of pain and injustice; to fight the sickness in mankind without becoming sickened.

The Black Act, as it was called, was passed, effective July 1, 1907. Indians were given thirty days to register or face the penalties. Gandhi promptly organized for resistance. To provide any waverers with a chance to withdraw, he readministered the oath of resistance to the three thousand who had taken it at the meeting in September, and through the columns of *Indian Opinion* obtained pledges from hundreds more. Through his newspaper he also instituted a practice that was to be an indisposable characteristic of every *Satyagraha* campaign thereafter. He spelled out his plans plainly and unreservedly, not only for the instruction of his co-workers but as a means of serving forthright notice on his opponents.

On the day the registration offices opened, picketing Indians appeared waving posters ("Loyalty to the king demands loyalty to the King of Kings ... Indians Be Free"). Gandhi placed volunteers outside the permit offices to dissuade the faint of heart, but the volunteers were forbidden to be violent or even discourteous to those who insisted on registering. The first Indian to be arrested became a hero; others immediately clamored to join him in jail. Taken aback, the Transvaal government extended the date of registration.

In late December, Gandhi, with twenty-six of his colleagues, was sentenced to two months' simple imprisonment. But where the government's intent was to halt the Indians by locking up their leader, the result was precisely the opposite. Morale remained high, the boycott grew, and before long the Johannesburg jail, built to accommodate fifty, was crowded with a hundred and fifty-five *Satyagrahis*.

Gandhi scarcely had time to adjust to prison routine before he was rushed to Pretoria for a conference with the Governor General, Jan Christian Smuts. Still in prison garb, he stood as Smuts read him the terms of a compromise: The Asiatic Registration Act would be repealed if Indians agreed to register voluntarily. With a smile, Smuts informed Gandhi that he was free and that the other prisoners would be released the next morning.

Within a few hours after his return to Johannesburg, Gandhi called a meeting to explain the agreement he had reached with Smuts. His followers were confused. Some were bitter and all felt let down. Why had he agreed to such a compromise? They demanded to know. Registration, he explained, was aimed at keeping Indians from moving into the Transvaal illegally; since the *Satyagrahis* did not intend to sneak immigrants into the province, why not register? "To bow to compulsion reduces the individual dignity and stature ... but collaboration freely given is generous and hence ennobling." But why had he not insisted that the registration act be repealed before, rather than after, voluntary registration? By conceding to Smuts, had he not played into the hands of the government? What if the government broke faith? "A *Satyagrahi*," Gandhi told them, "bids good-bye to fear.... Even if the opponent plays him false twenty times, the *Satyagrahi* is ready to trust him the twenty-first time, for an implicit trust in human nature is the very essence of his creed."

His manner calmed most of the group except for a six-foot Pathan named Mir Alam. Rising from his seat, he accused Gandhi of having taken a bribe of 15,000 pounds, then, without waiting for a reply, bellowed, "With Allah as my witness, I will kill the man who takes the lead in applying for registration."

Gandhi eyed him gently. The audience quieted to a hush, waiting. "I will be the first to register," Gandhi said and sat down.

On a morning soon thereafter Gandhi walked down Von Brandis Street to the registration office. On his way he was accosted by Mir Alam and several of his friends. Apparently with every intent to kill, the giant Pathan struck Gandhi a heavy blow on the head. Gandhi dropped to the sidewalk, unconscious. On his lips were the same words that forty-one years later would be his last: "*He Rama*"—"Oh, God."

Passersby rescued him from further attack. On recovering, his first act was to register, causing thousands of others to follow his example. His second was to obtain the release of Mir Alam and his accomplices, who were being held under arrest. "They thought they were doing right," he told incredulous friends. "I have no desire to prosecute them."

A month went by and it became clear that Smuts was backing out on his part of the compact. Instead of repealing the Black Act, the Transvaal legislature passed a new measure extending its penalties to all future immigrants from India. "Foul Play," called Gandhi in an article in *Indian Opinion*. He wrote Smuts, recalling their conversation. Smuts ignored him.

Had he to do it over again, he would still have trusted Smuts. As a matter of principle, he could not allow himself to predicate any action on distrust. But now the important thing was to make Smuts understand that the Indian community had no intention of acquiescing to a brazenly unjust law. By way of educating Smuts, he staged a huge bonfire in the Hamidia mosque.

There 2000 Indians threw their registration certificates into a cauldron of burning paraffin, a demonstration of protest that the *Daily Mail* correspondent compared to the Boston Tea Party. It ended with a telling sign of solidarity when Mir Alam stepped forward to shake Gandhi's hand.

For some time, prominent Indians in Natal who had an old right of domicile in the Transvaal had been pleading with Gandhi to let them test the Transvaal immigration ban. Convinced of their commitment, he now agreed. First he sent one across the border, then another, and then dozens, one of whom was his eldest son, Harilal. Each was arrested and sentenced to three months at hard labor. When Gandhi joined them, scores of well-to-do Indian barristers and merchants immediately turned up at police stations stating that they had no registration certificates and demanding that they too be imprisoned, which they were. At one time 2500 Transvaal Indians were in prison. Another 6000 had either been expelled or forced to flee under threat of expulsion. Active defiance continued throughout 1908.

This time Gandhi got a rough taste of prison life. He was worked from seven in the morning till sundown, digging with a spade in the hard ground. Uncomplaining, he cleaned the toilets and, in an effort to improve the prison fare for his seventy-five co-inmates, volunteered to do most of the cooking.

Freed in December 1908, he was re-arrested for a three-month term beginning in February and transferred to another prison. It was during this sentence that he first read Henry David Thoreau's *Essay on Civil Disobedience* in which the American stated his case for withholding taxes from a government he considered immoral. Much of what Gandhi read in *Civil Disobedience* so moved him that he copied the lines in his own hand, the better to fix them in his mind. In later years, whenever referring to his many stays in prison, he was given to quoting Thoreau as an apt summary of his own attitude: "I did not feel for a moment confined, and the walls seemed a great waste of stone and mortar."

Out of jail, Gandhi moved to enlist world opinion. Maintaining a steady series of exposés in *Indian Opinion*, he dispatched Henry Polak to India while he himself took off for England. His trip was timely, for plans were under way to merge the four African colonies into the Union of South Africa. London, he was sure, was the best place to lobby for Indian rights.

Viewed long-range, his mission was quite productive. Because of his efforts, British editors and statesmen were once again reminded of the disparities between British ideals and colonial policies. The Indian issue in South Africa, no less than the question of freedom of India itself, was forced to the surface with such skill that from that time forward it could never again be ignored or dismissed by any major political party.

But on his return, he was given several reasons to be disheartened. The British liberals who tried to mediate between the *Satyagraha* Association and the Boers reported a complete breakdown in understanding. On the personal side, he faced a critical decline in income. He had put all his savings in the movement, and since 1906 he had had little time for his law practice. Furthermore, in the absence of visible victories, wealthy Indians had begun to lose interest, and he was hard put to find enough funds to care for the dispossessed families of the imprisoned *Satyagrahis*.

Salvation came in the form of a tall, thick-set square-headed German with a handlebar mustache and pince-nez. His name was Hermann Kallenbach and he described himself variously as architect, Buddhist, pugilist, and wrestler. In Gandhi's words he was a man "of strong feeling, wide sympathies, and childlike simplicity." He had the additional virtue of being wealthy. He had joined the movement the year before and had proved so competent that Gandhi had come to use him as a deputy.

Now, when Gandhi suggested that perhaps the most economical arrangement would be to lodge the dependents of his displaced followers on a communal farm, Kallenbach bought a thousand acres twenty-one miles from Johannesburg and gave them rent free to the movement. They called it Tolstoy Farm after the Russian novelist, Leo Tolstoy, whose essays on Christ's social gospel were an implicit endorsement of nonviolence and renunciation. Depending on the number of *Satyagrahis* in jail, the Farm's population varied between fifty and a hundred.

It would be a mistake to assume that the importance of Tolstoy Farm was only as a haven for *Satyagrahis*. As strange as it may have seemed to the Boers of Transvaal, the fact that it existed at all — the fact that a small band of Indians preferred a life of grim austerity, practicing a rare kind of brotherhood — was not without its effect. On General Smuts and others of his persuasion, Tolstoy Farm impressed itself like an animated grievance petition, and to the masses of Indians who were quietly readying themselves for another round of *Satyagraha* its very survival was their inspiration.

In 1912 Gokhale came to South Africa to investigate Indian grievances. Gandhi met him in Capetown and happily served as his secretary, bearer, and valet throughout the one-month tour. After a conference with the ministers of the new Union of South Africa, Gokhale was convinced that everything had been settled. "The Black Act will be repealed," he told Gandhi. General Smuts had even promised to lift the annual tax on serfs who became free laborers.

Gandhi shook his head. "I doubt it very much," he said. "You do not know the ministers as I do."

Gandhi was right. Hardly had Gokhale left the shores of South Africa when General Smuts reneged again. It would not be possible to abolish the three-pound tax on the ex-indentured laborers, Smuts told the South Africa parliament. European feeling in Natal, he said, was too strongly opposed.

The next year there was an added insult when a justice of the Cape Colony supreme court ruled that only Christian marriages would be recognized as legal. In effect, Hindu, Moslem, and Parsi marriages were invalidated and all Indian wives were declared concubines.

This time it was the women who took the lead.

First, a party of sixteen "sisters" left Phoenix for the Transvaal, eager to confront a government that had so dishonored Indian women. Among them was Kasturbai. "What defect is there in me which disqualifies me for jail?" she demanded when Gandhi tentatively suggested that perhaps she was too weak for the journey.

On September 23, 1913, they were arrested and imprisoned for crossing the border without a permit.

A few days later, Gandhi sent a party of eleven women from Tolstoy Farm into Natal. Obeying his instructions, they proceeded to the Newcastle coal mines where they successfully incited the Indian miners to strike. At this point the women were arrested and the mine owners turned off the lights and water in the company houses. Hurrying to the scene, Gandhi advised the laborers to leave their quarters and pitch camp in the open.

In a few days, about five thousand Indians, all jobless and homeless, were on Gandhi's hands. The *Satyagraha* Association did not have the resources to feed them, nor did the few Christians in the area who had been attracted to their plight. As a way out of the dilemma, Gandhi proposed that the strikers march to the Transvaal and be "safely deposited in jail." He telegraphed his intent to the Natal government, suggesting "the peace army" be arrested before it broke camp. The authorities did not oblige him.

In a little more than a day, on a ration of a pound and a half of bread and an ounce of sugar, the strikers hiked thirty-six miles from Newcastle to Charlestown, close to the Transvaal border. While they paused, Gandhi tried once to arrange for a peaceful settlement. He telephoned General Smuts's office, telling the General's secretary, "If he promises to abolish the tax, I will stop the march." After checking with Smuts, the secretary replied, "The General will have nothing to do with you."

Gandhi called his forces together and gave them the battle plan. Tomorrow they would cross the border. If, as seemed likely, the Transvaal government refused to arrest them, they would advance to Tolstoy Farm by eight day-marches of twenty miles each. Food would be shipped to every day's campsite. There would be hardships. If any among them were of faint heart, now was the time to reconsider. At the close, he repeated the three standard rules of conduct: *Do not resist arrest; if the police flog you, don't fight back; keep clean.* The next morning, November 6, Gandhi headed a column of 2037 men, 127 women, and 57 children. It was, to quote *The Saturday Post,* "an exceedingly picturesque crew." Most were barefooted. Many of the women carried babies on their backs.

They crossed the border without incident, but they had hardly settled themselves for the night when an officer arrived with a warrant for Gandhi's arrest. At the police station, Gandhi posted bail and rushed back to the camp in time for the next day's march. Twenty miles later, he was re-arrested, this time by a magistrate. Gandhi laughed: "It seems I've been promoted."

Again he was released. But by the fourth day Transvaal authorities were growing uneasy and at Volksrust they ordered him held without bail.

The marchers continued without him as far as Balfour Station. There they were halted, herded into three waiting trains, and shipped back to Natal. But instead of being imprisoned they were forced into wire-enclosed stockades, which the government declared to be "out-stations" of the Dundee and Newcastle jails. And, instead of being put to the usual hard labor, they were sentenced to work at their old jobs in the mines. Workers who refused were whipped. Miners in the north and west who struck in sympathy were chased back to work by mounted military police.

Meanwhile in Volksrust, Gandhi, Polak, and Kallenbach were each sentenced to a year at hard labor. Transferred to Pretoria, Gandhi was put in an unlit cell ten feet long and seven feet wide. He was denied a bench, refused permission to talk, and, when summoned to the court for evidence, handcuffed and manacled like a criminal.

But by now South Africa's "blood and iron" policy was too much for a civilized world to contain. Fifty thousand men were on strike, and thousands more in jail. Gokhale toured India, mobilizing moral and financial support. Editorial opinion in both Britain and India was outraged. Breaking the imperial rule of non-interference, the British viceroy in India demanded a commission to inquire into Indian grievances.

Giving in, Smuts released Gandhi and immediately announced the appointment of a commission. Gandhi noted the appointees and promptly branded it a fraud, "a packed body, intended to hoodwink the government and public opinion both of England and of India." (One of its three members had been a leader of the crowd that tried to lynch him on his return to Durban in 1897.) He insisted that one or more Indians, or at least someone known to be pro-Indian, be added.

Sensing victory, but aware that the fight was not yet won, he called a mass meeting that was noteworthy in one particular. He appeared in a knee-length white smock, an elongated loincloth, and sandals. Rarely thereafter was he ever seen in Western clothes.

Smuts would not agree to expand the commission. Seeing no alternative, Gandhi announced a massive protest march from Durban on January 1, 1914. By coincidence, however, the white employees of all South African railways went on strike. With the nation paralyzed, Gandhi's reaction was to cancel the march. It was against the principles of *Satyagraha*, he explained, to take advantage of an opponent's weakness.

In answer to an invitation, Gandhi went to Smuts's office, recalling the broken pledge of 1908 and on his guard against fresh deception. Smuts, it appeared, was as eager as Gandhi to talk terms and to make the terms clear and binding. "This time we want no misunderstanding," Smuts said. "Let all the cards be on the table." Through meetings and correspondence, every clause of the impending agreement was meticulously examined. The resulting document became the Indian Relief Act.

For Gandhi, the crusade was over. The three-pound tax on former indentured Indian laborers was abolished. Non-Christian marriages were legalized; though indentured contract labor would cease in 1920, free Indians could continue to enter the Union, and wives could come from India to join their husbands in South Africa. Though it was admittedly a compromise, Gandhi saw the agreement as a vindication of the principle of racial equality and a clear demonstration of the power of *Satyagraha*.

"Return to India within twelve months," Gokhale had told him on his visit in 1912. Now Gandhi was free to obey. But before he left, he had one thing yet to do. While in jail, he had made a pair of sandals. He sent them as a parting gift to General Smuts.

Give Me Liberty

Rose Wilder Lane

In this essay, Rose Wilder Lane (1886-1968), daughter of the author of the famous Little House on the Prairie *series, describes her "fundamentalist American" reaction to the concept of the planned social order as she found it during her European travels in the early 1920s. This piece first appeared in the* Saturday Evening Post *in 1936, as a part of a series of articles titled "Credo," and later appeared as a pamphlet entitled* Give Me Liberty *(Boonton: Liberty Library, 1946, 9th edition, Sec. VI, pp. 28–35) from which it is taken. Lane was a freelance writer, journalist, and author of the earliest biographies of Henry Ford, Charlie Chaplin, and Jack London. Her most well known book was* The Discovery of Freedom: Man's Struggle Against Authority *(1943).*

When I asked myself, "Am I truly free?" I began slowly to understand the nature of man and man's situation on this planet. I understood at last that every human being is free; that I am endowed by the Creator with inalienable liberty as I am endowed with life; that my freedom is inseparable from my life, since freedom is my control of my own life-energy, for the uses of which I, alone, am therefore responsible.

But the exercise of this freedom is another thing, since in every use of my life-energy I encounter obstacles. Some of these obstacles, such as time, space, weather, are eternal in the human situation on this planet. Some are self-imposed and come from my own ignorance of realities. And for all the years of my residence in Europe, a great many obstacles were enforced upon me by the police power of the men ruling the European States.

I hold the truth to be self-evident, that all men are endowed by the Creator with inalienable liberty, with individual self-control and responsibility for thoughts, speech and acts, in every situation. The extent to which this natural liberty can be exercised depends upon the amount of external coercion imposed upon the individual. No jailer can compel any prisoner to speak or act against that prisoner's will, but chains can prevent his acting, and a gag can prevent his speaking.

Americans have been able to use more of man's natural freedom of thought, of choice, and of movement than other people. We inherited no limitations of caste to restrict our range of desires nor of ambition to that of our father's "class."

We had no governmental bureaucracy to watch our every move, to make a record of friends who called at our homes and the hours at which they arrived and left, in order that the police might be fully informed in case we were murdered. We had no officials who, in the interests of a just and equitable collection of gasoline taxes, stopped our cars and measured the gasoline in the tanks whenever we entered or left an American City.

We were not obliged, as Continental Europeans have been, to carry at all times a police card, renewed and paid for at intervals, bearing our pictures properly stamped and stating our names, ages, addresses, parentage, religion and occupation.

American workers were not classified; for a century and a half they were not required to carry police cards recording the places where they had worked, and permitting them to work. They have no places of amusement separate from those of higher classes, and their amusements are not subject to interruption by raiding policemen inspecting their workingmen's cards and acting on the assumption that any workingman is a thief whose card shows he has not worked during the past week.

In 1922, as a foreign correspondent in Budapest, I accompanied such a police raid. The Chief of Police was showing the mechanisms of his work to a visiting operative from Scotland Yard. We set out at ten o'clock at night, leading sixty policemen who moved with the beautiful precision of soldiers.

They surrounded a section of the workingmen's quarter of the city and closed in, while the Chief explained that this was ordinary routine; the whole quarter was combed in this way every week.

We appeared suddenly in the doorways of workingmen's cafes, dingy places with sawdust on earthen floors where one musician forlornly tried to make music on a cheap fiddle and men and women in the gray rags of poverty sat at bare tables and economically sipped beer or coffee. Their terror at the sight of uniforms was abject. All rose and meekly raised their hands. The policemen grinned with that peculiar enjoyment of human beings in possessing such power.

They went through the men's pockets, making some little jest at this object and that. They found the Labor cards, inspected them, thrust them back in the pockets. At the policeman's curt word of release, the men dropped into chairs and wiped their foreheads.

In every place, a few cards failed to pass the examination. No employer had stamped them during the past three days. Men and women were loaded into the patrol wagon.

Now and then, at our entrance, some one tried to escape from back door or window and ran, of course, into the clutch of policemen. We could hear the policemen laughing. The Chief accepted the compliments of the British detective. Everything was perfectly done; no one escaped.

Several women frantically protested, crying, pleading on their knees, so that they had almost to be carried to the wagon. One young girl fought, screaming horribly. It took two policemen to handle her; they were not rough, but when she bit at their hands on her arms, a third slapped her face. In the wagon she went on screaming insanely. I could not understand Hungarian. The Chief explained that some women objected to being given prostitutes' cards.

When a domestic servant had been several days without work, the police took away the card that identified her as a working girl and permitted her to work; they gave her instead a prostitute's card. Men who had not worked recently were sentenced to a brief imprisonment for theft. Obviously, the Chief said, if they were not working, they were prostitutes and thieves; how else were they living?

Perhaps on their savings? I suggested.

Working people make only enough to live on from day to day, they cannot save, the Chief said. Of course, if by any remarkable chance one of them had got some money honestly and could prove it, the judge would release him.

Having gone through all the cafes, we began on the tenements. I have lived in slums of New York and of San Francisco. Americans who have not seen European slums have not the slightest idea of what slums are.

Until dawn, the police were clambering through those filthy tenements and down into their basements, stirring up masses of rags and demanding from staring faces their police cards. We did not capture so many unemployed there, because it costs more to sleep under a roof than to sit in a café; the very fact that these people had any shelter argued that they were working. But the police were thorough and awakened everyone. They were quiet and good-humored; this raid had none of the violence of an American police raid. When a locked door was not opened, the police tried all their master keys before they set their shoulders to the door and went in.

The Scotland Yard man said, "Admirable, sir, admirable. Continental police systems are marvelous, really. You have absolute control over here." Then his British pride spoke deprecatingly, as it always speaks. "We could never do anything like this in London, don't you know. An Englishman's home is his castle, and all that. We have to have a warrant before we can search the premises or touch a man's person. Beastly handicap, you know. We have nothing like your control over here on the Continent."

This is the only police search of workingmen's quarters that I saw in

Europe. I do not believe that regimentation elsewhere went so far then as to force women into prostitution, and it may be that it no longer does so in Hungary. But I do know that the systematic surrounding and searching of workingmen's quarters went on normally everywhere in Europe, and that unemployment was assumed to push them over the edge of destitution into crime.

Like everyone else domiciled in Europe, I was many times stopped on my way home by two courteous policemen who asked to see my identification card. This became too commonplace to need explanation. I knew that my thoroughly respectable, middle-class quarter was surrounded, simply as a matter of police routine, and that everyone in it was being required to show police cards.

Nevertheless, I question whether there was less crime in police-controlled Europe than in America. Plenty of crimes were reported in brief paragraphs of small type in every paper. There is no section of an American city which I would fear to go into alone at night. There were always many quarters of European cities that were definitely dangerous after nightfall, and whole classes of criminals who would kill any moderately well-dressed man, woman or child for the clothes alone.

The terrible thing is that the motive behind all this supervision of the individual is a good motive, and a rational one. How is any ruler to maintain a social order without it?

There is a certain instinct of orderliness and of self-preservation which enables multitudes of free human beings to get along after a fashion. No crowd leaves a theatre with any efficiency, nor without discomfort, impatience and wasted time, yet we usually reach the sidewalk without a fight. Order is another thing. Any teacher knows that order cannot be maintained without regulation, supervision and discipline. It is a question of degree; the more rigid and autocratic the discipline, the greater the order. Any genuine social order requires, as its first fundamental, the classification, regulation and obedience of individuals. Individuals being what they are, infinitely various and willful, their obedience must be enforced.

The serious loss in a social order is in time and energy. Sitting around in waiting rooms until one can stand in line before a bureaucrat's desk seems to any American a dead loss, and living in a social order thus shortens every person's life. Outside the bureaucrat's office, too, these regulations for the public good constantly hamper every action. It is as impossible to move freely in one's daily life as it is to saunter or hasten while keeping step in a procession.

In America, commercial decrees did not hamper every clerk and customer, as they did in France, so that an extra half-hour was consumed in every department-store purchase. French merchants are as intelligent as American, but they could not install vacuum tubes and a swift accounting system in a central cashier's department. What is the use? they asked you. They would still be obliged to have every purchase recorded in writing in a ledger, in the presence of both buyer and seller, as Napoleon decreed.

It was an intelligent decree, too, when Napoleon issued it. Could French merchants change it now? It is to laugh, as they say; a phrase with no mirth in it. That decree was entangled with a hundred years of bureaucratic complications, and besides, think how much unemployment its repeal would have caused among those weary cashiers, dipping their pens in the prescribed ink, setting down the date and hour on a new line and asking, "Your name, madame?" writing. "Your address?" writing. "You pay cash?" writing. "You will take the purchase with you? Ah, good," writing. "Ah, I see. One reel of thread, cotton, black, what size?" writing. "You pay for it how much?" writing. "And you offer in payment — Good; one franc," writing. "From one franc, perceive, madame, I give you fifty centimes change. Good. And you are satisfied, madame?"

No one considered how much unemployment this caused to the daily multitudes of patiently waiting customers, nor that if these clerks had never been thus employed they might have been doing something useful, something creative of wealth. Napoleon wished to stop the waste of disorganization, of cheating and quarreling, in the markets of his time. And he did so. The result is that so much of France was permanently fixed firmly in Napoleon's time. If he had let Frenchmen waste and quarrel, and cheat and lose, as Americans were then doing in equally primitive markets, French department stores certainly would have been made as briskly efficient and time-saving as America's.

No one who dreams of the ideal social order, the economy planned to eliminate waste and injustice, considers how much energy, how much human life, is wasted in administering and in obeying the best of regulations. No one considers how rigid such regulations become, nor that they must become rigid and resist change because their underlying purpose is to preserve men from the risks of chance and change in flowing time.

Americans have had in our country no experience of the discipline of a social order. We speak of a better social order, when in fact we do not know what any social order is. We say that something is wrong with this system, when in fact we have no system. We use phrases learned from Europe, with no conception of the meaning of those phrases in actual living experience.

In America we do not have even universal military training, that basis of a social order which teaches every male citizen his subservience to The State and subtracts some years from every young man's life, and millions of man-power years annually from the modern industrial production which today is the source of a country's military power.

An apartment lease in America is legal when it is signed; it is not necessary to take it to the police to be stamped, nor to file triplicate copies of it with the collector of internal revenue, so that for taxation purposes our incomes may be set down as ten times what we pay for rent. In economic theory, no doubt it is not proper to pay for rent more than ten percent of income, and perhaps it is economic justice that everyone so extravagant as to pay more should be fined by taxation. It was never possible to quarrel with the motives behind these bureaucracies of Europe; they were invariably excellent.

An American could look at the whole world around him and take what he wanted from it, if he were able. Only criminal law and his own character, abilities and luck restrained him.

That is what Europeans meant when, after a few days in this country, they exclaimed, "You are so free here!" And it was the most infinite relief to an American returning after long living abroad, to be able to move from hotel to hotel, from city to city, to be able to rush into a store and buy a spool of thread, to decide at half past three to take a four o'clock train, to buy an automobile if one had the money or the credit and to drive it wherever one liked, all without making any reports whatever to the government.

But anyone whose freedom has been, as mine has always been, freedom to earn a living if possible, knows that this independence is another name for responsibility.

The American pioneers phrased this clearly and bluntly. They said, "Root, hog, or die."

There can be no third alternative for the shoat let out of the pen, to go where he pleases and do what he likes. Individual liberty is individual responsibility. Whoever makes decisions is responsible for results. When common men were slaves and serfs, they obeyed and they were fed, but they died by thousands in plagues and famines and wars. Free men paid for their freedom by leaving that false and illusory security.

The question is whether personal freedom is worth the terrible effort, the never-lifted burden, and the risks, the unavoidable risks, of self-reliance.

Resist Enumeration
Scott McDonald

Fundamentalist Christians have long called attention to Revelation 13: Verses 16 and 17, which describe the mark that all people shall receive, and which all shall be required to have. The author points out the many ways that modern society numbers committed Christians and urges them to heed the Biblical admonishments not to comply. Scott McDonald was a licensed building contractor in Alabama until he refused to provide his Social Security number for his license renewal. He has also sued the State of Alabama for demanding that his twin sons provide Social Security numbers as a precondition to applying for their drivers' licenses. He is also founder of the website, Fight the Fingerprint, from which this essay is taken. (See http://www.networkusa.org/fingerprint/ page6/fp-resist.html.)

The Social Security Number has become a *de facto* National Identification Number. It is now used to register, locate, and track nearly every single person living in America. However, governmental requirements to universally number citizens for identification purposes run contrary to Biblical principles. When the Social Security Act was first being considered the religious community raised strong objections to using a number for identification. To offset the objections, proponents of the Social Security Act gave assurance that the numbers would never be used for general identification purposes. It was for this reason that Social Security Cards, for many years, included the statement "NOT FOR IDENTIFICATION" printed boldly upon the face of the cards.

Today, more and more people are being confronted by ever-increasing demands to "identify" themselves, particularly when dealing with government agencies, by using their social security number. As the demands for SSNs steadily increase, more and more people are beginning to ask why — why does the government need all this personal information linked to my SSN? And why am I being pressured into getting a social security number for my children?

The Bible provides answers to these questions, along with instruction on how we should respond to the increasing demands for citizens to be numbered. God's People are admonished, by clearly stated example, to resist being numbered by government. We're told that King David wanted to "know the number of the people" under his authority (2 Samuel 24:2). And, Satan caused David to number all Israel (1 Chronicles 21:1). God's Word further states that David's command to number Israel "was evil in the sight of God" (1 Chronicles 21:7). Because of the people's acquiescence to the king's enumeration plan, God sent a plague *upon the people* (1 Chronicles 21:14).

The "People" are now, once again facing new demands from the modern day "kings" to be numbered and registered. And again it is the responsibility and duty of the PEOPLE to resist; regardless of how powerful or "godly" the particular ruling authority claims (or appears) to be, and regardless of the sincerity of their justifications. For, it is the *people* who will be held accountable if they do not resist.

There are also other references in the Bible to "numbering" people, but an important distinction is made between the different types of numbering that are discussed. For example, soldiers were often counted (numbered) but they were accounted for "by their name" (Numbers 1:19-23). And, there were censuses taken (numbering) of the non-citizen (alien) population for the purpose of establishing the amount of tax that was to be levied upon them (2 Chronicles 2:17). These examples do not represent "numbering" or "registering" of God's People (the citizens) as is related in 1 Chronicles 21:1 and 2 Samuel 24:2 which resulted in God's punishment.

Now, as before, Satan has risen up to deceive and mislead political leaders, and he has provided them with ample causes and justifications for numbering the citizens. Having believed the lie these present-day leaders are now promoting their own new numbering agendas -which, they assure us, will collectively "cure all the world's problems."

Citizens Were "Conned"

In 1996, this country witnessed what was referred to as the "Republican Revolution." At that time the "conservatives" in Congress vowed to reduce the overall size of government by making it more "efficient." But what we got instead was the "Contract with America" which should more appropriately be known as the "Contract On the Nation" (CON). This "CON" saddled the country with numerous new registration and enumeration requirements. As a result of the CON, every person must register with the government using a social security number in order to get a job (New Hires Database Registry); to get married or divorced; to get any type of license (Child Support laws); to get a birth certificate (Welfare Reform and Immigration Control); to enroll in public school (Federally Funded Grants); or to open a bank account or transfer money (Financial Crimes and Child Support Enforcement). This was the period also when the requirement for inclusion of an SSN for dependent children became mandatory on tax returns.

Another consequence of these recent federal Acts: parents feel pressured to number their children. Typically, parents are "coerced" (or tricked) into numbering their children at birth before they leave the hospitals. Then, they're frightened into fingerprinting and registering their children so that they'll be able to "identify" the child (or their remains) should the child ever be "abducted." And when parents take their child to "register" for school one of the first items of information requested is the child's social security number.

Where Are the Churches?

As Biblically offensive as the new numbering requirements are the corporate churches are offering little or no resistance. For, to do so would certainly jeopardize a church's tax-exempt status. In fact, so much as speaking publicly against government numbering requirements could cause a church to lose tax-exempt privilege. And with all the new government numbering and reporting requirements being put in place as a condition for being granted tax-exempt status, churches are certainly going to face even greater demands for collection of numbers from their members for tax accountability purposes.

It's no secret that the IRS is incrementally working towards achieving the capability to pre-determine each and every person's annual tax liability. Ultimately, taxpayers will not need to fill out even a single tax form — the IRS will do all the calculations for them. But, in order to realize their ultimate goal, the IRS must be able to obtain a record of every financial transaction engaged in by every single taxpayer — including their "charitable contributions."

In 1995, the project manager for the IRS's Document Processing System, Coleta Brueck, described the so-called "Golden Eagle" return. She said the government was working on a computer upgrade that would enable the agency to automatically gather all relevant aspects of a person's finances, sort it into appropriate categories, and then tally the tax due. "One-stop service," as Brueck put it. The information would also be fed to other government agencies, as well as states and municipalities, which would draw upon it for their own purposes. She vowed "absolutely" that this will one day happen, apparently assuming that Americans would be grateful to be relieved of the burden of filing any taxes. The government would simply take its due. Brueck is reported to have said that the system in place at the time the statement was made already provided most of the needed capability. She said:

> We know everything about you that we need to know. Your employer tells us everything about you that we need to know. Your activity records on your credit cards tell us everything about you that we need to know. Through interface with Social Security, with the DMV, with your banking institutions, we really have a lot of information, so why ... at the end of the year or on April 15, do we ask the Post Office to encumber itself with massive numbers of people out there, with picking up pieces of paper that you are required to file?... I don't know why. We could literally file a return for you. This is the future we'd like to go to [*Chicago Tribune*, January 20, 1995, also *Wired* Magazine article, "E-Money (That's What I Want)," by Steven Levy December 1994].

This particular IRS program was eventually de-funded by Congress, however the agency clearly has not abandoned the concept.

At some point in the near future, in order to maintain their tax-exempt status, churches in America will be required to start collecting social security numbers from parishioners so that their "tithe contributions" can be reported to the IRS. Only then will the IRS be able to calculate the exact amount of the person's annual "tithe tax rebate." Will the church then resist?

The Global Plan for Enumeration

There are also ongoing efforts now under way on the global scale to impose numbering and registration requirements upon ALL people of the world. There is, in fact, a universal "registration requirement" included as a part of the United Nations' "International Covenant on Civil and Political Rights." As found under Article 24, item number 2 the U.N. Treaty states that: "Every child shall be registered immediately after birth...."

And, political and corporate leaders from twenty of the world's most powerful countries have organized a group known as the Organization for Economic Cooperation and Development (OECD). The group was formed specifically for the purpose of drafting a "Constitution of a Single Global Economy." The OECD's agreement, known as the "Multilateral Agreement on Investment" (MAI), will establish a global economic framework within which any country, and any industry, desiring to compete in the world economy will be required to comply with. And these Power brokers are in a position to make it happen.

Another global organization known as the Global Chipcard Alliance has agreed to standardize all cashless electronic funds transfer cards known as "SmartCards." These cards, already in use in some countries, contain a tiny computer chip that facilitates and records every financial transaction. The Global Chipcard Alliance recently announced that it had agreed on a soon-to-be-unveiled "logo" which, they assure us, will eventually become universally recognized as representing buying and selling. They refer to the new transaction "logo" as the "service mark." No one will be able to access the

SmartCard financial system unless they are first registered in the system and use SmartCards bearing the Alliance's "mark."

New Technologies

Biometric identification technologies have now been developed which electronically scan a person's unique individual features (such as a fingerprint, face, or retina) and convert the data into a "number" facilitating automated identification, enumeration, and registration. Biometric identification is currently being used in the administration of various government services and programs such as food stamp programs, immigration control, and driver licensing. Just within the past few years, pioneering companies in the Smart-Card industry have announced plans to incorporate biometric identification technologies into their card systems for verification and authorization purposes.

The Final Chapter

Enumeration for self-aggrandizement — the registering of people for the sole purpose of giving "the king" a sense of self-fulfillment and the people a sense of "security" — is what we've been experiencing the past few years. This is representative of the type of numbering that God's People are warned against in 2 Samuel and 1 Chronicles.

All of the many new enumeration and registration technologies and requirements now being implemented merely serve to provide the necessary social conditioning for future "bigger — better" schemes. The generations that will grow up having been "numbered at birth" will not know how or why to resist. Implementation of a universal identification and financial transactions system is taking place incrementally, but at an ever-increasing pace. Nevertheless, participants in the coming global economic system *will have made* a conscious decision to accept the new standardization and unification scheme. And, they will, thereby, have made a conscience choice to be identified, enumerated, and registered by the system.

For the first time in the history of civilization, we now have the technology, the capability, and apparently the willingness, to number and register every single human being on earth, (presently estimated at being somewhere around six billion people). All the necessary technology now exists to establish the "Beast System" spoken of in Revelation 13. But, Revelation 20:4 reminds us of the horrible consequences of participating in such an ungodly system. John tells us: "If anyone worships the beast and his image, and receives a mark on his forehead or upon his hand, he also will drink of the wine of the wrath of God, which is mixed in full strength in the cup of his anger; and he will be tormented with fire and brimstone in the presence of the Lamb. And the smoke of their torment goes up forever and ever; and they have no rest day and night, those who worship the beast and his image, and whoever receives the mark of his name" (Revelations 14:9-11). And John further states: "And I saw the souls of those who had been beheaded because of the testimony of Jesus and because of the Word of God, and those who had not received the mark…" (Revelations 20:4). These could only be described as believers (Christians) who'll be beheaded for giving a "testimony of Jesus" and for refusing to be registered with the System. Those people who believe they'll find "safety and security" in registering, numbering, and identifying with the coming (global) System are living under strong delusion. The state cannot secure for the people what God has reserved solely to His own sovereign authority.

Editor's Addendum
by Carl Watner

Although this article mentions biometric identification, it does not discuss the latest technology of implantable micro-chips. Applied Digital Solutions, Inc., a Florida company, has been developing and marketing miniature digital transceivers, which are capable of storing limited bits of information. One of these silicon chips, known as the VeriChip, is about the size of the point of a typical ballpoint pen, and can be placed under the skin by syringe. The VeriChip is designed to store a verification number, which when retrieved by a handheld scanner can be used to access remote data bases for information about a person's identity and/or health history. The first person in the world to be implanted was a British scientist, Professor Kevin Warwick, on August 25, 1998. Sensors were set up "to pinpoint his location and even switch lights on automatically when he enter[ed] a room on campus." In late September 2001, Richard Seelig, a New Jersey surgeon, injected himself with two of these chips, one in his left forearm, and the other near the artificial hip in his right leg. He was inspired with the idea after seeing firefighters at the World Trade Center write their Social Security numbers on their forearms in magic marker. In Boca Raton, Florida in May 2002, Jeffrey and Leslie Jacob, and their teenage son, Derek, became the first family in America where both parents and child were implanted with the VeriChip.

Currently the Applied Digital Solution chips are being marketed primarily as the Digital Angel, a locator device — which is externally worn (like a watch or bracelet) by humans, but which has been implanted in millions of animals. The Digital Angel acts like a bar code that allows a scanner to read the information stored on the radio-frequency identification chip. Once the chip is read, its number can be fed into a computerized database to learn more about its bearer. The Digital Angel has been integrated with global positioning satellites so it can be used to locate kidnap victims, track animals, to determine the location of valuable property, and to monitor people with Alzheimer's disease or other at-risk medical conditions. The Digital Angel is also designed to operate as a "Wander Alert" (indicating when someone has moved beyond a predetermined boundary), and "Ambient Temperature Alert" (when a dramatic unexpected change is recorded in an individual's environment).

The combination of subdermal micro-chip and Global Positioning technology have made seamless global surveillance a real possibility.[1] Imagine how close to the prophecy of Revelation we would be if each child were implanted at birth, just as they are now "required" to have a state-issued birth certificate. Each newborn would receive a *mark* in their hand or in their forehead. In literally a generation or two (as soon as the "unmarked" [read: unimplanted] died off), the government would be literally capable of knowing everyone's whereabouts and identity. Thus, the ominous aspect of these chips is readily apparent. Both the VeriChip and the Digital Angel chips could be easily "forced" on prisoners and on mental patients hospitalized by court order. They could also be "required" of all military personnel. The potential for "mission creep" is incalculable. It remains to be seen if subdermal chips are actually the fulfillment of the Biblical prophecy about "the mark of the beast", but they certainly are a case of science fiction having evolved into hard fact. For further commentary on this issue see "Opinion: Will Microchip Implants = 666? Has the Mark of the Beast Arrived?" at http://www.raidersnewsupdate.com/opinion.htm.

Notes

1. See Jim Redden, *Snitch Culture* (Venice, Calif.: Feral House, 2000), pp. 4, 53, and 160.

National I.D. for
All Public Servants

Patricia Neill

*Several authors, among them Simon Davies, a contributor to this volume,
have noted that totalitarian regimes want to know everything about everyone,
but wish to reveal nothing about themselves. In a peculiar reversal of roles, Patricia Neill, a freelance writer living in Southern Indiana, puts forth a "tongue in
cheek" call to number ALL politicians. bureaucrats, and government employees.
How would they like to be placed under the same sort of all-encompassing surveillance that we ordinary Americans are experiencing or are about to experience? For many years, the author of this essay was managing editor of* Blake/An
Illustrated Quarterly *at the University of Rochester. Her essay was first posted
on the internet at http://www.curleywolfe.net/cw/RA_980725.shtml.*

By the power vested in me as one of We the People, without whose consent this country cannot possibly be governed, I hereby declare that what this
country really needs is an permanent identification number for all politicians, of all levels of government from the president down to "local" school
boards, including the millions of unelected bureaucrats. All "public servants"
from Cabinet members to federal agents of all the hordes of federal agencies,
to judges and prosecutors, governors, mayors, country administrators, down
to the local police and dog catchers shall be issued a permanent identification
number as soon as they take their oath of office and begin work.

The permanent identification number can be used to track all of these
politicians' and bureaucrats' actions, since they will not be able to do ANY-
THING without that number. We will be able to tally their votes, their performance of the work we hired them to do, in fact, every action taken by our
"public servants" will be open to the view of the public. We should be able
to see their bank accounts, their medical histories, times they went to see a

277

shrink, how many visits to the local red light district, phone calls to their bookies, every time they file a memo, write a regulation, conceive of legislation, attempt some obfuscation, stop a car for a traffic violation, go to the pharmacy for medication — ALL actions will require the use of their permanent identification number.

Every financial transaction will be open and public knowledge. Since billions of dollars disappear from various official budgets every year, in every federal agency, and probably in many state and local agencies as well, ALL financial transactions of "public servants"— in their official capacity as our hired help, AND in their private lives, will be made public. Thus we will be able to track the transfer of our money to their pockets, which is no doubt what happens to those billions of dollars that "go missing" every year, as reported again and again by the Government Accounting Office.

Every single action taken by a "public servant," official, or private business, will be tracked, noted, and the data entered into a database kept open to the public. We the People, who pay for all this "government," need to be able to see exactly what transpires when an IRS agent seizes someone's house. We'll be able to note when the home was taken, for what purposes, when it was auctioned, and where the money went. Whenever a EPA bureaucrat attempts to regulate private property out of existence, we'll know, since our "public servants" will be unable to function at all without using their permanent identification number. Whenever one of the myriad Monica Lewinskys goes to the White House, she'll have to use her number to even get through the door. This data will be automatically sent to the database.

The technology already exists, as we know because our "public servants" have expressed their fervent and demented desire to use it on U.S. citizens. This database shall be accessible to all Americans on the Web. Suggestions as to how to set up the Webpages are welcome.

I believe this is an idea whose time has come. As an ordinary citizen, there is absolutely no reason for me to have a national permanent ID number. Who cares what I do or don't do? Who should care, besides me and mine? However, it seems to me to be essential, in order for citizens to be properly vigilant concerning the actions of our "public servants," and to act responsibly upon the knowledge this vigilance will bring, that ALL of our "public servants" must henceforth receive a permanent identification number that they will agree to use for every action they take, official or private, if they wish to work for us. It is a way to ensure accountability of our "public servants"— something sorely lacking in our current form of government.

If they have no wish to work for us, fine. They remain private citizens, and thus need not be accountable except in the usual ways private citizens must be accountable in their personal and business lives. Once they retire from public life, their number retires as well.

What do you say, folks? Anyone like this idea besides me?

An American Refusenik
Claire Wolfe

American refusal to cooperate with the British during the first half of the 1770s led to the American Revolution. Is it possible that non-compliance and disobedience might result in another revolution, or a new civil rights movement (against national ID), or simply a new term of disapproval for those people who either will not or cannot sign up for their national ID? In this article, which first appeared in the Net publication Sierra Times, *Claire Wolfe discusses the problems of those who "rock the boat" when it comes to national ID.*

You walk past a bank. Out of the blue, you're overwhelmed with a sense of being an exile from ordinary life. The bank would never give an account to the likes of *you*. You can't get a job. Theoretically, you're "permitted" to, but practically nobody will hire you.

When a cop car appears in your rear-view mirror, you get more than the standard flash of nerves, even if your driving is angelically perfect. Because you don't have a driver's license.

Get a mortgage? Rent an apartment? Buy a gun? Invest in stocks? Rent a car? Get a fishing license? Board an airplane? Cross an international border? Rent a video? Some of these simple, "normal" things you can't do at all. Some you can do after fighting exhausting battles, enduring extra scrutiny, or researching obscure strategies. Sometimes you can do them if you fork over two or three times more than "normal" people have to pay.

Year by year, life closes in. The bank that reluctantly welcomed you five years ago now orders your account closed due to new regulatory policies. The company that insured you for a decade suddenly says you're too "high risk." When you hear that the government is going to require you to have a "unique identifying number" to go to a doctor, you don't worry about your privacy. You tremble for your very survival in a world where doctors could be prosecuted simply for examining you.

If you finally hit bottom, you know people like *you* won't qualify for the aid even drunks or ex-cons get as a matter of course — not even from most churches or private charities.

And what's your crime? What did you do to bring down upon yourself this hell of isolation and insecurity, this bleak, Stalinist-style internal exile?

You committed the worst crime anyone can commit in a bureaucratized, sociologized, international treatified, standardized, police-statized, hyper-controlled, hyper-securitized world.

You lived by your principles.

For readers who are still Innocents in TV Land, the life I just described isn't any science-fiction future or the dreary, long-past fate of a Russian dissident. This is how life is in the United States today, for thousands— maybe millions— of people who've done a simple thing: refused to accept a universal citizen ID number and/or refused to get a driver's license once they realized it had ceased to be a certification of their driving skill and had become, as the American Association of Motor Vehicle Administrators triumphantly acknowledges, a de facto national ID document.

Before you ID-bearers scoff at these ID-challenged idiots: Ask not why ID resisters cause themselves such unnecessary trouble, but why such a small thing as refusing a number or a government ID card should inevitably result in such oppression — in a nation that claims to be free.

Why should the vast choices of once-free life be channeled into *one* choice: Comply or live forever as a pariah?

And it's getting worse. As de facto national ID gradually morphs (or is abruptly changed) into in-fact-o national ID (complete with One Big Database, scanners, and facial recognition systems on every street corner) bureaucrats— or even mindless computer systems— gain a godlike power

Duncan Frissell, who wrote a *Sierra Times* article on national ID that I wished I'd written, points out that national ID is "*not* really about identity. It is about authorization. A modern national ID system will require Americans to obtain federal government permission to travel, work, rent or buy housing, obtain medical care, use financial services, and make many purchases." And of course, that means the federal government can also *stop* you from doing those things if, for instance, you're a deadbeat dad, you have overdue parking tickets, you fit a "suspicious" profile, or there's simply a glitch in the system.

We're halfway to ID hell now, but soon to take a giant leap further — into giving government instant, moment-to-moment control over daily activities.

But why resist?

By resisting, you've essentially (and ironically) done to yourself the next-to-worst that the government might have done, had you complied with its ID requirements then later been discovered to have a decades-old misdemeanor conviction, or the "wrong" political attitudes— made "normal" life exceptionally difficult for yourself and your family.

Of course, if you've resisted, you understand what the scoffers don't: that the very difficulty is one of the key reasons for resistance. How powerful and controlling are you going to allow institutions to become before you draw your personal line in the sand? How much more authority over your life are you going to allow them to accrue, simply because bucking their system is too inconvenient? Or because you trust the lying politicians who promise government ID will protect you from harm? Or because you foolishly choose not to understand the danger you're facing?

Frissell also hit the tyrant on the head when he called ID resisters political refuseniks. This is an important distinction, and one from which resisters can draw hope and courage.

The *American Heritage Dictionary* defines refusenik as "a Soviet citizen, usually Jewish, denied permission to emigrate." The term has expanded to include many groups and individuals who suffer at the hands of their governments for taking a stand on principal. Sunni Maravillosa, who was first to suggest that people in the freedom movement apply the term to themselves, gives one of the best descriptions of refuseniks in her essay "Newspeak." Many of the original Soviet refuseniks, she wrote:

> ... continued to re-apply until they were finally permitted to emigrate; the longest period on record is of a refusenik who waited 20 years before being able to leave. Their lives — already unpleasant — became more challenging once it became known that they wanted to leave the country, but for most the desire to live in freedom surpassed the obstacles placed before them. It was their refusal to cooperate — to live under the communist system — that led to the state's refusal to allow them to leave.

Only through adamant resistance could the refuseniks have achieved their goals. Had they gone along to get along, they might not have been singled out for special punishment. But they'd have had to endure dreary oppression unto death — as we all will if we permit national control in the guise of national ID.

How many American ID refuseniks are there now? How many will there be as people gradually wake up to the dangers of a comprehensive, instantaneous national ID system?

Sometimes it feels to resisters as if there were no more than a thousand, a hundred, a dozen others in the world. This form of resistance isn't something most people shout from the rooftops. It isn't organized. It's not done at public protest rallies, like the burning of draft cards once was.

Who else is out there?

Frissell estimates that up to 20 percent of the U.S. population will eventually become an ID outlaw class—composed both of principled resisters and hapless souls who've been shut out of the system for various reasons.

When you feel alone it's hard to grasp the idea of so many potential compatriots. Yet Frissell also points out that some 20 percent of the population *already* doesn't use the banking system — an astonishing figure when you consider how difficult it can be to get by without checks or credit cards.

And there are other signs that resistance — on principle or just for the hell of it — is broader and deeper than it sometimes seems. When Ohio police conducted checkpoints to catch unlicensed drivers they discovered that one in eight — nearly 13 percent — were not licensed. (Not merely failing to carry their licenses, but scoffing at that very form of government ID.)

Seemingly unrelated figures also might also shed some light. For example, unofficial IRS estimates of the number of income-tax non-filers runs as high as 35 million. No doubt most of that number is people who just don't bother, and a few million are people who refuse to file on principles unrelated to ID resistance. But one of the many things you can't do if you refuse to use (or have) a universal citizen ID number is file your taxes.

So who knows? The numbers of ID resisters may already be far larger than most would guess. Whatever it is, it's certainly going to grow as people realize that ID control isn't about ID, but about control.

I write a column for *Backwoods Home Magazine* called "Living the Outlaw Life." I chose that name as a constant reminder. Though a few readers object, I believe that all true freedom lovers *will* break the law — a lot of laws. Simply put, if we tried to follow all the millions of laws and regulations in the U.S. we'd not only be attempting the impossible (since ordinary people break laws unknowingly every day), but we'd be selling our souls to tyranny.

Only through resistance can we create pockets of personal freedom — dangerous but liberating (after all, who really wants to deal with snitch banks or work for some gray-cubicle, pee-in-a-bottle corporation?). Only through mass resistance do we have a hope of regaining political freedom.

Frissell is right (great minds) when he sees the outlaw class growing after imposition of national ID. He points out that the very size of that class will foster an ever-larger underground economy — in which terrorists and ordinary criminals will thrive (giving the lie to the government's false claims of protection), as well as millions of former good citizens driven into the ranks of outlawry.

It's ironic that in the name of conformity and false security, the nation is choosing to punish and make pariahs out of some of its best and brightest — the highly intelligent, principled, liberty-loving folks who best perceive the consequences of every policy. Nevertheless, that's exactly what's happening. Little girls and boys who once respected policemen, were polite to their teachers, honored their parents, and earned merit badges for good citizenship are now astonished to find themselves on the side of the lawbreakers. (Not criminals, mind you, but *law* breakers.)

But we haven't changed. We're still the best of citizens. It's just that our country has no use for the best any more.

We are America's refuseniks. All-American Outlaws. And we should be proud of that.

Red Tape
Blood Donor K

*In this short essay, the author, a member of the Catholic Worker move-
ment, recounts his experiences donating blood at Bellevue City Hospital in New
York City. Though he had no official ID, he did ultimately manage to contribute
blood. However, he observes that in the society in which we live apparently "some
people's blood is redder than other's" because of the ID they carry. This article
appeared in* The Catholic Worker, *January-February 2002, page 6.*

The day after Thanksgiving, I went to Bellevue City Hospital to give
blood. For me, it is an easy Work of Mercy, with a chance to lie down,
schmooze, eat Fig Newtons, watch daytime TV, get a door prize. The city
blood banks are always desperate, and I knew supplies were low again after
the generous outpouring following the World Trade Center attack.

Since September 11, there have been bag checks at the entrance to Bellevue. This time, we were put into two lines, one for employees, one for others, and everyone was asked for ID. When I said I don't carry any, the guard
told me it is against the law in NYC, but let me in anyway.

My first thought was that this by-law must be part of the post-September
11 measures, and mused about civil disobedience. My second thought was that
the city must have written down a practice that is not new for poor people, however little protested. People have told me, lots of times, about being moved from
park benches or stopped on the street by police, on this point of ID. Sometimes,
they are taken down to central booking, only to be let go or charged with something else. (Of course, people without immigration papers are particularly vulnerable to this procedure.) It has never really been about security, as much as
what former-Mayor Giuliani euphemistically called a "quality of life" issue.

Whatever an officer or guard may claim (and who can protest on the
spot?), the ID requirement, I am told, has never been, and is not yet, on the
city books. It is a threat to keep "undesirables" at bay. It seems to me the same

thing was going on at Bellevue, expanding an established practice under the guise of security. (And, how could this method possibly enhance real safety?) Presumably, I was not picked on because I do not fit any profile.

One irony is that I forgot that I did have ID that day — my donor card. It is possible they already have my DNA. Despite the fact that I have been on the clinic records for several years now, once inside, another identity crisis arose. Just as I was all set and registered, the administrator told me they now require a social security number before they can accept blood. Once more, I assumed the change was brought in after September 11, with the confusion over the overwhelming supply, as well as memories of tainted blood scandals elsewhere.

When I asked why, though, I was told it is to verify the information I had given. Like what? My age was the only candidate. But, surely, such social security information (not to mention prison records or job histories or income tax returns or citizenship) has nothing to do with the quality of the blood. In the circumstances, it is not extreme to wonder what they might do with this information. Again, I got by the same way I got in. Or, maybe they threw away the blood, as too insecure coming from someone who will not fill in a social security number, no matter what the reason.

My story is a minor incident, not a huge violation of civil rights (and a lawyer friend pointed out there is no constitutional right to give blood!) under the new draconian laws. The officials may well just want to show they are on the job. At the same time, it shows what frail, arbitrary functions of power "rights" are in practice, not given in human nature or natural law. Also, it is not true that precautions came in because everything has changed since September 11. Things are heating up, but we are not at the beginning — nor, likely, the end — of a slippery slope. I would say the techniques of identity are a sign of the times, in a society that very much believes — more and more up-front — that some people's blood is redder than others'.

Why I Refuse to
Be Numbered

Anonymous

This short essay was submitted to The Voluntaryist *(and published in whole number 116), after its author heard about the preparation of this anthology. In this chapter, Anonymous points out that he/she wants no contact with the U.S. government: neither to pay taxes nor to receive benefits. Being numbered by the government is one of the primary ways it keeps tabs on its taxpayers and welfare recipients. To the author, being numbered by the government is analogous to being made a slave. The author prefers to remain "unknown" because of the subversive nature of his/her ideas, which question the legitimacy of the State and challenge its right to exist.*

Counting by governments has been going on for many centuries. However, it is only in recent decades that individuals in the United States have been faced with government numbering. One historian of the public health movement observed that it was not until the federal government began disbursing Social Security checks that there was any financial incentive to have a state-issued birth certificate and federally-issued number.[1] (Under the Social Security Administration rules it became important to be able to prove when you were legally entitled to receive benefits. It was not until the early 1960s that federal tax returns were required to carry an identification number.) The point is that as citizen-numbering has evolved, the government has used the carrot and stick approach: get a number — receive government largess; refuse a number — be penalized and be ineligible to receive government benefits; refuse a number — be excluded from many activities which may only be described as government-granted privileges (issuance of a driver's license, access to licensed-physician medical care, access to state and federally-chartered bank services, etc.). To the normal, obedient citizen receiving a number is as innocuous and innocent as being inoculated against certain diseases at birth. It also automatically puts each and every productive citizen into the position of being tracked and spied upon as the government makes sure that the citizen pays his or her taxes.

I refuse to be numbered because I want no part of paying taxes or receiving any of the benefits that government bestows. I want to be responsible for myself and my family. America was built on that attitude and will survive only as long as that attitude persists. It is impossible in the nature of things, as described by the law of the conservation of energy, for more energy to come out of a social system than goes in. Someone has to produce goods and services, in order for there to be goods and services to be distributed. History is replete with examples of economic systems dying when there is no longer enough incentive for the producers to produce any more than they need for their bare survival. Although government bureaucrats may assume that goods and services automatically replicate themselves, like fruit on a tree, I assure them that the tree will eventually wither and die if it is mistreated or abused. The high standard of living which Americans enjoy will disappear if the economic inputs of the producers are not encouraged.

Although we have been taught that the whole purpose of government is to protect us from criminals and foreign invaders, in reality the purpose of government is to conquer and control us. There are benefits to be found in wide-spread social cooperation and the social division of labor, but benefits can only arise if trade and exchange are voluntary. By the very nature of things, if someone must be forced to trade or exchange with me (or I with them) it must be obvious that they (or I) do not see enough advantage to the trade to willingly engage in it. This analysis applies as much to groups that provide security from criminals and foreign invaders as it does to buying food at the store or buying shoes for your children. Government is the only organization in our society that regularly and legitimately obtains its money from compulsory levies—what it euphemistically describes as taxes. What happens to those who refuse to pay their taxes? Their bodies are put in prison or their property is seized by the government, or both. As much as the government tries to disguise it, taxation is robbery and violates the common sensical and moral dictum against stealing. (If everyone stole, eventually there would be nothing left to steal.)

The underlying premise of government taxation is the idea that you and your property belong to the State. You are its slave. Whatever the government allows you to keep is simply a result of its "generosity": What you produce is not yours by right, but by sufferance of the government. I do not want to be a slave; nor do I want to participate in a social system which enslaves others. I do not want to give my sanction to government. I do not want to support any coercive institution. I do not want to steal or be stolen from. I do not want to put others in jail for refusing to trade with me; nor do I want others to put me in jail for refusing to trade with them. Stealing (taxes) and coercion are not activities that lead to social harmony or prosperity. They are not activities that can be universalized. My objection to government (however good it may appear, or however many benefits it may distribute — which illusion can only be maintained by refusing to consider how much property it has first stolen, for government has nothing of its own) is to its coercive nature. I object to the compulsory manner in which government operates — regardless of how beneficial it appears — regardless of how necessary it considers itself — regardless of how many people embrace it. If government is so good, let it prove itself on the free and open market; let it depart from the coercive arena in which it now operates.

It might be argued that I consent to be numbered in many voluntary transactions. Every receipt I receive from Wal-Mart has a transaction number; every insurance policy has a contract number. While that is true, it ignores the main point of my objection to government numbering. I am not Wal-Mart's slave; I am not Hartford Insurance's slave. I may or may not choose to trade with them. I may or may not use a number to identify myself to them; but I do not have that option when it comes to dealing with the government. Slavemasters desire to control everything they can and numbering systems which allow no activity to be untaxed, unrecorded, or unnoticed are important to their success in controlling their slaves and expropriating their property.

It should be more than obvious now: I refuse to be numbered because I refuse to accept the badge of slavery. To be a number is to be a slave. I refuse to be a slave.

Note

1. "The national Social Security Act proved to be a great stimulus to accurate birth certification. Many people never considered a birth certificate to be of any importance until old age assistance, unemployment insurance, and other ramifications of the Social Security Act demonstrated to them that it was necessary to have this official proof of their existence." Wilson G. Smillie, *Public Health Administration in the United States* (3rd ed.), 1947, p. 191.

Slavery and National ID

Carl Watner

If one accepts the premise that the State owns the people (an assumption which seems to be prevalent today), rather than its opposite (that government is the agent; the people the principals), then it follows that the citizen is a slave of the government and must blindly obey. In this original contribution to this anthology, editor Carl Watner argues that when slavery was the norm every Negro was suspect. Practically everywhere in antebellum America, Negroes (off the plantation) had to prove their bona fides, either by possessing a valid pass from their master or by registering with the police and/or showing their "freedom" papers to the slave patrols. A free Negro without his certificate of freedom was considered a fugitive, apprehended, and returned to slavery. Query: If national ID were in place today, what would happen to those conscientious objectors or others who went about in public without their IDs? Isn't it likely they would be treated in just the same manner as the Negro of yesteryear?

Jim Fussell, in a review of "group classification on National ID cards," observed that in the pre–Civil War United States "'Free Passes', Freedom papers, and Deeds of manumission" functioned as ID's for the freed Negro.[1] This observation sparked my interest in the relationship between national ID and the history of slavery, and it is these two subjects which I would briefly like to comment upon in this paper.

The whole basis of chattel slavery, as it was known in the South, was the ownership of one person by another. Although some Negroes owned other blacks, for the most part slavery in the United States before the Civil War was largely along racial lines: white ownership of black people. All Negroes were presumed to be slaves, unless they could prove otherwise. The burden of proof was on the Negro. People with white skin never had to prove to anyone that they were free. In other words, the presumption was that if your skin was black, you were considered *prima facie* a slave, or else a runaway, or fugitive. The only way of proving that you were a free person was to show your deed of manumission (under which your owner had freed you), or some sort of certificate of freedom (often issued by the clerk of a county court) attesting to your free status.

Nearly all of the Southern states and several of the Northern states had laws which reflected this presumption. Slaves were not to leave their owner's land unless they had permission. In Connecticut, "[a]ny slave found wandering about without a pass was to be arrested as a runaway. Pennsylvania forbade blacks to travel more than ten miles from home without a pass.... Philadelphia directed its constables to arrest Negroes found in the streets on Sunday unless they had a pass from their owners."[2] Laws were often passed requiring all free blacks to register with local officials, in and some cases to post bond for their good behavior, and to ensure they would not become a charge upon the community. The District of Columbia had a particularly egregious ordinance passed on April 14, 1821 (effective June 1, 1821). It required all free blacks in the city to register annually with the Mayor and

> to enter into bond with one good and responsible free white citizen, as surety, in the penalty of twenty dollars, conditioned for the good, sober, and orderly conduct of such person or persons of color, and his or her family, for the term of one year following the date of such bond, and that such person or persons, his or her family, nor any part thereof, shall not, during the said term of one year, become chargeable to the Corporation in any manner whatsoever, and that they will not become beggars in or about the streets.

"Only after the bond was posted would the mayor issue a license to permit such free blacks to reside in the city for one year.... [F]ree Negroes were not permitted to change their places of residence until after such changes had been entered on their licenses by the registrar."[3] Similar regulations existed in such cities as Nashville, TN, Montgomery, AL, Baton Rogue, LA, Raleigh, NC, and Petersburg, VA.[4]

As I have pointed out in other essays for this anthology, the whole premise of National ID is that the government owns the citizen, and must provide the citizenry with identification, beginning with a state-issued birth certificate. In principle, this is just the same as it was during the time of American slavery. Every Negro was presumed a slave unless the government (or his master, actually ex-master) documented that he was a free person. If a freed Negro lost his "papers," then he was automatically considered a slave. If a Negro wanted to assert his natural born freedom, including the right not to carry government papers, his existence could be quite perilous, just as it would be to an American today who refused to carry government papers proving his or her identity.

It is next to impossible to function in our statist economy without a birth certificate, a drivers license, or a social security number issued by the government. If a person should try to operate in such a manner, he or she will surely eventually be apprehended by the authorities for "failing to register one's birth," for "driving without a license," or for "failing to provide a social security number." If, and when, a national or state ID program is implemented in the United States, the situation will be worse, because then it will undoubtedly become a crime to "fail to register" and "fail to carry one's state or federal ID card on one's person at all times."

Despite the danger to themselves, historians point out that many free Negroes refused to comply with the numerous municipal registration codes or the demand that they carry papers. "Many simply never bothered to register," "probably few carried freedom papers," and most instinctively preferred to avoid white officials.[5] "In 1853, St. Louis authorities attempted to chase alien free Negroes out of the city and to force native free Negroes to register. Police raided well-known free Negro haunts, whipped unregistered freemen, and shipped them beyond city limits.... The raids continued for almost a year, although they ended in failure."[6] Negroes in Virginia were no more compliant. "In Amelia County Virginia, for example, a consecutively numbered register of free Negroes kept between 1800 and 1865 listed about 150 freemen. In 1860, however, almost 200 resided in the county and many more had been born, had been manumitted, and had migrated into and out of the area during those years."[7]

Are the colored freemen of the 19th Century trying to tell us Americans of the 21st Century something that we might do? It is surely food for thought.[8]

Notes

1. Jim Fussell, "Global Survey (Jo to Vi) of Group Classification on National ID Cards, at http://www.preventgenocide.org/prevent/removing-facilitating- factor-sIDcards/survey/index2. See "USA (Pre-Civil War).

2. Edgar J. McManus, *Black Bondage in the North* (Syracuse: Syracuse University Press), 1973, p. 73 and p. 74.

3. Leonard P. Curry, *The Free Black in Urban America* (Chicago: University of Chicago Press), 1981, p. 86 and p. 301 (footnote 17) citing Washington, City Council, *Laws of the Corporation of the City of Washington* [1821] (Washington: Way and Gideon) 1821, pp. 110–111. The complete law is found at Chapter 133 of Laws Passed by the Eighteenth Council of the City of Washington, Approved April 14, 1821, Sections 1–21 (pp. 109–116). Secs. 11 and 12 (pp. 113–114) deal with change of residence regulations.

4. Ira Berlin, *Slaves Without Masters: The Free Negro in the Antebellum South* (New York: Oxford University Press paperback) 1981, pp. 319.

5. Ibid., p. 327.

6. Ibid., p. 330.

7. Ibid., p. 328. By the time of the Civil War there was a large number of free Negroes in the United States. "There were 59,000 free Negroes in the United States at the time of the first decennial census in 1790.... By [1860] the number had climbed to 488,000...." Over 40% of them lived in the South. John Hope Franklin and Alfred

A. Moss, Jr., *Free Slavery to Freedom: A History of Negro Americans* (New York: Alfred A. Knopf, Fortieth Anniversary Edition), 1988, p. 137.

8. What, might we ask, are the supposed benefits of government identification and documentation? Among other things it appears that our income can be traced and taxed; our children can be tracked from birth and forced to attend public schools; and our ages and the ages of our children can be known so that all of us might be subject to the military draft in time of war.

ID Without Big Brother

Sunni Maravillosa

No one knows for sure what future form ID may take; however, if this book has any success in sparking resistance to government enumeration, maybe we will find that it has also helped spawn new, non-governmental forms of identification. No longer might the state be involved in issuing birth and death certificates, or even drivers licenses. However, given the fact that some people will still want ID, in what manner will the free market provide identification, certification, and authentication services? This original essay, prepared especially for this anthology, offers one futuristic scenario full of provocative solutions to this question. Sunni Maravillosa is a psychologist and writer. She is the editor of Free-Market.Net's "Freedom Book of the Month" feature, a columnist for Sierra Times, *and the publisher of* Doing Freedom! *'zine.*

Sit back, clear your mind, and imagine the following for a few minutes...

After years of intensive education, aided by the homeschooling movement and the increasingly brazen actions and attitudes of federal and local government officials, the nightmare of living in an Orwellian society was cast off in this country in 2070. The sweet air of freedom has taken its place. Now, the year 2084, there are no state agencies and bureaucrats, and few rules that govern transactions between consenting adults.

The result is a wonderfully prosperous, mildly chaotic environment where individuals transact their own business as they see fit, and with rare exceptions handle problems with others peaceably and between themselves. Businesses of all sorts are thriving once again. Among the most successful— and competitive— businesses are those that deal with the identification needs of the individuals who live in the town we'll examine, known as Agora.

Wait a minute — what was that? There's no state government, but there's still ID? Do free individuals really need to have some means of identification? Why? And what for?

To answer those questions, we first need to go back, way back, before technology came along. Being social animals, we've always had a need to trust others: parents for food, shelter, and love; mates for love, and help with creating and maintaining a home and family; clan members for more general support and help fighting off other clans. As human society became more complex, we began transacting business with individuals we didn't know personally. Trust and word of mouth were the primary means by which such impersonal transactions were carried out; if you'd done business with Sam the fisher (who, in later times, would be known as Sam Fisher) and were happy with the result, you told others about that and they were more likely to trust Sam and do business with him. Similarly, if Alfred the cooper (again, the job title morphing into a last name in later times) cheated customers or made barrels of inferior quality, word would get around and folks wouldn't trust him with their business.

"My word is my bond" and handshakes that sealed transactions were early means of ensuring an individual was who he claimed to be, and could deliver the good or service promised. As society became larger and more complex, written means of verifying personal information came about; letters of introduction and recommendation are two examples. These were common into the early 1900's; letters of recommendation are still relied upon in some circles (e.g., admission to a university).

The history behind the development of identification is explored in other chapters in this volume, so let's not get bogged down in the details. The point is that there has almost always been a need at some time or other in an individual's life to prove one's identity, or entitlement to some kind of consideration (performing specific financial transactions, club membership, employment, and so forth). For these things—for your protection as well as that of the party involved with you in the transaction—some form of identification is a good idea. So, what uses would citizens of Agora have for identification?

Uses of Identification

"Identification" has long been a misnomer for the functions IDs have performed. Their actual purposes far exceed simple identification. However, keeping with popular and historical use, Agora residents continue to use the term to apply to the various items they use to perform a wide range of functions.

The first function of ID is **authentication**. This type of ID simply verifies that a certain name, symbol, or sign identifies a specific individual. To get such ID is fairly easy; one simply provides documentation that already links a name with their person. Or, with a certain number of individuals willing to accompany you and physically attest that you are said individual, you can get this type of ID. Of course, given the contrary nature Agorans are well known for, many eschew an ID for authentication purposes. As a result, letters of introduction have found a renewed popularity. In fact, they've become something of an art form, with many people creating unique papers used solely for this purpose; they also frequently include fancy calligraphic designs around the text. These features have the added benefit of keeping fraud down in this medium. Electronic verification, similar to 20th-century PGP-signed documents and other online transactions, is also very common.

Note that nothing prevents an individual from thus acquiring several names, if one so chooses. And indeed, if the purpose is not to defraud or harm anyone, does it really matter if an individual works as a computer analyst by the name of "Mason Jackson" by day, and is a stripper — "Ticonderoga Dick" — at a bar by night? By using various labels for different aspects of activities, an individual thus affords him- or herself more privacy than the one-size-constricts-all system most 20th century nations used. As a result, the word 'pseudonym' has all but vanished as Agorans make use of these formerly "secret identities" to establish differing personae in various cultural circles.

Another function of ID is **certification**, which attests to: physical attributes, skills, or talents an individual possesses; accomplishments or achievements reached; or training successfully completed. Such IDs replaced many government-mandated licenses and diplomas. Certificates are widely used by private companies for a dizzying array of functions. One demonstrates a specific level of financial solvency without divulging details—for example, having an account in good standing (a minimum of 500 grams of gold on reserve) at the First Free Bank of Agora. Another shows that an individual completed coursework in hair styling from Digby's Design House of Hair with at least a minimum level of competence.

The much-reviled drivers licenses have completely gone away, as Agorans came to understand its roots as a tool of control by the state rather than affirming driving competence. (See Carl Watner's chapter in this volume for an excellent history of drivers licenses.) Instead, a smart card automatically deducts road usage fees the road owner charges; insurance isn't required, but having it or showing proof of financial responsibility often gives a driver discounts on road fees.

Letters of recommendation are another type of certification. They've expanded beyond their 20th century uses, and are widely employed as a basis of credentialing individuals, or to attest to a level of skill worthy of a higher than usual fee for some good or service. Many companies collect letters of recommendation from satisfied customers regarding their employees' work, and allow potential customers to peruse them in order to find the employee who is best suited for the job they have. That's how Adam Beebe chose master Victorian artisan Oliver Hornsby of Architects Unlimited to renovate his family's house. Banks issue "credit credentials," which are based on an individual's or company's credit history with the bank, so that another individual or institution is satisfied that the entity in question is unlikely to default on a loan or other credit arrangement up to a certain amount.

The final broad function of ID is **authorization**—specifying what an individual may do in a general or specific circumstance. Authorizations provide proof of "legitimacy," rather like a bond or surety guarantee. Think of it this way: this form of ID helps ensure that its bearer is entitled to some good or service (has paid for membership in a health club, for example), or may engage in some specific action (accessing funds in a bank account). Or it might demonstrate that you have a right to be in a particular location for a specific purpose, as many corporate employee IDs do.

The need for identification hasn't changed since the state was banished in Agora; nor have the types of identification that an individual may need. However, without the state in the ID business, the sources of identification are more varied.

Sources of Trust

All of the previously described functions require some level of trust behind them — whether in the individual bearing a document or the issuing entity that created a document. While private companies fill various roles in creating these documents, other means of generating trust are used as well. For example, an individual's use of a particular name in a given setting leads to a reputation being established under that name. As others come to know that name and individual, they may vouch for him or her under certain circumstances (as in letters of introduction or recommendation). Thus, trust is built up by a history of trusted individuals using and passing along the trusted information. This is the idea behind the signing of PGP keys, and has successfully extended far beyond that in Agora, both in the physical and digital world.

While such "distributed" sources of trust can be slower to generate confidence, once a level of trust has been reached its reliability is considered as good as— if not better than— more centralized sources of trust. This method harkens back to the old days of hand-shaking as an authentication or certification procedure, and is very much a person-to-person means of spreading or corroborating information.

More centralized sources of trust are legion in Agora, and, rather than try to cover them all here, let's simply look at some of the places where Agora residents can get identification that offers any amount of verification or trust along the continuum.

Sources of Identification

If an employer wants to restrict access to sensitive areas— or even to the entire property — the employer decides what kind of information is required (i.e., authentication or authorization), how to verify an individual's credentials and identity, and what form the ID is to take. If their needs can't be met inside the company, it contracts with an outside source for ID creation. These kinds of IDs are privately issued, for private purposes. None of this is new.

Another type of ID is one that is used for public purposes. The term "ID" really doesn't describe all the functions these bits of information perform. A better term is "certificate," such as a diploma, or a seal, such as the Underwriter's Laboratory (UL) seal found on electronics for years. Instead of having letter-salad government bureaus act as certifying authorities, private agencies like UL have proliferated, and do their job much better than the FDA and USDA ever did.

A major element of the issuing agencies' success is the competitive nature of the business; each wants to have the highest safety margin, so each company works very hard to maintain the highest standards of testing or certification. Companies are free to choose which company (or companies) they use to certify their goods or services; issuing companies that don't maintain acceptable standards go out of business, as claims against them take away both profits and trust. Of course, a company may choose not to engage in certification testing. This means individuals are free to choose untested goods, and sometimes they do. Uncertified sources that are worthwhile continue to do business, while those that don't tend to go out of business fairly quickly as the "distributed" trust chain spreads the word.

One difference from the 20th-century public-purpose IDs is that they aren't required of the individual. They're a means of demonstrating some kind of legitimacy to a consumer, among other functions. An example of an individually-possessed certificate like this is the debit card. Issued by the individual's bank and paired with an "access code" (AC, formerly known as a "PIN"), they authorize the holder as someone entitled to access the funds in that account.

Since there's no state, there are of course no state-issued IDs. Travel is much more free, with few communities requiring "passports" or similar ID. Countries which continue to function as old nation-states either accommodate Agorans' lack of such documents, or don't permit such individuals' entry into the country. Not too many free individuals are keen to go to such places, anyway. In other areas that have rejected totalitarianism and collectivism, letters of introduction and credit serve Agorans just as well as they do at home.

If an individual wants an ID that attaches a specific label to her, she has several companies to choose from. IDs R Us is a national chain that has minimal requirements for such ID, and offers fast service and low prices. However, because it has minimal requirements, its safety record isn't that great, and many firms do not place much trust in their IDs. The most successful authentication ID issuer is Spooner's Identity Emporium. This company also has minimal requirements for low-level, name-only ID, but it takes the additional steps of verifying the ID-seeker's history under that name, as well as the reputation of those who vouch for the ID-seeker. The company publishes a monthly list on its web site — usually a very short list, given its careful processing — of individuals whose SID (for Spooner ID) has been revoked, along with the reason for revocation. Successful challenges to a SID revocation have been very few.

Of course, if an individual doesn't like the requirements of one company, she's free to use another company for her ID needs. Or, she's free to go without such ID. Many citizens of Agora do not have an authentication ID card beyond what their employers might require. The use of precious metals as currency, and the proliferation of barter and barter rings (wherein individuals and companies can make direct and indirect trades of goods and services with a high level of trust) have virtually eliminated the need for checks and credit cards. Debit cards have remained popular, as carrying around a pocketful of silver or gold coin can get uncomfortable.

Similarly, most private firms have turned to companies like Spooner's Identity Emporium to handle their ID and certification needs. This doesn't, however, create a huge database under one label, unlike past days where lots of information could be had by just knowing an individual's Social Security Number. Having a SID and a Spooner-researched employer ID are entirely separate entities, and no computer hacker can determine anything beyond the basic SID check, **if** they're fortunate enough to get past the Gyrfalcon Privacy Guardian (GPG) security measures placed on the computer files.

The exception is financial institutions, which are reluctant to part with their customers' information after the Banking Revolt of 2069, which marked the beginning of the fall of totalitarian government. Having seen the general public's willingness to shed banker blood over matters of financial privacy, all financial transactions are automatically accorded very high levels of privacy and security. Even requests for information from legitimate users (such as a bank customer seeking a loan at another bank) are carefully checked before being granted.

Of course, these improvements haven't done away with all security concerns. Occasional lapses in a security company's privacy policy have led to improper disclosures of confidential information, but these breaches have been very limited because of the decentralized nature of identification information and issuers. Arbitrators (replacing the thoroughly corrupted justice system) have been very hard on companies that have had security breaches, which has helped keep standards high. Those that can't handle the heat of strict security get tossed out of its kitchen; those that remain offer a variety of services at a variety of prices, enabling consumers to choose the level of security that's comfortable or needed. Each ID company in Agora must try to outdo its competition in providing the best service and the best privacy security at the least cost; otherwise it will lose business and eventually cease operations if it does not attract and retain enough customers.

ID Appearance

As has been suggested already, the appearance of these various forms of trust-giving information varies greatly. Sure, an Agoran may get a Spooner ID with a photograph of him- or herself, but that kind of "ID" is largely used for gags or as favors at retro "TwenCen" parties. Technological developments have made electronic transactions—from authentication to authorization— commonplace, and more secure than the old Internet.

Much more common is the "smart card." A smart card is a small container of information; it can house several different identities (for authentication purposes), certificates, and authorizations. Best of all, technology has rendered the bland-looking, standard-issue plastic card a thing of the past (this advance is known as 'de-ellisoning', which refers to the rejection of the omnipotent National ID). Individuals and companies can choose among a surprising array of materials to house their ID chips, including biological material (fingernails are a common location, because they're quite durable and slow-growing). If two Agorans' "cards" look the same, it's most likely a statistical coincidence. A plastic key chain may house ID chips, or perhaps they're in the pretty blue-green metal bracelet the lady wears. Or could they be in the scrap of paper she keeps tucked securely in her side arm's holster? Is that simply a fashionable hat, or is the brim the gentleman's repository of identification and certification chips?

The only way to know is to test the items, generally by a swipe across an authentication reader. However, since these are essential features of each ID-issuing company's security and privacy measures, their distribution and use is carefully controlled. Other security procedures in place protect privacy by requiring a specific kind of reader, or that an authentication key signal be received, before the card will provide requested information. These are only the publicized aspects of security. Several others exist and are used in varying ways that help reduce unauthorized access to information on a chip, as well as fraudulent creation of chips and/or cards.

Of course, one isn't required to keep all one's sensitive information on a single smart card. The problems with "identity theft" make that an obviously poor security choice, one the old government played right into. Agorans can choose to do that if they wish; most prefer to disperse security information among a variety of resources, and often have backups too. And let's not forget the widespread use of letters of introduction and recommendation; they provide important information in a different format.

Conclusion

Identification is a key — an important key that can unlock various pieces of a person's life. Through it come an individual's public identity (or identities), credentials, and the activities she or he may legitimately undertake in certain circumstances. While it doesn't play the large role that ID cards did in most 20th-century nation-states, Agora citizens understand well the problems inherent in the state's approach to ID. That was a large part of the Orwellian stranglehold on individuals, and was decisively rejected. Relying on birth certificates, which bore no information to directly link the holder to the person affirmed born at the time and place stated on the certificate; Social Security cards, which held nothing more than a name and a Social Security Number; and driver's licenses (containing — or verified by — the hated SSN) as the backbone of the entire nation's identification system was a farce doomed to fail.

Instead, trust is placed back at the heart of the authentication, certification, and authorization functions of whatever sort of ID is used. Individuals again take responsibility for much of their own needs, relying upon distributed trust systems such as vouching for one another, letters of recommendation, and choosing which company to trust with certification testing of the products they consume. Their continued demand for solid information and service, coupled with the profits private companies can generate, have made ID services a very popular and competitive market sector. The harsh penalties that befall companies that can't maintain high standards of service for either individual or corporate information needs helps keep them striving to improve security measures and their general trustworthiness.

By transferring the ID service industry to the free market, individuals get a wide choice of services, competitive prices, and more barriers between various elements of their private lives. Businesses get better ID services and security. Distributed trust systems offer an alternative means of gaining and verifying trust within a given culture or society. Although the forms of ID possible in the future are much more speculative than the examples given here — nanotechnology alone offers vistas beyond many imaginations — ID without Big Brother is a classic example of a free-market "win-win" scenario.

Acknowledgments: I would like to thank Carl Bussjaeger, Brad Felton, Jeff Jordan, Dale Stimson, Don L. Tiggre, Carl Watner, and Claire Wolfe for the thought-provoking discussions and ideas they have provided on this subject.

Epilogue: National ID
and the Police State

Claire Wolfe *and* Aaron Zelman

In the last pages of their book (written and published after the September 11th destruction of the World Trade Center), the authors of The State vs. The People *(Hartford: Mazel Freedom Press, 2001, pp. 478–479) point out that some sort of national ID is a fundamental prerequisite of every totalitarian state. Most Americans don't realize this, and, even if they did, they still appear ready to trade liberty for security. However, as some observers have noted, this is not really a trade-off. The only true security is in accepting and attempting to meet the responsibilities of liberty. Everyone must do that for him or herself; no one can do it for another. Only as individuals in society move toward freedom themselves, will their society become more safe and more free. Distributed by Jews for the Preservation of Firearms Ownership. Box 270143. Hartford, WI 53027.*

The national ID card is a keystone in the building of a police state. Proponents have pushed for it for 70 years—from the days when they still assured us so solemnly (even writing into law) that our Social Security numbers would never be used for ID purposes. Police-state advocates are not going to stop now — especially not now that technology has made the card and its related database more valuable to them than ever. As they do with "gun-control" laws or congressional pay raises, legislators, bureaucrats, and their friends in industry will keep bringing this up again and again until they have their way. Congress will eventually pass national ID card legislation at midnight with only three members present (just as they passed the Brady law). Or they'll hide it as one paragraph in a many-thousand page appropriations bill, which your "representative" will vote for without reading (as they did with milder ID legislation in 1996). Or some federal agency will suddenly discover that — lo and behold! — it already has the authority under some new interpretation of an existing statute to impose a national ID card without legislative consent.

And unlike congressional pay raises, you won't just be paying with your tax dollars. You'll be paying with the last scraps of your freedom. (And what will you do when your grandchildren look you in the eyes and ask what you did to stop such evil from happening?) Implementation of the national ID card will be the end to freedom. After that, everything else will just be a minor cleanup detail for the minions of the police state.

Within the lifetime of everyone reading this book, freedom has diminished, sometimes steadily and almost imperceptibly, sometimes in thundering steps. With the most real and dreadful crisis Americans have ever faced on their home shores, police-state advocates have the excuse they need to take almost anything they wish from us. We will never get it back.

True, at the end of every other freedom-stealing war or crisis since the War Between the States, the most odious and visible restrictions on freedom have been withdrawn once the crisis has passed. Rationing ends, emergency detentions cease, internment camps close. But the vast majority of the "emergency measures" put in place remain — like the World War II "victory tax" payroll withholding that's still taken out of your paycheck each week. The agencies created to deal with the crisis of the day — like the ATF and the CIA — remain, grow and become as brutal and intrusive as Congress, the courts, the media, and the public allow. The national ID card, and most of what we've written about in this chapter and this book, will remain long after the crisis that gave birth to these horrific abuses of liberty.

Before the September attacks, Americans had been on the verge of realizing that government was the problem, not the solution. In the midst of crisis, every poll showed that Americans not only trusted their government to retaliate against the attackers, but as we saw above, they had increased confidence in the government's ability to protect them from terrorism.

Think about that. After watching 7,000 people die due in part to failures of FAA-guided airport security, failures of CIA and FBI intelligence, and the INS's failure to effectively screen and monitor suspicious immigrants — Americans have more faith in government's protective power than ever.

Is there any help for a country whose citizens are this dumbed down, this numbed down, this passive, this willing to help build a Fourth Reich — who nod their heads like ceramic dashboard doggies each time some power broker repeats the Big Lie that the reich's tyrannies are being imposed on them — and on us all — solely "to preserve freedom?"

The few Americans who truly love and understand freedom must continue the fight for liberty because if we don't, it's lost forever. But after what our own government is inflicting on us, using this tragedy as an excuse — after what our own fellow citizens are not only tolerating, but begging for — it's almost certain that only our children or grandchildren will have any chance of winning back American liberty.

We wish that future generation of freedom fighters well. We pray for them and hope they fare better than our generation will.

For Further Reading

There is a wide selection of ID items that were not among those chosen for reprinting in this anthology. The following entries will be helpful to those interested in prsuing this subject further.

Anderson, Poul. "Sam Hall" in *The Best of Poul Anderson*. New York: Pocket Books, 1976. First published in *Astounding Science-Fiction* (1953). The genesis of this story was the author's travels in Europe, and "the requirement of filling out a silly little [police] card wherever [he] spent the night."

Anonymous. "This Far: No More!" *The Voluntaryist*, whole no. 68, June 1994, p. 3. Discusses conscientious objection to the use of Social Security numbers.

Brown v. Texas. 443 U.S. 47 (1979). Chief Justice Burger, delivering the opinion of a unanimous Court, pointed out that "the guarantes of the Fourth Amendment do not allow" "demanding identification from an individual without any specific basis for believing he is involved in criminal activity" (443 U.S. 47, 53).

Caplan, Jane, ed. *Written on the Body: The Tattoo in European and American History*. Princeton: Princeton University Press, 2000. Some of the articles in this anthology focus on the penal use of tattooing and branding to identify prisoners and convicts.

_____, and John Torpey, eds. *Documenting Individual Identity: The Development of State Practices in the Modern World*. Princeton: Princeton University Press, 2001. This is a valuable collection of essays, some of which deal with the history of fingerprinting, the history of passports, and identity cards and genocide in Rwanda.

Cole, Simon. *Suspect Identities: A History of Fingerprinting and Criminal Identification*. Cambridge: Harvard University Press, 2001.

Conrat, Maisie, and Richard. *Executive Order 9066: The Internment of 110,000 Japanese Americans*. Los Angeles: California Historical Society, 1972. Includes photographs of American citizens wearing their numbered "relocation" tags.

Davies, Simon G. "Touching Big Brother: How Biometric Technology Will Fuse Flesh and Machine." *7 Information Technology and People* (1994), pp. 38–47. Includes "Case Studies" of several government biometric programs.

Des Forges, Alison. *"Leave None to Tell the Story": Genocide in Rwanda*. New York: Human Rights Watch, 1999. Points out that the law which "required that all Rwandans be registered according to ethnic group" contributed to the genocidal killings (p. 3).

Eaton, Joseph W. *Card-Carrying Americans: Privacy, Security, and the National ID Card Debate*. Totowa: Rowman & Littlefield, 1986. Argues the pros and cons of national ID before the War on Terrorism was ever imagined.

Etzioni, Amitai. "Big Brother or Big Benefits?: ID Cards and Biometric Identifiers," Chapter 4 in *The Limits of Privacy*. New York: Basic Books, 1999. Arguments outlining the benefits of a national ID program.

Frissell, Duncan. "What's Our National Identity?" *The Sierra Times*, December 12, 2001, at http://www.sierratimes.com/archives/files/dec/06/eddf120601.htm. Observes that "a national ID card is not really about identity. It is about authorization" and "social controls" imposed by Congress and the administrative bureaucracies in this country.

Fussell, Jim. "Sample Documents," at http:/www.preventgenocide.org/prevent/removing-facilitating-factors/IDcards/samples/. Excellent digital photos of national ID cards from around the world, illustrating "Group classifications."

Gabb, Sean. "A Libertarian Conservative Case Against Identity Cards," at http://www.btinternet.com/~old.whig/pamphlet/idcards.htm. First published by Libertarian Alliance, London, 1994, as Political Notes 98, ISBN 1 85637 268 5. Lengthy critique of ID card programs.

Garfinkel, Simson. "Authorized Uses of Social Security Numbers," in *Database Nation*. Sebastopol: O'Reilly & Associates, 2000, pp. 33–34. This chart lists the "mission creep" history of Social Security numbers from 1943 through 1996.

_____. "Nobody Fucks with the DMV," at http://www.wired.com/wired/archive/2.02/dmv.html. Points out in this February 1994 article from *Wired* that "the DMV has a unique means of forcing citizens to comply with [all sorts of] state edicts [most of them unrelated to one's operation of a motor vehicle]," by refusing to renew one's drivers license.

Ham, Shane, and Robert D. Atkinson. "Using Technology to Detect and Prevent Terrorism." Progressive Policy Institute Briefing at http://www.ppionline.org/ppi_ci.cfm?knlgAreaID=124&subsecID=307&contentID=250070. Advocates increased use of technology and national ID for homeland security.

Hart, Kitty. *Return to Auschwitz: The Remarkable Life a Girl Who Survived the Holocaust*. New York: Atheneum, 1982. The author, now Kitty Hart-Moxon, recounts the story of how she and her mother were tattooed in Auschwitz, and how she preserved their tattoos in formaldehyde. See pp. 23 and 62.

Inada, Lawson Fusao, ed. *Only What We Could Carry: The Japanese American Interment Experience*. Berkeley: Heyday Books, 2000. See the Photo Essay on p. 57: Hiro Niwa's evacuation tag #13664.

Kirn, Walter. "The Mother of Reinvention: The real reason Americans detest the idea of a national ID card." *The Atlantic Monthly*, May 2002, pp. 28–29. "In American legal and cultural tradition one essential privilege of citizenship is not having to prove it [one's identity] on demand."

Kolender v. Lawson. 461 U.S. 352 (1983). Justice Brennan of the U.S. Supreme Court, concurring, wrote that "Merely to facilitate the general law enforcement objective of investigating and preventing unspecified crimes, States may not authorize the arrest and criminal prosecution of an individual for failing to produce identification or further information on demand by a police officer" (461 U.S. 352, 363).

Levi, Primo. *Survival in Auschwitz*. New York: Summit Books, 1985. See Chapter 2, "On the Bottom," the section titled *Haftling*. Imprisoned by the Germans during World War II, Levi was tattooed with number 174517. This autobiography describes "the dehumanizing process that goes along with being thought of as a number."

Metclaf, Geoff. "Mark of the Beast?" at http://www.WORLDNETDAILY.com/news/article.asp?ARTICLE_ID=26217. This internet news article from January 2002 discusses subdermal bio-chip implants—such as the Digital Angel, which serves as an ID device and global personal global positioning satellite devices (like the VeriChip)—in light of the Biblical warnings in Revelation 13, verses 16 and 17.

Methorst, H. W., and J. L. Lentz. "Population Administration and the Family-Individual-Card System in the Netherlands." *2 Population* (1935), pp. 42–65. The authors define the purpose of a national population register as *"the registration of a person in such a way that the public authorities constantly have at their disposal ... all the data relating to that person which may be important for the fulfilling of their task"* (p. 42, italics in original).

Okubo, Mine. *Citizen 13660.* Seattle: University of Washington Press, 1989. See pp. 19–23. A Japanese-American imprisoned during World War II, Ms. Okubo was assigned government number 13660 during her confinement.

Pearl, Raymond. "Tabular Review of Some of the Most Important Events in the History of Biostatistics," in *Introduction to Biometry and Statistics.* Philadelphia: W. B. Saunders, 3rd ed., 1940. First published in 1923, this chronological chart lists many of the most important dates and events in the field of government enumeration. See pages 22–25.

Rice v. Connolly. Queen's Bench Division [1966] 2QB414, [1966] 2All ER 649, [1996] 3 WLR 17, 130 JP 322. This English decision is often cited for the point that "the whole basis of the common law is the right of the individual to refuse to answer questions put to him by persons in authority, and a refusal to accompany those in authority to a particular place; short, of course, of arrest."

Russell, Steve. "The New Outlawry and Foucault's Panoptic Nightmare." 17 *American Journal of Criminal Justice* (1993), pp. 39–50. Judge Russell discusses Michael Foucault's view of the surveillance institutions in modern society.

Smith, L. Neil. "Toward a National Disidentification Movement." Privately circulated essay, December 2001. The author points out that "The United States of America has an internal passport system fully as stringent as any former communist nation...." It is our system of state-issued drivers licenses.

Thomas, Dorothy Swaine. "Determining Population in Intercensal and Postcensal Years by Means of Continuous Population Registers." 28 *Journal of American Health* (January 1938), pp. 28–35. Discusses use of population registers in Sweden and the Netherlands.

Torpey, John. *The Invention of the Passport: Surveillance, Citizenship, and the State.* New York: Cambridge University Press, 2000. Deals with the history of the passport as an identification and travel document.

Twight, Charlotte. "Systematic Federal Surveillance of Ordinary Americans," in Charlotte Twight, *Dependent on D.C.* New York: Palgrave for St. Martin's Press, 2001, pp. 235–278. This is a revised version of her earlier essay, which appears in this anthology.

Van Drunen, Newton. "Statement of Newton Van Drunen for the Hearing on Federal Identification Fraud." U.S. Senate Oversight Hearing on Fraudulent Identification and Penetration of Benefit Programs, June 16, 1982. In "Appendix," Joseph W. Eaton, *Card-Carrying Americans; Privacy, Security, and the National ID Card Debate.* Totowa: Rowman and Littlfield, 1986. A prisoner at Sandstone Federal Prison explains how he learned to counterfeit IDs in the prison print shop.

Watner, Carl. "The Exit Option." *The Voluntaryist*, whole no. 37, April 1989. This article briefly discusses the history of passports, restrictions on international travel, and the option of leaving the country in which one holds citizenship.

_____. "Man Without a Country." *The Voluntaryist*, whole no. 49, April 1991. This article details the life of Garry Davis of the World Service Authority, who refuses to use government passports.

_____. "Un-Licensed, Un-Numbered, Un-Taxed." *The Voluntaryist*, whole no. 68, June 1994. This article describes Pastor Paul Revere of the Embassy of Heaven Church, Sublimity, OR, who refuses to recognize the jurisdiction of political governments, or their rights to number, license, or tax him.

Index